THE PUBLIC LAW OF WALES

Welsh Planning Law and Practice

THE PUBLIC LAW OF WALES

Welsh Planning Law and Practice

Graham Walters

UNIVERSITY OF WALES PRESS
2017

www.uwp.co.uk

British Library CIP Data
A catalogue record for this book is available from the British Library.

ISBN 978-1-78683-155-2
eISBN 978-1-78683-156-9

Typeset by Marie Doherty
Printed by CPI Antony Rowe, Melksham

Series Preface

For several centuries after the union of the two countries under the Tudors, the laws which applied in England and the laws which applied in Wales were almost exactly identical. Although administered differently in Wales by the courts of Great Session, the laws were not different. Only in the nineteenth century, barely half a century after the abolition of the Great Sessions in 1830, did laws begin to be made for Wales which did not apply in neighbouring England. The number of such laws however remained small when compared with those which were common to both countries. England and Wales was a single law district with a single law – the law of England and Wales, which was in reality English law.

Devolution has changed that situation significantly. The creation of the National Assembly for Wales and its subsequent acquisition of primary law-making powers has meant that there is now a growing number of differences between the laws which apply in Wales and those which apply in England. Although in the majority of cases, the laws of the two countries remain the same, there is an increasing divergence in the rules relating to those matters which have been devolved. In truth, there are now three bodies of law in England and Wales: one which applies only in Wales; a second which applies only in England, and a third which applies in both countries. Whenever the National Assembly legislates for Wales or the United Kingdom Parliament legislates only for England, the divergence increases. As that divergence increases, so does the importance that lawyers, law students and the public should be able to inform themselves of what the law is in Wales. People need to know the laws which govern their lives from the perspective of the society in which they live. In both countries, lawyers need to know what the law is on either side of the border

The temptation has been to present the law which applies in Wales in terms of the law which applies in England, while merely noting the differences. As divergence increases, that approach becomes not merely unhelpful from a Welsh perspective, but unacceptable. The purpose of this series therefore is to present to the professions and to the public an account of the law as it applies in Wales in the areas where there is now divergence, and in so doing to both redress the deficit and provide the foundation for a legal literature to serve the distinct needs of Wales.

Thomas Glyn Watkin

Contents

Foreword

The modern law relating to town and country planning in England and Wales has its roots in the Town and Country Planning Act 1947. This Act of the United Kingdom Parliament was one of a number of statutes passed in the years immediately after the cessation of war that was to have a profound influence over the lives of the citizens of the United Kingdom. By virtue of the 1947 Act owners of land were required to obtain permission from local planning authorities to develop their land except in very limited circumstances. Development of land encompassed two concepts: the making of a material change of use of the land in question or the carrying out of building and other defined operations on or over the land. An individual's right to use or build upon his land as he pleased was henceforth to be curtailed.

Decisions about whether or not planning permission for development was to be granted were entrusted in the first instance to local planning authorities. Invariably, these authorities were local councils or bodies which were given specific powers by the 1947 Act. This was an explicit recognition by Parliament that decisions about development of land, at least at first instance, were best made locally.

Against this background it is hardly surprising that as soon as law-making powers were devolved by the United Kingdom Parliament to law-making institutions in Northern Ireland, Scotland and Wales, the law relating to town and country planning was considered fit for consideration by those devolved institutions. The Government of Wales Act 1998 conferred express powers upon the National Assembly for Wales to legislate in respect of town and country planning.

That is not to say that the National Assembly thereby became the sole legislator in respect of town and country planning in Wales. The Town and Country Planning Act 1990, which was the governing statute for England and Wales at the time of the creation of the National Assembly, was not repealed in so far as it related to Wales. The result has been that those affected by or interested in the law relating to town and country planning have needed to look both to Acts of the United Kingdom Parliament and to the legislation of the National Assembly in order to ascertain the law as it is in force in Wales. Currently, the Town and Country Planning Act 1990 enacted by the United Kingdom Parliament stands side by side with the Planning (Wales) Act 2015 enacted by the National Assembly.

Those familiar with this area of the law will know that primary legislation is just the starting point in seeking a thorough understanding of the applicable law. In this field secondary legislation is detailed and complex, ministerial guidance is routinely issued to assist in the interpretation of the law or published planning policy and, of course, since 1947, there has been an ever-growing body of case law which has grappled with the plethora of disputes thrown up by this complex area of the law.

Thus, the time is ripe for a comprehensive analysis of the law of town and country planning as it relates to Wales. Graham Walters is extremely well placed to provide that analysis. Throughout his career as a barrister in Cardiff he has demonstrated a keen interest and genuine expertise in planning law. The reader of *Welsh Planning Law and Practice* will find invaluable guidance about the substantive law and procedure. Practitioners in the field will find that it fills a large void; those who are interested in the development of Welsh law will find a comprehensive account of a dynamic process.

Sir Wyn Williams
Former Presiding Judge for Wales
February 2017

Preface

The Wales Act 2017 recognises that there is a body of law made by the National Assembly for Wales and the Welsh Ministers and that it forms part of the law of England and Wales. Legislation on town and country planning as a devolved subject is an important part of that body of law. However, the simple statement of the constitutional position belies the practical difficulties in identifying the law as it actually applies in Wales. Recently, the Law Commission has noted concerns about the complexity and inaccessibility of the law and referred to a succession of piecemeal changes and the increasing divergence between planning law in England and in Wales.

This book is part of the Public law of Wales series designed to serve the distinct needs of Wales following devolution and that growing divergence between the law as it applies in Wales and in England. It aims to provide a comprehensive guide to the sources and structure of Welsh planning law and provide a route through the complexity. It is not a comparative study but deals with legislation and policy affecting land in Wales, placing them in the context of shared principles and concepts and the case law common to England and Wales.

This is not, or not just, an academic exercise. Planning is a practical matter affecting important aspects of daily life and the desirability of public engagement in the planning process is well recognised. The aim is to promote recognition of the body of Welsh planning law, to aid accessibility for all who practise in or who are, or want to be, involved in shaping development in Wales and to assist understanding of this important subject.

Given the range and extent of source material, it can of necessity serve only as an introduction to certain topics but it is hoped that references are placed clearly in their context and are readily identified to enable further reading where necessary. Generally the law is as stated in November 2016, although it has been possible to add references to the Wales Act 2017 assuming its enactment as approved and amended following the third reading in the House of Lords.

Graham Walters
Cardiff

Copyright acknowledgements

Table of Cases

EWCA Civ 1365, [2006] 1 WLR 334, [2006] 1 P & CR 522, [2005] All ER (D) 291 (Nov) **5.30**

Pioneer Aggregates (UK) Ltd v Secretary of State for the Environment [1985] AC 132, 1984] 3 WLR 32, [1984] 2 All ER 358, 82 LGR 488, 48 P & CR 95, 128 Sol Jo 416, [1984] 2 EGLR 183, [1984] LS Gaz R 2148, 272 Estates Gazette 425, [1984] JPL 651 **6.52**

Pressland v Hammersmith and Fulham LBC [2016] EWHC 1763 (Admin). **11.29**

Pye v Secretary of State for the Environment Transport and Regions [1998] 3 PLR 72, (1999) PLCR 28 [1998] 19 LS Gaz R 25 **11.36**

Pyx Granite Co. Ltd. v. Ministry of Housing and Local Government [1958] 1 QB 554, [1958] 2 WLR 371, [1958] 1 All ER 625 **14.20**

R v Beard [1996] EWCA Crim 396, [1997] 1 PLR 64 **20.6**

R v Bristol CC ex p Anderson (1999) 79 P & CR 358, [1999] 25 LS Gaz R 30, (1999) Times, 5 July, [2000] PLCR 104 **14.24**

R v Clarke [2002] EWCA Crim 753, [2002] All ER (D) 36 (Mar) **20.7**

R v Clayton [2014] EWCA Crim 1030, [2014] 1 WLR 3994, [2014] 2 Cr App Rep 296, 178 CL&J 351, [2014] All ER (D) 02 (Jun) **20.13**

R v Epping and Harlow General Commissioners, ex p Goldstraw [1983] 3 All ER 257, [1983] STC 693, 57 TC 536 **23.3**

R v Flintshire County Council, ex parte Somerfield Stores Ltd [1998] PCR 336 **7.19**

R v Hillingdon LBC ex p Royco Homes Ltd [1974] 1 QB 720, [1974] 2 All ER 643, 72 LGR 516, 28 P & CR 251, 138 JP 505, 118 Sol Jo 389, 231 EG 739 **14.38**

R v Leicester City Council, ex p Powergen UK Ltd (2000) 81 P & CR 47, [2000] NPC 57, [2000] EGCS 64, [2000] JPL 1037, [2000] All ER (D) 696 **11.37**

R v Leominster DC ex p Pothecary (1997) 76 P & CR 346, [1997] 3 PLR 91, [1997] NPC 151, [1997] 45 LS Gaz R 28, [1998] JPL 335, (1997) Times, 18 November **5.10**

R v Monopolies and Mergers Commission, Ex p Argyll Group Plc [1986] 1 WLR 763, [1986] 2 All ER 257, 130 Sol Jo 467, [1986] LS Gaz R 1225 **23.13**

R v Newbury DC (1993) 65 P & CR 438 **11.17**

R. v Rochdale MBC ex parte Milne (No. 1), R. v Rochdale MBC ex parte Tew [2001] JPL 407, [2000] JPL 54, [2001] Env LR 22, [1999] 3 PLR 74 **8.27**

R. v Rochdale MBC ex parte Milne (No. 2) (2001) 81 P & CR 365, [2001] JPL 470 [2001] Env LR 406, [1999] 20 LS Gaz R 41, [1999] EGCS 70, **8.27**

R v Secretary of State for the Home Department ex parte Daly [2001] UKHL 26, [2001] AC 532, [2001] 2 WLR 1622,, [2001] 3 All ER 433, [2001] 26 LS Gaz R 43, (2001) Times,

Table of Acts and Measures

Table of Statutory Instruments

List of Circulars

List of Abbreviations

CIL	Community Infrastructure Levy
CPR	Civil Procedure Rules 1998
DMP(W)O	Town and Country Planning (Development Management Procedure) (Wales) Order 2012
EIA Regs	Town and Country Planning (Environmental Impact Assessment) (Wales) Regulations 2016
GOWA	Government of Wales Act 2006
NAW	National Assembly for Wales
NAWC	National Assembly for Wales Circular
NDF	National Development Framework
PA 2008	Planning Act 2008
PCPA 2004	Planning and Compulsory Purchase Act 2004
PPW	Planning Policy Wales (current edition is ed. 9 November 2016 and references to specific parts of PPW in the text are to this edition.)
TAN	Technical Advice Note
TCPA 1990	Town and Country Planning Act 1990
WAG	Welsh Assembly Government
WG	Welsh Government
WGC	Welsh Government Circular
WOC	Welsh Office Circular

Chapter 1

History and Structure of Devolution

INTRODUCTION

For present purposes the formal process of devolution in Wales starts with the Government of Wales Act 1998. This established the National Assembly for Wales and made provision for legislative and executive powers and functions to be exercised within the devolved subject areas. One area of devolved responsibility was town and country planning. The Assembly held its first session on 12 May 1999 and the Act was brought into force progressively by a series of six commencement orders from 1998 to 2001. Key functions were transferred by the National Assembly for Wales (Transfer of Functions) Order 1999.[1] 1.1

The current position is that new legislation in planning may be enacted by Acts of the National Assembly for Wales, statutory instruments are made by Welsh Ministers subject, where applicable, to approval by the Assembly, and ministerial functions generally in the field of planning are exercised by Welsh Ministers. The national body for planning guidance is the Welsh Ministers and policy statements and circulars are issued by them. Certain functions, notably development consent relating to nationally significant infrastructure projects and powers regarding the Community Infrastructure Levy, are not devolved and remain exclusively with the UK Parliament or UK Ministers.[2] 1.2

The Planning (Wales) Act 2015 is the first Welsh Act in this subject area. It amends certain parts of the principal planning Acts and continues the steady progress toward a distinct Welsh planning system. It therefore helps establish a central part of the body of Welsh law on planning although, of course, the framework remains UK legislation and many important provisions apply equally to England and Wales. 1.3

The Wales Act 2017 makes significant changes to the devolution settlement. The major changes are in the constitutional arrangements and the scope of devolved powers generally rather than in the practical operation of the planning system but in planning terms the changes will, in particular, affect responsibility for the Community Infrastructure Levy. The text here was written before the Act became law and deals with the position before its enactment and operation but, where essential, reference has been included to the effect of the Act in anticipation. Looking further ahead, significant change in land use planning may be anticipated 1.4

[1] SI 1999 No. 672.

[2] The Wales Act 2017 changes the legal basis of devolution. In planning terms the change will, in particular, affect powers regarding the Community Infrastructure Levy (see below).

with consideration of a codifying Planning Act. The Welsh Government has for some time indicated a desire to move towards consolidation of key legislation in this area and it is being advanced in the current programme of the Law Commission. Its work is at an early stage but is also referred to below.

1.5 This book is not a study of constitutional law and reference should be made to a specialist text for that purpose. However, to understand the law relating to planning in Wales, and in particular to understand the references to the various sources of law and policy as now applying, it is necessary to understand the historic and constitutional position. The position now established is summarised below at paragraphs 1.29–1.33, although, as stated, further devolution legislation will become operative and is referred to in summary. More detailed consideration of the scope and exercise of the specific devolved powers in connection with planning will be found in Chapters 2 and 4.

1.6 Following consideration of the process of devolution below, the following chapter considers the main elements of the Planning (Wales) Act 2015 and seeks to place Welsh planning law and practice in its UK context. The text then considers the law applicable in Wales and the key statutes, namely the Town and Country Planning Act 1990, the Planning and Compulsory Purchase Act 2004, the Planning Act 2008 and the Planning (Wales) Act 2015: the first two of these are referred to as TCPA 1990 and PCPA 2004 respectively in the text below.

HISTORY

1.7 Constitutionally Wales is part of the United Kingdom. The legal union of England and Wales dates back to the Laws in Wales Acts of 1535 and 1542. Until the Welsh Language Act 1967 indeed a reference to England in a statute included Wales.[3]

1.8 Geographically Wales is defined in the Interpretation Act 1978, Sch. 1 as the administrative areas created by the Local Government Act 1972, s. 20. These are the twenty-two unitary authorities defined as principal areas (counties or county boroughs) now established by virtue of the Local Government (Wales) Act 1994. In the Government of Wales Act 2006, Wales includes the sea adjacent to Wales as far as the seaward boundary of the territorial sea.[4] Article 6 of the National Assembly for Wales (Transfer of Functions) Order 1999[5] makes specific provision for the sea within the Severn and Dee estuaries adjacent to Wales and the Government of Wales Act 2006, s. 58(1A) excludes the transfer of ministerial functions exercisable in the Welsh zone beyond the seaward limit of the territorial sea. For practical purposes in planning, therefore, the local authority council boundary is the boundary.

[3] See Wales and Berwick Act 1746.

[4] Section 158(1). There is power to further define the boundary within British fishery limits under s. 158(3).

[5] SI 1999 No. 672.

The power to pass primary legislation, that is, the legislative competence of the National Assembly for Wales, is now governed by the Government of Wales Act 2006 by reference to defined subjects listed under the headings in Schedule 7 to the Act.[6] Heading 18 in Part 1 is 'Town and country planning'. The UK Parliament retains power to legislate on any matter whether devolved or not but it will not normally legislate on a devolved matter without the consent of the Assembly.[7] 1.9

Historically legislative power was in the UK Parliament alone although it is necessary to refer to the territorial application and commencement date in Wales of the UK laws and the express terms of the text to confirm the specific operation of individual provisions in Wales. England and Wales is a single legal jurisdiction and Acts of the UK Parliament and of the National Assembly for Wales extend to the whole jurisdiction but this is not to be confused with the question of whether a particular provision applies in the circumstances in question.[8] In addition, UK ministers exercised executive powers throughout Wales. Separate Welsh departments within the UK government existed from early in the twentieth century, most notably the Welsh Office with a Secretary of State for Wales, which was created in 1964 and survives in a form today. 1.10

The Government of Wales Act 1998 created the National Assembly for Wales and made provision for the transfer to and exercise of functions by the Assembly. Section 21 provided that the Assembly was to have the functions transferred to or made exercisable by the Act or conferred or imposed on the Assembly by the Act or any other Act. Ministerial functions were to be transferred in accordance with section 22, allowing the Assembly to have exclusive operation, to have power concurrently with the Minister of the Crown or specifying that the Minister could act only with the agreement of or after consultation with the Assembly. The result was that both secondary legislative and executive functions were exercised by the National Assembly for Wales. 1.11

Schedule 2 provided that one of the fields in which functions were to be transferred was Town and Country Planning. Other fields where functions were transferred – for example, agriculture and forestry, ancient monuments and historic buildings, the environment and highways – could impact on planning matters.[9] 1.12

Practical effect was given to this by the National Assembly for Wales (Transfer of Functions) Order 1999,[10] which came into force on 1 July 1999. The 1999 Order transferred functions under relevant statutes, including TCPA 1990, to the National Assembly for Wales subject to the exceptions and qualifications specified in Schedule 1 to the Order. Similarly, functions under other legislation relevant 1.13

[6] Government of Wales Act 2006, s. 108.

[7] This convention is formally recognised by the Wales Act 2107.

[8] For the meaning of geographical extent when referring to legislation on the UK Government legislation website, see its Glossary.

[9] Legislation in these areas will therefore become significant and the recent Environment (Wales) Act 2016, for example, is intended to link in with policies pursued under the Planning (Wales) Act 2015.

[10] SI 1999 No. 672.

to planning (e.g. Planning (Listed Buildings and Conservation Areas) Act 1990 and the Town and Country Planning (Costs of Inquiries etc.) Act 1995) were also transferred to the extent specified. A limited number of functions were transferred subject to concurrent exercise with the Secretary of State as specified in Schedule 2. Functions under related statutory instruments as specified were also transferred. There have been a number of subsequent orders transferring functions but for planning purposes relevant amendments are in the National Assembly for Wales (Transfer of Functions) Order 2000.[11] These continue to determine the extent of devolved functions following the further reforms of the 2006 Act.[12]

1.14 The Government of Wales Act 2006 amended the 1998 Act and provided for a separate executive, the Welsh Ministers, responsible for exercising devolved functions. The Order making powers of the Assembly were also transferred to the Welsh Ministers subject to appropriate procedures for Assembly approval. The majority of the provisions of the 2006 Act came into force immediately after the Assembly election held in May 2007.

1.15 The 2006 Act also extended the legislative powers of the Assembly. Section 94 provided that laws could be made by an Assembly Measure where provision could be made by an Act of Parliament but subject to the Assembly's legislative competence. Legislative competence was defined by reference to Schedule 5. Initially, therefore, there was power to pass secondary legislation within the devolved fields and also to make primary legislation subject to the limitations on competence and the insertion of a relevant matter into Schedule 5 by a Legislative Competence Order or Act of Parliament. Further provision was made by Planning Act 2008, section 202, which amended Schedule 5, adding legislative competence for plans relating to the development and use of land in Wales.

1.16 Section 107 of the 2006 Act provided for laws by Acts of the National Assembly for Wales subject to a referendum on commencement of the power.[13] The referendum of 2011 was in favour and this brought into operation the law-making powers of Part 4 of the Act superseding the previous power to make Measures: the effective date was 5 May 2011. Primary legislation since that date is accordingly by an Act of the National Assembly for Wales. There were no Measures specific to planning passed during the relevant period, 2007–2011, although they may be encountered in related fields, such as local government, playing fields, waste and housing. The Welsh Language (Wales) Measure 2011 is of general import and impacts on planning issues and processes generally and is considered in Chapter 3.

[11] SI 2000 No. 253. This varied the 1999 Order regarding planning by substituting the provisions in Schedule 1 to the 1999 Order. The effect was that functions under TCPA 1990, s. 270 regarding the electronic communications code network were not devolved.

[12] Again subject to the further transfer orders under the 2006 Act which do not, however, affect planning.

[13] Section 103.

An Act must be within the legislative competence of the Assembly,[14] defined as relating to a subject listed in Schedule 7, Part 1 to the 2006 Act and not within one of the exceptions listed in the Schedule.[15] The exceptions listed anywhere in the Schedule apply to all the subjects whether or not contained in the particular subject heading in question.[16] 1.17

There are certain general restrictions in section 108 of the Act. A provision must not apply otherwise than to Wales or concern functions exercisable other than in relation to Wales.[17] It is outside legislative competence if it breaches any restriction in Part 2 of Schedule 7 having regard to any exception in Part 3, it extends otherwise than to England and Wales or it is incompatible with Convention rights as defined in the Human Rights Act 1998, s. 1 or Community law.[18] 1.18

An Act may also provide for the enforcement of a provision which is within the Schedule or if it is otherwise appropriate for making such a provision effective or is otherwise incidental or consequential on such a provision. Whether any provision relates to a listed subject or an exception is to be determined by reference to the purpose of the provision, having regard, amongst other things, to its effect in all the circumstances.[19] 1.19

The proper approach to devolved powers was considered by the Supreme Court in *Re Agricultural Sector (Wales) Bill: Attorney General for England and Wales v Counsel General for Wales*,[20] where it was said: 1.20

> the scheme of the conferred powers model adopted for Welsh devolution, as embodied in the [2006 Act], is to limit the legislative powers of the Assembly in relation to subjects listed in Schedule 7 by reference to the express exceptions and limitations contained in the Act, rather than via some dividing up of the subjects in Schedule 7 along lines not prescribed in the legislation. Under section 108(4) and (7), the Assembly has legislative competence if the Bill relates to one of the subjects listed in Part 1 of Schedule 7, provided it is not within one of the exceptions. In most cases, an exception will resolve the issue. Where however there is no exception, as in the present case, the legislative competence is to be determined in the manner set out in section 108. Provided that the Bill fairly and realistically satisfies the test set out in section 108(4) and (7) and is not within an exception, it does not matter whether in principle it might also be

[14] Section 108.

[15] The provisions for legislative competence in s. 108 and Sch. 7 were considered by the Supreme Court in *Re Recovery of Medical Costs for Asbestos Diseases (Wales) Bill* [2015] UKSC 3.

[16] Section 108(4)(a). However, where a provision relates to a devolved tax it is not outside the competence by reason only of the fact that it falls within an exception listed under another heading (see s. 108(4A), inserted by Wales Act 2014).

[17] Section 108(4)(b).

[18] Section 108(6).

[19] Section 108(7).

[20] [2014] UKSC 43 at para. 67.

capable of being classified as relating to a subject which has not been devolved. The legislation does not require that a provision should only be capable of being characterised as relating to a devolved subject.

1.21 Town and Country Planning is a heading in Schedule 7[21] under which subjects are listed in the following terms: 'Town and country planning, including listed buildings, and conservation areas. Caravan sites. Spatial planning. Mineral workings. Urban development. New towns. Protection of visual amenity.' There is a specific exception to exclude 'Development Consent under the Planning Act 2008'.[22] Subjects under related heading areas (e.g. agriculture and ancient monuments) are also listed in the Schedule. The Planning (Wales) Act 2015, for example, identified the Act as relating to subjects listed under five headings in Schedule 7, namely Town and Country Planning, Local Government, Environment, Public Administration and the Welsh Language.

1.22 Notwithstanding that a subject is listed in Schedule 7, the UK Parliament may legislate on any matter relating to Wales. However, by convention, if any law relates to a devolved matter the prior consent of the National Assembly is required: this is given by a Legislative Consent Motion of the Assembly.[23]

1.23 In respect of other powers, section 58 provides for the transfer to the Welsh Ministers of any function so far as exercisable by a Minister of the Crown in relation to Wales, with provision for concurrent exercise and agreement or consultation where functions are not transferred. This thus transferred executive and secondary law-making powers previously exercised by the National Assembly for Wales to the Welsh Ministers. Further, the Welsh Ministers may by order make provision which has an effect in relation to Wales that corresponds to the effect an England-only provision of the Planning Act 2008 has in relation to England and conferring power on the Welsh Ministers to do anything in relation to Wales that corresponds to anything the Secretary of State has power to do by virtue of an England-only provision of that Act.[24]

1.24 The First Minister and Welsh Ministers are collectively known as the Welsh Ministers.[25] These Ministers and the Counsel General and Deputy Welsh Ministers were named the Welsh Assembly Government in the Act although from May 2011 they were known simply as the Welsh Government and this became the formal title with effect from 17 February 2015.[26] For the purposes of the subject matter

[21] See subject number 18 in the Schedule, as amended.

[22] See the Government of Wales Act 2006, Sch. 7, Pt 1, para. 18, as amended by the Localism Act 2011, Sch. 13, para. 79.

[23] See the Memorandum of Understanding and Supplementary Agreements between the United Kingdom Government, the Scottish Ministers, the Welsh Ministers, and the Northern Ireland Executive Committee (Oct. 2013).

[24] See the Planning Act 2008, s. 203, which also gives details of the England-only provisions and the procedure for Orders by the Welsh Ministers.

[25] Government of Wales Act 2006, s. 45.

[26] See Wales Act 2014, s. 4: in Welsh it is Llywodraeth Cymru.

of this book the formal power when exercising a function will generally be that of the Welsh Ministers and appeals and legal proceedings should therefore use the title Welsh Ministers.

By section 80 a community obligation of the United Kingdom is also an obligation of the Welsh Ministers in the exercise of their functions and by section 81 there is a general exclusion of acting contrary to the European Convention on Human Rights. 1.25

Those functions which had been transferred to the National Assembly for Wales following the 1998 Act were transferred to the Welsh Ministers by section 162 and paragraphs 30 and 32 of Schedule 11 to the 2006 Act. Accordingly, the terms of the Transfer of Functions Orders referred to above and the relevant exclusions apply to the exercise of functions by the Welsh Ministers. In addition there have been specific subsequent transfers either under the 2006 Act or by particular statutes. The Schedule contains transitional provisions for continuance of powers exercised under the 1998 Act. 1.26

The Transfer of Functions Orders specify those sections of TCPA 1990 where powers are not devolved. The exclusions essentially relate to certain functions concerning development with government authorisation, development on operational land of statutory undertakers and acquisition of special categories of land with concurrent powers regarding directions relating to national security. Reference should be made the Order[27] for the full terms. 1.27

In summary, therefore, the sources of Welsh planning law and practice reflect the developing legal and constitutional position of Wales as a result of over fifteen years of significant change and will continue to be affected by ongoing devolution. As far as concerns town and country planning, the majority of powers and functions are devolved. The relevant sources are listed below together with a description of the situation as presently existing. 1.28

CURRENT POSITION AND STATUS OF LAW AND POLICY

The result of the history above is that planning legislation applying in Wales comprises UK Parliament Acts and statutory instruments, statutory instruments from 1999 to 2007 made by the National Assembly for Wales, statutory instruments made since 2007 by Welsh Ministers (approved as appropriate by the National Assembly for Wales), Measures of the Assembly made between 2007 and 2011, and Acts of the National Assembly for Wales since May 2011. 1.29

The principal statutes governing the law and practice of planning in Wales are TCPA 1990, PCPA 2004, the Planning Act 2008 and the Planning (Wales) Act 2015. The latter makes significant alterations to the text of the three principal Acts as applicable in Wales and, although many provisions of these Acts are common 1.30

[27] Note that the terms of the 1999 Order regarding the 1990 Act exclusions were substituted under Schedule 3 to the 2000 Order.

to England and Wales, it is necessary to confirm the application to and operation of individual provisions in Wales. Relevant subordinate legislation is now generally of Welsh origin leading to separate rules, regulations and orders, for example governing planning applications and appeal procedures.

1.31 As noted above, other legislation of the National Assembly for Wales impacts on the planning process and decisions and the 2015 Act is one element of the overall strategy for land use and the environment in Wales. The 2015 Act expressly links in with the sustainability objectives of the Well-being of Future Generations Act 2015. Further, the principle of sustainable development is complemented by the provisions of the Environment (Wales) Act 2016. Development management for listed buildings and scheduled monuments and historical features generally is subject to changes made by the Historic Environment (Wales) Act 2016.

1.32 National policy was that of the UK Government until 1999. Guidance until that date reflected that position with circulars generally issued by the Welsh Office with a separate reference (WOC) although usually, but not invariably, worded as the English counterpart. National policy from 1999 until 2007 was the responsibility of the National Assembly for Wales.[28] Guidance was by circulars bearing the prefix 'NAW'[29] and by certain other statements and documents, a list of which is contained in the Welsh Government Index of Planning Policy and Guidance (revised December 2015).[30] From May 2007 policy and guidance has been the responsibility of the Welsh Ministers and circulars were identified as by the Welsh Assembly Government until 2011 and from then simply as the Welsh Government, with circulars prefixed 'WAGC' and 'WGC' respectively.

1.33 Key national policy is to be found in Planning Policy Wales, Minerals Planning Policy Wales and the various Technical Advice Notes. High level strategic guidance, whether or not specifically related to land use, is contained in the *Wales Spatial Plan: People, Places, Futures 2004* (updated 2008) adopted further to PCPA 2004, section 60. This is not part of the statutory development plan framework and, although local planning authorities must have regard to it in preparing local development plans, there is no requirement that local development plans conform with the Wales Spatial Plan.

1.34 This work deals with the legal position in Wales, not the differences between England and Wales, and the law and practice of planning in Wales is not considered by comparing the position in Wales with the position in England. Nevertheless, it is helpful to highlight where the process of devolution has taken planning in Wales to date, and the next chapter seeks to summarise key structural, procedural and substantive differences between Wales and England.

[28] Although the first edition of Planning Policy Wales pre-dated devolution and was issued in 1992.

[29] However, in places Welsh Government websites refer to these circulars by the prefix 'NafWC': 'NAW' is more usual and is the term in the Index and is used throughout this text.

[30] Since this date four circulars have been cancelled and replaced by the WG Development Management Manual, section 23.

In addition, there will be further significant change when the Wales Act 2017 is operative. The Act amends key provisions of the Government of Wales Act 2006 and will replace the existing conferred powers model with a reserved powers model and give additional powers to the National Assembly for Wales and the Welsh Ministers.[31] Accordingly, the basis of legislative competence and executive competence described in this chapter will be changed. 1.35

The Act inserts new provisions into the 2006 Act, declaring that the National Assembly and the Welsh Ministers are permanent parts of the constitutional arrangements of the United Kingdom. It provides that the law that applies in Wales includes a body of law made by the Assembly and Welsh Ministers and expressly recognises their ability to make law forming part of the law of England and Wales. GOWA 2006, section 107 is amended to recognise that the United Kingdom Parliament will not normally legislate with regard to devolved matters without the consent of the Assembly. The detailed provisions of the Act are beyond the scope of this work but for present purposes it should be noted that there is a general reservation of responsibility for the courts, civil and criminal proceedings and judicial review of administrative action.[32] The Act therefore retains the single legal jurisdiction for England and Wales. 1.36

The Act sets out the new limits of legislative competence replacing the existing section 108 of the Government of Wales Act 2006. It contains provisions regarding the territorial extent and application of legislation, allowing competence for ancillary provisions in defined circumstances, and for compatibility with other obligations. Critically, an Assembly Act will be outside legislative competence if it relates to any reserved matter as defined in the new Schedule 7A. 1.37

Schedule 7 will be replaced by new Schedules 7A and 7B which, as stated, operate on the basis that matters are devolved unless otherwise provided. The structure is for reservations, exceptions and carve-outs so that, in the words of the Bill Explanatory Notes: 'The reservations, less the exceptions, plus the carve outs equals the totality of the matters reserved to the UK Parliament'.[33] Accordingly, a reservation describes a subject matter in relation to which only the UK Parliament can pass primary legislation and any consequent secondary legislation as regards Wales. Schedule 7A contains both general and specific reservations. An exception describes a subject which would otherwise be reserved but which is stated to be within the legislative competence of the Assembly, but an exception may be subject to carve-out (an exception to the exception) so that it is effectively reserved. 1.38

It will be appreciated that a provision in an Assembly Act which is in relation to a subject matter within competence may affect the law in relation to a reserved matter. In that event the particular provision would be subject to the ancillary 1.39

[31] The description here of the Act is based on the text of the Bill as at 18 January 2017 following the final reading in the House of Lords and assumes its enactment in that form.

[32] See revised Schedule 7A, para. 8 to GOWA 2006.

[33] See para. 41: the Notes refer to the Bill as first introduced into Parliament in June 2016.

purpose test.[34] So, for example, giving effect to a planning matter may modify the law on a reserved matter and the issue then would be whether the provision was ancillary and whether it has a greater effect than is necessary to give effect to the planning provision.

1.40 The specific reservations are in Part 2 of Schedule 7A and section M3 is concerned with development and buildings, providing that planning generally is reserved but only for certain types of development. It states that planning, including the subject matter of Parts 2 to 8 of the Planning Act 2008, is reserved but only in relation to relevant nationally significant infrastructure projects, certain overhead electric lines, and railways other than those which start, end and remain in Wales. The significant change concerns the Community Infrastructure Levy, which will become a devolved matter.

1.41 The practical effect will be to continue devolution generally in the field of planning subject to the major exceptions for relevant nationally significant infrastructure projects as defined in section 14 of the 2008 Act. The precise scope of nationally significant infrastructure projects will depend on the extent of competence under the new arrangement and there are some modifications extending the scope of devolved powers which will affect development consent. These are in Part 2 of the Act, which refers to harbour facilities within section 24 of the 2008 Act and to generating stations with 350mw capacity or less. Associated development consent within section 115 of the 2008 Act is amended regarding designated generating stations and overhead electric lines.

1.42 Executive functions are the subject of a new section 58A inserted into the 2006 Act. Executive ministerial functions, that is a function of Her Majesty exercisable by a Minister of the Crown other than one conferred or imposed by legislation or the prerogative, are exercisable by Welsh Ministers so far as exercisable within devolved competence and where they are ancillary to executive functions conferred on Welsh Ministers exercisable outside devolved legislative competence. Functions are exercisable by Welsh Ministers alone unless the function is one listed for exercise concurrently.

STATUTORY INTERPRETATION

1.43 Finally, mention should be made about the general approach to devolved legislation.

1.44 The Government of Wales Act 2006, section 112 enables scrutiny of legislation by the Supreme Court to ensure that it is within legal competence. In addition, and quite distinct from the question of competence, section 114 empowers the Secretary of State to intervene on specified grounds, for example, that a Bill would have an adverse effect on the operation of the law as it applies in England.

1.45 Section 112 enables the Counsel General or the Attorney General to refer the question whether a Bill or provision in a Bill is within the Assembly's legislative

[34] See GOWA 2006, s. 108A.

competence to the Supreme Court within four weeks of its passing or subsequent approval on amendment.

Attorney General v National Assembly for Wales Commission and others[35] concerned a reference by the Attorney General in relation to sections 6 and 9 of the Local Government Byelaws (Wales) Bill and functions to be exercised by the Assembly and the Secretary of State concurrently in accordance with the National Assembly for Wales (Transfer of Functions) Order 1999. It was held that section 6 of the Bill removed a pre-commencement function of the Secretary of State and was therefore outside legislative competence. However, the provision was incidental to or consequential on the purposes of the Bill and for that reason fell within the competence: the primary purpose of the Bill was to remove the requirement for the confirmation of byelaws by the Welsh Ministers and there would be no point in so doing if the Secretary of State retained the power. 1.46

Reliance was also placed on the principle of construction in section 154(2) of the Government of Wales Act 2006 which requires any provision to be read as narrowly as is required for it to be within competence or within the powers relied on, if that is possible. 1.47

In other respects the approach to legislation and interpretation is as for UK legislation generally and, as noted, the planning legislation fits into the overall structure of UK Acts. 1.48

In a recent case, *Stevens (t/a* KCS Asset *Management) v Blaenau Gwent BC*,[36] statutory interpretation was considered against a submission that there was a gap in the legislative framework in Wales. It was said that there was a gap in the permitted development legislation applicable to Wales as article 3(1) of the Town and Country Planning (General Permitted Development) Order 1995 (the 1995 GPDO) refers to legislation that no longer exists (regulations 60 to 63 of the Conservation (Natural Habitats etc.) Regulations 1994 (1994 Regulations)). It was not amended to make any reference to the Habitats Regulations 2010. 1.49

Patterson J held that in accordance with the Interpretation Act 1978, sections 20(2) and 23(1), references to an enactment refer to the enactment as amended and the same rule applies to subordinate legislation as to the primary Act and accordingly there was no gap. She continued: 1.50

> Were there to be any doubt, member states are obliged to interpret domestic legislation in a manner that gives effect to European legislation where European legislation has competence. It follows that Article 3(1) of the 1995 GPDO must be construed so as to refer to legislation currently in force in Wales, that is the 2010 regulations, to give effect to the intention of the Habitats Directive so as to preserve, protect and improve the quality of the environment, including the conservation of natural habitats and of wild fauna and flora.

[35] [2012] UKSC 53, [2013] 1 AC 792.

[36] [2015] EWHC 1606 (Admin).

Chapter 2

Devolution and Planning – An Overview

INTRODUCTION

The previous chapter outlined the history and structure of the devolution settlement generally and noted how planning is a devolved subject. This chapter considers the overall results of that process and seeks to place Welsh planning law and practice in the wider UK context, with a brief overview comparing major elements of the planning system in the two countries. Significant differences between Wales and England are therefore dealt with as an introduction to the later chapters, which present the law and practice as it applies in Wales. 2.1

Key concepts and procedures in planning are the same in England and Wales and will be readily familiar to practitioners wherever situated. The meaning of development, when development is commenced, conditional permission, full and outline permission, section 106 obligations, breach of planning control, and appeals and statutory challenge, for example, are essentially the same. However, the formal sources of law and policy are different and certain processes, for example, permission in principle, do not apply in Wales. The principal planning Acts for each are the same but with a significant, and increasing, number of differences in the applicability of particular provisions. The development management provisions are not identical and the range of enforcement measures differ. Secondary legislation and policy have different sources and can only be approached by following the detailed wording of the particular applicable rule, regulation, order or policy. 2.2

The main differences stem from the different structure of government and administration and the framework of development plans and national policy, and significant variations are highlighted below. Sustainable development in both is a 'golden thread', although in Wales it is part of a wider legislative pattern. In terms of content one may single out the form and role of local and other development plans and the differences in approach to regional, local and community involvement. The central role of the Welsh Ministers should be noted, and this includes expressed concern over the deliverability of functions at local authority level, the status of the national policy as a development plan document and the degree of actual engagement in the local development plan process. Developments of national significance are dealt with by the Welsh Ministers, not the local planning authority, although the definition largely corresponds to that for nationally significant infrastructure projects requiring development consent from the Secretary of State in England and so is less significant in substance. 2.3

AREAS OF DIVERGENCE

2.4 Responsibility for planning in the UK lies with the Secretary of State for Communities and Local Government. In Wales the formal powers lie with the Welsh Ministers and departmental responsibility is with the Cabinet Secretary for Environment and Rural Affairs.

2.5 Wales has a unitary structure of local authorities under the Local Government (Wales) Act 1994. The authority for each administrative area is a principal authority and will be either a county council or county borough council[1] and is the local planning authority in Wales.[2] The more complex division in England with London Boroughs, metropolitan and non-metropolitan counties with county and district councils and some two-tier administrations is not replicated in any form. Nevertheless, preparation of local plans and control over development in England are single-tier, district council, functions with only mineral planning and specified exceptions lying with counties. Where there is a unitary council in England it will have all local planning authority functions and this corresponds to the Welsh position.[3]

2.6 Regional strategies for England have been abolished except for Greater London but the Planning (Wales) Act 2015 enables the Welsh Ministers to create strategic planning panels that will be responsible for a strategic plan creating an intermediate level between the Welsh Government and local planning authorities for development plans, but not for any other planning function.

2.7 In both England and Wales in an area of a National Park the National Park Authority will be the sole local planning authority[4] and provisions regarding enterprise zones,[5] urban development zones,[6] housing action areas[7] and the Homes and Communities Agency[8] apply, although the functions of this last-mentioned body are carried out by the Welsh Government. Below local planning authority level there is no equivalent in Wales of neighbourhood development orders, including community right to build orders, or neighbourhood development plans, and the provisions of TCPA 1990, sections 61E–61Q and Schedules 4B and 4C are applicable only in England.

2.8 Community interest in Wales is accommodated by the need for well-being plans introduced by the Well-being of Future Generations Act 2015 to replace community strategies. However, pilot projects are being undertaken to assist town and community councils in developing Place Plans, which are intended as

[1] The term 'City' may appear in the title.

[2] TCPA 1990, s. 1(1B).

[3] See TCPA 1990, s. 1 generally.

[4] TCPA 1990, s. 4A, subject to the further terms of that section.

[5] TCPA 1990, s. 6.

[6] TCPA 1990, s. 7.

[7] TCPA 1990, s. 8.

[8] TCPA 1990, s. 8A.

Supplementary Planning Guidance but will not have development plan status. Consultation for development plans and for individual planning permission may require or involve community or town councils.

The statutory duty to decide in accordance with the development plan unless material considerations otherwise require is fundamental in both regimes but in Wales there is particular emphasis on the formal plan as the definition of development plan under PCPA 2004, section 38 is different for England and for Wales. In Wales the development plan is the local development plan for an area.[9] However, in due course, when amendments made by the Planning (Wales) Act 2015 become fully operational, the development plan will be the National Development Framework for Wales, the strategic development plan for any strategic planning area and the local development plan, contrasting with the position in England. 2.9

The local planning authority development plan in Wales is different in form and of course subject to different regulations, policy and guidance, leading to differences in the detailed processes. Steps in the plan preparation and matters to which regard must be had are set out in the Act[10] and in the Town and Country Planning (Local Development Plan) (Wales) Regulations 2005.[11] 2.10

In Wales the local planning authority is under a duty to prepare a plan setting out its objectives in relation to the development and use of land and its general policies to implement them. It may set out specific policies for any part of its area.[12] There must be a sustainability appraisal and this must include an assessment of the likely effects of the plan on the Welsh language.[13] 2.11

The Welsh Government must be consulted in the course of plan preparation and has powers to intervene under PCPA 2004, section 65 where the plan is unsatisfactory, and has default powers under section 71. Particular attention should be paid to the evidence base so that the plan is based on 'up-to-date relevant and proportionate information'[14] in accordance with the review requirements of section 61. Policy requirements are set out in Chapter 2 of Planning Policy Wales including statements as to the form and content of the plan. 2.12

The plan must be submitted to an independent examination to determine if it complies with statute and is sound.[15] 2.13

In England the statutory regime is under Part 2 of PCPA 2004 (sections 13–37) whereas, as noted, Part 6 is applicable in Wales. Outside Greater London, the development plan comprises the development plan documents and any neighbourhood 2.14

[9] Transitional provisions enable reliance on the previous adopted plan, the Unitary Development Plan or earlier plan as not all authorities have a UDP, until replaced by adoption of a local development plan. The intent is for the NDF to be operational from March 2020.

[10] I.e. PCPA 2004, ss. 62–63, as amended.

[11] SI 2005 No. 2839, as amended.

[12] PCPA 2004, s. 62(1)–(3).

[13] PCPA 2004, s. 62.

[14] See PPW 2.2.1.

[15] PCPA 2004, s. 64.

development plan.[16] The local planning authority is obliged to prepare and maintain a local development scheme, one requirement of which is to specify the development plan documents.[17] These documents will be the local plan[18] and must set out the authority's policies relating to the development and land use in their area.[19] In preparing the plan the local planning authority must have regard to national policies and other strategies[20] and it must be independently examined in order to assess whether it is sound (s. 20). Policy is in the National Planning Policy Framework ('NPPF'), paragraphs 150–185, which set out what the local plan should do and the test of soundness in terms somewhat different from the Welsh counterparts.

2.15 The Secretary of State has default power to intervene and powers regarding examination of the plan although the detailed wording of the provisions is not identical to the corresponding Welsh provisions.

2.16 A further distinction is the introduction in Wales of a category of developments of national significance. To an extent the developments in question are developments in Wales which, were the land in England, would be nationally significant infrastructure projects and are therefore a consequence of the more limited definition of these projects in Wales because of devolved powers. Nevertheless, the scope could extend to a wider group of developments and will lead to the grant of planning permission, not development consent. The application process has affinity with the provision which will allow developers at their option to apply for planning permission directly to government rather than to the local planning authority.

2.17 In addition, permission in principle, introduced in England by the Housing and Planning Act 2016, does not apply in Wales and it is expressly stated that a reference to permission in principle in any provision of TCPA 1990 in its application to land in Wales, or in its application to functions of the Welsh Ministers or other authorities in Wales, is to be ignored.[21]

PRIMARY LEGISLATION – GENERAL

2.18 Starting with primary legislation, numerous statutes impact on the planning process but in both Wales and England the key statutes are TCPA 1990, PCPA 2004 and the Planning Act 2008.[22] In addition, the Planning (Listed Building and Conservation

[16] PCPA 2004, s. 38(3). Neighbourhood development plan is defined in s. 38A.

[17] PCPA 2004, ss. 15 and 37(3).

[18] The definition of local plan is in reg. 6 of the Town and Country Planning (Local Planning) (England) Regulations 2012 (SI 2012 No. 767) and refers to the various documents which may form the plan. The regulations also contain details of the form and content of the plan.

[19] PCPA 2004, s. 17.

[20] PCPA 2004, s. 19.

[21] TCPA 1990, s. 58A(4).

[22] The Law Commission Consultation Paper on Planning Law in Wales published in July 2016 at para. 4.3 lists forty-eight Acts relating to planning and land use in Wales.

Areas) Act 1990 and the Planning (Hazardous Substances) Act 1990 apply to both.[23] EU law and policy, where it impacts on planning, is an integral part of the legal framework in Wales as in England, at least for the present, although it will be subject to the terms of withdrawal from EU membership.

There are, however, important differences in the application of certain provisions of the main Acts. Before looking at some of the major differences it is necessary to note how differences in the application of a statute in Wales and in England may arise. England and Wales is a single legal jurisdiction so that statutes will extend to England and Wales: the question is which provisions actually apply to the particular circumstances in question. 2.19

The different sources of law may not always be immediately apparent,[24] although, increasingly, individual provisions are expressed as applying in England or in Wales, as the case may be. For example, TCPA 1990, sections 61W and 61Z both refer to pre-application consultation, with the former expressly stated to refer to land in England and the latter to land in Wales, and in each case the section heading identifies this. Comparison of the two, however, illustrates that the precise wording is not the same. In addition, as noted above, a provision may state that any reference is to be ignored in relation to land in Wales.[25] 2.20

The territorial application, if not apparent from the heading, may be limited by the detailed wording of the statutory provision. TCPA 1990, section 74A, for example, only applies to a condition attached to planning permission for land in England. The time limits in sections 91 and 92 are separately identified for England and for Wales, with different subsections referring to each. 2.21

The language in each section may not be a sufficient indicator, however, and it may be necessary to refer to a general interpretation clause or to have knowledge of the general applicability of other provisions. A reference in a section to a neighbourhood development order, for example as in TCPA 1990, section 108, would not be relevant to Wales as such orders do not apply, although section 108 generally is applicable. 2.22

More confusingly, a provision once confined to England in terms may be extended by later amendment in Wales. Remaining with section 108 therefore, the amendment to this by the Planning Act 2008, section 189 was applicable only in England but, by relying on the power in section 203 of the 2008 Act to make provision in Wales corresponding to an English provision, TCPA 1990, section108 was amended by the Planning Permission (Withdrawal of Development Order or Local Development Order) (Compensation) (Wales) Order 2012, article 2[26] so that it applies in Wales. 2.23

[23] These Acts, together with the Planning (Consequential Provisions) Act 1990, are defined as the planning Acts in s. 336 of TCPA 1990.

[24] The complexity is commented on in the Law Commission Consultation paper on Planning Law in Wales.

[25] TCPA 1990, s. 58A(4).

[26] SI 2012 No. 210.

2.24 Use of the term 'Welsh Ministers' would be definitive[27] but a reference to 'Secretary of State' would not as there has been a general transfer of functions to Welsh Ministers in the field of planning, as noted in the previous chapter, and the original reference may remain in the text of the Acts.

2.25 Apart from this, commencement orders for Wales are made independently by the Welsh Ministers and in England by the Secretary of State and the operative dates may be widely apart (for example, temporary stop notices commenced in England in March 2005 and in Wales in June 2015) or lead to commencement in, say, England but no operative date as yet in Wales (for example, as with TCPA 1990, sections 70A and 70B conferring power to decline applications).

2.26 An indication of where the principal Act, TCPA 1990, contains provisions applying differently in England and Wales follows but it is helpful first to look at the different impacts of key post-devolution Acts, in particular as they have amended or modified the 1990 Act.

2.27 As far as concerns PCPA 2004, there are marked differences in application. Part 6 is specifically concerned with plans in Wales. It makes provision for the Wales Spatial Plan, strategic planning and local development plans: in turn there have been later amendments to this Part by the Planning (Wales) Act 2015. Part 2, local development, relates only to England, leading to structural differences in development plan documents. The definition of development plan in section 38 is separately worded for Wales and England[28] and the neighbourhood development plan provisions apply only in England.

2.28 The development control provisions, other than for local development orders, broadly apply but care is needed to confirm the particular application and effective commencement and amendment to TCPA 1990.

2.29 The Planning Act 2008, dealing primarily with non-devolved matters, applies equally in Wales and England. Responsibility for nationally significant infrastructure projects, however, depends upon a matter being the responsibility of the UK Parliament and Ministers and not devolved. Therefore it affects only major energy projects and certain harbour development in Wales. Details of the differences in classification of nationally significant infrastructure projects in England and Wales and related differences in the development consent regime are dealt with in Chapter 8 as they are essential to an understanding of the regime in Wales. The Wales Act 2017 makes further changes affecting responsibility for energy and harbour developments, which are also referred to in Chapter 8.

2.30 The Localism Act 2011, Part 6[29] is concerned with planning but it is largely confined to England, save for those chapters dealing with nationally significant

[27] Subject, of course, to the date of commencement.

[28] Section 38(4), as amended, compared with subsection (2) for Greater London and (3) for England, with resulting differences in application of later sections of the Act.

[29] Sections 109–144.

infrastructure projects[30] and the Community Infrastructure Levy:[31] these are not devolved subjects and the provisions therefore apply in England and Wales. Other provisions of Part 6 are not generally applicable in Wales. For example, neighbourhood development orders do not apply in Wales and consequently sections 61E–61Q of TCPA 1990 are confined to England. Notable exceptions are section 125, inserting section 172A into TCPA 1990, relating to assurances regarding prosecution following service of an enforcement notice and the amendment to various enforcement time limits and penalties in TCPA 1990 made by section 126, which, however, has a lower maximum fine in Wales than in England. A full list of the territorial application is at Annex A to the Explanatory Memorandum to the Act. The amendments to TCPA 1990, PCPA 2004 and Planning Act 2008 made by the Act, where applicable in Wales, are dealt with in the later chapters below as appropriate.

Various later statutes, to the extent that they affect planning, for example, the Growth and Infrastructure Act 2013, the Enterprise and Regulatory Reform Act 2013, the Infrastructure Act 2015 and the Housing and Planning Act 2016, generally apply only to England. Insofar as they amend TCPA 1990, this leads to appreciable differences in application and key ones are mentioned below. 2.31

Significant amendments to town and country planning in Wales are in the Planning (Wales) Act 2015. It proceeds largely by amending TCPA 1990 and PCPA 2004, the new provisions therefore marking an important distinction between England and Wales, although the subject matter of some of the provisions correspond to England-only provisions found in those Acts or elsewhere and they may mirror England-only amendments made by different statutes. 2.32

The Historic Environment (Wales) Act 2016 amends the Planning (Listed Buildings and Conservation Areas) Act 1990 with regard to Wales and is considered in Chapter 24. One point of note is that conservation area consent for demolition works in Wales remains and has not been merged with planning permission as the amendments made by the Enterprise and Regulatory Reform Act 2013 apply only in England. 2.33

Before giving a brief comparison it is appropriate to consider the overall aim and structure of the 2015 Act as it marks a significant step toward a distinct planning system. One overarching feature is the degree of centralisation, with the Welsh Ministers having an enhanced role, and the objective of streamlining the planning process has led to differences of detail at the procedural level. 2.34

30 Chapter 6, ss. 128–142.

31 Chapter 2, ss. 114–115. The levy will not be a reserved matter under the terms of the Wales Act 2017 and so will become a devolved responsibility on implementation of the Act.

PLANNING (WALES) ACT 2015

2.35 The focus of the Act was stated to be on 'delivery structures, processes and procedures' and it is a framework Act providing for the detailed working to be contained in later Rules, Regulations and Orders. The current policy approach to use of the new powers for subordinate legislation is in the Welsh Government's published statements of policy intent. A number of topics have been or are to be the subject of consultation papers and will evolve further with time. The intended timescale for implementation can be found in the Positive Planning Implementation Plan published by the Welsh Government in December 2015.[32]

2.36 The precise mechanisms are therefore largely subject to later implementation by secondary legislation and will progressively establish the distinctive character of planning in Wales. However, the Planning (Wales) Act 2015 makes numerous amendments to TCPA 1990, inserting new provisions, and makes amendments to other statutes, in particular to PCPA 2004. The result can appear somewhat unwieldy, with a lengthy list of newly inserted sections, identified by suffixes, to be taken into account.

2.37 There is a stated intention to move to consolidating legislation. This topic is currently being considered by the Law Commission as part of its Twelfth Programme, which included planning law in Wales. The approach adopted has been in terms of simplification and codification and should be considered together with the Commission's Final Report on the Form and Accessibility of the Law Applicable in Wales.[33] The current situation is that a scoping consultation paper was published on 30 June 2016[34] with the intent of publishing a final consultation paper in early 2017, with a final report thereafter.

2.38 The Act is divided into nine parts, of which the five key ones for present purposes are development planning, pre-application procedure, applications to Welsh Ministers, development management, and enforcement and appeals.

2.39 Structurally of major significance is the introduction of a three-tier policy framework with the adoption of the National Development Framework and Strategic Development Plans (where appropriate), which will have statutory development plan status. This is dealt with in Part 3 (sections 3–16). The National Development Framework will replace the Wales Spatial Plan and deals with development and land use issues of national significance. It will be prepared and published by the Welsh Ministers and a draft is to be laid before the National Assembly for Wales and any resolution of the Assembly is to be taken into account by the Ministers in adopting the plan.

2.40 Strategic Development Plans, which lie between national and local plans, are for those areas where considered appropriate concerning issues crossing local

[32] See also the April 2016 update.

[33] Law Commission No. 366, dated 29 June 2016.

[34] Law Commission Consultation Paper No. 228.

planning authority boundaries. The Minister has stated that there would only be around two strategic development plans.[35]

Pre-application procedure is strengthened by measures in Part 4 (sections 17–18) for consultation and for assistance from the local planning authority, or Welsh Ministers where they are the decision-making body, before an application is formally made and to enable fees to be charged for this service.[36] 2.41

Part 5 (sections 19–27) provides for two situations where an application for permission may be made directly to Welsh Ministers in the first instance. It introduces a new category of permission for developments of national significance lying between development consent orders and local planning authority decisions. The further provisions enable developers to make an application for planning permission directly to the Welsh Ministers where a planning authority is consistently performing badly within the criteria laid down by the Welsh Ministers. 2.42

Part 6 (sections 28–42) deals with development management. It contains provisions as to the requirements for an application, decisions on applications and the duration of permissions. Notable provisions concern consideration of the Welsh language and these are dealt with in Chapter 3 of this text. 2.43

Part 7 (sections 43–51) contains new provisions for an enforcement warning notice and measures concerning appeals against planning decisions and enforcement notices. 2.44

The Act contains a number of more general and miscellaneous provisions in Parts 1, 2 and 8, including a restriction on the right to apply for registration of town and village greens, amending the Commons Act 2006. These lie outside the scope of this work. 2.45

Commencement of these provisions is in accordance with section 58 and subsequent Commencement Orders. Three Commencement Orders have been made at the time of writing.[37] Taken together, the result is that the majority of the provisions of the Act came into force on dates between 6 July 2015 and 16 March 2016 subject to saving and transitional provisions, although certain provisions are in force only insofar as they relate to developments of national significance and secondary consents. The law as stated below states the position applying where all relevant acts or steps post-date commencement of the applicable provision and ignores the transitional provisions. 2.46

[35] See Minister for Natural Resources, plenary debate, 7 October 2014. Three possible areas are referred to elsewhere.

[36] England-only arrangements in this regard were introduced by the Localism Act 2011.

[37] The Planning (Wales) Act 2015 (Commencement No. 1) Order 2015 (SI 2015 No. 1736), the Planning (Wales) Act 2015 (Commencement No. 2 and Transitional and Saving Provisions) Order 2015 (SI 2015 No. 1987) and the Planning (Wales) Act 2015 (Commencement No. 3 and Transitional Provisions) Order 2016 (SI 2016 No. 52).

2.47 The remaining provisions of the Act are in force only so far as is necessary for enabling the Welsh Ministers to exercise any function of making regulations or orders by statutory instrument under any enactment as amended by them.[38]

2.48 The provisions not fully in force therefore are sections 5–10, which refer to aspects of strategic planning and the National Development Framework and strategic development plans; certain detailed amendments further to section 16 and Schedule 2 ; section 23 referring to the option to make a planning application to the Welsh Ministers; section 39 which is concerned with the way in which the local planning authority discharges its functions by committee or otherwise; and sections 47, 48 and 50, all of which refer to aspects of appeals.

2.49 Those provisions operative only in relation to developments of national significance and secondary consents (and therefore not in force in relation to other application to Welsh Ministers) are sections 24–27, section 33 (decision notices), section 34 (notification of development), section 50 (inquiry procedure) and Schedules 3 and 4 (procedure).

2.50 Secondary legislation of significance relying on powers in the 2015 Act include the Town and Country Planning (Pre-Application Services) (Wales) Regulations[39] and the set of five regulations to implement the provisions concerning developments of national significance. The latter came into force on 1 March 2016 and are referred to in Chapter 10 of the text below.

2.51 For the purposes of this work, the fact that provisions are not fully in force is noted and the absence of any consequential rules, regulations and orders should minimise possible confusion although the pace of change inevitably means that care will be needed to follow provisions as progressively introduced.

TOWN AND COUNTRY PLANNING ACT 1990

2.52 The main differences in the text of TCPA 1990 applicable in England and in Wales are highlighted below.

2.53 In England the option to apply for planning permission to the Secretary of State is in sections 62A–62C, in Wales the provisions are in sections 62M–62O but are not yet in force. Developments of national significance in Wales are subject to a separate regime under TCPA 1990, sections 62D–62L. This overlaps with development that may be subject to development consent in England but it is a distinct regime leading to planning permission.

2.54 The pre-application consultation provisions in Wales are TCPA 1990, sections 61Z–61Z2 but sections 61W–61Y in England and appeals regarding validity of planning applications in Wales are in sections 62ZA–ZD. Thereafter, the terms of section 62 which enable a development order to make provision governing planning applications, including their form and content, distinguish England and Wales

[38] See s. 58(2).

[39] See Chapter 12.

for certain purposes: a relevant application is one to which section 61W applies and is therefore confined to England and subsections (9)–(11) refer expressly to a 'relevant Welsh application'. The consultation provisions of section 100A apply only in Wales.

The powers to decline applications in sections 70A and 70B are not in force in Wales, although the power to decline retrospective applications in section 70C is in force as amended. Provisions regarding notices were added for Wales by the 2015 Act – see TCPA 1990, sections 71ZA and 71ZB. 2.55

Section 73(5) prohibits extending time for carrying out development without complying with a condition and is expressed to apply only to land in England. In Wales there is no prohibition on a section 73 application which in effect extends the time for commencement provided the application itself is made before expiry of the time limit. Amendments by the Planning (Wales) Act 2015, section 35, inserting subsections (3ZA)–(3ZD) into TCPA 1990, section 91, mean that the new section 73 permission will last for the unexpired period of the original permission, unless otherwise stated. 2.56

Similarly, section 74A, concerning deemed discharge of conditions, applies only to the development of land in England and local financial considerations are of English-only concern as TCPA 1990, section 70(2)(b) is expressly excluded by section 70(2A) in Wales. TCPA 1990, section 78A enables a local authority to serve a notice of its decision after an appeal has been lodged and is fully operative in Wales but in England the commencement only enables the making of rules, regulations or orders. 2.57

The time limits in sections 91 and 92 are differently worded for England and for Wales. The applicable period for the duration of planning permission in England is three years and in Wales is five years.[40] The time for approval of reserved matters in each is three years but in England the development must be begun within two years of the final approval, whereas in Wales it must be begun within five years or, if later, within two years of final approval.[41] 2.58

Moving to other parts of the Act, the enforcement provisions are not identical: sections 171BA–171BC, referring to planning enforcement orders, apply only in England, while enforcement warning notices under section 173ZA apply only to land in Wales. The appeal provisions in section 174 contain differently worded subsections for England and Wales. 2.59

Sections 195 and 196, appeals on applications for certificates of lawful use and development, have certain specific subsections relating to Welsh Ministers. Section 196A is inapplicable as it was inserted by a provision of the Enterprise and Regulatory Reform Act 2013 which relates to conservation areas in England. 2.60

The validity provisions of sections 284, 288 and 289 contain additional provisions referring expressly to the exercise of powers specifically by Welsh Ministers. Sections 303 and 303ZA concerning fees and section 303A concerning the costs 2.61

[40] Section 91(5)(a) and (b).

[41] Section 92(2).

of certain inquiries refer specifically to the position in Wales. Generally, of course, the text of ancillary provisions in the Act must be read subject to the extent of devolution of relevant powers and functions to Welsh Ministers and a number of the miscellaneous provisions in Part XV relate separately to England or Wales as identified in the heading (e.g. section 322 costs, England and section 322C costs in Wales).

SECONDARY LEGISLATION

2.62 Secondary legislation under the devolved powers regarding planning will be by separate Orders, Rules and Regulations for each of England and Wales as the majority of executive functions under TCPA 1990 and PCPA 2004 have been transferred to the Welsh Ministers. So, for example, development management procedure is subject to the Town and Country Planning (Development Management Procedure) (England) Order 2015[42] in England and the Town and Country Planning (Development Management Procedure) (Wales) Order 2012[43] in Wales, and the arrangement of the Orders is not identical.

2.63 Pre-devolution statutory instruments have also been amended since 1999 so that the provisions are no longer the same. For example, the Town and Country Planning (Use Classes) Order 1987 applies in England and Wales but modifications in England are not all applied in Wales: for instance, class A3 is differently worded and classes A4 and A5 do not apply in Wales. Wales-only amendments were made in 2002, 2006 and 2016.[44]

2.64 Permitted development in Wales is governed by the Town and Country Planning (General Permitted Development) Order 1995[45] as amended. In England it has been replaced by the 2015 Order[46] which consolidated the original Order and its various amendments and made further fresh amendments including permitted development rights to facilitate change to residential use, allow change of use from shops to financial and professional services and to restaurants, cafes and leisure uses.

2.65 Procedure generally is subject to the Town and Country Planning (Development Management Procedure) (Wales) Order 2012 as amended and in England by the 2015 Order.

[42] SI 2015 No. 595.

[43] SI 2012 No. 801.

[44] SI 2002 No. 1875, SI 2006 No. 1386 and SI 2016 No. 28.

[45] SI 1995 No. 418.

[46] SI 2015 No. 596.

POLICY FRAMEWORK

Turning to national guidance and policy, nationally significant infrastructure projects, wherever situated, are subject to national policy statements. Apart from this, in Wales the strategic framework is set by the Wales Spatial Plan[47] and national policy comprises Planning Policy Wales (PPW), Technical Advice Notes, circulars and policy clarification letters. This structure will be modified by the National Development Framework, which will sit alongside Planning Policy Wales and will have Development Plan status to form the core central element of national strategic planning when adopted further to PCPA 2004.[48] 2.66

In England, policy is set out in the National Planning Policy Framework and additional matters are in topic-specific guidance. The NPPF should be read in conjunction with the policy for traveller sites, and waste policies are dealt with in the National Waste Management Plan for England. As is well known, the NPPF was introduced in 2012 to replace over one thousand pages with a text of around fifty pages, and replaced forty-four policy documents. Its purpose is as guidance for local planning authorities and decision-takers both in drawing up plans and as a material consideration in determining applications. 2.67

The result is that PPW is a lengthier document with more descriptive elements explaining the planning system and more detailed statements on the key subjects addressed, although more abbreviated in the latest (ninth) edition, with reliance in places on the Development Plan Manual. However, its essential purpose is the same as for the NPPF and both seek to set out national policy to ensure sustainable development, although in Wales this is in accordance with the statutory obligation of the Well-being of Future Generations (Wales) Act 2015. This is reflected in the different texts of PPW and NPPF on sustainability. Historically, although Green Belts are recognised national policy, the reliance on them is widely divergent and there is still only one area of Green Belt in Wales.[49] 2.68

47 Made further to PCPA 2004, s. 60.

48 See ss. 60, 60A and 60B, inserted by s. 3 of the Planning (Wales) Act 2015.

49 An area between Cardiff and Newport.

Chapter 3

Welsh Language and the Planning System

INTRODUCTION

This chapter addresses two issues: use of the Welsh language in the course of the planning process and its role as a material consideration in planning policy and decision-making. 3.1

The progressive implementation of the Welsh Language (Wales) Measure 2011 and of the amendments made by the Planning (Wales) Act 2015, sections 2, 3, 6, 11 and 31 will materially alter the formal position. 3.2

In broad summary, the English and Welsh languages have equal status. In legal proceedings a person has a right to use Welsh or English. The use of the languages by public bodies was in accordance with their published Welsh language scheme but will be in accordance with formal standards in accordance with the 2011 Measure when fully operational with compliance enforced by the Welsh Language Commissioner. 3.3

In practice, throughout the planning process the use of Welsh or English depended on area, although the choice of language was that of the contributor in question, and where matters are heard in public a simultaneous translation service should be, and is generally, available. The translation of formal documents in planning was not consistent: some development plans are in English and Welsh and some are not and applications depended on individual circumstances with no particular clarity as to who would provide translation in individual cases. The implementation of Standards applying to all local planning authorities should lead to a more uniform approach. 3.4

Whether or not the Welsh language is a material consideration in planning policy is the subject of guidance, notably TAN 20, and some local planning authorities have specific Welsh language planning policies and these accordingly may impact on individual developments. The Planning (Wales) Act 2015 refers to the role of the Welsh language generally and in preparing a development plan and in applications for planning permission. 3.5

OFFICIAL STATUS OF THE WELSH LANGUAGE

The legal position of the Welsh language in recent history can be taken as starting with the Welsh Language Act 1967 (now repealed), followed by the Welsh Language Act 1993 (also largely repealed) and continued with the Government of Wales Act 1998. The key current legislative provisions are the Government of 3.6

Wales Act 2006 and the Welsh Language (Wales) Measure 2011, together with amendments made by the Planning (Wales) Act 2015.

3.7 As indicated, not all relevant provisions are fully operational and the particular commencement is referred to below, although of course the legal status of and right to use the Welsh language have been established for many years.

3.8 The official status of the Welsh Language now contained in section 1 of the Measure came into force on the date of the Measure[1] and there is power for Welsh Ministers to make specified regulations and orders including those relating to the Welsh Language Commissioner. Regulations (see below) were passed in March 2015 and notice was issued to the Welsh Ministers, all county council and county borough councils and the three national park authorities in September 2015 of what they are expected to do to comply with the standards. By 30 March 2016 these bodies were to comply with the standards, which will replace their statutory schemes. Other bodies are required to comply by later Regulations.

3.9 The Welsh language has official status in Wales by the Welsh Language (Wales) Measure 2011, section 1(1). Without prejudice to this general principle, legal effect is given to this status by enactments imposing duties or conferring powers. These are described in the further provisions of the section. For present purposes, the particular matters of relevance are enactments giving equal standing to the Welsh and English language texts of Measures and Acts of the National Assembly for Wales and subordinate legislation,[2] those which confer a right to speak the Welsh language in legal proceedings in Wales[3] and those which create standards for the use of the Welsh language in the delivery of services and policy making.[4]

3.10 Taking these in turn, the Government of Wales Act 2006, section 35[5] provides that the official languages of the National Assembly are English and Welsh and they must be treated on a basis of equality.

3.11 The right to use Welsh in legal proceedings in Wales is contained in the Welsh Language Act 1993, section 22, which refers both to spoken Welsh and to documents. In civil proceedings this is reflected in the Practice Direction Relating to the Use of the Welsh Language in Cases in the Civil Courts in Wales.[6] For criminal proceedings the matter is governed by the Criminal Procedure Rules, rule 3.26.

3.12 It will be noted that the right in section 22 of the Welsh Language Act 1993 is for use in legal proceedings in Wales: it has been held that this referred to the geographical location of the proceedings and did not apply to appeal proceedings heard outside Wales for the determination of disputes commenced in Wales.[7]

1 9 February 2011.

2 Section 1(3)(c).

3 Section 1(3)(b).

4 Section 1(3)(e).

5 As amended by the National Assembly for Wales (Official Languages) Act 2012.

6 Current version last updated 1 April 2013.

7 *Williams v Cowell (t/a The Stables)* [2000] 1 WLR 187.

There is no definition of 'legal proceedings' in the Act and decisions on applications by local planning authorities or Welsh Ministers could fall outside the term, which is concerned with courts and tribunals. All such decisions and actions would, however, have been subject to the Welsh Language Scheme adopted by each of them. Inquiries held under the Planning Acts were covered by the Planning Inspectorate Welsh Language Scheme. Standards required under the Measure now apply to all these functions of local planning authorities, the Welsh Ministers and the Planning Inspectorate. The structure of the Measure concerning Standards is dealt with below. 3.13

In addition, section 113 of the Measure is concerned with interference with the freedom to use Welsh, a matter which may be investigated by the Welsh Language Commissioner. 3.14

WELSH LANGUAGE STANDARDS

The content of the various schemes adopted by relevant bodies differed. In practice, development plans and policy documents may be in English or in English and Welsh and persons use either language orally or in written documents as they choose. Translation is made available for public hearings but there was no formal requirement that documents generally are to be in both languages or for translation where provided in one only. The Planning Inspectorate's revised scheme was approved by the Welsh Language Commissioner in September 2014 and relates to the situation before compliance with Standards was required. The current position is that standards will be in accordance with the compliance notice issued to the Welsh Government under the Welsh Language Measure 2011. In general terms the Measure will require no less favourable treatment of the Welsh language and steps to promote its use. 3.15

The Measure established the office of the Welsh Language Commissioner, whose principal aim is to promote and facilitate the use of the Welsh language[8] and who has powers of inquiry[9] and can instigate and intervene in legal proceedings, although this does not of itself create any cause of action.[10] 3.16

The Measure requires persons and bodies as specified in one of Schedules 5, 6, 7 and 8 to comply with standards. A person is required to comply with a standard if six conditions laid down by section 25 are met. The conditions are the subject of the further provisions of Chapters 3–6 of Part 4 of the Measure. Section 26 of the Measure enables the Welsh Ministers to specify the standards and section 39 enables provision that a standard is specifically applicable by authorising the Welsh Language Commissioner to issue a compliance notice requiring the recipient to comply with a standard. 3.17

[8] Section 3.

[9] Section 7.

[10] Section 8.

3.18 Those who may be required to comply are listed in the Measure[11] and include the Welsh Government and local authorities and also other bodies who may be consultees in the planning process. The application to organisations is in stages and, as affects planning, the Welsh Ministers and local planning authorities are in the first stage.

3.19 The first Regulations, the Welsh Language Standards (No. 1) Regulations 2015[12] were made in March 2015. They will apply to the functions of the Welsh Ministers, county and county borough councils and National Park Authorities at various stages of the planning process. Under the Measure, standards apply separately to service delivery, policy making, operational matters, promotion and record keeping and it is necessary to consider the particular function for the content of the obligation. They have applied since 30 March 2016.

3.20 These standards therefore provide the essential content of the requirement for key personnel in the planning process to use and facilitate the use of the Welsh language. Compliance will be the responsibility of the Welsh Language Commissioner who can apply sanctions. There will be appeal to the Welsh Language Tribunal.

3.21 The Local Development Plan Manual Edition 2 (August 2015) refers to the standards and future practice at paragraph 2.8.1, saying:

> Many of the Standards are likely to be relevant to all stages of the process of preparing and revising LDPs but particularly to the way in which LPAs publicise proposals, consult with the public, communicate with those making representation and make arrangements for the conduct of examination proceedings. Use of the Welsh language in communications should be identified in the Community Involvement Scheme.

3.22 The key relevant parts of the compliance notice for planning purposes provide for correspondence to be in Welsh where responding to Welsh or where requested and notices and general communications will be bilingual. Historically, simultaneous translation services at hearings and inquiries was regarded as the responsibility of the local planning authority and would be available depending on the known circumstances and, if requested, would be made available. The availability of translation services at public meetings is required under the standards, being the responsibility of the person arranging the meeting. Written evidence will generally be the responsibility of the person presenting it and in the language of their choice and the former Scheme made clear that the Planning Inspectorate would not translate written documents submitted to them. Public notices and policy documents produced by a person to whom the standards apply must be in Welsh.

[11] See s. 33 and Schs 5–8.

[12] SI 2015 No. 996.

WELSH LANGUAGE AS A MATERIAL CONSIDERATION

The second issue is the extent to which the Welsh language is a material consideration in planning, whether for policy and development plans or when considering applications for planning permission. 3.23

Historically, Welsh Office Circular 53/88 'The Welsh Language – Development Plans and Planning Control' said that the language, like other social issues, could be a material consideration in planning and this provides the background to the current position. 3.24

Policy, pending changes which will follow implementation of the Planning (Wales) Act 2015 measures referred to below, is in TAN 20 Planning and the Welsh Language.[13] This is directed at how the planning system considers the implications of the Welsh language when Local Development Plans (LDPs) are prepared, saying 'Depending on what significance is assigned to the Welsh language in a plan area or part of the area, one of the issues that LDPs may need to address is how the land use planning system can be used to consider and, if necessary, mitigate any effects of development on the Welsh language and the sustainability of Welsh language communities.' Of the adopted Local Development Plans a roughly equal number have specific Welsh language policies as do not. 3.25

TAN 20 also explains how the sustainability appraisal is used to assess the impact of the development plan on the Welsh language. Further guidance from the Welsh Government is in 'A Practical Guide for the consideration of the Welsh language in Development Plans' and this points out that in relation to the Welsh language and planning, the Equality Act 2010 and the Human Rights Act 1998 will be relevant and decision-makers should be mindful of the wider legal implications. 3.26

The policy and guidance is thus not directly concerned with individual applications for development although mention is made of the position of the Welsh language as a material consideration in decision-making. 3.27

Local authorities were obliged to prepare single integrated plans in accordance with their Welsh language schemes and will now have to comply with the standards set under the 2011 Measure. TAN 20 states[14] that LDPs should express, in appropriate land use planning terms, those elements of the single integrated plan that relate to the development and use of land, provided that those elements conform with national and international policy and obligations, including national objectives regarding the Welsh language, and so far as compatible with EU law or the European Convention on Human Rights. It continues to state that where a single integrated plan has identified the protection and/or enhancement of the Welsh language as a priority for an area, the LDP should consider this priority insofar as it is relevant to the use of land and should do so through the sustainability appraisal and associated site assessment processes during plan preparation. 3.28

[13] Issued in October 2013, it replaces the earlier version issued in 2000.

[14] Paragraph 2.2.2.

3.29 Specifically, the policy-making standards of the 2015 Regulations[15] would require an assessment of the effects, if any, whether positive or adverse, on opportunities for persons to use the Welsh language and treating the Welsh language no less favourably than the English language when formulating, revising or reviewing policy.

3.30 Where the Welsh language is not considered to be of any significance, the basis for this should be stated in the plan. However, all LDPs should include a short reasoned justification of the regard had by the local planning authority to social, economic and environmental considerations, including the needs and interests of the Welsh language, and how any policies relating to the Welsh language interact with other plan policies.[16] Where Welsh language is considered to be a significant part of the social fabric, the local planning authority should ensure that plan strategy, policies and land allocations in the deposit LDP have regard to the needs and interests of the Welsh language[17] and appropriate Welsh language indicators should be identified in the LDP and monitored.[18]

3.31 The advice reasserts the need to comply with general legal obligations at paragraph 3.7.4 warning: 'policies which take into account the needs and interests of the Welsh language should not seek to introduce any element of discrimination between individuals on the basis of their linguistic ability. Planning policies should not seek to control housing occupancy on linguistic grounds.'[19] It then continues to address mitigation measures as an element sustaining communities and expressly allows for Welsh language infrastructure to be included in the Community Infrastructure Levy charging schedule.

3.32 Paragraph 4.1.2 says:

> In determining individual planning applications and appeals where the needs and interests of the Welsh language may be a material consideration decisions must, as with all other planning applications, be based on planning grounds only and be reasonable. Adopted development plan policies are planning grounds, including those which have taken the needs and interests of the Welsh language into account. Planning applications should not be subject to Welsh language impact assessment, as this would duplicate LDP site selection processes where LDP objectives indicated the need for such an assessment.

3.33 Both at the development plan stage and, where applicable, in deciding individual development applications it is necessary therefore to consider positive- and anti-discriminatory provisions of general legal effect. The Equality Act 2010, the

[15] See Sch. 2.

[16] Paragraph 3.7.2. See below in relation to the Well-being of Future Generations Act 2015 and a fourth element, namely cultural considerations.

[17] Paragraph 3.7.2.

[18] Paragraph 3.11.2.

[19] This is re-affirmed in PPW at 4.13.5.

Human Rights Act 1998 and the European Convention on Human Rights are accordingly of potential significance.

The Equality Act 2010, section 9 defines race as a protected characteristic but Welsh is not an ethnic group and the Welsh should not be divided according to whether they are English-speaking or Welsh-speaking.[20] Any discrimination therefore would likely be indirect not direct and may also impact on the public sector duties in Part 11 of the Act. 3.34

Human Rights Act concerns will centre on the prohibition of discrimination in Article14 of the European Convention on Human Rights when linked to the enjoyment, for example, of the right to possessions under Article 1 of the First Protocol. The implications for the free movement of workers and citizens and for the provision of services, all of which are provided in the terms of the Treaty on the Functioning of the European Union, may also fall for consideration.[21] Finally, the EU Charter of Fundamental Rights and Freedoms prohibit discrimination on the grounds of language[22] and provides that linguistic diversity must be respected.[23] 3.35

The Planning (Wales) Act 2015 was amended during its passage to take account of concerns that the Act should give proper consideration to the Welsh language at appropriate stages of the planning process. More extensive amendments had been proposed during its progress through the Assembly, including a requirement to use Welsh language impact assessments before decisions on classes of development to be specified by Welsh Ministers. The amendments made are however more limited. The Act as passed distinguishes between strategic decisions and impacts at development plan level and individual applications. In the latter, the test remains materiality within the adopted development plan framework and national policy. 3.36

The Welsh language provisions of the 2015 Act affect planning matters in three ways: first, the language may be an element in the overall sustainability requirements of section 2, which refer to the goals of the Well-being of Future Generations (Wales) Act 2015; secondly, the preparation of each of the development plan documents must address use of the Welsh language; and, finally, impact on the language may need to be considered when deciding applications for planning permission. 3.37

Section 2 of the Act is in force from 1 April 2016 subject to the saving that it does not apply to any local development plan submitted for examination prior to that date.[24] It applies to the Welsh Ministers, a local planning authority or any other public body exercising functions under Part 6 of PCPA 2004 regarding a 3.38

[20] See *Gwynedd County Council v Jones* [1986] ICR 833.

[21] This is of course dependent on the extent to which relevant provisions or principles are continued or adopted on withdrawal from EU membership following the 'leave' vote in the June 2016 referendum.

[22] Article 21

[23] Article 22.

[24] See SI 2015 No. 1987, arts 5 and 6.

development plan or any function under Part 3 of TCPA 1990 in relation to an application for planning permission. By section 2(2) that function must be exercised, as part of carrying out sustainable development in accordance with the Well-being of Future Generations (Wales) Act 2015, for the purpose of ensuring that the development and use of land contribute to improving the economic, social, environmental and cultural well-being of Wales.

3.39 The duty under section 2 of the Well-being of Future Generations (Wales) Act 2015 itself refers to sustainable development as involving action aimed at achieving the well-being goals of section 4. Amongst those goals (being part of the cultural element of sustainable development) is 'A society that promotes and protects culture, heritage and the Welsh language, and which encourages people to participate in the arts, and sports and recreation.' Planning Policy Wales has been updated to reflect the impact of this Act.

3.40 The Planning (Wales) Act 2015, section 2(5) states that the sustainability obligation does not alter whether regard is to be had to any particular consideration under section 70(2) of TCPA 1990 or the weight to be given to any such consideration and this is repeated in the amendment made by section 31 of the 2015 Act (see below).

3.41 This proviso reflects the concern that the material considerations when dealing with an application for development must be planning matters, that is they relate to the use of the land, whereas certain impacts (e.g. personal impacts on existing users) may fall outside that which may properly be taken into account.[25]

3.42 Although in particular cases language may be considered a personal circumstance, more usually it will be a social or cultural factor of wider import. It could thus fall within the principle in *R (Copeland) v London Borough of Tower Hamlets*[26] where Cranston J said:

> Promoting social objectives may be a material consideration in the planning context. Planning controls in order to promote social objectives are considerations which can relate to physical land use. Whether a social objective is relevant in a particular case turns on the circumstances. As long as the promotion of the social goal is lawfully within the planning sphere it matters not that it falls elsewhere as well.

3.43 The Planning (Wales) Act 2015 will also expressly require consideration of the Welsh language at the development plan preparation stage by amendments to PCPA 2004.

3.44 At national level, section 60B of PCPA 2004 will require the Welsh Ministers to include an assessment of the likely effects of the policies on the use of the

[25] See *Westminster City Council v Great Portland Estates Plc* [1985] AC 661.

[26] [2010] EWHC 1845 (Admin) at paragraph 22.

Welsh language as part of their sustainability appraisal of the National Development Framework.[27]

At the regional level, there is an equivalent requirement on a strategic planning panel when carrying out its sustainability appraisal of a strategic development plan.[28] This is by additional provisions in PCPA 2004, inserted by section 6 of the Planning (Wales) Act 2015, but this is in force only to the extent that it enables regulations and orders to be made. 3.45

At the local level, section 11 of the Planning (Wales) Act 2015 requires the local planning authority survey under section 61 of PCPA 2004 to include review of the extent to which the Welsh language is used in the area.[29] In addition it inserts a new subsection (6A) into section 62 of the 2004 Act so that the sustainability appraisal for a local development plan will have to include an assessment of the likely effects of the plan on the use of the Welsh language in the area of the authority.[30] 3.46

Individual applications for development are dealt with by section 70(2)(aa) of TCPA 1990 requiring the local planning authority to have regard to any considerations relating to the use of the Welsh language so far as material to the application. This does not alter whether regard is to be had to any particular consideration under section 70(2) or the weight to be given to any consideration. The position thus remains that what is in fact material depends upon the individual facts and circumstances: issues regarding materiality generally are considered in Chapter 13. 3.47

[27] The new provisions dealing with the Framework (PCPA 2004, ss. 60, 60A and 60B, inserted by s. 3 of the 2015 Act) are in force from 4 January 2016 but the replaced s. 60 continues to have effect as if s. 3 had not been commenced: see SI 2015 No. 1987, arts 2 and 7.

[28] Section 60I(8).

[29] This part, introduced by section 11(1) and (2) of the 2015 Act, is in force from 4 January 2016: see SI 2015 No. 1987, art. 3.

[30] Subject to the saving that it does not apply to any local development plan submitted for examination before that date.

Chapter 4

Planning Bodies

INTRODUCTION

The key roles in the planning system of Wales are occupied by the Welsh Ministers and the twenty-five local planning authorities. The local planning authority is also the mineral planning authority and there is power to act through Joint Planning Boards. Certain policy-making functions, when the provisions are fully operational, may be exercised at a tier between national and local level by Strategic Planning Panels. 4.1

Power to pass primary legislation and to oversee the Welsh Ministers lies with the National Assembly for Wales and the history and extent of devolution and the legislative powers of the National Assembly have been considered earlier. The UK Parliament and Government act in the limited range of non-devolved planning functions. As an executive agency of government, the Planning Inspectorate carries out core functions on behalf of the Welsh Ministers or Secretary of State. Judicial control is through the court system common to England and Wales. 4.2

UK PARLIAMENT AND GOVERNMENT

The provisions conferring legislative powers on the Assembly do not affect the formal power of the UK Parliament to pass laws affecting Wales.[1] However, by convention the UK Parliament will not normally legislate with regard to devolved matters without the agreement of the Assembly.[2] Subject to this consideration, where the National Assembly for Wales has legislative competence it will pass the relevant laws. Amendments to the legislative competence of the National Assembly for Wales can be by a UK Act or by Order in Council, which is subject to approval by each House of Parliament.[3] 4.3

In the case of executive functions, Ministers of the Crown exercise functions in respect of the matters that are not devolved but devolved matters are the responsibility of the Welsh Ministers. Detailed Guidance has been issued by the UK Government on the working of the devolution settlements and reference 4.4

[1] See e.g. GOWA 2006, s. 107(5).

[2] Memorandum of Understanding and Supplementary Agreements between the United Kingdom Government, the Scottish Ministers, the Welsh Ministers, and the Northern Ireland Executive Committee (Oct. 2013), para. 14. See now GOWA 2006, s. 107(6), inserted by Wales Act 2017, s. 2.

[3] GOWA 2006, s. 109.

should be made to it for operation of the system between departments of the two governments.[4] It should be noted that the terms of devolution governing legislative competence and those concerning executive functions are not identical: this non-alignment can lead, for example, to UK Ministers having functions, for example to grant consents, relating to matters which are within the Assembly's legislative competence and this may raise issues of proper scrutiny.

4.5 Most of the functions of the Secretary of State for Wales were transferred in 1999 on commencement of the Government of Wales Act 1998 and the remaining role is essentially in safeguarding devolution and representing Welsh interests more generally. Functions that are not devolved remain the province of the relevant UK Minister although some functions are carried out concurrently. The two main areas of town and country planning that are not devolved are responsibility for nationally significant infrastructure projects and for the Community Infrastructure Levy.[5]

4.6 As has been seen earlier, the legislative competence of the National Assembly for Wales excludes development consent under the Planning Act 2008.[6] However, the categories of project subject to this procedure are more narrowly defined in Wales than in England, with development consent applying only to certain energy and harbour projects. In addition, the removal of the need for authorisation under other statutes and the definition of associated development are different. These differences are best explored in connection with development consent orders generally because of the level of detail, and reference should be made to Chapter 8. Policy for the projects is the responsibility of the UK Government, which has published National Policy Statements.

4.7 Authority over the Community Infrastructure Levy does not, at the time of writing, lie with the Welsh Ministers and regulations are made by UK Ministers in accordance with Part 11 of the Planning Act 2008. The levy is dealt with in Chapter 16 below.

4.8 There are in addition certain specific exclusions of Welsh ministerial powers under TCPA 1990 so that the powers remain with the relevant Secretary of State. The relevant exclusions are listed in the National Assembly for Wales (Transfer of Functions) Order 1999, Schedule 1, as amended.[7] Government authorisation under sections 36 and 37 of the Electricity Act 1989[8] is excluded. Other authorisations[9] are excluded except to the extent that they were functions of the Secretary of State for Wales. However, an order for a new railway or tramway entirely in Wales

[4] Guidance, issued by the Cabinet Office and Wales Office in February 2013 and updated, is on the UK Government website.

[5] As noted elsewhere, the Wales Act 2017 will result in the levy becoming a devolved matter.

[6] See GOWA 2006, Sch. 7, Pt 1, para. 18, as amended by Localism Act 2011, Sch. 13, para. 79.

[7] SI 1999 No. 672, as amended by SI 2000 No. 253, which substituted that part of Sch. 1 as related to TCPA 1990.

[8] See TCPA 1990, s. 90(2).

[9] I.e. under TCPA 1990, s. 90(1).

under the Transport and Works Act 1992 is made by the Welsh Ministers.[10] In the case of development by statutory undertakers on operational land, the particular provisions modifying the operation of TCPA 1990[11] are not devolved, again except in so far as they were functions of the Secretary of State for Wales and, where he was the appropriate Minister under the Act, only those functions relating to water and sewerage undertakers were transferred. The provisions concerning the use and development of consecrated land, burial grounds and open spaces are excluded,[12] as are certain powers regarding compensation and entry on to Crown land.[13]

NATIONAL ASSEMBLY FOR WALES

The legislative competence of the National Assembly for Wales has been considered in Chapter 1 and above and the Government of Wales Act 2006, section 108 and Schedule 7 give legislative competence for Acts of the Assembly relating to town and country planning excluding development consent. 4.9

The Assembly scrutinises secondary legislation, excluding cases where ministerial approval only is required, so that rules, regulations and orders generally may be considered by the Assembly and are subject to either negative or affirmative resolution or occasionally the super affirmative procedure. The affirmative procedures both require Assembly approval of the legislation, whereas the negative enables introduction of a motion to annul an instrument which has, or will, otherwise come into force. 4.10

In addition, the National Development Framework must be laid before the Assembly and regard must be had to any resolutions or recommendations[14] and the Welsh Government is generally accountable to the Assembly. 4.11

WELSH MINISTERS

The Welsh Ministers exercise functions in relation to planning in accordance with Part 2 of the Government of Wales Act 2006 and the National Assembly for Wales (Transfer of Functions) Order 1999[15] as amended. Between 1999 and May 2007 these functions were carried out by the National Assembly for Wales. In addition, the Welsh Ministers have power to make rules, regulations and orders in devolved matters in those cases where power is specifically conferred. This is subject to 4.12

[10] TCPA 1990, s. 90(2A), which is not excluded under the Order.

[11] TCPA 1990, ss. 263(3) and (4), 266, 268 and 336(3). See paras 9.35–9.36, below.

[12] TCPA 1990, ss. 238(10(a), 239(1)(a) and 241(1)(a), respectively.

[13] TCPA 1990, s. 279(5) and (6).

[14] See Chapter 5 below.

[15] SI 1999 No. 672.

the supervisory and control powers of the National Assembly for Wales where so provided.

4.13 The Welsh Ministers have express power to make provisions consequential upon or supplemental to TCPA 1990, section 1 (local planning boards) and TCPA 1990, section 2 (joint planning boards). The latter provisions may amend or otherwise modify any enactment contained in, or made under, the planning Acts or the Planning and Compulsory Purchase Act 2004, any other enactment relating to functions exercisable by or in relation to local planning authorities and any other enactment relating to functions exercisable by local authorities of any description in connection with the development of land.[16] In addition, the Planning Act 2008, section 203 gives Welsh Ministers power to make provision in Wales corresponding to a number of England-only powers conferred by that Act. These deal with more minor or administrative powers. To date, four sets of subordinate legislation have been made dealing with compensation on withdrawal of a development order, non-material changes and correction of errors, procedure, and overriding easements and statutory undertakers.[17]

4.14 The Welsh Ministers are the First Minister and those appointed by him as a Welsh Minister under section 48 of the Government of Wales Act 2006.[18] They are responsible for all matters of national policy and guidance and can call-in an application for decision. They have powers in connection with local development plans and in certain circumstances may make or confirm orders revoking or modifying planning permission.[19]

4.15 In addition, they decide applications where the project is of national significance and, when the Planning (Wales) Act 2015 Act is fully operational, they will publish the National Development Framework, which is a development plan document, and will have power to decide applications for planning permission in those cases where an applicant is able to elect to apply to them rather than to a local planning authority.

4.16 Appeal against local planning authorities' decisions lies to the Welsh Ministers. They are consultees in the development plan process, can call-in local development plans or issue directions requiring further steps or preventing adoption, and have numerous advisory and regulatory functions in connection with strategic planning

[16] TCPA 1990, s. 9, as amended by Planning (Wales) Act 2015, s. 42.

[17] See respectively the Planning Permission (Withdrawal of Development Order or Local Development Order) (Compensation) (Wales) Order 2012 (SI 2012 No. 210), the Town and Country Planning (Non-Material Changes and Correction of Errors) (Wales) Order 2014 (SI 2014 No. 1770), the Town and Country Planning (Determination of Procedure) (Wales) Order 2014 (SI 2014 No. 2773) and the Town and Country Planning (Power to Override Easements and Applications by Statutory Undertakers) (Wales) Order 2015 (SI 2015 No. 1794).

[18] Section 45(2). The First Minister, the Welsh Ministers, the Counsel General and the Deputy Welsh Ministers are collectively the Welsh Government by virtue of s. 45 of the Act, now termed 'the Welsh Government' by Wales Act 2014, s. 4, but the formal title for the exercise of powers, and the term used throughout this text, is 'the Welsh Ministers'.

[19] See TCPA 1990, ss. 96–100.

panels and the work of local planning authorities. They have certain reserve powers in place of the local planning authority, for example to issue an enforcement notice.[20] Orders, rules and regulations are made by the Welsh Ministers in accordance with the empowering statutes. The source and details of these functions and how they are exercised is dealt with later in this work.

PLANNING INSPECTORATE

The Planning Inspectorate is an executive agency of the UK Government with responsibilities across England and Wales. It is not an independent Welsh Government agency although it has a Welsh Directorate based in Cardiff. [21] 4.17

It is responsible for national infrastructure planning (through the National Infrastructure Directorate) and for public examination of strategic and local development plans. It has appeal functions in respect of planning applications, enforcement appeals and certain other appeals, subject to the delegation of authority to it by the Welsh Ministers. On appeal, the inspector will either have power to make the final decision or to make a recommendation to the Welsh Ministers. 4.18

STRATEGIC PLANNING PANELS

Strategic Planning Panels may be established for a designated strategic planning area by regulations made by the Welsh Ministers.[22] The relevant provisions are by additions to PCPA 2004 introduced by the Planning (Wales) Act 2015, which have been in force since 4 October 2015[23] although no panel has to date been created. A strategic planning area must comprise all of the area of one planning authority and all or part of the area of at least one other local planning authority.[24] Prior to making regulations the Welsh Ministers must consult relevant authorities and persons.[25] Designation follows a direction given to the local planning authorities concerned, obliging the authorities to consult and to submit a proposal for an area to be designated as a strategic planning area.[26] 4.19

The panels are responsible for the strategic development plan only and have no functions in connection with the grant of planning permission or planning enforcement. Strategic development plans are considered in Chapter 5. The stated 4.20

[20] See TCPA 1990, s. 182.

[21] The address is: The Planning Inspectorate, Crown Buildings, Cathays Park, Cardiff, CF10 3NQ.

[22] PCPA 2004, s. 60D.

[23] See SI 2015 No. 1736.

[24] PCPA 2004, s. 60D(2).

[25] PCPA 2004, s. 60F(1).

[26] PCPA 2004, s. 60E.

aim[27] is to allow 'larger than local issues such as housing demand, search areas for strategic employment sites and supporting transport infrastructure, which cut across a number of local planning authorities, to be considered and planned for in an integrated and comprehensive way'. Inclusion of policies in the strategic development plan would then avoid the need for repetition in the local development plan. The number of such areas will be few, reference being made to two or three with provisional identification focused on Cardiff, Swansea and the A55 corridor in North Wales.

4.21 Membership of strategic planning panels is governed by Schedule 2A to PCPA 2004[28] and the Strategic Panel (Composition of Panels and Qualifying Expenditure) (Wales) Regulations 2016[29] and by the regulations which establish the individual panel. It consists of local planning authority members and nominated members and two-thirds of the total membership must be members of the local planning authority. Nominated members are not entitled to vote at meetings of the Panel or its committees.[30]

4.22 Appointment of a local planning authority member is by the constituent authority from amongst its eligible members.[31] The number of members to be appointed by each constituent authority is to be specified in the regulations establishing the panel in question. Nominated members are named by a nominating body from the list of such bodies published for this purpose by the Welsh Ministers. The 2016 Regulations provide for the composition to include a minimum of 40 per cent each of men and women unless unachievable, with an obligation to review and report to the Welsh Ministers if the composition requirement is not met. The Welsh Ministers have default powers if they think that a panel or constituent local planning authority is failing or omitting to do anything necessary to comply.[32]

LOCAL PLANNING AUTHORITIES

4.23 The overall pattern of local government in Wales has been mentioned in Chapter 2. The local planning authority is the county council or county borough council for the area.[33] The local planning authority is also the mineral planning authority.[34] Within the area of a National Park the National Park Authority is the sole planning

[27] See Explanatory Memorandum to Planning Bill (Wales) April 2015 (dated Oct. 2014) at para. 3.29.

[28] Inserted by s. 4(2) of and Sch. 1 to the Planning (Wales) Act 2015.

[29] SI 2016 No. 18.

[30] PCPA 2004, Sch. 2A, para. 13.

[31] Defined in Sch. 2A.

[32] See SI 2016 No. 18, reg. 8 (notification of failure or omission) and reg. 9 (direction to take appropriate steps).

[33] TCPA 1990, s. 1(1B).

[34] TCPA 1990, s. 1(4B).

authority (this includes mineral planning authority functions).[35] The structure is thus a unitary one in accordance with the arrangements for the administration of local government established by the Local Government (Wales) Act 1994, with the result that there are twenty-two local authorities and three National Park Authorities exercising planning functions in Wales.

The three National Park Authorities are those for Snowdonia, the Pembrokeshire Coast and the Brecon Beacons.[36] They have published joint supplementary planning guidance in July 2014, which acts as a guide to the specific local development plan policies and is a helpful introduction to development in their areas. 4.24

Details of the distribution of local planning authority functions in Wales are in Schedule 1A to TCPA 1990. These include provisions for situations where the local planning authority is not the highway authority, for consultation with community councils[37] and provisions affecting the definition of local planning authority in certain enforcement matters. 4.25

Where an application for development is not within the area of a local planning authority but does affect land in its area, the authority will be a statutory consultee.[38] 4.26

There is power to designate an enterprise zone authority,[39] an urban development corporation[40] and a housing action trust[41] as the local planning authority for its subject area but the current designations do not establish any such body as the local planning authority. Home and Communities Agency[42] functions in Wales are exercised by the Welsh Ministers. 4.27

If it appears to the Welsh Ministers that it is expedient that a joint board should be established as the local planning authority for two or more areas, each of which is the whole or part of a Welsh county or county borough, they may by order constitute those areas or parts as a united district for the purposes of this Act and constitute a joint board as the local planning authority for that united district.[43] The joint board is known as a joint planning board.[44] This formerly did not apply 4.28

[35] TCPA 1990, s. 4A(1) and (2).

[36] See the National Park Authorities (Wales) Order 1995 (SI 1995 No. 2803).

[37] See below and Chapters 5 and 12.

[38] Town and Country Planning (Development Management Procedure) (Wales) Order 2012 (SI 2012 No. 810), art. 14 and Sch. 4.

[39] Section 6. There are eight enterprise zones designated in Wales, namely Anglesey, Cardiff Airport and St Athan, Central Cardiff, Deeside, Ebbw Vale, Haven Waterway, Port Talbot Waterfront and Snowdonia.

[40] TCPA 1990, s. 7.

[41] TCPA 1990, s. 8.

[42] See TCPA 1990, s. 8A.

[43] TCPA 1990, s. 2(1B).

[44] TCPA 1990, s. 2(1C).

to any area or part of an area which is in a National Park[45] but section 41 of the Planning (Wales) Act 2015 enables Welsh Ministers by regulations to make provision for joint planning boards for an area including all or part of a National Park.[46]

4.29 In addition there is power for the Welsh Ministers to make an amalgamation order under section 162 of the Local Government (Wales) Measure 2011 although no such order has yet been made.[47] This relates to local authority functions generally by establishing a new local government area. Authorities may also merge voluntarily.[48] Reform of local government administration is a matter of ongoing consideration: there is no current intent to compel merger although individual functions may be amalgamated.[49]

4.30 Local planning authorities may agree to prepare a joint development plan[50] but in this case they remain separate planning authorities. The Welsh Ministers may also direct two or more local planning authorities to prepare a joint local development plan, although a direction cannot be given to a National Park Authority.[51] Subject to any withdrawal or variation, the authorities to which the direction is given must act jointly in exercising their functions under the 2004 Act relating to local development plans.

4.31 The detailed arrangements for the discharge of functions by local planning authorities are subject to the general requirements on local authorities, including the general power of delegation under the Local Government Act 1972, section 101 and the general arrangement of functions under the Local Government Act 2000, Local Government (Wales) Measure 2011 and Local Authorities (Executive Arrangements) (Functions and Responsibilities) (Wales) Regulations 2007.[52] However, variation between authorities in the arrangements and concern over lack of continuity and consistency has led to specific planning provisions introduced by section 39 of the Planning (Wales) Act 2015, and sections 101 and 102 of the 1972 Act have effect subject to these provisions[53] and regulations to be made under them. The provisions will replace the individual arrangements adopted by the different local authorities.

[45] TCPA 1990, s. 2(1D).

[46] The Order itself would be made further to TCPA 1990, s. 2(1B). Section 42 contains power to make any consequential or supplementary provision amending or modifying enactments relating to local planning authority functions.

[47] Specific proposals were made but were withdrawn for further consideration in 2016.

[48] Local Government (Wales) Act 2015, s. 3.

[49] See White Paper *Reforming Local Government* (2014) and subsequent Welsh Government statements: earlier aims to reduce the number of authorities to around half led to disagreement and have been dropped. The latest proposal is to retain the same number of authorities but to progress joint provision of certain services or functions. Voluntary merger will also be considered.

[50] PCPA 2004, s. 72.

[51] PCPA 2004, s. 72(A1) and (A2): the result is that a joint planning board including the whole or part of the area of a National Park will have development management functions but not those relating to the local development plan.

[52] SI 2007 No. 399, as amended by SI 2013 No. 2902.

[53] TCPA 1990, s. 319ZC(1).

The provisions amend TCPA 1990 to give new powers to the Welsh Ministers to make regulations prescribing the size and composition of planning committees and to introduce a national scheme of delegation in respect of a function of a local planning authority in relation to planning applications.[54] Section 319ZA of TCPA 1990 accordingly provides that the Welsh Ministers may by regulations require a relevant local planning authority to make arrangements under section 101 of the Local Government Act 1972 for a function exercisable in relation to an application under the 1990 Act[55] to be discharged by a committee, sub-committee or officer of the authority. The regulations may prescribe the terms of the arrangements and any permitted variations and when the arrangements are in force the function may only be exercised in accordance with them.[56] 4.32

Section 319ZB of the 1990 Act enables Welsh Ministers by regulations to prescribe requirements relating to the size and composition of a committee or sub-committee discharging those functions. The local authority may not arrange for a relevant function to be discharged by a committee or sub-committee that fails to satisfy a requirement of the regulations.[57] 4.33

Where a local planning authority itself wishes to carry out development it is subject to the Act and requires permission in the ordinary way subject to some minor modifications.[58] However, development by them requiring government authorisation may be granted deemed planning permission under the terms of the authorisation[59] and the definition of development makes express reference to certain works by them[60] and certain works are permitted as general permitted development.[61] 4.34

MINERAL PLANNING AUTHORITIES

The local planning authority is also in Wales the mineral planning authority.[62] Accordingly, development plan functions and planning decisions involving minerals and mineral extraction will be with the relevant county or county borough council or National Park Authority. 4.35

[54] See s. 319ZD.

[55] Being the definition of 'relevant function' in s. 319ZD: it therefore includes applications for planning permission under ss. 70, 73 and 73A and for certificates of lawfulness of existing use or development under s. 191 or approval of reserved matters or under a condition.

[56] TCPA 1990, s. 319ZA(2) and (3).

[57] TCPA 1990, s. 319ZB(2).

[58] TCPA 1990, s. 316, and see Chapter 12.

[59] TCPA 1990, s. 90.

[60] TCPA 1990, s. 55(2).

[61] Town and Country Planning (General Permitted Development) Order 1995, SI 1995 No. 418.

[62] TCPA 1990, s. 1(4B).

4.36 TCPA 1990, section 315 enables modification of provisions of the Act in relation to development consisting of the winning and working of minerals or involving the depositing of mineral waste. The provisions in question are specified in Parts I and II of Schedule 16 to the Act. Modification is by regulations under the section and the power has been transferred to the Welsh Ministers.[63]

4.37 Modification was made by the Town and Country Planning (Minerals) Regulations 1995[64] and the effect of EIA on old mineral permissions is the subject of the Town and Country Planning (Environmental Impact Assessment) (Undetermined Reviews of Old Mineral Permissions) (Wales) Regulations 2009[65] and the additional provisions of the Town and Country Planning (Environmental Impact Assessment) (Wales) Regulations 2016.[66] Additional notification obligations where land contains coal, gas, oil, silver or gold are in article 17 of the Town and Country Planning (Development Management Procedure) (Wales) Order 2012.[67]

4.38 As regards mineral planning generally, national policy is not dealt with in Planning Policy Wales but by Minerals Planning Policy Wales (December 2000). This is supplemented by the ten Minerals Planning Policy guidance notes issued before devolution and the two Minerals Technical Advice Notes (MTAN 1 Aggregates and MTAN 2 Coal) issued subsequently.

STATUTORY UNDERTAKERS

4.39 Statutory undertakers means 'persons authorised by any enactment to carry on any railway, light railway, tramway, road transport, water transport, canal, inland navigation, dock, harbour, pier or lighthouse undertaking or any undertaking for the supply of hydraulic power and a relevant airport operator'.[68] This definition applies equally in Wales save that TCPA 1990, section 262(3) has been amended to refer expressly to the Natural Resources Body for Wales.

4.40 They have a particular position in planning, and development by them requiring government authorisation may be granted 'deemed planning permission' under the terms of the authorisation.[69] Development by them on their operational land is subject to special procedures outside the ordinary grant of planning permission being dealt with by governmental authorisation or by permission granted by the Secretary of State and the appropriate Minister.[70] In addition, the definition of

[63] National Assembly for Wales (Transfer of Functions) Order 1999, art 2 and Schedule 1.

[64] SI 1995 No. 2863.

[65] SI 2009 No. 3342.

[66] SI 2016 No. 58: see reg. 52 and Sch. 7.

[67] SI 2012 No. 801, as amended ('DMP(W)O').

[68] TCPA 1990, s. 262(1).

[69] TCPA 1990, s. 90.

[70] TCPA 1990, ss. 262–268, and see paras 9.37–9.38.

development makes express reference to certain works by statutory undertakers[71] and particular types of work are identified as general permitted development.[72]

OTHER BODIES

Numerous other bodies have specific responsibilities impacting on the planning process, for example as statutory consultees. The description of consultees for development plan preparation is given in the Town and Country Planning (Local Development Plan) (Wales) Regulations 2005,[73] which refer to general and specific consulting bodies and community consultees in regulation 2.[74] Applications for planning permission and related applications require consultation in accordance with the specific procedural requirements, which are dealt with as appropriate in the later chapters. Of particular relevance at this stage are community councils. 4.41

Community councils and town councils are part of the overall local government structure. There are around 750 councils with widely differing populations, varying from 155 to over 45,000 people[75] and together they represent approximately 70 per cent of the population of Wales. They have responsibility for certain local services and will be involved as part of the wider community process, for example as a partner to the public services board that will prepare the well-being plan: a local planning authority must have regard to this plan in preparing its local development plan. However, community councils have no specific formal powers in planning matters and, as noted above, there is no Welsh equivalent of neighbourhood orders or plans, which give a role to the councils' English counterparts, parish councils. Their statutory recognition in the planning process is as a consultee. 4.42

A local development plan must be prepared in accordance with the authority's community involvement scheme, that is, its statement of policy regarding involvement of specified persons.[76] A community council will be a consultee in the local development plan process.[77] As a community consultee,[78] it must be consulted as part of the pre-application process for major applications[79] and it may receive 4.43

[71] TCPA 1990, s. 55(2).

[72] Town and Country Planning (General Permitted Development) Order 1995 (SI 1995 No. 418).

[73] SI 2005 No. 2839, as amended by Town and Country Planning (Local Development Plan) (Wales) (Amendment) Regulations 2015 (SI 2015 No. 1598), and SI 2016 No. 59.

[74] See para. 5.41, below.

[75] See the 'Research Study into the Role, Functions and Future Potential of Community and Town Councils in Wales' report of the University of Aberystwyth, August 2003 at para. S7.

[76] PCPA 2004, s.63(1) and (2).

[77] They are a specific consultation body being within the definition of relevant authority in reg. 2 of the Town and Country Planning (Local Development Plan) (Wales) Regulations 2005.

[78] DMP(W)O, art. 2, as amended by SI 2016 No. 59, art. 3.

[79] DMP(W)O, art. 2D.

notice of applications, enabling it to make representations before any application for permission is granted, in accordance with TCPA 1990, Schedule 1A.[80]

4.44 As local representatives at the level closest to the population, the councils have an important role to play in making representations and responding to planning policies and applications affecting their community. Involvement is formally encouraged by the Welsh Government, with implementation of the Planning (Wales) Act 2015 placing greater emphasis on community engagement. Training to meet the needs of the councils is given by Planning Aid Wales in partnership with the Welsh Government and One Voice Wales.[81] Proposals for place plans as Supplementary Planning Guidance will give a more formal role when the stated intention to move to their introduction is implemented following the pilot schemes currently being undertaken.

4.45 Two further particular bodies may be singled out because of their significant environmental responsibilities. As part of their general responsibilities, for example, both Natural Resources Wales and Cadw are consultation bodies for the purposes of strategic environmental assessments,[82] as well as in other situations.

4.46 The natural environment is an area of Welsh Government responsibility for which it will be a statutory consultee. Natural Resources Wales was formed in 2013 combining the former Environment Agency Wales, Countryside Council for Wales and the Forestry Commission Wales. It is a statutory body created by the Natural Resources Body for Wales (Establishment) Order 2012[83] and carries out functions, including certain statutory functions of the Welsh Ministers, as prescribed by the Natural Resources Body for Wales (Functions) Order 2013.[84] Its general purpose is now defined as one to pursue sustainable management of natural resources in Wales and to apply the principles of sustainable management of natural resources.[85] It is a specific consultation body for local development plan preparation[86] and it has published detailed guidance on the nature of applications of which it should be notified for comment. It will have key functions under the Environment (Wales) Act 2016 to produce the State of Natural Resources Report, giving an assessment of natural resources and how well they are managed in a sustainable way and Area Statements setting out the priorities, risks and opportunities for managing natural

[80] See para. 2 of the Schedule and DMP(W)O, art. 16. See also art. 14 and DMP(W)O, Sch. 4.

[81] The national representative body for community and town councils: membership is at the option of the council.

[82] See Environmental Assessment of Plans and Programmes (Wales) Regulations 2004 (SI 2004 No. 1656).

[83] SI 2012 No. 1903.

[84] SI 2013 No. 755.

[85] See art. 4 of the Order, as substituted by Environment (Wales) Act 2016, s. 5.

[86] See Town and Country Planning (Local Development Plan) (Wales) Regulations 2005 (SI 2005 No. 2839), as amended.

resources sustainably. As with other public bodies, it must carry out sustainable development.[87]

Cadw[88] is the Welsh Government body responsible for the historic environment and is part of the Economy, Science and Transport Department. It has responsibilities where appropriate on behalf of the Welsh Government regarding relevant planning applications and under the Planning (Listed Buildings and Conservation Areas) Act 1990. Changes to this latter Act and related legislation are in the Historic Environment (Wales) Act 2016 and are considered in Chapter 24. The Act deals with scheduled monuments protected by the Ancient Monuments and Archaeological Areas Act 1979 and with buildings and land with special status under the Planning (Listed Buildings and Conservation Areas) Act 1990: it will add protection for other aspects of the historic environment, for example registered historic parks and gardens. 4.47

Cadw and other bodies will not be replaced but greater coordination is considered necessary and the Act will establish an Advisory Body for the Welsh Historic Environment to provide independent expert advice to the Welsh Ministers on the formulation, development, resourcing and delivery of historic environment policy and strategy. 4.48

As stated, legal proceedings are brought in the appropriate court of the court service, although it should be noted that administrative court and planning court proceedings are typically issued and heard in Wales in accordance with Civil Procedure Rules PD54 Administrative Court (Venue). There is an Administrative Court Office in Cardiff.[89] 4.49

Complaints relating to the exercise of planning functions may be subject to investigation by the Public Services Ombudsman for Wales. 4.50

87 Well-being of Future Generations (Wales) Act 2015, s. 3.

88 Derived from the Welsh word for keeping or preserving.

89 See Chapter 22 below on legal challenge and statutory appeal, esp. paras 22.28–22.30.

Chapter 5

Development Plans

INTRODUCTION

Development management is a plan-led system and the development plan is accordingly at its core. This chapter looks at the definition of development plans and outlines the process of preparation and adoption of the plans. 5.1

Historically, the sole development plan was the plan prepared by a local planning authority applying to its administrative area. Amendments by the Planning (Wales) Act 2015 introduce a national document of development plan status and enable the introduction of regional development plans, known as strategic development plans. The key measures are in PCPA 2004, Part 6, as amended. 5.2

STATUTORY POSITION OF DEVELOPMENT PLANS

The central role of the development plan is established by two complementary provisions. TCPA 1990, section 70(2) states that in dealing with an application for planning permission regard is to be had to the provisions of the development plan so far as material to the application and to any other material considerations. PCPA 2004, section 38(6) provides that if regard is to be had to the development plan for the purposes of any determination to be made under the planning Acts, the determination must be made in accordance with the plan unless material considerations indicate otherwise. 5.3

This role is reinforced by the fact that all development plans are to be kept under review and expire at the end of the plan period. The National Development Framework must specify the period for which it is to have effect and it ceases to be the framework on the expiry of that period.[1] Provisions to like effect apply to a strategic development plan[2] and to local development plans.[3] In addition, conformity is aided by the power for the Welsh Ministers to give directions referring applications to them rather than being determined by the local planning authority (call-in).[4] Until 2012 this led to a requirement to notify the Welsh Ministers if the authority were minded to grant permission which was not in accordance with the development plan but this was removed by the Town and Country Planning 5.4

[1] PCPA 2004, s. 60(6) and (7).

[2] PCPA 2004, s. 60I(4) and (10).

[3] PCPA 2004, s. 62(3B) and (9).

[4] TCPA 1990, s. 77.

(Development Management Procedure) (Wales) Order 2012.[5] Article 20 of the Order now provides that a local planning authority may, in such cases and subject to such conditions as may be prescribed by directions given by the Welsh Ministers, grant permission for development which does not accord with the provisions of the development plan in force in the area. Directions and guidance are given by the Town and Country Planning (Notification) (Wales) Direction 2012, replacing departure application criteria with new criteria.[6]

5.5 The role of the development plan in the determination of individual applications and the scope of directions is considered in Chapter 13 below.

MEANING OF DEVELOPMENT PLAN

5.6 The development plan for an area is the local development plan adopted or approved for that area.[7]

5.7 When amendments introduced by section 9 of the Planning (Wales) Act 2015 are fully into force, the development plan will be the National Development Framework for Wales, the strategic development plan for any strategic planning area that includes all or part of an area and the local development plan for that area.[8] Strategic development plans are a new creation and the National Development Framework replaces the former Wales Spatial Plan, which contained national land use policy but lacked development plan status. Pending due introduction of a National Development Framework or any strategic plan, the local development plan is therefore the only document of this formal status. At the time of writing not all local planning authorities had adopted Local Development Plans[9] and the relevant plan would under transitional provisions be the latest adopted plan for that area.[10]

5.8 There is thus a clear hierarchy of national, regional and local policies and strategies. The National Development Framework is to concentrate on development and land use issues of national significance and strategic development plans will provide where necessary for an integrated and comprehensive approach when issues cut across local planning authority boundaries. A strategic development plan must be in general conformity with the National Development Framework for Wales[11] and a local development plan must be in general conformity with both that and

[5] SI 2012 No. 801.

[6] WGC 7/12. See Chapter 9 below.

[7] PCPA 2004, s. 38(4).

[8] See PCPA 2004, s. 38(4), as substituted by Planning (Wales) Act 2015, s. 9.

[9] The most up-to-date published figures, to January 2016, show that eighteen Local Development Plans had been adopted.

[10] I.e. the Unitary Development Plan where adopted or predecessor plans in the case of Isle of Anglesey CC, i.e. the relevant structure and local plans.

[11] PCPA 2004, s. 60I(3).

the strategic development plan for any strategic planning area that includes all or part of the area of the local planning authority.[12]

The intent is that where a strategic development plan covers an area it will be unnecessary for the local development plan to repeat its provisions. This will lead to a reduced plan focusing only on local matters and site-specific allocations, with general questions of the provision and scale of facilities being confined to the strategic plan. The National Development Framework will identify key locations in accordance with Welsh Government land use priorities. 5.9

The plans will have equal status although questions may arise as to interpretation where there is apparent inconsistency. PCPA 2004, section 38(5) says that if to any extent a policy contained in a development plan for an area conflicts with another policy in the development plan, the conflict must be resolved in favour of the policy that is contained in the last document to be adopted, approved or published (as the case may be). In addition, principles have been developed for construction where there is a conflict or perceived conflict between different provisions of the same plan and these could be applied to resolve issues in this situation.[13] 5.10

THE NATIONAL DEVELOPMENT FRAMEWORK

The National Development Framework[14] derives from section 3 of the 2015 Act, which substituted four new sections (60, 60A–60C) for the original section 60 of PCPA 2004. These provisions of the Act came into force on 4 January 2016 with the exception of the review provisions of section 60C, subject to the saving that the replaced section 60 continues to have effect as if not replaced.[15] The current intent is for the Framework to be operative from March 2020 after completion of the various stages of the formal preparation and publication process. 5.11

The Welsh Ministers are under a duty to prepare and publish the Framework.[16] It sets out the Welsh Ministers' policies in relation to the development and use of land[17] and may specify development which is to constitute development of national 5.12

[12] PCPA 2004, s. 62(3A).

[13] See e.g. *City of Edinburgh Council v Secretary of State for Scotland* [1997] 1 WLR 1447; *R v Leominster DC, ex parte Pothecary* (1997) 76 P & CR 346; and *R (TW Logistics Ltd) v Tendring DC* [2013] EWCA Civ 9, where the court, dealing with a single development plan, said that it is for the planning authority to decide which policy should be given greater weight in relation to a particular decision. The court cited Ouseley J in *R (Cummins) v Camden LBC* [2001] EWHC 1116 (Admin) at [164]: 'It may be necessary for a Council in a case where policies pull in different directions to decide which is the dominant policy: whether one policy compared to another is directly as opposed to tangentially relevant, or should be seen as the one to which the greater weight is required to be given.'

[14] 'NDF' or 'Framework' in the text.

[15] SI 2015 No. 1987, arts 2 and 7. Pending full commencement of s. 9 of the 2015 Act, amending PCPA 2004, s. 38(4), the development plan does not include the NDF.

[16] PCPA 2004, s. 60(1).

[17] PCPA 2004, s. 60(2).

significance for the purposes of section 62D of the 1990 Act.[18] In each case reasons must be given for the policies and provisions.[19]

5.13 In addition to identifying key locations for development, the role of the NDF is to provide a national land use framework for strategic and local development plans, provide coordination and give the development plan context for Welsh Ministers' decisions on developments of national significance. It will set out area- or location-specific policies, which before its publication would be found in Planning Policy Wales and Technical Advice Notes. The intent is to revise PPW so that it sits alongside the NDF as the primary national policy documents. They will be supported by a *Development Plan Manual* and a *Development Management Manual*.[20]

5.14 The Welsh Ministers must publish a statement of public participation setting out the consultation to be carried out in preparing the NDF[21] and this must include provision about the form of the consultation. The consultation must include a draft of the Framework and allow a period of twelve weeks for representations.[22]

5.15 Before publishing the NDF, the Welsh Ministers must carry out a sustainability appraisal, which must include an assessment of the likely effects of its policies on the Welsh language.[23] They must afterwards lay the draft before the National Assembly for Wales, which then has a sixty-day period for consideration.[24] The Welsh Ministers must have regard to any Assembly resolution or Assembly committee recommendation made in that period and may then publish the NDF.[25] The publicity and opportunity to comment may be contrasted with the current informal system, which relies on responses to consultation drafts of policy documents or revisions.

5.16 There is an obligation to keep the NDF under review with a five-year review period and the Welsh Ministers may revise it at any time.[26] The procedure for revision is as for publishing the Framework itself, following the steps in sections 60A and 60B.[27] If the Welsh Ministers decide not to revise, following publication of a draft, or fail to carry out the necessary steps to revise within the review period, they must publicise their position and the reasons for it.[28]

[18] PCPA 2004, s. 60(3). Section 62D provides that applications for certain major developments are made to the Welsh Ministers and not local planning authorities: see below.

[19] PCPA 2004, s. 60(4).

[20] See Welsh Government Positive Planning Implementation Plan (Dec. 2015), p. 7. The *Development Management Manual* was published in November 2016.

[21] PCPA 2004, s. 60A(1).

[22] PCPA 2004, s. 60A.

[23] PCPA 2004, s. 60B. The sustainability appraisal will include a Strategic Environmental Assessment and a Habitats Regulations Assessment.

[24] PCPA 2004, s. 60B(3) and (5).

[25] PCPA 2004, s. 60B(4), (6) and (7).

[26] PCPA 2004, s. 60C.

[27] PCPA 2004, s. 60C(3).

[28] PCPA 2004, s.60(4)–(7).

Legal challenge to the National Development Framework is permissible only by application to the High Court on the grounds that it is not within the appropriate power or a procedural requirement has not been complied with.[29] 5.17

STRATEGIC DEVELOPMENT PLAN

Strategic development plans are designed to overcome difficulties from cross-border planning issues that are not effectively resolved by a single local planning authority. 5.18

There are twenty-two principal councils in Wales as local planning authorities and three National Parks with planning responsibility within their boundaries. The question of merger and the power for the Welsh Ministers to make an amalgamation order under section 162 of the Local Government (Wales) Measure 2011 were referred to earlier. In the specific context of planning there is power for authorities to prepare joint development plans,[30] although only Gwynedd County Council and the Isle of Anglesey County Council are adopting this approach. In addition, there should be collaboration between neighbouring authorities when preparing plans[31] and there is power to merge local planning services. A regional approach is also evident for certain specific issues, for example minerals and waste management. Nevertheless, the conclusion was reached that there was a need for an additional power to give an integrated and comprehensive approach to those issues that cut across formal local authority boundaries. The stated intention[32] is to adopt this approach for larger issues such as housing demand, search areas for strategic employment sites and supporting transport infrastructure. Three areas have been identified provisionally as benefiting – Cardiff Capital Region, Swansea Bay City Region and the A55 corridor in North Wales. 5.19

The legislation enables the designation of strategic planning areas and panels and requires the panel to prepare a strategic development plan for its area. The relevant provisions are sections 60D–60J of and Schedule 2A to PCPA 2004, inserted by sections 4–6 of and Schedule 1 to the Planning (Wales) Act 2015: these are in force so as to enable the making of regulations and orders. Strategic planning panels have been considered in Chapter 4, above. 5.20

The panel must prepare a strategic development plan setting out its objectives in relation to the development and use of land in its area and its policies for the implementation of those objectives.[33] The panel must keep under review the matters which may be expected to affect the plan[34] and the obligation to consider review of the plan after publication of the National Development Framework 5.21

[29] PCPA 2004, s. 113(1) (c), (2) and (3) – see Chapter 22.

[30] PCPA 2004, s. 72.

[31] See e.g. PCPA 2004, s. 61(5) and PPW 2.5.

[32] See Planning (Wales) Act 2015 Explanatory Memorandum, paras 3.29 and 3.30.

[33] PCPA 2004, s. 60I (1) and (2).

[34] PCPA 2004, s. 60H, applying s. 61(2)–(5) as they apply to a local planning authority.

contained in section 68A of the 2004 Act applies to strategic development plans as it does to local development plans.[35]

5.22 The strategic planning panel is only concerned with plan preparation and review and matters incidental to that and has no other planning functions so all applications are to, and decisions are made by, the local planning authority or, where applicable, the Welsh Ministers.

5.23 The procedure for preparation, independent examination and adoption of a strategic development plan is the same as for local development plans because sections 63 to 68 of PCPA 2004 apply to strategic development plans as they apply to local development plans.[36] They are considered later and reference should be made to the section on local development plans. A strategic development plan is operative as such only in so far as it is adopted by resolution of the panel or approved by Welsh Ministers under PCPA 2004, sections 65 or 71[37] and ceases on the expiry of the plan period.[38]

5.24 In preparing the plan the strategic planning panel must have regard to current national policies, the National Development Framework for Wales, the strategic development plan for any adjoining strategic planning area, and the local development plan for each area, all or part of which is included in the panel's area.[39] Note that there is no express reference to the local development plan of an area adjoining but not part of the panel area. The panel must also have regard to the resources likely to be available for implementation and any other matters prescribed by regulation.[40] A sustainability appraisal must be carried out and reported[41] and this must include an assessment of the likely effects of the plan on the use of the Welsh language in the strategic planning area. A strategic development plan must be in general conformity with the National Development Framework.[42]

5.25 Legal challenge to a strategic development plan is permissible only by application to the High Court on the grounds that it is not within the appropriate power or a procedural requirement has not been complied with.[43]

LOCAL DEVELOPMENT PLAN

5.26 A local development plan is the development plan adopted by the local planning authority or approved by Welsh Ministers in accordance with PCPA 2004, sections

[35] PCPA 2004, s. 60J(1) and (3).

[36] PCPA 2004, s. 60J(1) and (3).

[37] PCPA 2004, s. 60I(8).

[38] PCPA 2004, s. 60I(9).

[39] PCPA 2004, s. 60I(6).

[40] PCPA 2004, s. 60I(6)(e).

[41] PCPA 2004, s. 60I(7).

[42] PCPA 2004, s. 60I(3).

[43] PCPA 2004, s. 113(1) (c), (2) and (3) – see Chapter 22.

62–78.[44] Adoption by the authority is governed by section 67 of PCPA 2004 whilst residual powers of approval lie with the Welsh Ministers under section 65 or section 71. A plan is a development plan only if adopted by the authority by resolution or approved under either of the two latter provisions.[45] Joint local development plans may be prepared by two or more local planning authorities, in which event anything to be done by one of the authorities in connection with the plan must be done by each of them.[46] Welsh Ministers may direct two or more local planning authorities to prepare a joint local development plan.[47]

General guidance is contained in the *Local Development Plan Manual* (Edition 2, August 2015)[48] although this does not have the status of national policy. Policy is contained in Planning Policy Wales Chapter 2. Detailed provisions as to the form, content and procedure applicable are prescribed by the Town and Country Planning (Local Development Plan) (Wales) Regulations 2005,[49] as amended.[50] 5.27

A local planning authority must prepare a local development plan that sets out its objectives in relation to the development and use of land in its area and the general policies for their implementation.[51] It may also set out specific policies in relation to any part of the area. The plan must specify the period for which it is to have effect and ceases to be a local development plan on the expiry of that period.[52] 5.28

The plan must be in general conformity with the National Development Framework for Wales and the strategic development plan for any strategic planning area that includes all or part of the area of the authority.[53] Whether something is 'in general conformity' with another plan is a matter of degree and of planning judgment taking into account the practicalities of the statutory system of planning control. This was established by the Court of Appeal in *Persimmon Homes (Thames Valley) Ltd v Stevenage BC*,[54] which was concerned with the general conformity of local plans with structure plans, Laws LJ stating that it would not be workable to construe the phrase as meaning simply 'in character' with and that a balanced approach was required to accommodate such factors as the long lead-in times of plans and the fact that the exigencies of good planning policy are liable to change. 5.29

In preparing a local development plan the authority must have regard to current national policies, the National Development Framework for Wales, the strategic development plan for any strategic planning area that includes all or part of 5.30

[44] As amended by the Planning (Wales) Act 2015. See PCPA 2004, s. 38(4).

[45] PCPA 2004, s. 62(8).

[46] PCPA 2004, s. 72.

[47] PCPA 2004, s. 72(A1).

[48] At the date of writing there is a stated intent to revise the Manual.

[49] SI 2005 No. 2839.

[50] See SI 2011 No. 971, SI 2013 No. 755 and SI 2015 No. 1598.

[51] PCPA 2004, s. 62(1) and (2).

[52] PCPA 2004, s. 62(3B) and (9).

[53] PCPA 2004, s. 62(3A).

[54] [2005] EWCA Civ 1365 at para. 28.

the area of the authority or adjoins that area, any published area statement,[55] any relevant local well-being plan, the resources likely to be available for implementing the plan and such other matters as are prescribed.[56]

5.31 Local well-being plans replace community strategies in accordance with the Well-being of Future Generations (Wales) Act 2015.[57] Community strategies were required for all authorities except the National Park Authorities further to the Local Government Act 2000 and were met by the single integrated plan produced in accordance with the Local Government (Wales) Measure 2009. Local well-being plans will be prepared by public services boards, there being one board for each local authority area.[58] In the case of National Park Authorities the local well-being plan will be that of the public services board that includes any part of the authority's area.[59] The local well-being plan is complementary to the local development plan and should express those elements which relate to land use provided that they are in conformity with national and international policy and obligations.[60]

5.32 In addition, the plan must have regard to Waste Strategy for Wales, Local Transport Plans and other policies prepared under section 108 of the Transport Act 2000, Local Housing Strategies and objectives for major accident prevention and limitation, and any marine plan affecting the authority's area.[61] Policies for reasonable requirements in furtherance of energy policies may be included in accordance with the Planning and Energy Act 2008, section 1.

5.33 The local planning authority must have regard to any guidance issued by the Welsh Ministers in exercising any of their functions under this part of the Act.[62] In *R (TW Logistics Ltd) v Tendring*[63] Lewison LJ said:

> when a decision maker is required to 'have regard' to a particular factor he complies with his legal duty if at some stage in the decision making process, he conscientiously considers that factor, on the clear understanding that it is a factor relevant or potentially relevant to his decision. In other words, he must take that factor into account during the decision making process.

5.34 As stated, regard must be had to the resources necessary to implement the plan and a sustainability appraisal is required.[64] The sustainability appraisal addresses the

[55] Published further to Environment (Wales) Act 2016, s. 11.

[56] PCPA 2004, s. 62(5) and (8).

[57] PCPA 2004, s. 62(5)(d), as substituted.

[58] Well-being of Future Generations (Wales) Act 2015, ss. 39 and 29.

[59] PCPA 2004, s. 62(7), as substituted.

[60] See PPW 2.1.7.

[61] Town and Country Planning (Local Development Plan) (Wales) Regulations 2005, reg. 13, as amended.

[62] PCPA 2004, s. 75.

[63] [2013] EWCA Civ 9 at para. 19.

[64] PCPA 2004, s. 62(6).

economic, environmental and social effects of the plan and must include all steps necessary to comply with the SEA Regulations.[65] Detailed Guidance on the preparation of the Sustainability Appraisal is contained in the *Local Development Plan Manual*. The sustainability appraisal must include an assessment of the likely effects of the plan on the use of the Welsh language in the local authority area[66] and the survey required under section 61 of the 2004 Act must include the extent to which the Welsh language is used in the area.[67]

The extent to which an adopted development plan can be challenged, in particular because of alleged inadequacies of the environmental and sustainability appraisals, was considered in *Shadwell Estates Ltd v Breckland DC*:[68] the case involved issues relating to the English local plan process but the general point applies that challenge is on conventional *Wednesbury* grounds[69] and only if an environmental document is so deficient that it cannot be described as the document as defined by the legislation will the courts intervene. 5.35

PPW 2.3.1 states that local development plans should contain sufficient policies and proposals to provide the basis for deciding planning applications. More detailed thematic or site-specific guidance relating to the specific interpretation of the plan may be by selective use of Supplementary Planning Guidance but this is not part of the development plan – although it may be a material consideration under PCPA 2004, section 38(6). It expressly states[70] that 'the Welsh Government and the Planning Inspectorate will give substantial weight to approved SPG which derives from and is consistent with the development plan, and has been the subject of consultation.' 5.36

LOCAL DEVELOPMENT PLAN PROCESS

The plan process may be divided into its component stages as part of a cyclical process, beginning with and returning to review. It is described as an integrated process incorporating the sustainability appraisal and reflecting without repeating policies and strategies whether national, regional or local. 5.37

[65] Environmental Assessment of Plans and Programmes (Wales) Regulations 2004 (SI 2004 No. 1656); and see PPW 2.4.4.

[66] PCPA 2004, s. 62(6A).

[67] PCPA 2004, s. 61(2)(a).

[68] [2013] EWHC 12 (Admin) at paras 71–8.

[69] *Wednesbury* unreasonableness will be met at various points in the text. It refers to the decision in *Associated Provincial Picture Houses Ltd v Wednesbury Corporation* [1948] 1 KB 223, where it was said that the court is entitled to interfere with a decision where the decision-makers have taken into account matters which they ought not to take into account, or, conversely, have refused to take into account or neglected to take into account matters which they ought to take into account. Once that question is answered in favour of the decision-makers, it may be still possible to say that they have nevertheless come to a conclusion so unreasonable that no reasonable authority could ever have come to it.

[70] Paragraph 2.3.4.

5.38 There are seven identified stages in the process.[71] In turn they are: the evidence stage, which involves reviewing, developing and maintaining a robust evidence base and monitoring the current development plan. Next is preparation and publication of the delivery agreement, followed by pre-deposit plan preparation. This is the important consultation stage extending to all relevant aspects including the issues, preferred strategies, alternatives and allocations. The plan is then placed on deposit, following which it is submitted for independent examination. The three final stages are the inspector's report, adoption and monitoring, review and revision.

5.39 Each of these stages is the subject of detailed provisions in accordance with the 2005 Regulations.[72] Reference should be made to the *Manual* for detailed consideration of the plan process. Further information is in the Planning Inspectorate 2015 publications, *Local Development Plan Examinations: Procedure Guidance* and *LDPs: Preparing for submission – Guidance for Local Planning Authorities*.

5.40 The plan is to be prepared in accordance with the local planning authority's community involvement scheme, that is the involvement of prescribed and other interested persons in the process,[73] and the authority's timetable for the plan. Both of these are embodied in the delivery agreement produced by the authority.

5.41 The procedural requirements provide for publication to enable public consultation and refer to general consulting bodies by reference to the interest affected and identify specific consultation bodies.[74] Further details of both categories of consultee are in Annex B to the *Local Development Plan Manual*. Among the specific consultation bodies are the Welsh Government, Natural Resources Wales, Network Rail Infrastructure Limited, adjoining local authorities and community and town councils,[75] Local Health Boards, UK government departments and statutory undertakers. General consultation bodies are voluntary bodies, bodies representing racial, ethnic or national groups, or religious groups, or disabled persons, or those representing business or Welsh cultural interests.[76]

5.42 The process requires the Welsh Government to be consulted and it may make representations at relevant stages and may, as statutory consultee, be represented at the public examination. In addition, it possesses formal powers to intervene in the process.[77] The local planning authority must make an annual report to the Welsh Ministers on the extent to which the objectives of the plan are being achieved.[78]

[71] See *Local Development Plan Manual*.

[72] Town and Country Planning (Local Development Plan) (Wales) Regulations 2005 (SI 2005 No. 2839).

[73] PCPA 2004, s. 63.

[74] Town and Country Planning (Local Development Plan) (Wales) Regulations 2005 (SI 2005 No. 2839), regs 14–16A.

[75] These are relevant authorities within the meaning of reg. 2 of the 2005 Regulations.

[76] Regulation 2.

[77] PCPA 2004, ss. 65 and 71.

[78] PCPA 2004, s. 76.

Section 64 requires the plan to be submitted to the Welsh Ministers for independent examination. The authority must not submit a plan unless it has complied with the relevant requirements and thinks that it is ready for public examination[79] and must send 'prescribed information' to accompany the examination.[80] The purpose of the examination is to determine if the plan satisfies the requirements of sections 62 and 63 and the Regulations and that it is sound.[81] 5.43

The formal procedural steps have been referred to above. The procedural test is referred to in the Appendix to the Planning Inspectorate Examinations Guidance, where it refers to early screening to ensure compliance with the delivery agreement, and completion of a sustainability appraisal including the Strategic Environmental Assessment and of an Appropriate Assessment under the Habitats Regulations.[82] 5.44

Soundness is not defined but it involves the three categories of consistency, coherence and effectiveness. It is a matter of planning judgment under the examination process and not a matter for the court, which is concerned only with established matters of legal review.[83] However, there is no presumption of soundness and if there was no evidence to support an essential element of the plan at examination, so that the inspector reached a conclusion that was not properly open to him, the plan will fail to meet the statutory requirements.[84] 5.45

The *Local Development Plan Manual*[85] identifies three questions to determine soundness and gives examples of subsidiary questions under each. The first question is 'Does the plan fit?', asking if it has regard to relevant documents and objectives. Coherence is considered by asking 'Is the plan appropriate?' and includes issues such as the strength of evidence, whether it addresses key issues and whether it meets assessed needs and contributes to achieving sustainable development. Finally it asks, 'Will the Plan deliver?' and raises questions of viability and deliverability. 5.46

Review must be carried out if after consideration the authority thinks it should be reviewed and at such other times as the Welsh Ministers prescribe.[86] There is power to revise the plan after review[87] and the local planning authority must consider whether to carry out a review following publication of the National Development Framework or a revised framework or of a strategic development plan or revised plan for all or part of the area of the local planning authority.[88] 5.47

79 PCPA 2004, s. 64(2).

80 PCPA 2004, s. 64(3).

81 PCPA 2004, s. 64(5).

82 The Guidance refers to the 1994 Regulations, although they have of course been replaced by the 2010 Regulations.

83 *Grand Union Investments Ltd v Dacorum BC* [2014] EWHC 1894 (Admin) at para. 56.

84 *Blyth Valley DC v Persimmon Homes (North East) Ltd* [2008] EWCA Civ 861.

85 See Section 8.

86 PCPA 2004, ss. 68A and 69.

87 PCPA 2004, s.70(1).

88 PCPA 2004, s. 68A.

5.48 The person appointed for the public examination can make recommendations[89] which may lead to modifications to the published plan.[90] In addition the Welsh Ministers can issue a direction that a plan must be modified and the authority must then comply.[91] The Welsh Ministers may also issue a direction that a plan must be submitted to it for approval before adoption[92] and they may then approve, modify or reject the plan.[93] Further, a direction may be issued to revise a plan[94] or direct a local planning authority to withdraw a plan at any time before adoption.[95]

5.49 Where there has been no direction to withdraw, a local planning authority may withdraw a plan at any time before adoption but subject to further provisions depending on the stage reached in the process,[96] and the plan may be revoked at any time by the Welsh Ministers at the request of the local planning authority.[97] A default power enables the Welsh Ministers to hold an independent examination if they think that the authority is failing or omitting to do anything necessary in connection with the preparation, revision or adoption of the plan.[98]

5.50 The local planning authority may adopt a local development plan as originally prepared if the person appointed to carry out the independent examination of the plan so recommends or as modified in accordance with the modifications so recommended.[99] It may not be adopted if the Welsh Ministers issue a direction not to do so.[100] Adoption is by resolution of the authority.[101] A plan may be adopted with revisions as recommended where the procedure in Regulation 13A and Part 4A or Regulations 14–16 and Part 4 is followed.[102] A plan may also become operative on approval by Welsh Ministers under sections 65 or 71. On approval or adoption by the local planning authority the plan supersedes any existing LDP, which then ceases to have effect.[103]

5.51 Challenge to the validity of the plan or any part of the process may be made in a claim under PCPA 2004, section 113. This provides that a challenge to the validity of, *inter alia*, a local development plan or any local development plan document may only be made to the High Court on the grounds that the document is not

[89] PCPA 2004, s. 64(7).
[90] PCPA 2004, s. 67(2).
[91] PCPA 2004, s. 65(1).
[92] PCPA 2004, s. 65(4).
[93] PCPA 2004, s. 65(9).
[94] PCPA 2004, s. 70.
[95] PCPA 2004, s. 66.
[96] PCPA 2004, s. 66A.
[97] PCPA 2004, s. 68.
[98] PCPA 2004, s. 71.
[99] PCPA 2004, s. 67(1) and (2).
[100] PCPA 2004, s. 67(4).
[101] PCPA 2004, s. 67(3).
[102] See also reg. 25A.
[103] 2005 Regulations, reg. 25(3).

within the appropriate power or a procedural requirement has not been complied with, and must be made within six weeks of the relevant date. In the case of a local development plan this will be the date of adoption or approval.[104] The court's jurisdiction under section 113 is thus limited to the traditional public law grounds of review.[105] This is considered in Chapter 22 below.

[104] The section was considered in *IM Properties Development Ltd v Lichfield DC* [2014] EWHC 2440 (Admin), where it was held that once a document had been submitted for examination it was a development plan document within s. 113 and could only be challenged in accordance with its provisions.

[105] *Grand Union Investments Ltd v Dacorum BC* [2014] EWHC 1894 (Admin).

Chapter 6

The Need for Planning Permission – Development

INTRODUCTION

Planning permission is required to carry out any development of land.[1] 6.1

Development is defined in TCPA 1990, section 55 in general terms, although 6.2 the Act gives specific instances of what is to be treated as development and instances of what is not. In addition there are a limited number of exceptions to the requirement for permission,[2] that is, cases where permission is not required although the activity is development of the land. The Act then provides how planning permission may be granted depending on the nature of the development: this includes planning permission generally by order for certain categories of development.

Nationally significant infrastructure projects require development consent, not 6.3 planning permission[3] and there are additional provisions defining relevant development for these purposes in section 32(2)–(3) of the Planning Act 2008: the effect of these is considered in Chapter 8 (on development consent orders), below.

This chapter therefore deals with the essential question of whether or not 6.4 something constitutes development: if an activity is not development of land there is no planning law restriction on carrying it out. It also considers the statutory exceptions where development is involved but permission is not required. If permission is required the grant of permission is considered in Chapter 9, which deals with both general permitted development and individual grants of permission. Advertisements are subject to specific provisions, which are considered at the end of this chapter.

TCPA 1990 binds the Crown[4] and development by the Crown will require 6.5 permission subject to certain exceptions. The procedure, where different, and exceptions regarding Crown development, are referred to in Chapter 12. Similarly, development on land by a local planning authority, either alone or jointly with others, is controlled by TCPA 1990 but subject to any specific modification by regulations, and this is also considered in Chapter 12.

[1] TCPA 1990, s. 57(1).

[2] See s. 57(1) and the exceptions in subsections (2)–(4).

[3] Planning Act 2008, s. 33(1)(a).

[4] TCPA 1990, s. 292A.

MEANING OF DEVELOPMENT

6.6 Development means the carrying out of building, engineering, mining or other operations in, on, over or under land or the making of any material change in the use of any buildings or other land.[5] Land means any corporeal hereditament, including a building.[6] Although it is said that development involves change, in fact the wording in the statute is simply 'development' and this is an ordinary word which probably requires no gloss. The issues that do arise stem from the more complicated statutory structure of definitions, clarifications and exceptions.

6.7 The definition refers to both operational development and material change in use. It is generally considered that operations will involve physical alteration to land whilst a change in use does not physically interfere with it.[7] However, a particular development may include both forms of development and the distinction between the two is not always clear. It may be necessary to obtain planning permission for both depending upon the precise circumstances. For example, in *West Bowers Farm Products v Essex CC*[8] the development was the construction of an extensive reservoir involving the extraction of sand and gravel which was to be removed from the site and sold. It was held that a single process may for planning purposes amount to two activities. Whether it does so or not is a question of fact and degree. If it involves two activities, each of substance, so that one is not merely ancillary to the other, then both require permission. On the facts, the construction of the reservoir and the extraction of minerals each required planning permission. Further, it was said that the same activity may also constitute both an operation and a material change of use.

6.8 In *R (Lowther) v Durham County Council*[9] it was held, considering *West Bowers*, that there is no reason why two or more activities should not constitute a single use covered by a single planning permission.

6.9 Where planning permission is granted for the erection of a building, it may specify its purpose: if it does not, the permission includes permission to use the building for the purpose for which it is designed.[10] However, 'use' does not include the use of land for the carrying out of any building or other operations on it, so that a specific permission will be required for those operations.[11]

[5] TCPA 1990, s. 55(1).

[6] TCPA 1990, s. 336(1).

[7] See *Parkes v Secretary of State for the Environment* [1978] 1 WLR 1308: physical alteration generally involves a degree of permanence for the purposes of s. 55 but care must be taken where other provisions concerning development are concerned: see e.g. s. 56 below and *Malvern Hills DC v Secretary of State for the Environment* (1983) 46 P & CR 58.

[8] (1985) 50 P & CR 368.

[9] [2001] EWCA Civ 781.

[10] TCPA 1990, s. 75(2) and (3).

[11] TCPA 1990, s. 336(1).

What is development is not to be construed too narrowly. In *R (Save Woolley Valley Action Group Ltd) v Bath and North East Somerset Council*[12] it was held that development was to be interpreted broadly so as to include, wherever possible, projects which required an Environmental Impact Assessment under Council Directive 85/337/EEC.[13] The Court here also considered the extent to which deciding whether or not something was development was a matter of strict legal definition or one of judgment. It was held that whether or not the poultry units at issue constituted 'development' under section 55 was not a question of jurisdictional fact to be determined by the court. The court said that in *R (A) v London Borough of Croydon, Secretary of State for the Home Department and another Intervening*,[14] the Supreme Court had distinguished between an evaluative question, which Parliament intended to be decided by the decision-maker, and an objective question to which there was a right or wrong answer, which was not a matter of opinion. In the case of an objective question, upon which the exercise of executive power depends, the court will decide whether or not the requisite precondition has been satisfied. However, the question whether or not the poultry units constituted 'development' within section 55 was an evaluative question, which required an exercise of judgment by the local planning authority. 6.10

The general view thus is that the question of whether or not there is development is a question of fact and degree challengeable only within the traditional public law confines rather than a matter of law for the courts to determine. 6.11

OPERATIONAL DEVELOPMENT – GENERAL

Operations comprise building, engineering, mining or other operations. These may overlap and it is not necessarily essential in an individual case to determine which of the forms of operational development is involved.[15] 6.12

BUILDING OPERATIONS

Building operations include demolition of buildings, rebuilding, structural alterations or additions to buildings and other operations normally undertaken by a person carrying on business as a builder.[16] This is to be read subject to the exclusions in section 55(2) referred to below. Building is defined as including any structure or erection, and any part of a building but does not include plant or machinery 6.13

[12] [2012] EWHC 2161 (Admin).

[13] See now Directive 2011/92/EU. The current regulations are SI 2016 No. 58.

[14] [2009] UKSC 8, [2009] 1 WLR 2557.

[15] See e.g. *James v Secretary of State for Wales* (1998) 76 P & CR 62.

[16] TCPA 1990, s. 55(1A).

comprised in a building.[17] In the case of demolition works, the provisions are subject to any direction of the Welsh Ministers in accordance with section 55(2)(g).

6.14 The approach generally adopted is to consider whether what is on the land is a building, within the definition, and, if it is, then the work to erect or create it will be considered a building operation. Three factors – size, permanence and degree of physical attachment – are relevant in deciding what is a building or structure. In *Skerritts of Nottingham Ltd v Secretary of State for the Environment Transport and Regions (No. 2)*[18] the Court accepted this test as formulated in earlier authorities, noting that the necessary flexibility was met by referring to the degree of permanence. On the facts, a marquee which remained on a lawn from February to October but was removed for the winter season had the necessary degree of permanence so as to be a building under the Act.

6.15 In *R (Hall Hunter Partnership) v First Secretary of State*[19] polytunnels of substantial size and proportion, attached by legs screwed into the ground but remaining in one location only for three to seven months in a year, were properly regarded as development. Further consideration was given to the element of permanence in the *Save Woolley Valley Action Group* case[20] where the issue was the mobility and temporary or permanent fixing to the ground of the poultry units.

6.16 Certain operations or uses are not to be taken as involving development.[21] In the immediate context, maintenance, improvement or other alteration which affect only the interior of a building or which do not materially affect its external appearance are not development.[22] The exclusion of internal development is subject to restriction by development order. The relevant provision is article 2A of the Town and Country Planning (Development Management Procedure) (Wales) Order 2012,[23] which excludes from the scope of section 55(2)(a) increases in floor area by more than 200 square metres for buildings for the retail sale of goods other than hot food. This, therefore, is included within the definition of development. In *Sage v Secretary of State for the Environment, Transport and the Regions and another*[24] the House of Lords held that the exception to 'development' in the section applied only to operations carried out on a completed building for its 'maintenance, improvement or other alteration', and did not apply to work carried out by way of completing an incomplete building.

6.17 In practice, it is appropriate to consider also the extent to which works of enlargement, alteration or improvement to a dwelling house, although within the

[17] TCPA 1990, s. 336(1).

[18] [2000] JPL 1025.

[19] [2006] EWHC 3482 (Admin).

[20] See above.

[21] See TCPA 1990, s. 55(2).

[22] TCPA 1990, s. 55(2)(a): making good war damage and the creation of underground space are excluded and they are therefore development.

[23] As inserted by SI 2015 No. 1330.

[24] [2003] UKHL 22, [2003] 1 WLR 983.

definition of development, might be permitted by article 3 of and Schedule 2 to the Town and Country Planning (General Permitted Development) Order 1995[25] as being within the curtilage of the dwelling, not exceeding the relevant dimensions and otherwise meeting the terms of the permission.

Certain highway works and works to sewers, mains, pipes, cables and other apparatus by a local authority or statutory undertaker are also excluded from being development and are referred to under engineering operations, below.[26] 6.18

DEMOLITION

Demolition is development under TCPA 1990, section 55(1A) but there is an exception for the demolition of any description of building specified in a direction given by the Welsh Ministers to local planning authorities generally or to a particular local planning authority.[27] 6.19

The Town and Country Planning (Demolition – Description of Buildings) Direction 1995, which was attached to WOC 31/95, excepted certain categories of demolition. Its aim was that the total demolition of dwelling houses and buildings attached to them outside conservation areas and gates, walls and fences within such areas remained development and would be dealt with as appropriate as general permitted development. Paragraphs 2(a)–(d) provided that demolition of any listed building, any building in a conservation area, any scheduled monument and any building other than a dwelling or one attached to a dwelling were taken not to involve development by the Direction. Control over the first three categories would be exercised under other Acts.[28] 6.20

Certain parts of the 1995 Direction referred to above were held unlawful by the Court of Appeal in *Save Britain's Heritage v Secretary of State for Communities and Local Government*.[29] The Court granted declarations that demolition of buildings was capable of constituting a project within Annex II of Council Directive 85/337/EEC (EIA Directive) and that paragraphs 2(1)(a)–(d) of the Direction were unlawful and should not be given effect. The 1995 Direction has not been re-issued but must be read subject to this ruling as explained in the Welsh Government letter of 18 April 2011 to planning officers headed 'Planning Control over Demolition'.[30] 6.21

[25] SI 1995 No. 418.

[26] TCPA 1990, s. 55(2)(b) and (c).

[27] TCPA 1990, s. 55(2)(g).

[28] See Listed Buildings and Conservation Areas Act 1990 and Ancient Monuments and Archaeological Areas Act 1979, and Chapter 24, below.

[29] [2011] EWCA Civ 334. The case refers expressly to the English Circular, DoE 10/95: the circular was jointly issued by the relevant departments.

[30] See Index of Planning Policy Guidance for Wales (Dec. 2015) for reference. It has been issued in amended form in relation to England only by a 2014 Direction.

6.22 The effect of this is that demolition generally is development. The exceptions that remain from the Direction are for certain minor development, that is, the demolition of a building the cubic content of which, measured externally, does not exceed 50 cubic metres, or it is or involves the demolition of the whole or any part of any gate, fence, wall or other means of enclosure, except where they are in a conservation area.

6.23 In practical terms the need for an application for planning permission will depend on whether permitted development rights[31] apply to the demolition. If the development is EIA development such rights will not apply.[32] Subject to this, demolition of a building is generally permitted subject to the conditions and further definitions laid down.[33] Demolition of all or any part of any gate, fence, wall or other means of enclosure is also permitted.[34] Application should always be made to the local planning authority to determine if prior approval is required for the method of demolition and restoration.[35] As stated, demolition affecting listed buildings and in conservation areas is subject to separate control and will require the appropriate consent.[36]

6.24 Where other descriptions, e.g. engineering or other operations, are more apt to describe the activity, it is inappropriate to give demolition a wide meaning.[37]

ENGINEERING OPERATIONS

6.25 Engineering operations include the formation or laying out of means of access to highways.[38] Works for maintenance or improvement within the boundaries of a road when carried out by a highway authority are exempt save for works not exclusively for maintenance where they may have significant adverse effects on the environment.[39] Works by local authorities or statutory undertakers for the purpose of inspecting, repairing or renewing sewers, mains, pipes, cables or other apparatus are also declared not to constitute development.[40]

6.26 To opposite effect, section 55(4A) provides that the placing or assembly of a tank in inland waters for fish farming where it would not otherwise involve

[31] See Chapter 9, below and the Town and Country Planning (General Permitted Development) Order 1995, Sch. 2, Pt 31.

[32] Town and Country Planning (General Permitted Development) Order 1995, art. 3.

[33] See the Order, Sch. 2, Pt 31, Class A.

[34] See Order, Sch. 2, Pt 31, Class B, which thus extends to those in conservation areas.

[35] Notice to the local authority of intended demolition is generally required by the Building Act 1984, s. 80.

[36] See Chapter 24, below.

[37] See *Coppen (Trustees of Thames Ditton Lawn Tennis Club) v Bruce-Smith* (1999) 77 P & CR 239.

[38] TCPA 1990, s. 336(1).

[39] TCPA 1990, s. 55(2)(b).

[40] TCPA 1990, s. 55(2)(c).

development of the land below shall have effect as if the tank resulted from carrying out engineering operations.

Other than this there is no further statutory guidance and, unlike building operations where the focus is on the building or structure produced, it may not be as easy to identify the product of the works and attention must be paid to the operations themselves. Drainage and waste disposal works can be particularly problematic. The complexity of the operation and the extent to which it may have required expert engineering involvement can be relevant to the question of whether or not development is involved – see e.g. *Coleshill & District Investment Co. Ltd v Minister of Housing and Local Government and another.*[41] 6.27

MINING OPERATIONS

Mining operations include the removal of material of any description from a mineral working deposit, from a deposit of pulverised fuel ash or other furnace ash or clinker or from a deposit of iron, steel or other metallic slags and the extraction of minerals from a disused railway embankment.[42] Mineral working deposit and minerals are themselves further defined,[43] and the definition makes clear that it refers to the winning and working of minerals in, on or under the land. There is an exclusion for peat where it is cut for purposes other than sale. 6.28

OTHER OPERATIONS

The House of Lords, in *Coleshill & District Investment Co. Ltd v Minister of Housing and Local Government and another,*[44] doubted that 'other operations' was simply to be construed *ejusdem generis* with the preceding specified operations on the grounds that it was difficult to discover any common genus to building, engineering or mining operations, although it was said that the use of the words together suggests that the operations do have some relationship with one another. 6.29

It is therefore a residual category dependent on the particular facts and circumstances. The erection of poultry units was considered to be capable of being 'other operations' in *R (Save Woolley Valley Action Group Ltd) v Bath and North East Somerset Council.*[45] 6.30

[41] [1969] 1 WLR 746 at p. 754.

[42] TCPA 1990, s. 55(4).

[43] See TCPA 1990, s. 336(1).

[44] [1969] 1 WLR 746.

[45] Above.

MATERIAL CHANGE IN USE

6.31 In addition to carrying out operations, the making of any material change in use of any buildings or other land is development.[46] As stated, use does not include use for carrying out any building or other operations.[47] Land and buildings have the meaning as above.

6.32 Certain specific uses are expressly identified in the Act so that there are three categories of use which are not to be taken to involve development and three others which are development.

6.33 The uses excluded from being development are, first, the use of any buildings or other land within the curtilage of a dwelling house for any purpose incidental to the enjoyment of the dwelling house as such.[48] Secondly, there is excluded the use of any land for the purposes of agriculture or forestry (including afforestation) and the use for any of those purposes of any building occupied together with land so used.[49] Finally, in the case of buildings or other land which are used for a purpose of any class specified in an order made by the Welsh Ministers under this section, the use of the buildings or other land or, subject to the provisions of the order, of any part of the buildings or the other land, for any other purpose of the same class is not development.[50]

6.34 The relevant Order for the purposes of the last exception is the Town and Country Planning (Uses Classes) Order 1987[51] and article 3 of the Order gives effect to the exception in section 55(2)(f). It provides that a change of use from a purpose within a specified class to any other purpose of the same class is not to be taken as development. Development is therefore concerned with purposes which do not fall within any specified use class (termed 'unique uses' rather than the former '*sui generis* uses') and changes to a use in a different class, although in certain cases the Order does permit change of use from a defined use in one class to that in another. In *Belmont Riding Centre v First Secretary of State*,[52] Richards J said 'the use classes order has no application to a mixed use: the mixed use does not itself fall within any class and a finding of material change of use is not avoided simply by showing that a component falling within a particular class has been substituted for another component falling within the same class.' This was quoted with approval in *Fidler* (see below).

6.35 Two particular uses are expressly declared, for the avoidance of doubt, to involve a material change of use. The use as two or more separate dwelling houses of any building previously used as a single dwelling house is a material change in the

[46] TCPA 1990, s. 55(1).

[47] TCPA 1990, s. 336(1).

[48] TCPA 1990, s. 55(2)(d).

[49] TCPA 1990, s. 55(2)(e).

[50] TCPA 1990, s. 55(2)(f), and see Town and Country Planning (Use Classes) Order 1987, art. 3(1).

[51] SI 1987 No. 764, as amended.

[52] [2003] EWHC 1895 (Admin) at para. 80.

use of the building and of each part of it which is so used.[53] Secondly, the deposit of refuse or waste materials on land is a material change, notwithstanding that the land is comprised in a site already used for that purpose, if the superficial area of the deposit is extended, or the height of the deposit is extended and exceeds the level of the land adjoining the site.[54]

Finally, the use for the display of advertisements of any external part of a building which is not normally used for that purpose shall be treated for the purposes of section 55 as involving a material change in the use of that part of the building.[55] Advertisements, whether or not constituting development, are subject to distinct rules and regulations. The result is that advertisements within the regulations will not require planning permission although unauthorised advertising may be development subject to the regulations and to general planning control. Advertisements are considered separately below. 6.36

GENERAL APPROACH TO MATERIAL CHANGE IN USE

In *Fidler v First Secretary of State*,[56] Carnwath LJ accepted that the following four principles to approach the issue of material change were not in dispute: 6.37

> The orthodox approach is for the decision maker to identify the appropriate 'planning unit' to be considered for the purpose of deciding whether or not there has been a material change in the use of land;
>
> The appropriate planning unit may embrace an area of occupation within which a variety of activities are carried on and comprise a composite or mixed use, where the individual components may fluctuate in their intensity from time to time, but are not confined within separate and physically distinct areas of land;
>
> Whether or not there has been a material change in the use of land is to be considered by reference to the character of the use or uses to which the land is put. A material change in the character of the use of land is capable of resulting, wholly or in part, from changes in the intensity of the use or uses of or activities carried out on land. Such changes may be material for planning purposes even though the generic use or uses of the land in question have not changed;
>
> Whether the use of land has changed in any manner that is material for planning purposes is a question of fact and degree for the decision maker to determine in the light of all the circumstances of the case.

The separate elements in this approach can now be considered in turn. 6.38

[53] TCPA 1990, s. 55(3)(a).

[54] TCPA 1990, s. 55(3)(b).

[55] TCPA 1990, s. 55(5).

[56] [2004] EWCA Civ 1295.

PLANNING UNIT

6.39 The term 'planning unit' does not appear in statute but has a long history in considering material change in use. *R (Sellars) v Basingstoke & Deane Borough Council*[57] held that the identification of the appropriate planning unit (whether larger or smaller than the land specified in the application) was also an essential part of the decision whether a certificate of lawful use should be granted.

6.40 Planning unit embraces two different elements: temporal, which refers to the planning history of the site; and geographical, which refers to the physical area of land under consideration.[58]

6.41 In *Burdle v Secretary of State for the Environment*,[59] Bridge J set out some non-exhaustive tests as follows:

> First, whenever it is possible to recognise a single main purpose of the occupier's use of his land to which secondary activities are incidental or ancillary, the whole unit of occupation should be considered. That proposition emerges clearly from *G. Percy Trentham Ltd. v. Gloucestershire County Council [1966] 1 W.L.R. 506*, where Diplock L.J. said, at p. 513: 'What is the unit which the local authority are entitled to look at and deal with in an enforcement notice for the purpose of determining whether or not there has been a "material change in the use of any buildings or other land"? As I suggested in the course of the argument, I think for that purpose what the local authority are entitled to look at is the whole of the area which was used for a particular purpose, including any part of that area whose use was incidental to or ancillary to the achievement of that purpose.'
>
> But, secondly, it may equally be apt to consider the entire unit of occupation even though the occupier carries on a variety of activities and it is not possible to say that one is incidental or ancillary to another. This is well settled in the case of a composite use where the component activities fluctuate in their intensity from time to time, but the different activities are not confined within separate and physically distinct areas of land.
>
> Thirdly, however, it may frequently occur that within a single unit of occupation two or more physically separate and distinct areas are occupied for substantially different and unrelated purposes. In such a case each area used for a different main purpose (together with its incidental and ancillary activities) ought to be considered as a separate planning unit.
>
> To decide which of these three categories apply to the circumstances of any particular case at any given time may be difficult. Like the question of material change of use, it must be a question of fact and degree. There may indeed be an almost imperceptible change from one category to another. Thus, for example, activities initially incidental to the main use of an area of land may grow in scale

57 [2013] EWHC 3673 (Admin).

58 See e.g. *Jennings Motors Ltd v Secretary of State for the Environment* [1982] QB 541.

59 [1972] 1 WLR 1207 at p. 1212.

> to a point where they convert the single use to a composite use and produce a material change of use of the whole. Again, activities once properly regarded as incidental to another use or as part of a composite use may be so intensified in scale and physically concentrated in a recognisably separate area that they produce a new planning unit the use of which is materially changed. It may be a useful working rule to assume that the unit of occupation is the appropriate planning unit, unless and until some smaller unit can be recognised as the site of activities which amount in substance to a separate use both physically and functionally.

The concept has no relevance to the change from use as a single dwelling to use as two or more separate dwelling houses within section 55(3).[60] 6.42

Finally, it should be noted that the House of Lords has held that where the grant of planning permission, whether it be permission to build or for a change of use, was of such a character that the implementation of the permission led to the creation of a new planning unit, existing use rights attaching to the former planning unit were extinguished.[61] 6.43

CHARACTER OF USE

As made clear in the statement of Carnwath LJ cited above, the central question is whether the character of the use has changed. 6.44

In *East Barnet Urban District Council v British Transport Commission*,[62] Lord Parker CJ stated: 'It seems clear to me that under the Acts . . . what is really to be considered is the character of the use of the land, not the particular purpose of a particular occupier'. This approach has been adopted in subsequent cases and was expressly confirmed, citing earlier authority, by the Court of Appeal in *Hertfordshire CC v Secretary of State for Communities and Local Government*[63] and later applied by the Court of Appeal in *Westminster City Council v Secretary of State for Communities and Local Government, Oriol Badia v Property Investment (Developments) Ltd.*[64] 6.45

SINGLE ACTIVITY AND MULTIPLE ACTIVITIES

Land may be used for more than one activity. Where physically separate and distinct areas of land are occupied for substantially different and unrelated purposes each 6.46

[60] *Van Dyck v Secretary of State for the Environment* (1993) 66 P & CR 61.

[61] *Newbury District Council v Secretary of State for the Environment, Newbury District Council v International Synthetic Rubber Co. Ltd* [1981] AC 578.

[62] [1962] 2 QB 484 at p. 491.

[63] [2012] EWCA Civ 1473, Pill LJ at paras 9–11.

[64] [2015] EWCA Civ 482.

area will generally be regarded as a separate planning unit.[65] However, different activities may take place within the same planning unit. This 'mixed activity' may properly be described as a composite use involving the various activities, there may be more than one primary use so that they are treated independently, or one or more may be a primary use and another or others ancillary. Whether a change is material will depend on the overall test of alteration in character taking into account the use before and after the 'change'. Subdivision of the planning unit may be a material change in use.[66]

6.47 The concept of ancillary or incidental use was extensively considered at first instance in *Harrods Ltd v Secretary of State for the Environment, Transport and Regions*[67] and passages were cited at some length on appeal (see *Harrods Ltd v Secretary of State for the Environment, Transport and Regions*[68]), where Schiemann LJ said that he broadly concurred. So, at first instance, Sullivan J said:

> The ancillary use principle was developed by the courts as a response to practical realities on the ground: the factory containing administrative offices; the car park associated with the office building; the storage area associated with the shop. It gives the occupier a valuable measure of flexibility to respond to changing needs. But restricting that degree of flexibility to ancillary uses which are 'ordinarily incidental' to the primary use of the planning unit as a whole does not prevent the introduction of the extraordinary, or the unusual. It merely subjects it to the need to apply for planning permission. If, on consideration of an application for planning permission, it is found that there are no good reasons to refuse permission . . . then planning permission will be granted. If there are good reasons to refuse planning permission, it must be in the public interest that those reasons should be able to prevail and not be 'sidestepped' by the application of an unqualified 'incidental/ancillary' use test.

6.48 In upholding the decision on appeal, the Court said: 'It is not appropriate to concentrate on what is incidental to this particular shop, given the way *it* is run, and given *its* needs. The right approach is to see what shops in general have as reasonably incidental activities'.

INTENSIFICATION OF USE

6.49 In *Hertfordshire County Council v Secretary of State for Communities and Local Government and Metal and Waste Recycling Limited*,[69] Pill LJ said that it was not disputed that

[65] See *Burdle*, above.

[66] See e.g. *Wakelin v Secretary of State for the Environment and another* (1983) 46 P & CR 214.

[67] [2001] EWHC Admin 600 at para. 97.

[68] [2002] EWCA 412 at paragraph 22.

[69] [2012] EWCA Civ 1473 at para. 9.

intensification of a use is capable of constituting a material change in use. What is necessary, however, is that the test for deciding whether there has been a material change is whether there has been a change in the character of the use. Elias J in *R (Manning) v South Lakeland District Council*[70] approached the matter as follows:

> Perhaps the key point here is that the impact of a particular use is an integral part of the character of that use, so that even though the relevant use itself may not change, save in the intensification itself, that will, in an appropriate case, be capable of constituting a change in character.

In *Birmingham Corporation v Minister of Housing and Local Government and Habib Ullah*[71] the fact that throughout the use was residential was not decisive and the change from a single dwelling to a house let in lodgings was capable of being a material change in use. 6.50

CESSATION AND RETURN TO AN EARLIER SITUATION

Questions may arise in connection with operations or use where an earlier activity has ceased: is a resumption of that activity development requiring planning permission or is there a return to what was earlier lawful so that planning permission is not required? In these cases the answer may be that the resumption of operations or use is in fact not fresh development or, although a material change from the immediately preceding activity or use of the land, does not in fact require planning permission. The exceptions to the need for planning permission in TCPA 1990, section 57 are examples of the latter (see below) and in practice will often fall to be decided where this issue arises, but certain matters of general principle need to be considered. 6.51

In *Pioneer Aggregates (UK) Ltd v Secretary of State for the Environment*[72] planning permission had been granted in 1950 and the owner carried out quarrying until 1966, when it notified the local planning authority that it would cease operations, and in 1967 site restoration of the quarry was completed. In 1978 a new owner wished to carry out quarrying and enquired whether planning permission was needed. The local planning authority considered that the 1950 permission had been abandoned or alternatively that the development had been completed. The House of Lords held that there is no principle in planning law that a permission capable of being implemented according to its terms can be abandoned; the commercial decision to cease operations on land where there is a valid planning permission cannot by itself extinguish the permission unless the permission in terms so provides. On 6.52

[70] [2005] EWHC 242 (Admin) at para. 8.

[71] [1964] 1 QB 178.

[72] [1985] AC 132.

the second issue it was found that the permission was for one single development, which had not been completed.

6.53 The *Pioneer* case was concerned with the situation where there was a grant of planning permission. Where there was an existing or established use of land, the use could be abandoned. In *Hartley v Minister of Housing and Local Government*[73] it had been held that cessation for a considerable time with no evinced intention to resume the use may as a matter of fact be abandonment so that a later resumption was a material change of use. This was applied, and *Pioneer* distinguished as applying to grants of permission, in *White v Secretary of State for the Environment*.[74]

6.54 It should also be noted that although the 'intervening' use may not have been development requiring permission, for example because it is excluded by section 55(2)(e), return to the original use may still require permission: it does not follow from the fact that the change to the intervening use was not development that a change from it back to the original is also excluded by the subsection.[75]

6.55 Where the permission was temporary it was said in *Avon Estates Ltd v Welsh Ministers*[76] that it is very difficult to conceive of a condition on a temporary permission under section 72 which could sensibly relate to a development, once that development has ceased to be authorised by the permission.

EXCEPTIONS

6.56 Finally, it should be noted that TCPA 1990 makes specific provision for three categories of case where planning permission is not required although there may have been development. So section 57 provides:

> (2) Where planning permission to develop land has been granted for a limited period, planning permission is not required for the resumption, at the end of that period, of its use for the purpose for which it was normally used before the permission was granted.
> (3) Where by a development order or a local development order planning permission to develop land has been granted subject to limitations, planning permission is not required for the use of that land which (apart from its use in accordance with that permission) is its normal use.
> (4) Where an enforcement notice has been issued in respect of any development of land, planning permission is not required for its use for the purpose for which (in accordance with the provisions of this Part of this Act) it could lawfully have been used if that development had not been carried out.

[73] [1970] 1 QB 413.

[74] (1989) 58 P & CR 281.

[75] *JL Engineering v Secretary of State* (1994) 68 P & CR 504.

[76] [2011] EWCA Civ 553.

In determining what is normal use of land no account is taken of a use in breach of Part III of the Act or in breach of previous planning control.[77] 6.57

ADVERTISEMENTS

Erecting or displaying an advertisement may be operational development or a material change use. As noted above, TCPA 1990, section 55(5) expressly provides that, without prejudice to regulations made under the Act for the control of advertisements, the use of the external part of any building not normally used for that purpose for the display of advertisements shall be treated as involving a material change in use of that part of the building. 6.58

Where the display of advertisements in accordance with regulations made under section 220 involves development, planning permission is deemed to be granted for it and no application is necessary under Part III (sections 55–106C) of the Act.[78] The result is that where the display is within the regulations, control is governed by them rather than by the general provisions of the Act; but in other cases both regimes may apply. 6.59

Advertisement is defined in TCPA 1990, section 336 somewhat tortuously, the essential feature being a display for advertising. The full definition is that it means: 6.60

> any word, letter, model, sign, placard, board, notice, awning, blind, device or representation, whether illuminated or not, in the nature of, and employed wholly or partly for the purposes of, advertisement, announcement or direction, and (without prejudice to the previous provisions of this definition) includes any hoarding or similar structure used or designed, or adapted for use and anything else principally used, or designed or adapted principally for use, for the display of advertisements, and references to the display of advertisements shall be construed accordingly.

There is power to make regulations[79] and the current regulations are the Town and Country Planning (Control of Advertisements) Regulations 1992,[80] with policy and guidance in WOC 14/92 and TAN 7 on Outdoor Advertisement Control. The Regulations apply to the display of any advertisement. Deemed consent is granted for defined advertisements, that is those specified in Schedule 3, Part 1 to the Regulations.[81] Subject to this, an express application must be made to the local planning authority.[82] 6.61

[77] TCPA 1990, s. 57(5).

[78] TCPA 1990, s. 222.

[79] See TCPA 1990, ss. 220 and 222.

[80] SI 1992 No. 666.

[81] Regulation 6.

[82] Regulation 9.

6.62 A local planning authority shall exercise its powers under the Regulations only in the interests of amenity and public safety, taking account of any material factors. In particular, in the case of amenity, it must take account of the general characteristics of the locality, including the presence of any feature of historic, architectural, cultural or similar interest, disregarding, if they think fit, any advertisement being displayed there. In the case of public safety, the factors are the safety of any person who may use any road, railway, waterway, dock, harbour or aerodrome and whether any display of advertisements is likely to obscure, or hinder the ready interpretation of, any road traffic sign, railway signal or aid to navigation by water or air.[83]

6.63 Procedure, including consultation requirements, is in regulations 9–17, which includes a right to appeal to the Welsh Ministers under TCPA 1990, sections 78 and 79 subject to modifications in Part III of Schedule 4: those sections as modified are expressly set out in Part IV of the Schedule. Power to decline an application under section 70A also applies as modified by Part I of the Schedule, the modified section being set out in Part II.

6.64 Display of an advertisement in contravention of the Regulations is a criminal offence.[84] In addition, the local planning authority can issue a notice for discontinuance of a display for which deemed consent is granted where necessary to remedy a substantial injury to amenity of the locality or a danger to members of the public.[85] An express consent can be modified or revoked where expedient.[86] The local planning authority also have power to remove or obliterate any placard or poster displayed in contravention of the Regulations.[87]

[83] Regulation 4.

[84] Regulation 27.

[85] Regulation 8.

[86] Regulation 16.

[87] TCPA 1990, s. 225.

Chapter 7

The Commencement of Development

INTRODUCTION

If development is permitted it may become important to decide when the operations or use started. The main practical importance is in determining if the time limit condition on a planning permission imposed under TCPA 1990, section 91 or 92 has been met, although it may be necessary in other contexts. 7.1

The key issue is whether what has been done on site is done under the authority of the permission; if not, it may be unlawful. The main questions are how much, or how little, work is sufficient, how does it relate to the permission and what is the effect if it is not in accordance with a condition of the permission? 7.2

Notice requirements before beginning certain specified development have been introduced recently.[1] The notice will identify the permission and should clarify key factual questions concerning the activity and its commencement. 7.3

DATE OF CARRYING OUT DEVELOPMENT

Development shall be taken to be begun on the earliest date on which any material operation comprised in the development begins to be carried out.[2] This applies for the purposes of sections 85(2), 86(6) and 87(4) (simplified planning zones), section 89 (enterprise zones), section 91 (duration of planning permission), section 92 (outline permissions) and section 94 (completion notices) of TCPA 1990. 7.4

It is to be noted that this is distinct from the date when development is 'initiated', as referred to in TCPA 1990, section 56(1): this is concerned with separate provisions concerning compensation and is now obsolete.[3] Case law refers to the start, beginning, commencement or implementation of development, generally interchangeably: the latter is the most helpful in appreciating the purpose of the provisions although the precise context and statutory provision in issue should be considered. The text of TCPA 1990, section 71ZB refers to 'beginning', although the heading uses the term 'initiation'. 7.5

[1] TCPA 1990, s. 71ZB, as inserted by Planning (Wales) Act 2015.

[2] TCPA 1990, s. 56(2).

[3] See e.g. *Welwyn Hatfield CBC v Secretary of State for Communities and Local Government* [2011] 2 AC 304 at para. 12.

7.6 Where development consists of the winning and working of minerals, Schedule 1 to the Town and Country Planning (Minerals) Regulations 1995[4] modifies TCPA 1990, section 56(2) so that for the purpose of sections 91, 92 and 94 development shall be taken to be begun on the earliest date on which the winning and working of minerals to which the relevant grant of planning permission relates begins.

7.7 Material operation is defined as:

> (a) any work of construction in the course of the erection of a building;
> (aa) any work of demolition of a building;
> (b) the digging of a trench which is to contain the foundations, or part of the foundations, of a building:
> (c) the laying of any underground main or pipe to the foundations, or part of the foundations, of a building or to any such trench as is mentioned in paragraph (b);
> (d) any operation in the course of laying out or constructing a road or part of a road;
> (e) any change in the use of any land which constitutes material development.[5]

7.8 Change of use which is material within the above is further defined so as to exclude certain categories of development, one such category being development permitted by and in accordance with a condition or limitation of a general or local development order.[6]

7.9 These provisions are concerned with whether the operations are within the terms of a planning permission and this is determined by reference to the wording of TCPA 1990, section 56: it is not the same as whether the operations are development so as to require planning permission in the first place, which, as has been seen, involves consideration of the permanence of the steps taken.[7]

7.10 The test for what is material is now generally regarded as objective, that is, it does not depend on the intentions of the developer.[8] The Court of Appeal in *Staffordshire CC v Riley*[9] held that an objective test was to be applied and Pill LJ agreed with the statement in the Scottish case of *East Dunbartonshire Council v Secretary of State for Scotland*[10] that the test was whether what had been done had been done in accordance with the relevant planning permission, and, secondly, whether it was material, in the sense of not being *de minimis*. There was no justification, in the terms or in the structure of the legislation, for the imposition of

[4] SI 1995 No. 2863.

[5] TCPA 1990, s. 56(4).

[6] TCPA 1990, s. 56(5).

[7] See *Malvern Hills DC v Secretary of State for the Environment* (1983) 46 P & CR 58.

[8] See e.g. *Riordan Communications Ltd v South Bucks District Council* (1999) 81 P & CR 85 and *Ashfield v National Assembly for Wales* [2003] EWHC 3309 (Admin).

[9] [2001] EWCA Civ 257.

[10] [1999] 1 PLR 53.

an ill-defined requirement that the specified operation should be carried out with some particular intention.

As to the nature of operations necessary to satisfy the test, the general approach was given in *Malvern Hills District Council v Secretary of State for the Environment and another*,[11] where Eveleigh LJ said: 7.11

> The specified operations are not necessarily very extensive. Very little need be done to satisfy the section. That which is done, however, must genuinely be done for the purpose of carrying out the development. Section 43 is a benevolent section that aims at avoiding hardship to a developer who is genuinely undertaking the development.

The test therefore is not essentially focused on the extent of the work done but on its relationship with the permitted development. In *Thayer v The Secretary of State for the Environment and Wycombe District Council*,[12] Purchas LJ said 'one only has to pose the question: If [the operation] was not executed in furtherance of the planning permission, to what purpose was it directed?' This is a matter of fact and degree. The proper approach is to consider not just the existence of differences between the plans and the operations relied on, but also to consider the significance of those differences. It is insufficient just to mark and measure the existence of differences.[13] 7.12

DEVELOPMENT IN BREACH OF CONDITION

One of the recurring issues is the legal effect of operations that are not strictly in accordance with the permission and its conditions. Development that fails to comply with the conditions attached to a permission cannot be the commencement of the development. 7.13

In *Henry Boot Homes Ltd v Bassetlaw DC*,[14] Keene LJ said: 7.14

> there is an established principle of law that in order for operations to amount to the commencement of development under a planning permission, those operations must be authorised by the permission in question, read together with its conditions. In general, operations carried out in breach of a condition cannot be relied upon as material operations capable of commencing the development within the meaning of s.56(2). This principle, sometimes referred to as the

[11] (1982) 46 P & CR 58 at p. 70.

[12] [1992] JPL 264.

[13] *Commercial Land Ltd v The Secretary of State for Transport, Local Government and the Regions* [2002] EWHC 1264 (Admin).

[14] [2002] EWCA Civ 983 at para. 37.

Whitley principle, goes back at least to the decision in *Etheridge v Secretary of State for the Environment*.[15]

7.15 The *Whitley* principle refers to the formulation by Woolf LJ in *FG Whitley & Sons Co. Ltd v Secretary of State for Wales*,[16] where he said:

> It is only necessary to ask the single question: are the operations (in other situations the question would refer to the development) permitted by the planning permission read together with its conditions? The permission is controlled by and subject to the conditions. If the operations contravene the conditions they cannot be properly described as commencing the development authorised by the permission. If they do not comply with the permission they constitute a breach of planning control and for planning purposes will be unauthorised and thus unlawful.

7.16 In *R (Hart Aggregates Ltd) v Hartlepool BC*,[17] Sullivan J cautioned against excessively strict application of the principle, saying:

> The court should be wary of applying the principle in an unduly rigid fashion and thereby pushing it to such an extreme that, far from giving effect to the underlying purpose of the legislation (in this case the provisions in the 1990 Act and the Town and Country Planning (Minerals) Regulations 1971 relating to the date when development authorised by planning permissions must begin if the permission is not to lapse), actually frustrates it by leading to absurd and wholly unforeseen results.

7.17 Having reviewed the authorities and the extent to which a condition was a relevant condition precedent, he concluded:[18]

> I believe that the statutory purpose is better served by drawing a distinction between those cases where there is only a permission in principle because no details whatsoever have been submitted, and those cases where the failure has been limited to a failure to obtain approval for one particular aspect of the development. In the former case, common sense suggests that the planning permission has not been implemented at all. In the latter case, common sense suggests that the planning permission has been implemented, but there has been a breach of condition which can be enforced against. I appreciate that these are two opposite ends of a spectrum. Each case will have to be considered upon its

15 (1983) 48 P & CR 35.

16 (1992) 64 P & CR 296 at p. 301.

17 [2005] EWHC 840 (Admin) at para. 41.

18 See para. 65.

own particular facts, and the outcome may well depend upon the number of conditions that have not been complied with.

There are exceptions to the general *Whitley* principle and these were conveniently summarised in by Keene J in *Leisure Great Britain Plc v Isle of Wight Council*[19] and cited in *Greyfort Properties Ltd v Secretary of State for Communities and Local Government*[20] by Richards LJ. The position is that the principle is of general application but there may be defined exceptions, the categories of which are not closed. 7.18

There are three accepted specific exceptions. First, if a condition requires an approval before a given date and the developer has applied by then for the approval, which is subsequently given so that no enforcement action could be taken, work done before the deadline and in accordance with the scheme ultimately approved can amount to a start to development.[21] Secondly, where the wording of a number of conditions required the submission and approval of schemes but left the local planning authority with discretion in the way in which it dealt with them and where the developer has complied with what was in fact required by the authority.[22] Thirdly, a condition may in substance be complied with where the relevant report had been submitted and approved but the formalities, including a written notice of approval, had not been achieved by the time work began on site.[23] 7.19

A more general exception arises where it would be unlawful under public law principles for the local planning authority to take enforcement action in respect of the operations: here they are effective to commence operations.[24] 7.20

In connection with the first exception above, note that an application can be made under TCPA 1990, section 73 to develop land without complying with a condition previously imposed. This does not apply if the previous planning permission was granted subject to a condition as to the time within which the development to which it related was to be begun and that time has expired without the development having been begun.[25] However, there is no prohibition on a section 73 application which in effect extends the time for commencement provided the application itself is made before expiry of the time limit.[26] Amendments by the Planning (Wales) Act 2015, section 35, inserting subsections (3ZA)–(3ZD) 7.21

[19] (2000) 80 P & CR 370.

[20] [2011] EWCA Civ 908 at paras 6–11.

[21] See *Whitley* itself.

[22] See e.g. *Agecrest v Gwynedd CC* [1998] JPL 325.

[23] See *R v Flintshire County Council, ex parte Somerfield Stores Ltd* (1998) P & CR 336.

[24] See *R (Hammerton) v London Underground Ltd* [2002] EWHC 2307 (Admin) and *Greyfort*, above, para. 11.

[25] TCPA 1990, s. 73(4).

[26] Section 73(5), which serves to prevent this, applies in England but has not been brought into force in Wales. See Planning (Wales) Act 2015, s. 35(7), inserting the words 'for the development of land in England' into s. 73(5) – yet to be brought into force – for the duration of s. 73 permissions.

into TCPA 1990, section 91, mean that a section 73 permission will last for the unexpired period of the original permission, unless otherwise provided.

7.22 The application of the general public law exception to the *Whitley* principles where EIA development was at issue was considered in *Ellaway v Cardiff CC*.[27] Permission had been granted subject to a number of pre-commencement conditions and the local planning authority had purported to discharge all bar one of them. The claimant alleged that the discharge had been unlawful as in breach of the Environmental Impact Regulations. In response, the planning authority resolved not to take enforcement action and the claimant sought to challenge the lawfulness of that decision and those discharging the conditions. Wyn Williams J held that the *Whitley* principle and its exceptions were firmly grounded in domestic law and that there was no basis to conclude that the authority had acted unlawfully when it invoked an exception to the *Whitley* principle in order to justify discharging the pre-commencement conditions.

NOTICE BEFORE BEGINNING DEVELOPMENT

7.23 Recent provisions have introduced a requirement to give notice before beginning certain development and this should clarify or resolve some of the issues above. The requirement will apply where there is a relevant planning permission defined as one of a description specified by a development order.[28] Such a permission is deemed to be granted subject to the condition that the notice requirements must be complied with.[29] Consequently, development begun without due notice will not be in accordance with the permission.

7.24 The requirements are to give the local planning authority notice, stating the date on which the development is to begin, the details of the permission and any other matter specified by a development order, and to display a copy of the decision to grant permission at or near the place of the development at all times when the development is being carried out.[30] The form of notice to the local planning authority and for on-site display are as specified by a development order[31] and the decision notice must set out the duties under the section.[32]

7.25 To date the requirement applies only in the case of developments of national significance.[33] The particular form of notice and requirements as to display are set out in the Order specifying this as development under section 71ZB and in the

[27] [2014] EWHC 836 (Admin).

[28] TCPA 1990, s. 71ZB(1) and (6).

[29] TCPA 1990, s. 71ZB(5).

[30] TCPA 1990, s. 71ZB(1) and (2).

[31] TCPA 1990, s. 71ZB(3).

[32] TCPA 1990, s. 71ZB(4).

[33] Developments of National Significance (Procedure) (Wales) Order 2016 (SI 2016 No. 55), art. 31.

amendments to the Town and Country Planning (Development Management Procedure) (Wales) Order 2012.[34]

COMPLETION NOTICES

Where development has been begun before the expiration of the relevant time limit but it has not been completed within that period the local planning authority may serve a completion notice.[35] The effect of the notice is that the planning permission will cease to have effect on the expiry of the period specified in the notice, which must not be less than twelve months. The permission then becomes invalid but this does not affect any development carried out under the permission before that date.[36] A notice can only be served where the authority is of the opinion that the development will not be completed within a reasonable period. 7.26

A notice does not take effect until confirmed by the Welsh Ministers.[37] Before confirmation, the person served with the notice and the local planning authority must be given an opportunity to appear before the Ministers or a person appointed by them if the person served so requires.[38] 7.27

The Welsh Ministers also have power to serve a completion notice themselves where it is expedient.[39] 7.28

34 SI 2012 No. 801, art. 24B, as amended by SI 2016 No. 59.

35 TCPA 1990, s. 94.

36 TCPA 1990, s. 95(4) and (5).

37 TCPA 1990, s. 95(1).

38 TCPA 1990, s. 95(3).

39 TCPA 1990, s. 96.

Chapter 8

Development Consent Orders

INTRODUCTION

Development consent is required for development that is or forms part of a nationally significant infrastructure project.[1] This replaces the need for planning permission and certain other consents.[2] Development has the same meaning as in TCPA 1990 but specific inclusionary provisions are added by the Planning Act 2008, section 32(2) and (3). These refer to certain changes of use involving: petroleum products or natural gas; airport use; and specified works, including demolition affecting listed buildings, scheduled monuments and in conservation areas which would not otherwise be development. 8.1

The definition of nationally significant infrastructure projects in Wales is different from that in England as devolved matters are excluded.[3] This is considered below. 8.2

Development consent may also be granted for associated development: the definition of that in Wales is confined to the construction of surface works, boreholes or pipes associated with underground gas storage within the Planning Act 2008, section 17(3) (see below).[4] In addition, a development consent order may authorise compulsory acquisition of land and interests in land.[5] 8.3

Where development consent is required other specified authorisations or permissions are not required or may not be granted.[6] The application of this differs in England and Wales and is considered below. In addition, an order granting development consent may remove a requirement for a prescribed consent or authorisation to be granted where the relevant body has consented to the inclusion of the provision.[7] 8.4

[1] Planning Act 2008, s. 31. The Act is referred to as PA 2008 in subsequent footnotes in this chapter.

[2] PA 2008, s. 33.

[3] See the Welsh Government ministerial letter of 2 April 2009 to local planning authorities on the application of the Planning Act 2008 to the Planning Function in Wales and Annex 1 of its enclosures for guidance.

[4] PA 2008, s. 115(4).

[5] PA 2008, ss. 122–134.

[6] PA 2008, s. 33.

[7] PA 2008, s. 150: see Infrastructure Planning (Interested Parties and Miscellaneous Prescribed Provisions) Regulations 2015 (SI 2015 No. 462), reg. 5(2) and Sch. 2, Pt 2, which applies in Wales. Schedule 2, Pt 1 is applicable in England and Wales.

MEANING OF NATIONALLY SIGNIFICANT INFRASTRUCTURE PROJECT

8.5 In Wales, nationally significant infrastructure projects mean the construction of certain electricity generating stations, above ground electric lines, gas storage facilities, pipe-lines other than those constructed by a gas transporter and harbours.[8] The definition in England is more extensive and a brief comparison is appropriate.

8.6 The Planning Act 2008, section 14 lists sixteen types of development in the fields of energy, transport, water, waste water and waste which may be nationally significant infrastructure projects. They are subject to the later detailed stipulations of sections 15–30 of the Act regarding their scale and scope. There is power for the Secretary of State to add a new type of project but this is confined to England.[9] Of the sixteen, subject to further detailed description, the majority if situated in Wales are not subject to the development consent regime. Therefore, in Wales they continue to be decided under TCPA 1990 subject to amendments by the Planning (Wales) Act 2015 which are highly relevant here as they create a category of nationally significant development. This category overlaps with those projects requiring Development Consent in England but the application required is to the Welsh Ministers for the grant of planning permission.

8.7 Projects in Wales within the detailed classification are generating stations within section 15, electric lines above ground within section 16, underground gas storage further to section 17, cross country pipe-lines other than by a gas transporter as provided by section 21, and harbour facilities in accordance with section 24. The definition therefore excludes projects relating to LNG facilities, gas reception facilities and gas pipe-lines, highway, airport and railway developments, water and waste facilities within the further provisions of this Part of the Act. In each case the projects within the definition in Wales are subject to the same detailed constraints of the relevant provision as for projects in England, except in the case of underground gas storage, which is subject to a different definition in section 17(3) rather than section 17(2).

8.8 The result is that the development consent regime will apply in Wales to the following description of projects.

8.9 The construction or extension of a generating station will be within the definition if it is in Wales, does not generate electricity from wind, is not offshore and has a capacity of more than 50 megawatts[10] or is an offshore generating station in territorial sea waters adjacent to England or Wales or in a Renewable Energy Zone and has a capacity of more than 100 megawatts.[11] A Welsh offshore generating

[8] PA 2008, s. 14.

[9] PA 2008, s. 14(3)–(7).

[10] PA 2008, s. 15(1) and (2), as amended by SI 2016 No. 306.

[11] PA 2008, s. 15(3) and (4).

station authorised under the Transport and Works Act 1992, section 3 does not require development consent.[12]

An electricity line is a nationally significant infrastructure if it is an installation above ground wholly or partly in Wales unless the nominal voltage is expected to be less than 132 kilovolts or it is within premises occupied or controlled by the installer.[13] 8.10

Development is also within the definition if the developer is a gas transporter starting to use underground gas storage facilities in Wales in natural porous strata where the expected working capacity is at least 43 million standard cubic metres or the maximum flow rate is expected to be at least 4.5 million standard cubic metres per day.[14] The construction of cross-country pipe-lines other than by a gas transporter will be nationally significant if one end is in England or Wales and the other is in England or Wales.[15] 8.11

The construction or alteration of harbour facilities in Wales or in territorial sea waters adjacent to England or Wales are similarly within the definition subject to capability to handle materials at least to the defined relevant quantity.[16] 8.12

RELATED CONSENTS

Where development consent is required for the development, consents under other statutory regimes, including of course planning permission, are not required.[17] There are differences again between the application of these provisions in Wales and in England, in addition to those differences which flow automatically from the fact that the definition of affected projects is not the same. The notable differences relate to the historic environment. Listed building consent, conservation area consent and consents under the Ancient Monuments and Archaeological Areas Act 1979 need not be obtained if the project for which development consent is required is in England: if the land is in Wales application for consent must be made in the ordinary way.[18] 8.13

In addition, where development consent is required the work may not be authorised by other specified consents.[19] These include orders relating to harbours, gas storage and railways and other transport under the Transport and Works Act 1990. Where highway works require development consent it is not possible to 8.14

[12] PA 2008, s. 34.

[13] PA 2008, s. 16.

[14] PA 2008, s. 17.

[15] PA 2008, s. 21 but subject to the further provisions of this section.

[16] PA 2008, s. 24.

[17] PA 2008, s. 33(1).

[18] PA 2008, s. 33(1)(f), (g), (i) and (j).

[19] PA 2008, s. 33(2).

make or confirm certain orders under the Highways Act 1980.[20] Special provision is made so that in Wales orders may be made authorising Welsh offshore generating stations under the Transport and Works Act 1992, section 3 and development consent is not required.[21]

8.15 The final point of distinction is in connection with PA 2008, section 150 and the extent to which a development consent order may remove the need for a prescribed consent or authorisation with the consent of the relevant consenting body. As noted, there are additional consents affected in Wales which are separately listed by the relevant Regulations.[22]

ASSOCIATED DEVELOPMENT

8.16 Development consent may be granted for development associated with the development for which the consent is required. This is broadly defined in England to include all associated development other than for dwellings, with the addition of consent for related housing development.[23] In Wales, associated development is confined to the carrying out or construction of surface works, boreholes or pipes associated with relevant underground gas storage.[24]

8.17 Before leaving this topic, it should be noted that the categories of nationally significant infrastructure projects will be affected by changes to devolved powers in the Wales Act 2017.[25] Part 2 of the Act contains specific provisions regarding development consent for harbour facilities within section 24 of the 2008 Act,[26] with the result that in Wales only a category defined as a reserved trust port will be within the regime. Development consent for generating stations within section 15 of the 2008 Act is also amended so that in Wales all onshore generating stations with a capacity of not more than 350 megawatts and all offshore generating stations will be the responsibility of the Welsh Ministers. Associated development consent within section 115 of the 2008 Act is amended regarding designated generating stations and overhead electric lines to reflect these changes.

[20] PA 2008, s. 32(4). It also extends to toll orders under New Roads and Street Works Act 1991, s. 6.

[21] See PA 2008, s. 34.

[22] See fn 7 above.

[23] PA 2008, s. 115(1), (2), (3), (4B) and (4C).

[24] PA 2008, s. 115(4).

[25] See Chapter 2.

[26] See section 33.

APPLICATION PROCEDURE – GENERAL

Application for development consent must be made to the Secretary of State on the prescribed form and be accompanied by prescribed documents.[27] The Secretary of State may issue guidance as to compliance with these requirements and may issue guidance on the pre-application procedure to which an applicant must have regard.[28] 8.18

Procedure is governed by the Planning Act 2008, Parts 5 (sections 37–54) and 6 (sections 55–119), whilst the content of orders and miscellaneous matters are dealt with in Part 7 (sections 120–159). Further detailed provisions are in the numerous Orders and Regulations made under the Act. Responsibility for most functions has been delegated to the Planning Inspectorate and this includes those relating to applications, the appointment of the examining authority and the examination. Communications should initially be addressed to the Planning Inspectorate and for most practical purposes statutory functions of the Secretary of State are exercised by the Planning Inspectorate, although the formal statutory designation is followed in the text below. Guidance states that all communications should be directed to the inspectorate in the first instance. 8.19

Advice and guidance on the process is on the dedicated National Infrastructure Planning website. This lists relevant secondary legislation, guidance and advice notes issued by the Planning Inspectorate and reference should be made to the relevant documents depending on the nature of the development, although certain key sources are identified below. Advice Notes from the Planning Inspectorate do not have any statutory status. 8.20

The Planning Inspectorate guidance divides the process into six stages: pre-application, acceptance, pre-examination, examination, recommendation and decision, and post-decision. The purpose was to streamline the process for major development and a strict timescale is adopted and this includes pre-application procedures. The result is that significant steps must be completed at the first stages of the process. The examination process involves an essentially inquisitorial role by the Inspectorate and differs from the adversarial approach of an inquiry. 8.21

The pre-application provisions of the Act[29] apply where a person proposes to make an application for an order granting development consent. Guidance may be issued on this procedure and the applicant must have regard to it[30] – the current guidance is *Planning Act 2008: Guidance on the pre-application process* 8.22

[27] PA 2008, s. 37(3): for forms, see the Infrastructure Planning (Applications: Prescribed Forms and Procedure) Regulations 2009, as amended by SI 2014 No. 2381.

[28] PA 2008, s. 50: the relevant guidance is the *Planning Act 2008: Guidance on the pre-application procedure*, updated March 2015. This refers to Chapters 1 (applications) and 2 (pre-application procedure) of Part 5 of the Act. Other guidance on further aspects of the process is listed on the National Infrastructure Planning website of the Planning Inspectorate.

[29] PA 2008, ss. 41–50.

[30] PA 2008, s. 50(3).

(published by Department for Communities and Local Government, March 2015). Key secondary legislation applying at this stage includes the Infrastructure Planning (Environmental Impact Assessment) Regulations 2009,[31] the Infrastructure Planning (National Policy Statement Consultation) Regulations 2009,[32] the Infrastructure Planning (Applications: Prescribed Forms and Procedure) Regulations 2009[33] and the Infrastructure Planning (Applications: Prescribed Forms and Procedure) (Amendment) Regulations 2014.[34]

8.23 The core requirement under Planning Act 2008, section 42 is for consultation with persons prescribed, local authorities and persons within section 44 and the guidance states that 'without adequate consultation, the subsequent application will not be accepted when it is submitted'.[35] Where the consultation is inadequate, the Secretary of State can recommend that further consultation is carried out.

8.24 The list of prescribed persons is in Schedule 1 to the Infrastructure Planning (Applications: Prescribed Forms and Procedure) Regulations 2009[36] and includes the Welsh Ministers, Natural Resources Wales and the Royal Commission on Ancient and Historical Monuments of Wales. Note that the Marine Management Organisation has responsibility in Wales for non-devolved matters, other functions under the Marine and Coastal Access Act 2009 being those of the Welsh Ministers. For these purposes, local authorities are county councils, county borough councils or National Park Authorities if the land in question is within its area or it is within another authority's area and there is a common boundary.[37] Persons within section 44 are owners, lessees, tenants or occupiers or persons who after diligent inquiry are known to be interested in or have power to sell, convey or release the land and those who would or might be entitled to claim compensation were the order implemented.

8.25 Information on consultees and the consultation process is in the statutory guidance. In particular, an application should include a Statement of Community Consultation detailing how local community consultation is to be conducted and this must be available for public inspection.[38] The applicant must have regard to the responses to consultation.[39]

8.26 An application for an order granting development consent must be made in the prescribed form, so far as necessary to secure that the application (including accompaniments) is of a standard that is satisfactory, specify the development to

[31] SI 2009 No. 2263, as amended by SI 2012 No. 787.

[32] SI 2009 No. 1302.

[33] SI 2009 No. 2264.

[34] SI 2014 No. 2381.

[35] See para. 19.

[36] SI 2009 No. 2264.

[37] PA 2008, s. 43.

[38] PA 2008, s. 47.

[39] PA 2008, s. 49.

which it relates, be accompanied by the consultation report referred to above and be accompanied by documents and information of a prescribed description.[40]

The applicant is also responsible for submitting a draft development consent order. Section 120 prescribes what may be in an order and further detail is in the statutory guidance paragraphs 97–105, in particular at paragraph 101 which contains a list of what may be included in an order. The order may contain requirements corresponding to planning conditions and model conditions are in the Infrastructure Planning (Model Provisions) (England and Wales) Order 2009.[41] In addition, where the draft order deals with authorisations otherwise separately granted but excluded by the 2008 Act, section 33, provisions which would be attached to those authorisations should be included. Flexibility to allow for cases where all the details cannot be specified at the time of application are allowed for under what is known as the 'Rochdale envelope'.[42] 8.27

Fees are payable in accordance with the Infrastructure Planning (Fees) Regulations 2010.[43] Advice on drafting is in the (non-statutory) Planning Inspectorate Advice Note 15, with additional preparation advice in Advice Note 13. 8.28

If the Secretary of State is satisfied with the procedures the application will be accepted. This decision must be made within twenty-eight days and is subject to the provisions of section 55 of the 2008 Act.[44] The Secretary of State may accept it only if he concludes that it is an application for an order granting development consent, that development consent is required for any of the development, that the applicant has complied with Chapter 2 of Part 5 (pre-application procedure) and that the application (including accompaniments) is of a standard that the Secretary of State considers satisfactory. In deciding if it is to a satisfactory standard he must have regard to the extent to which the application complies with the requirements in section 37(3) (form and contents of application) and any standards set under section 37(5), and that any applicable guidance given under section 37(4) has been followed in relation to the application.[45] Paragraph 115 of the Guidance states 8.29

[40] PA 2008, s. 37(3), as amended by Localism Act 2011, s. 137.

[41] SI 2009 No. 2265.

[42] See Guidance, paras 109–13 and Planning Inspectorate Advice Note Nine. The name is taken from two cases concerning application for outline permission for business park development in Rochdale subject to a requirement for an environmental statement: *R v Rochdale MBC, ex parte Milne (No. 1)* and *R v Rochdale MBC, ex parte Tew* [2001] JPL 407, [2000] JPL 54, [2001] Env LR 22, [1999] 3 PLR 74 and *R v Rochdale MBC, ex parte Milne (No. 2)* [2001] JPL 470, [2001] Env LR 406, (2001) 81 P & CR 365. In the later case, Sullivan J stated that the intention of the EIA Directive and Regulations was that the likely significant environmental effects of projects should be comprehensively assessed before consent was granted but that projects may evolve over time and the implications of this need for flexibility should be taken into account at the outset. It was for the decision-maker to decide whether the difficulties and uncertainties are such that the proposed degree of flexibility is not acceptable in terms of its potential effect on the environment.

[43] SI 2010 No. 106 (amended by SI 2013 No. 498).

[44] As amended by the Localism Act 2011.

[45] PA 2008, s. 55(5A).

that, in particular, applicants should be able to demonstrate that they have acted reasonably in fulfilling the requirements of the Act to take account of responses to consultation and publicity.

PRE-EXAMINATION PROCEDURE

8.30 Following acceptance, the process moves to a pre-examination phase. On acceptance, the applicant must notify persons in accordance with section 56 of the 2008 Act and publicise the application. The categories of persons to be notified are set out in section 57. The applicant must then, within fifty-six days, certify compliance.[46] Where the application includes a request for compulsory acquisition the applicant must also give a notice to the Secretary of State of the names and prescribed information of those affected.[47] Following this, the Secretary of State must invite each relevant local authority to submit a local impact report.[48]

8.31 The Secretary of State decides if the application is to be handled by a panel under Chapter 2 (sections 64–77) or a single appointed person under Chapter 3 (sections 78–85) of the 2008 Act[49] and under the rules either will be the Examining Authority.[50] The criteria for the choice of procedure is required to be published under section 61 of the 2008 Act and the Planning Act 2008 Guidance on examinations of applications for development consent sets out the factors at paragraphs 12–14 based on complexity and the level of public interest.

EXAMINATION

8.32 For this stage, key items of secondary legislation are the Infrastructure Planning (Interested Parties and Miscellaneous Prescribed Provisions) Regulations 2015,[51] Infrastructure Planning (Examination Procedure) Rules 2010[52] and the Infrastructure Planning (Decisions) Regulations 2010.[53] Where the order also contains provisions for compulsory purchase, these are subject to the Infrastructure Planning (Compulsory Acquisition) Regulations 2010.[54]

8.33 There are four items of guidance issued by the Secretary of State which are of particular importance but, unlike the pre-application guidance, they have no

[46] PA 2008, s. 58.

[47] PA 2008, s. 59.

[48] PA 2008, s. 60.

[49] PA 2008, s. 61.

[50] See the Infrastructure Planning (Examination Procedure) Rules 2010 (SI 2010 No. 103).

[51] SI 2015 No. 462.

[52] SI 2010 No. 103, as amended.

[53] SI 2010 No. 305.

[54] SI 2010 No. 104, as amended.

statutory status and responsibility for the examination of an application lies with the examining authority. The guidance is *Planning Act 2008: Guidance for the examination of applications for development consent*; *Planning Act 2008: Guidance related to procedures for the compulsory acquisition of land*; *Planning Act 2008: Guidance on associated development applications for major infrastructure projects*; and *Awards of costs: examinations of applications for development consent orders – guidance*.[55]

Turning to the examination process itself, the Planning Act 2008, Chapter 4 (sections 86–102) regulates procedure together with the Infrastructure Planning (Examination Procedure) Rules 2010,[56] which set out the detailed requirements. Generally, procedure is controlled by the examining authority but will be conducted by written representation unless oral representation is considered necessary on particular issues[57] or a party affected by a compulsory acquisition order requests a hearing.[58] Hearings are in public and conducted in accordance with section 94. Provision is made for preliminary meetings and for a strict timetable throughout the process. 8.34

Section 102 defines who is an interested party for the purpose of participating and making representations in an examination and this is subject to the further provisions of the Infrastructure Planning (Interested Parties and Miscellaneous Prescribed Provisions) Regulations 2015. An interested party will include a statutory party and these are listed in Schedule 1 to the Regulations, which identifies expressly whether it refers to England and Wales or one of them.[59] 8.35

The examination must be completed within six months of the start day[60] and a report of the examining body is to be made within three months of the deadline for the completion of the examination. 8.36

REPORT AND DECISION

The examining authority will report and make recommendations and the decision will be made by the appropriate Secretary of State, who may grant or refuse consent[61] and must give reasons.[62] Development consent extends to the development and associated development in accordance with section 115. If the Secretary of State differs from the examining authority on any material fact or takes into account any 8.37

[55] All published by the Department of Communities and Local Government.

[56] SI 2010 No. 103.

[57] PA 2008, ss. 87, 90 and 91.

[58] PA 2008, s. 92.

[59] PA 2008, s. 102 and reg. 3(2); and Sch. 1 to the 2015 Regulations.

[60] PA 2008, s. 98.

[61] PA 2008, s. 114.

[62] PA 2008, s. 116.

new evidence or fact, he must notify all interested parties, giving his reasons, and give them an opportunity to make representations in writing.[63]

8.38 Changes may be made to development consent orders after they have been made, in accordance with Schedule 6 to the Planning Act 2008, and the process is in accordance with the Infrastructure Planning (Changes to, and Revocation of, Development Consent Orders) Regulations 2011, as amended.[64]

8.39 Legal challenge to a development consent order can only be by a claim for judicial review made within six weeks.[65]

[63] Procedure Rules, r. 19.

[64] SI 2011 No. 2055, as amended by SI 2012 No. 635 and SI 2015 No. 760.

[65] PA 2008, s. 118.

Chapter 9

Grant of Planning Permission

INTRODUCTION

Planning permission is required to carry out any development of land.[1] As seen in the preceding chapter, it is not required for development requiring development consent under section 33(1) of the Planning Act 2008, that is, where it is for a nationally significant infrastructure project.[2] 9.1

Planning permission may be granted in a number of different ways and is defined to include permission granted in accordance with Part III of TCPA 1990 (that is, sections 55–106C).[3] It may be granted by a development order or local development order, by the adoption or approval of a simplified planning zone or designation of an enterprise zone, by application to the Welsh Ministers or by application to a local planning authority, or be deemed to be granted by government authorisation under section 90 of TCPA 1990.[4] This is without prejudice to any other provisions of the Act,[5] of which the most important examples are in connection with planning permission granted in enforcement appeals.[6] 9.2

Planning permission may be granted unconditionally or subject to conditions.[7] An application may provide all the details of the development ('full permission') or it may be an application for outline permission, that is one where details of specified reserved matters are to be submitted later for approval.[8] It may be made before or after the development has commenced or been carried out.[9] In addition, an application can be made for permission to develop land without complying 9.3

[1] TCPA 1990, s. 57(1). There are three specific exclusions from the requirement to obtain permission for development in TCPA 1990, s. 57(2)–(4). The exclusions refer to the resumption of a normal use after cessation of a temporary permission, to the normal use of land where permission has been granted subject to limitations by development order or local development order, or, where an enforcement notice has been issued, the use of land for a purpose which was lawful had the unlawful development not been carried out – these have been noted in Chapter 6, above.

[2] TCPA 1990, s. 57(1A).

[3] TCPA 1990, s. 336(1).

[4] TCPA 1990, s. 58(1) & (2). Note that functions under s. 90 are not devolved (see paras 4.10–4.11, above) and government therefore refers to the UK government.

[5] TCPA 1990, s. 58(3).

[6] TCPA 1990, s. 173; see Chapter 19, below.

[7] TCPA 1990, s. 70(1).

[8] TCPA 1990, s. 92.

[9] TCPA 1990, s. 73A.

with a condition imposed on an earlier planning permission,[10] or the conditions of a permission may necessitate further application for approval. Each of these raise distinct issues which are considered specifically in later chapters: this chapter is concerned solely with the description of the various methods by which permission may be granted. The procedure and decision-making process are also the subject of separate treatment later in the text.

DEVELOPMENT ORDERS

9.4 Development orders are defined in TCPA 1990, section 59. An order may be a general order applicable to all land or a special order applying only to such land or descriptions of land as is specified.[11] A development order may either itself grant permission for specified development or for specified categories of development or may provide for planning permission to be granted on application in accordance with the order.[12] General powers concerning matters that may be contained in a permission given by a general development order are in TCPA 1990, section 60.

9.5 The two relevant orders of general application are the Town and Country Planning (General Permitted Development) Order 1995 as amended[13] and the Town and Country Planning (Development Management Procedure) (Wales) Order 2012.[14]

9.6 The 1995 General Permitted Development Order, as amended, deals with the substantive grant of planning permission for certain classes of development. Schedule 2 to the Order details the development for which permitted development rights are conferred. The effect is that no specific application for permission is required for development within the description. In each case the general permission is subject to any exception, limitation or condition contained in the Schedule.[15] As noted in Chapter 2, the terms of this are not the same as in the current Order for England.[16]

9.7 Schedule 2 refers to minor operations, changes of use and temporary buildings and uses and then itemises a range of particular types of development which, subject to the terms of the Schedule, are permitted. Part 1 is a common example referring to development within the curtilage of a dwelling house. So, for example, rear and side extensions to dwelling houses may be permitted subject to the precise rules concerning such matters as overall height and size and proximity to a boundary. Historically, some parts of the Schedule were concerned only with England while

[10] TCPA 1990, s. 73.

[11] TCPA 1990, s. 59(3).

[12] TCPA 1990, s. 59(2).

[13] SI 1995 No. 418, amended by SI 2013 No. 1776, SI 2014 No. 592 and SI 2014 No. 2692.

[14] SI 2012 No. 801, as amended by SI 2015 No. 1330 and SI 2016 No. 59.

[15] See TCPA 1990, s. 60(1) and the GPDO Schedule.

[16] SI 2015 No. 596.

other parts dealt with England and Wales in separate terms.[17] These distinctions are carried forward in the terms of the current Town and Country Planning (General Permitted Development) (England) Order 2015, with additional changes reflecting other policy changes affecting England only.

Procedural matters are dealt with in the Town and Country Planning (Development Management Procedure) (Wales) Order 2012 and subject to further provisions of TCPA 1990. One recent requirement is for pre-application consultation for development of a description specified in a development order.[18] In addition, section 62R of TCPA 1990 provides that a development order may make provision regulating the way in which an application to the Welsh Ministers under the procedures introduced by the 2015 Act is to be dealt with, including provisions about consultation on and variation of an application. 9.8

The requirements above do not remove the need to comply with any other applicable procedures and two instances should be noted. First, regulations 10 and 11 of the Town and Country Planning (Environmental Impact Assessment) (Wales) Regulations 2016[19] preserve the position where those Regulations are applicable so that compliance with those, as appropriate, remains necessary. Secondly, regulation 73 of the Conservation of Species and Habitats Regulations 2010[20] provides that it is a condition of any planning permission granted by a general development order that development which is likely to have a significant effect on a European site or a European offshore marine site (either alone or in combination with other plans or projects) and is not directly connected with or necessary to the management of the site, must not be begun until the developer has received written notification of the approval of the local planning authority under regulation 75. 9.9

LOCAL DEVELOPMENT ORDERS

Local development orders are made by a local planning authority and grant planning permission for specified development or for development of any specified class so that individual application for permission is unnecessary.[21] Detailed Guidance on making an order has been given by the Welsh Government.[22] However, a study in 2014 commissioned by the Welsh Government[23] found that despite government encouragement no such orders had been made in Wales and the position has not 9.10

[17] Part 1 (dwelling house), Part 8 (industrial buildings), Part 32 (Schools, Colleges, Universities and Hospitals), Part 40 (Domestic Microgeneration Equipment), Part 41 (Office Buildings) and Part 43 (Shops, Financial or Professional Services Establishments) dealt separately with England and Wales.

[18] TCPA 1990, s. 61Z. Procedure generally is dealt with in Chapter 12.

[19] SI 2016 No. 58.

[20] SI 2010 No. 490.

[21] Section 61A of TCPA 1990. They are subject to the supplemental provisions of sections 61B–61D.

[22] WGC 003/2012.

[23] Local Development Orders: Impacts and Good Practice.

changed although use of the orders in connection with enterprise zones has been encouraged and may be anticipated.

9.11 The order may relate to all or any part of the land in the area of the authority or to any specified site and different provision may be made for different descriptions of land. A development order may specify any area or class of development in respect of which a local development order must not be made. However, an order must not be made so as to grant planning permission for development affecting a listed building or for development which is EIA development.[24]

9.12 TCPA 1990, Schedule 4A contains details of the procedure to be followed in making a local development order and the order may be revoked at any time. The Welsh Ministers may give a direction regarding adoption of orders and may require an order to be submitted to the Welsh Ministers who may then approve, reject or give a direction to modify the order.[25] They also have power to revoke an order.[26]

9.13 Planning permission granted by a local development order may be granted unconditionally, or subject to such conditions or limitations as are specified in the order.[27] If permission is granted for development of a specified description, the order may enable the local planning authority to direct that the permission does not apply in relation to development in a particular area, or any particular development.[28]

SIMPLIFIED PLANNING ZONES AND ENTERPRISE ZONES

9.14 Simplified planning zones are areas within a scheme made by a local planning authority in accordance with TCPA 1990, sections 82–88 and Schedule 7. Adoption or approval has effect to grant planning permission for development specified in the scheme, or for development of any class so specified, in relation to the zone, or any part of it specified in the scheme. The permission so granted is subject to any specified conditions, limitations or exceptions. Guidance is given by TAN 3 Simplified Planning Zones. There are currently no simplified planning zones in Wales.

9.15 Enterprise zones are designated in accordance with the Local Government Planning and Land Act 1980, Schedule 32. The Welsh Government has designated eight enterprise zones in Wales.[29] TCPA 1990, section 88 provides that an order designating an enterprise zone has effect, without more, to grant planning permission for specified development. This is subject to exclusions where EIA development is concerned and where the development is of national significance for the purposes

[24] Article 27(13) of the Development Management Procedure Order 2012.

[25] TCPA 1990, s. 61B.

[26] TCPA 1990, s. 61B(8).

[27] TCPA 1990, s. 61C(1).

[28] TCPA 1990, s. 61C(2).

[29] They are listed at para. 4.27, above.

of TCPA 1990, section 62D. The provisions do not preclude the grant of planning permission in an enterprise zone in any other way.

One feature is the aim to provide simplified planning procedures and the intent is to assist development opportunity by removing the need for a planning application for development in accordance with a local development order, and the aim is for planning permission to be dealt with by this process. 9.16

APPLICATIONS FOR PLANNING PERMISSION

Applications for planning permission for a development of national significance within the meaning of TCPA 1990, section 62D are made to the Welsh Ministers instead of the local planning authority.[30] Application for permission for other types of development may be made to the Welsh Ministers at the option of the applicant if they are qualifying applications so designated by Welsh Ministers under powers conferred by section 62L of TCPA 1990. This is subject to commencement of the relevant provisions. 9.17

All other applications for full or outline planning permission are made to the relevant local planning authority. As noted above, additional requirements applicable to development (e.g. environmental impact assessments), apply equally whichever body is formally required to determine the application. 9.18

DEVELOPMENTS OF NATIONAL SIGNIFICANCE

It has been noted that the category of nationally significant infrastructure projects in Wales is more limited in scope than in England and one consequence was that certain major projects fell for determination by local planning authorities. Sections 62D to 62L of TCPA 1990 contain provisions for a separate category of developments of national significance where an application is to be made to Welsh Ministers. These developments are those which are of greatest significance to Wales in terms of their potential impacts and include projects identified in the National Development Framework and those meeting the thresholds and criteria in subordinate legislation. The projects include projects treated as nationally significant infrastructure projects in England but not in Wales. The difference is that the developments require planning permission, not development consent, and the two are therefore subject to different regimes. 9.19

When compared with the regime for other planning applications, the key elements are that developments of national significance are dealt with at an examination by an inspector who makes a recommendation to the Welsh Ministers, and the application process and procedure has its own code. In this respect the system is akin to that for nationally significant infrastructure projects. 9.20

[30] TCPA 1990, s. 62D.

9.21 Regulations to implement these provisions came into force on 1 March 2016. The main items of subordinate legislation are the Developments of National Significance (Specified Criteria and Secondary Consents) (Wales) Regulations 2016,[31] the Developments of National Significance (Wales) Regulations 2016[32] and the Developments of National Significance (Procedure) (Wales) Order 2016,[33] augmented by two further measures, concerning fees[34] and application of provisions of TCPA 1990 to these applications.[35]

9.22 Regulation 3 of the Specified Criteria Regulations lists the description of development which is of national significance and developments which are listed relate to electricity generating stations, certain gas facilities, airports, railways, and specified water and waste facilities. The Welsh Ministers will also make the decision on consent which is related to the development, termed a secondary consent.[36]

9.23 Application is by notification to the Welsh Ministers complying with the requirements specified in the development order[37] and the Welsh Ministers will take steps in respect of the application as specified in a development order.[38]

9.24 Details of developments of national significance and the application process are in Chapter 10.

9.25 Further supplementary provisions, applicable also to optional applications to Welsh Ministers (see below), enabling directions requiring a local planning authority to do things in relation to an application and for notice to community councils are contained in sections 62P and 62Q of TCPA 1990.

OPTIONAL APPLICATION TO WELSH MINISTERS

9.26 When the relevant provisions are fully in force,[39] if the conditions laid down are met a developer will be able to choose to make an application for planning permission directly to the Welsh Ministers instead of to the local planning authority. The conditions are that the local planning authority is one designated for the purpose by the Welsh Ministers and the application is a qualifying application. Qualifying applications are ones for planning permission for development, provided that it is not development of national significance, and applications for approval of a reserved matter of an outline planning permission under TCPA 1990, section 92.

[31] SI 2016 No. 53.

[32] SI 2016 No. 56.

[33] SI 2016 No. 55.

[34] Developments of National Significance (Fees) (Wales) Regulations 2016 (SI 2016 No. 57).

[35] Developments of National Significance (Application of Enactments) (Wales) Order 2016 (SI 2016 No. 54).

[36] TCPA 1990, s. 62H.

[37] TCPA 1990, s. 62E.

[38] TCPA 1990, s. 62I(1).

[39] TCPA 1990, s. 62M.

An application for permission to develop land without complying with conditions subject to which a previous planning permission was granted which otherwise would be a qualifying application is not to be treated as such unless it is of a description prescribed in regulations made by the Welsh Ministers.[40]

A local planning authority can only be designated in accordance with the set procedure.[41] The intent is to designate only poorly performing authorities, criteria for which include the speed with which applications are determined by the authority and its appeal record. 9.27

A connected application may also be made directly to the Welsh Ministers provided that it is made on the same day as the principal application.[42] An application is connected if it is made under the planning Acts, relates to land in Wales, is of a description prescribed by regulations and is considered by the applicant to be connected to the principal application.[43] The Welsh Ministers must refer the application to the local planning authority if they consider that the application is not connected to the principal application or, although connected, the decision should not be made by the Welsh Ministers.[44] It must then be determined by the local planning authority as an application made on the date of referral.[45] 9.28

The procedure is to be prescribed by development order[46] and the exercise of functions by an appointed person is governed by Schedule 4D to TCPA 1990. 9.29

A decision on such application is final.[47] However, as with developments of national significance, amendments to sections 284 and 288 of TCPA 1990 will enable challenges to the decisions under that statutory procedure.[48] 9.30

CALL-IN

The Welsh Ministers have power to direct any local planning authority to refer an application to them[49] and have power to issue directions in this respect in accordance with the Town and Country Planning (Development Management Procedure) (Wales) Order 2012.[50] They have issued the Town and Country Planning (Notification) (Wales) Direction 2012,[51] which requires local planning authorities 9.31

[40] TCPA 1990, s. 62M(5) and (6).

[41] TCPA 1990, s. 62N.

[42] TCPA 1990, s. 62O(1) and (2).

[43] TCPA 1990, s. 62O(3): planning Acts is defined in s. 336(1).

[44] TCPA 1990, s. 62O(4) and (5).

[45] TCPA 1990, s. 62O(6).

[46] TCPA 1990, s. 62R. As indicated, no order has yet been made.

[47] See TCPA 1990, s. 62P.

[48] See Chapter 22, below.

[49] TCPA 1990, s. 77.

[50] SI 2012 No. 801.

[51] See Annex 1 to WGC 07/12.

to refer to Welsh Ministers all applications for notification development in Wales which the authority does not propose to refuse.[52] However, the Direction does not restrict the power of call-in generally in accordance with its call-in policy.[53]

9.32 Notification development means flood risk area development, significant residential development, minerals development, waste development and development which consists of the extraction of aggregates from new or existing sites within a National Park or an Area of Outstanding Natural Beauty, and significant residential development. Significant residential development is in turn defined as development which includes more than 150 dwellings or is residential development on a site measuring more than 6 hectares and does not accord with the provisions of the applicable development plan.

9.33 Where the local planning authority are required to refer an application to the Welsh Ministers they must not grant permission within a period of twenty-one days of receipt by Welsh Ministers of the required notification information except further to a notice from the Welsh Ministers.[54]

9.34 On notification the Welsh Ministers decide whether or not to call-in the application. Planning Policy Wales gives examples of development which may be considered for call-in.[55] This includes development in conflict with national planning policies. Other examples are development which could have wide effects beyond its immediate locality or which may give rise to substantial controversy beyond the immediate locality, development which is likely significantly to affect sites of scientific, nature conservation or historic interest or areas of landscape importance, and that which raises issues of national security or novel planning issues.

GOVERNMENT AUTHORISATION AND DEEMED PLANNING PERMISSION

9.35 Development by local planning authorities, National Park authorities and statutory undertakers may require specific government authorisation under a separate statutory regime. In this case authorisation may direct that planning permission for that development shall be deemed to be granted, subject to such conditions (if any) as may be specified in the direction.[56] Specific provision to like effect is made where consent is given under the Electricity Act 1989, section 36 or 37 and the Transport and Works Act 1992, section 1 or 3.[57] The deemed planning permission is treated for TCPA 1990 as if made on call-in.[58] The authorisation accordingly replaces the

[52] Article 3.

[53] WGC 07/12, para. 9.

[54] See arts 6 and 7 of the Notification Direction.

[55] See PPW 3.7.3.

[56] TCPA 1990, s. 90(1).

[57] TCPA 1990, s. 90(2)–(2A).

[58] TCPA 1990, s. 90(3) but excluding Pt XII of the Act.

need to apply for planning permission in the ordinary way. As noted above,[59] these powers may be specifically excluded from the general transfer of functions to the Welsh Ministers under TCPA 1990.

Further, in this context, by TCPA 1990, section 266 applications relating to operational land[60] which are referred to the Welsh Ministers under TCPA 1990, Pt III (call-in) or on an appeal against the refusal of an application or in enforcement cases, are dealt with both by the Welsh Ministers and the appropriate Minister, that is the one with departmental authority for the particular activity.[61] However, they shall not be required to deal with an application for permission if the authorisation of a government department is required except where it has already been granted and did not contain any direction as to the grant of planning permission.[62] There was thus concurrent authority in those remaining cases but this was amended in 2015 so that the functions are now dealt with solely by the Welsh Ministers unless otherwise directed.[63] 9.36

APPLICATIONS TO LOCAL PLANNING AUTHORITIES

Except for those applications above made in the first instance to the Welsh Ministers, application for planning permission for development is made to the local planning authority for the area in which the land in question is situated. As with applications to the Welsh Ministers for nationally significant development, there may be a requirement to engage in pre-application consultation: this applies in the case of major applications.[64] In addition there is a duty on the local planning authority to provide pre-application services whenever requested.[65] Subject to this the procedures are laid down in TCPA 1990, sections 62–76 and the Town and 9.37

[59] See Chapter 4: the result is that the general transfer of functions does not include consents under the Electricity Act 1989 and the Transport and Works Act 1992 and only the functions of the Secretary of State for Wales within s. 90(1) were transferred.

[60] Operational land is land used for the purpose of carrying on the undertaking or held for the purpose of carrying out the undertaking but, in the latter case, if acquired after 6 December 1968, only if there is or was specific planning permission for it: TCPA 1990, ss. 263 and 264. In the case of a universal postal service provider and the Civil Aviation Authority, the definition depends on regulations relating to them.

[61] The appropriate Minister is defined in TCPA 1990, s. 265. The National Assembly for Wales (Transfer of Functions Order) 1999, as amended, transferred the functions of the appropriate Minister to the Welsh Ministers only so far as they related to water and sewerage.

[62] TCPA 1990, s. 268.

[63] The Town and Country Planning (Overriding Easements and Other Rights and Applications and Appeals by Statutory Undertakers) (Wales) Order 2015 (SI 2015 No. 1794), art. 6, inserting a new s. 266(1B) into TCPA 1990, s. 266. This mirrors the earlier England-only provision of s. 266(1A).

[64] See para. 12.8, below.

[65] See TCPA 1990, ss. 61Z1 and 61Z2 and SI 2016 No. 61; see Chapter 12, below.

Country Planning (Development Management Procedure) (Wales) Order 2012.[66] Applications made to a local planning authority may be called-in by the Welsh Ministers in accordance with section 77 – see above.

9.38 An application for planning permission may be for outline permission in accordance with sections 91 and 92 of TCPA 1990, that is a planning permission for the erection of a building which is granted subject to a condition requiring the subsequent approval of the local planning authority with respect to one or more reserved matters.[67] Reserved matters are matters of access, appearance, landscaping, layout and scale in respect of which details have not been given in the application.[68] In addition, an application can be made for planning permission for the development of land without complying with conditions subject to which permission was previously granted,[69] for approval of other matters in accordance with a condition on a planning permission, and may be granted for development which has already been carried out.[70] The particular features of each of these are considered in Chapter 11.

EFFECT OF PLANNING PERMISSION

9.39 TCPA 1990, section 75(1) provides that planning permission is for the benefit of the land and of all persons for the time being interested in it. This is subject to the general provisions regarding the duration of permissions and to any provision in the permission and conditions may cut down the scope of its operation.

9.40 Where a development has been commenced but has not been completed in accordance with a time limit for commencement or is affected by an area ceasing to be a simplified planning zone or an enterprise zone before completion, a completion notice may be served under TCPA 1990, section 94 and under its terms the permission may cease to have effect.

9.41 The duration of permission is also subject to the powers of modification and revocation in TCPA 1990, sections 97 and 100. In addition, there is a general power to require the discontinuance of use or alteration or removal of buildings or works where it is expedient in the interests of the proper planning of an area including its amenity.[71]

66 SI 2012 No. 801.

67 See 1990 Act, s. 91 and SI 2012 No. 801, art. 2.

68 Article 2.

69 TCPA 1990, s. 73.

70 TCPA 1990, s. 73A.

71 TCPA 1990, s. 102.

Chapter 10

Developments of National Significance

INTRODUCTION

Applications for planning permission for a development of national significance within the meaning of TCPA 1990, section 62D are made to the Welsh Ministers instead of to the local planning authority. The statutory framework is in TCPA 1990, section 62D–62L. Further supplementary provisions, enabling directions requiring a local planning authority to do things in relation to an application and for notice to community councils, are contained in sections 62P and 62Q of TCPA 1990. 10.1

The main items of subordinate legislation are the Developments of National Significance (Specified Criteria and Secondary Consents) (Wales) Regulations 2016,[1] the Developments of National Significance (Wales) Regulations 2016[2] and the Developments of National Significance (Procedure) (Wales) Order 2016[3] augmented by two further measures concerning fees[4] and application of provisions of TCPA 1990 to these applications.[5] Detailed guidance has been given by a set of documents prepared by the Planning Inspectorate and accessible via the Welsh Government website. 10.2

SCOPE OF DEVELOPMENTS

Developments of national significance are developments meeting criteria specified by regulations or by the National Development Framework.[6] Permission for these developments includes all forms of planning permission for land in Wales, with the exception that it does not include outline permission.[7] In addition, an application for planning permission to vary the conditions attached to a previous planning permission will not be treated as development of national significance unless it is 10.3

[1] SI 2016 No. 53.

[2] SI 2016 No. 56.

[3] SI 2016 No. 55.

[4] Developments of National Significance (Fees) (Wales) Regulations 2016 (SI 2016 No. 57).

[5] Developments of National Significance (Application of Enactments) (Wales) Order 2016 (SI 2016 No. 54).

[6] TCPA 1990, s. 62D(3) and (4).

[7] I.e. further to TCPA 1990, s. 92, see TCPA 1990, s. 62D(5).

an application of a description expressly prescribed in the regulations.[8] The regulations provide that only applications meeting the overall criteria and made under TCPA 1990, section 73 in respect of a condition relating to a general time limit imposed by or under section 91 of the Act will be treated as nationally significant: applications regarding other conditions will not therefore be included.[9]

10.4 The Welsh Ministers also have power to determine secondary consents. These are consents related to the primary development which are necessary for or facilitate carrying it out and this enables all relevant authorisations to be dealt with at the same time. The detailed criteria are below.

10.5 The Application of Enactments Order[10] provides that specific provisions of TCPA 1990 relating to planning applications apply to these applications as if references to the local planning authority were references to the Welsh Ministers. They are the provisions relating to the duty to take account of material considerations,[11] to decline subsequent applications[12] and the general power to grant permissions and impose conditions.[13] Similarly, provisions regarding application for permission without complying with conditions previously imposed[14] and retrospective applications[15] apply where appropriate. Certain powers to make provision by development order are extended to the Welsh Ministers in these cases, as is the duty not to entertain an application not complying with requirements.[16]

CRITERIA

10.6 Regulation 3 of the Specified Criteria Regulations lists the description of development which is of national significance and the further regulations[17] then contain the more detailed definition and specification for each category, generally by reference to the capacity of the facility in question. The developments which are listed relate to electricity generating stations, underground gas storage facilities, LNG facilities, gas reception facilities, airports, railways, rail freight interchanges, dams or reservoirs, development for the transfer of water resources, waste water treatment plants and hazardous waste facilities. They apply only to the construction or alteration of the facilities, except that they refer in addition to the extension of

[8] TCPA 1990, s. 62D(6) and (7).

[9] TCPA 1990, s. 62D and reg. 51 of the Developments of National Significance (Wales) Regulations 2016.

[10] SI 2016 No. 54, art. 3.

[11] Section 70(2).

[12] Sections 70A(1) and (2).

[13] Sections 70 and 72(1).

[14] TCPA 1990, s. 73(2).

[15] TCPA 1990, s. 73A(1).

[16] TCPA 1990, s. 327A(2).

[17] Regulations 4–14.

an electricity generating station and include any development relating to airports or the transfer of water resources.

Development permitted by article 3 of the Town and Country Planning (General Permitted Development) Order 1995 is not of national significance. 10.7

The Welsh Ministers will also make the decision on consent which is related to the development, termed a secondary consent.[18] A secondary consent is a consent that is required under legislation, or is given under legislation, that relates to or is given in connection with the development or use of land in Wales or a notice is required by legislation to be given in relation to or in connection with the development or use of land in Wales and it is so prescribed by regulations.[19] Consent includes a permit, certificate, licence or other authorisation.[20] 10.8

The relevant consents are listed in the Schedule to the Developments of National Significance (Specified Criteria and Secondary Consents) (Wales) Regulations 2016 and refer to ancient monuments, listed buildings, conservation areas, certain consents relating to highway matters and to hazardous substances and two specific consents under the Commons Act 2006. The specified consents include planning permission, other than outline permission, and thus development which is not itself of national significance but which relates to such development will be a relevant consent dealt with by the Welsh Ministers. 10.9

A secondary consent is connected to a section 62D development application if it is required in order for that development to be carried out, would facilitate the carrying out of that development, or would facilitate any redevelopment or improvement or the achievement of any other purpose carried out on or in relation to land in connection with that development.[21] It is not therefore confined to consents, as widely defined, under the planning regime. 10.10

PROCEDURE AND DECISION

A person proposing to make an application must notify the Welsh Ministers and the local planning authority to whom the application would otherwise have been made of the proposal and the notification must comply with the development order. The requirements which may be specified may include the form and content of a notification, information to accompany the notification and the way in which and time at which the notification is to be given.[22] The process, including that for obtaining secondary consents, is governed by the Developments of 10.11

[18] TCPA 1990, s. 62H.

[19] TCPA 1990, s. 62H(1): only matters within the legislative competence of the Assembly and exercisable by a body exercising functions of a public nature can be included (s. 62H(2)).

[20] TCPA 1990, s. 62H(3).

[21] TCPA 1990, s. 62F.

[22] TCPA 1990, s. 62E.

National Significance (Wales) Regulations 2016[23] and the Developments of National Significance (Procedure) (Wales) Order 2016[24] together with the fees Regulations.[25] The Procedure Order contains details of the notification and application process itself, publicity, consultation, acceptance by the Welsh Ministers and duties on the local authority in whose area the site is, including the provision of local impact reports. In addition, it provides for variation of the application and details relating to the decision and notification when development commences.

10.12 Pre-application steps are an important feature of the process and the regulations provide for pre-application notification to the Welsh Ministers followed by consultation before submission of the application itself.[26] No step taken before the date of the formal application is to be treated as consultation under the Act.[27] A proposed application must be publicised by site notice, by written notice to owners and occupiers of adjoining land, in a local newspaper and on the applicant's website.[28] Consultation must be carried out[29] and specialist consultees,[30] but not others (for example, community consultees), must respond within forty-two days.[31] An application following this must include a pre-consultation report that gives details of the process and the account taken of responses.[32] These obligations are additional to the publicity and consultation requirements on the Welsh Ministers in determining the application.

10.13 In addition, these developments are qualifying applications for the provision of pre-application services[33] and the local planning authorities or the Welsh Ministers are under a duty to provide the services further to any request made to them.[34]

10.14 Notification of the proposed development must be on the prescribed form and contain the particulars required and be accompanied by a plan and either a statement that an environmental statement will be provided or a screening direction together with the fee.[35] Guidance points out that Environmental Impact Assessments and Habitats Regulation Assessments should be fully integrated with the pre-application process. Notice that the application is accepted or not accepted

[23] SI 2016 No. 56.

[24] SI 2016 No. 55.

[25] Developments of National Significance (Fees) (Wales) Regulations 2016 (SI 2016 No. 57).

[26] See Procedure Order, art. 7 and TCPA 1990, s. 61Z.

[27] TCPA 1990, s. 62E(5).

[28] Procedure Order, art. 8.

[29] TCPA 1990, s. 61Z(4) and Procedure Order, art. 9.

[30] See Procedure Order, art. 2 and Sch. 5.

[31] Article 10.

[32] Article 11.

[33] See TCPA 1990, s. 61Z1(4) and the Developments of National Significance (Wales) Regulations 2016.

[34] See Developments of National Significance (Wales) Regulations 2016, regs 7 and 8 and the request procedure in reg. 6.

[35] Procedure Order, art. 5.

as complying with the requirements must then be given within ten working days. If accepted, the application must be submitted within twelve months otherwise the notice will lapse.[36]

The procedure for the application itself is in Part 3 of the Procedure Order. 10.15

The application must be on the prescribed form or one substantially to like effect and contain the required particulars,[37] which must include a design and access statement.[38] Notice of receipt of a valid application must then be given and this activates the timetable for determining applications under TCPA 1990, section 62L.[39] The applicant must give notice of the application to all owners and tenants of the land to which it relates and certify compliance.[40] There are separate publicity requirements on each of the Welsh Ministers and the local planning authority.[41] In determining the application, the Welsh Ministers must take into account all representations received in response to these notices.[42] The duty to record the application in the register is on the local planning authority[43] and they must also forward any representation received to the Welsh Ministers as soon as practicable.[44] 10.16

The Welsh Ministers must consult any specialist consultee and may consult any other authority, body or person. They must take into account any representations received from a specialist consultee[45] and that body is under a duty to respond to the consultation.[46] 10.17

As in the case of nationally significant infrastructure projects, the Welsh Ministers must require each relevant local planning authority to submit a local impact report[47] and other local planning authorities may submit a voluntary local impact report[48] and, in either case, the Welsh Ministers must have regard to the reports in dealing with the application.[49] A local impact report is one meeting the tests in section 62K of TCPA 1990 and article 25. 10.18

The Welsh Ministers must determine the application and any decision on a secondary consent within the period of thirty-six weeks from the date of acceptance 10.19

36 Procedure Order, art. 6(3).
37 Procedure Order, art. 12.
38 Procedure Order, art. 14.
39 Procedure Order, art. 15.
40 Procedure Order, arts 16 and 17.
41 Procedure Order, arts 18 and 19.
42 Procedure Order, art. 28.
43 Procedure Order, art. 20.
44 Procedure Order, art. 21.
45 Procedure Order, art. 22.
46 Procedure Order, art. 23 and PCPA 2004, s. 54.
47 TCPA 1990, s. 62I.
48 TCPA 1990, s. 62J(3).
49 TCPA 1990, s. 62J(1) and (2).

of the application[50] although the timeframe may be extended.[51] The guidance states that to comply the report to the Welsh Ministers must be made within twenty-four weeks, the effect being that the timescale for the examination is seventeen weeks.

10.20 Applications for developments of national significance will be determined by an appointed person in accordance with Schedule 4D to TCPA 1990.[52] However, all post-determination procedures will be handled by local planning authorities and this includes decisions relating to the discharge of conditions.

10.21 The process of deciding the application is for examination by an appointed inspector who will report to the Welsh Ministers who then make the decision. The Developments of National Significance (Wales) Regulations 2016 deal with the functions of the person appointed for the purpose of the application and for conducting a hearing or inquiry. The decision as to a hearing or inquiry is that of the Welsh Ministers.[53] Thereafter, the Regulations set out in Part 7 the formal steps for a hearing and in Part 8 for an inquiry and lay down the applicable timescale.

10.22 As it is an examination, the inspector plays a leading role although the provisions differ from examinations for development consent orders. The key is that in deciding on the form of examination the Welsh Ministers give notice identifying the matters, if any, to be determined at a hearing or inquiry and any matters on which further representations are required. If further representations are required, the notice must state if they are required in writing, at a hearing or at an inquiry.[54] The notice will also state who is invited to attend any hearing or inquiry to be held. It may be that a combination of procedures is adopted with, for example, some issues being considered orally, and others dealt with by written representations. Although the process at hearing or inquiry will be in familiar format, including cross-examination at an inquiry, the focus will be only on those issues raised as requiring that form of oral consideration. Further information may be requested but this is subject to strict timescales and must not exceed 3,000 words on any particular matter.[55]

10.23 The formalities for publicity and holding the hearing or inquiry, pre-inquiry meetings, where applicable, site visits and procedure are detailed in the Regulations.

10.24 Where an application is granted subject to conditions or is refused, the full reasons for this must be clearly and precisely stated.[56] A decision on such application is final,[57] as are decisions on any secondary consent.[58] Accordingly, the

[50] See TCPA 1990, s. 62L.

[51] See TCPA 1990, s. 62L and regs 4 and 11.

[52] TCPA 1990, s. 62S.

[53] In accordance with TCPA 1990, s. 319B, see reg. 13 of the 2016 Regulations.

[54] SI 2016 No. 56, reg. 13.

[55] SI 2016 No. 56, reg. 15.

[56] Article 29 of the Procedure Order.

[57] TCPA 1990, s. 62P.

[58] TCPA 1990, s. 62F(5).

rights of appeal which might otherwise apply were the decision made by the body responsible in the absence of a development of national significance do not apply. However, Schedule 4, paragraphs 15 and 16 of the Planning (Wales) Act 2015 amend sections 284 and 288 of TCPA 1990 so that legal challenge by proceedings in the High Court may be brought under Part XII of TCPA 1990.

When the development granted by the permission is begun, notice must be displayed in accordance with TCPA 1990, section 71ZB.[59] 10.25

[59] Article 31 of the Procedure Order.

Chapter 11

Outline and Miscellaneous Applications

INTRODUCTION

The different ways in which full planning permission may be granted have been considered in Chapter 9. This chapter is concerned with the provisions governing particular types of application for planning permission or applications necessary under the terms of a permission to enable the development to be carried out. 11.1

The applications dealt with are: outline permissions; approval of reserved matters; applications for consent or approval, other than reserved matters, in accordance with a condition on a permission; applications for permission without complying with conditions attached to a previous permission; retrospective permissions; and applications for non-material amendment to an existing permission. 11.2

OUTLINE PERMISSION AND APPROVAL OF RESERVED MATTERS

Outline planning permission is the grant of permission in accordance with the provisions of a development order with the reservation for subsequent approval of matters not particularised in the application, these matters being reserved matters.[1] It is an application for planning permission subject to the procedural provisions considered in Chapter 12, although the information required on reserved matters is in accordance with article 3 of the Town and Country Planning (Development Management Procedure) (Wales) Order 2012.[2] Permission for developments of national significance to be granted by the Welsh Ministers does not include grant of an outline permission.[3] 11.3

The Order[4] defines an outline planning permission as one granted for the erection of a building subject to a condition requiring approval of one or more reserved matters. Reserved matters are in turn defined as access, appearance, landscaping, layout and scale. 11.4

Each of these are more exhaustively defined in article 2(1). Access, in relation to reserved matters, means the accessibility to and within the site for vehicles, cycles 11.5

[1] TCPA 1990, s. 92(1).

[2] SI 2012 No. 801 (DMP(W)O in the following footnotes). Details are not required of these under art. 5: see art. 5(3).

[3] TCPA 1990, s. 62D(5).

[4] DMP(W)O, art. 2(1).

and pedestrians in terms of the positioning and treatment of access and circulation routes and how these fit into the surrounding access network and 'site' means the site or part of the site in respect of which outline planning permission is granted or, as the case may be, in respect of which an application for such a permission has been made.

11.6 Appearance means the aspects of a building or place within the development which determine the visual impression the building or place makes, including the external built form of the development, its architecture, materials, decoration, lighting, colour and texture.

11.7 Landscaping means the treatment of land (other than buildings) for the purpose of enhancing or protecting the amenities of the site and the area in which it is situated and includes: (a) screening by fences, walls or other means; (b) the planting of trees, hedges, shrubs or grass; (c) the formation of banks, terraces or other earthworks; (d) the laying out or provision of gardens, courts, squares, water features, sculpture or public art; and (e) the provision of other amenity features.

11.8 Layout means the way in which buildings, routes and open spaces within the development are provided, situated and orientated in relation to each other and to buildings and spaces outside the development.

11.9 Scale means the height, width and length of each building proposed within the development in relation to its surroundings.

11.10 An application for outline planning permission reserving layout must state the approximate location of buildings, routes and open spaces included in the development proposed. Where scale is a reserved matter, it must state the upper and lower limit for the height, width and length of each building included in the development proposed and in the case of access it must state the area or areas where access points to the development proposed will be situated.[5]

11.11 Where the local planning authority are of the opinion that, in the circumstances of the case, the application ought not to be considered separately from all or any of the reserved matters, they must within the period of one month beginning with the receipt of the application notify the applicant that they are unable to determine it unless further details are submitted, specifying the further details they require.[6]

11.12 Outline permission shall be granted subject to a condition that application for approval of any reserved matter must be made not later than the expiration of three years from the date of grant of the permission[7] and, if not expressly so granted, the permission is deemed to be subject to such condition.[8]

11.13 It shall also be granted subject to a condition that the development must be begun no later than the expiration of five years from the date of the grant of outline planning permission, or, if later, the expiration of two years from the final

[5] DMP(W)O, art. 3(3)–(5).

[6] DMP(W)O, art. 3(2).

[7] TCPA 1990, s. 92(2)(a).

[8] TCPA 1990, s. 92(3).

approval of the reserved matters or, in the case of approval on different dates, the final approval of the last such matter to be approved.[9] Again, if not expressly so granted, the permission is deemed to be subject to such condition.[10]

Either period may be varied where appropriate by the authority substituting a longer or shorter period.[11] Separate periods may be specified for separate parts of the development.[12] The time limit applies only to reserved matters properly so called and not to conditions relating to other matters in respect of which post-permission approval is required by an express condition. 11.14

The time for applying for approval of reserved matters or for development in those cases where there is no express condition is varied where the outline permission is one made under section 73,[13] that is where it is for permission to develop land without complying with a condition attached to a previously granted permission. The position is that where the time periods depend on the deemed provisions of TCPA 1990, section 92 the permission will lapse unless action is taken before the end of those periods. Accordingly, it is provided that the deemed conditions are that application for approval must be made not later than the date on or before which the previous permission required application for approval[14] and in respect of the development that it must be begun not later than the date on or before which the previous permission required development to be begun.[15] 11.15

Where conditions are attached under section 92, development carried out after the date by which the conditions require it to be carried out shall be treated as not authorised by the permission and an application for approval of a reserved matter, if it is made after the date by which the conditions require it to be made, shall be treated as not made in accordance with the terms of the permission.[16] 11.16

Approval of an application for a reserved matter is a planning decision under TCPA 1990, section 336 and the application for approval has been held to be an application under Part III of the Act, and the approval itself may therefore be subject to conditions in accordance with section 70.[17] However, the Development Management Procedure Order generally refers to applications for planning permission and separately in places to 'applications', so that the two are for those purposes distinct. 'Applications' may in turn refer specifically to applications for approval of reserved matters or other types of application. In particular, the references to applications under article 4, that is to approval of reserved matters, 11.17

[9] TCPA 1990, s. 92(2)(c).

[10] TCPA 1990, s. 92(3).

[11] TCPA 1990, s. 92(4).

[12] TCPA 1990, s. 92(5).

[13] TCPA 1990, s. 92(3A)–(3E).

[14] TCPA 1990, s. 92(3A) and (3B).

[15] TCPA 1990, s. 92(3C) and (3D).

[16] TCPA 1990, s. 93(4).

[17] *R v Newbury DC* (1993) 65 P & CR 438.

are no longer included within the provisions governing valid applications and acknowledgements.[18]

11.18 An application for approval of reserved matters must be made in writing to the local planning authority on a form published by the Welsh Ministers (or a form substantially to the like effect) and include the particulars specified or referred to in the form. It must be accompanied by such plans and drawings, to an identified scale and showing north, as are necessary to deal with the matters reserved in the outline planning permission.[19] Applications may be made electronically[20] but, where not, must be accompanied by three copies of the form and the plans unless the authority indicate that fewer are required.

11.19 An application for approval of a reserved matter may be a qualifying application so that, where the other conditions are met, it may be made to the Welsh Ministers at the option of the developer in accordance with TCPA 1990, section 62M.[21]

11.20 A fee is payable when applying for approval of a reserved matter in accordance with the fees regulations.[22]

11.21 The extent of those duties to be discharged at the outline stage and those at the approval of reserved matters stage is important. In earlier cases the view had been expressed that there was no power at the reserved matters stage to carry out an environmental impact assessment. In *R (Barker) v Bromley London Borough Council*,[23] however, the House of Lords held that the 1988 Regulations failed properly to implement Council Directive 85/337/EEC and that there was power to require an assessment at the reserved matters stage. The Regulations have now been replaced by the 2016 Regulations, which extend to subsequent consents and accordingly allow for assessment at either stage.[24]

11.22 TCPA 1990, section 100A[25] contains measures that apply to the consultation process for reserved matters approval enabling, but not obliging, consultation with statutory consultees. A development order may provide that such an application is not to be determined before a defined period and for a substantive response from a statutory consultee who is consulted. A statutory consultee is any person required to be consulted under TCPA 1990, section 71 or 74 on the original application and that person may be subject to further requirements by order.

[18] See DMP(W)O, arts 8 and 22, as amended by SI 2016 No. 59.

[19] DMP(W)O, art. 4.

[20] See DMP(W)O, art. 32.

[21] TCPA 1990, s. 62M(4)(b).

[22] Town and Country Planning (Fees for Applications, Deemed Applications and Site Visits) (Wales) Regulations 2015 (SI 2015 No. 1522), as amended by SI 2016 No. 62, reg. 3.

[23] [2007] 1 AC 470.

[24] Town and Country Planning (Environmental Impact Assessment) (Wales) Regulations 2016 (SI 2016 No. 58), reg. 2 definition of subsequent application.

[25] Inserted by Planning (Wales) Act 2015, s. 37: SI 2016 No. 59 inserted new consultation provisions, arts 15A–15F of DMP(W)O.

The development management order has been amended so that where a person is consulted the local planning authority must provide specified information to the statutory consultee[26] and the response from a consultee must be made within twenty-one days of the receipt of the consultation documents or the last of them.[27] If a statutory consultee is consulted he is under a duty to give a substantive response[28] and the decision must not be made before the expiry of twenty-one days from receipt of the consultation documents. 11.23

A decision on a reserved matters application must give full reasons for a refusal or imposition of conditions, just as in the case of planning permission.[29] A decision may be appealed under the Town and Country Planning Act 1990, section 78, in which event articles 10 and 11 of the Order apply. 11.24

APPROVAL OF MATTERS OTHER THAN RESERVED MATTERS IN ACCORDANCE WITH A PLANNING PERMISSION

A condition may require the developer to obtain the later approval of the local planning authority for a defined aspect of the development. Such conditions must be distinguished from conditions relating to reserved matters which are subject to the particular provisions above. However, both are subject to consultation provisions under TCPA 1990, section 100A[30] and the Order. The terms of paragraphs 11.22 and 11.23 above are therefore equally applicable. 11.25

Guidance is given in WGC 016/2014 and procedure is referred to in the 2012 Order. The circular points out[31] that authorities should seek to ensure, where possible, that conditions other than those relating to reserved matters are self-contained, and do not require further approvals to be obtained before development can begin. Where necessary, however, a local planning authority may impose a condition requiring that details of a specified aspect of the development which was not fully described in the application (e.g. the provision of car parking spaces) be submitted for approval before the development is begun. 11.26

Applications are referred to as applications to discharge conditions in article 23 of the Order and the Circular states that an application should be made to a local planning authority using the 1APP standard application form and should identify the original permission, the relevant condition and the details which the local planning authority are to consider.[32] A local planning authority may reject an application for any consent, agreement or approval required by any condition 11.27

[26] DMP(W)O, art.15D.

[27] DMP(W)O, art. 15C, as amended by SI 2016 No. 59.

[28] Section 100A(2) and DMP(W)O, art. 15E sets out what constitutes a substantive response.

[29] DMP(W)O, art. 24.

[30] See TCPA 1990, s. 100A(5).

[31] See para. 5.11.

[32] See para. 4.28.

or limitation subject to which planning permission has been granted where the application fails to provide information or documents or materials so as to comply with the permission.[33] Notice must be given identifying the failure. Where satisfied an authority should issue confirmation of compliance.

11.28 The applicant has a right to appeal against a non-compliance notice to the Welsh Ministers on the grounds specified in section 62ZB(3). Procedure is in accordance with the Town and Country Planning (Validation Appeals Procedure) (Wales) Regulations 2016[34] and is by written representations. The notice of appeal and accompanying documents comprise the appellant's representations and the local planning authority's notice of invalidity comprises their representations, with power for the Welsh Ministers to require further information.

11.29 The authority must give notice to the applicant of its decision on the application itself within a period of eight weeks beginning with the date on which the application was received by the authority, or such longer period as may be agreed by the applicant and the authority in writing. The approval may itself be subject to conditions and these are conditions subject to which the permission is granted and enforceable as such.[35]

11.30 A decision may be appealed under the Town and Country Planning Act 1990, section 78 as for planning decisions generally, in which event articles 10 and 11 of the 2012 Order apply. An appeal lies against a refusal of the application and against the grant subject to conditions.[36]

11.31 The Welsh Ministers may make directions by development order as to the deemed discharge of conditions where approval has been applied for but time has elapsed without any decision.[37] In addition, an application for any consent, agreement or approval required by any condition or limitation subject to which planning permission has been granted is, like a reserved matters application, a relevant application under TCPA 1990, section 100A and a development order may provide for the time of decision and for matters regarding statutory consultees.

11.32 TCPA 1990, section 71ZA provides that where any consent, agreement or approval required by a condition or limitation is given or a condition or limitation is imposed, removed or altered, a revised version of the decision notice granting permission must be given.

[33] TCPA 1990, s. 62ZA.

[34] SI 2016 No. 60.

[35] See *Pressland v Hammersmith and Fulham LBC* [2016] EWHC 1763 (Admin).

[36] See TCPA 1990, s. 78(1)(b).

[37] TCPA 1990, s. 74A.

DEVELOPMENT WITHOUT COMPLIANCE WITH CONDITIONS PREVIOUSLY ATTACHED

Applications for planning permission to develop land without complying with conditions subject to which a previous application was granted are made further to TCPA 1990, section 73. This is a planning application subject to the same procedures as applications generally, except that article 5(1)(c) of the 2012 Order exempts it from the requirement to lodge plans. In addition, articles 12(4A) and 15ZA contain specific provisions regarding site notices and consultations before the grant of section 73 applications. 11.33

On such an application the local planning authority shall consider only the question of the conditions subject to which planning permission should be granted. They may grant planning permission subject to different conditions or unconditionally or, if they consider that it should be subject to the same conditions, refuse the application.[38] It leads to a fresh permission: as Pitchford LJ put it in *Lawson Builders Ltd v Secretary of State for Communities and Local Government*,[39] the section does not work by enabling new conditions to be grafted on to the old permission. 11.34

The section cannot be used to extend the time for beginning development where that time has expired without the development having begun.[40] However, there is no prohibition on a section 73 application which in effect extends the time for commencement provided the application itself is made before expiry of the time limit.[41] Amendments by the Planning (Wales) Act 2015, section 35, inserting subsections (3ZA)–(3ZD) into TCPA 1990, section 91, mean that a section 73 permission will last for the unexpired period of the original permission, unless otherwise provided. 11.35

The classic explanation of the nature of section 73 applications was given in *Pye v Secretary of State for the Environment Transport and Regions*[42] where Sullivan J said: 11.36

> Whilst section 73 applications are commonly referred to as applications to 'amend' the conditions attached to a planning permission, a decision under section 73(2) leaves the original planning permission intact and unamended. That is so whether the decision is to grant planning permission unconditionally or subject to different conditions under paragraph (a), or to refuse the application under paragraph (b), because planning permission should be granted subject to the same conditions.
>
> In the former case the applicant may choose whether to implement the original planning permission or the new planning permission; in the latter case, he is still free to implement the original planning permission.

[38] TCPA 1990, s. 73(2).

[39] [2015] EWCA Civ 122 at para. 22.

[40] TCPA 1990, s. 73(4).

[41] TCPA 1990, s. 73(5), which serves to prevent this, applies in England but not in Wales. See Planning (Wales) Act 2015, s. 35(7), inserting the words 'for the development of land in England' into s. 73(5).

[42] [1998] 3 PLR 72 at p. 85.

He continued:

> Considering only the conditions subject to which planning permission should be granted will be a more limited exercise than the consideration of a 'normal' application for planning permission under section 70 . . . how much more limited will depend on the nature of the condition itself.

11.37 The Court of Appeal concurred with this in *R v Leicester City Council, ex parte Powergen UK Ltd*[43] and said:

> When considering whether or not to grant planning permission for the development of land without complying with conditions subject to which a previous planning permission was granted, the authority must take into account the provisions of the development plan and any other material considerations. If one asks 'material to what?' the answer is—material to the application under section 73. Thus, for instance, if the application is to retain a use of land without complying with a condition imposed on a previous permission that the use should cease after five years it must be right to examine that application in the light of facts and policies as they are at the time of the decision on the new application.

11.38 It is established law that where two planning permissions exist (i.e. the original permission and the one granted under section 73) it is open to the developer to choose between them, subject only to the fact that steps taken under one of them may make it impossible to implement the other.[44]

11.39 The interaction of this provision and section 73A, referring to retrospective applications, was recently before the Court of Appeal in *Lawson Builders Ltd*.[45] Pitchford LJ said:

> it is implicit in the terms of sections 73 and 73A TCPA, read together, that in an appropriate case a planning authority considering an application under section 73 for planning permission to proceed with a development without complying with conditions attached to an existing permission may grant, under section 73A, retrospective planning permission for a development already carried out, subject to conditions imposed under section 70.

He added that it may be necessary to forewarn the applicant of the intent to do so in unusual circumstances.

[43] (2001) 81 P & CR 47 at p. 59 (para. 45).

[44] See e.g. acceptance of this in *R (Robert Hitchins Ltd) v Worcestershire CC* [2015] EWCA Civ 1060 at para. 19.

[45] [2015] EWCA Civ 122 at para. 36 and see para. 11.34, above.

The nature of the inquiry under each section was also considered and it was said[46] that: 11.40

> an application for retrospective planning permission under section 73A may, and often will, require engagement with wider planning considerations than those raised by a reconsideration of conditions imposed upon an existing permission under section 73. However, it would be a mistake to assume that a section 73 examination of conditions will never involve the study of wider planning considerations. Although the planning merits of the development in general will not be under consideration, the conditions may have been imposed so as to ensure compliance with an important aspect of policy. The task of the planning authority and the planning inspector under section 73 is *'only'* to judge whether the conditions originally imposed should be adhered to or varied but that task may require, depending upon the purpose of the condition, a wide ranging enquiry. As to section 73A, it can be seen from the terms of section 73A(2) that there is scope for wider or narrower examination of the planning merits depending upon the nature and stage of the development and the circumstances of the application.

Applications under TCPA 1990, section 73 are planning applications subject to the general provisions of the Act: the provisions of the section are expressly applied to these applications in cases where they are referred to the Welsh Ministers (call-in).[47] 11.41

RETROSPECTIVE APPLICATIONS

TCPA 1990, section 73A states that a local planning authority may grant planning permission for development carried out before the date of the application. 11.42

This applies to development carried out without planning permission, in accordance with planning permission granted for a limited period, or carried out without complying with some condition subject to which planning permission was granted.[48] The permission may be granted to have effect from the date on which the development was carried out or, if it was in accordance with a temporary permission, from the end of that period.[49] 11.43

As seen above, this application is distinct from an application under section 73 and it is not necessary to specify that the grant is under section 73A where it is clear that any grant had to be retrospective.[50] The scope of inquiry requires consideration 11.44

[46] At para. 31.

[47] TCPA 1990, s. 77(4).

[48] TCPA 1990, s. 73A(2).

[49] TCPA 1990, s. 73A(3).

[50] See *Lawson Builders Ltd v Secretary of State for Communities and Local Government* [2015] EWCA Civ 122.

of all material planning matters as on an application for development yet to take place, although what is material in any case depends on all the circumstances.[51]

11.45 Subject to this, it is a planning application governed by the same procedures as applications generally except that where the development was carried out without complying with a condition on a planning permission it is exempt from the requirement to lodge plans.[52]

11.46 Amendments to TCPA 1990, section 70C made by Planning (Wales) Act 2015, section 32 extend application of the section to Wales so that the local planning authority may decline to determine an application for planning permission if it would involve granting planning permission for any matter specified in a pre-existing enforcement notice as a breach of planning control. This applies to the whole or any part of the development in the notice and whether it relates to all or part of the land if the enforcement notice was issued before the planning application was received.

11.47 When conditions are imposed they may be needed to be drafted with time limits to accommodate the fact that development has been carried out.[53]

NON-MATERIAL AMENDMENTS TO PLANNING PERMISSION

11.48 Section 96A of TCPA 1990 was brought into force on September 2014 in Wales and guidance was given in July 2014.[54] It simply provides that a local planning authority may make a change to a planning permission if satisfied that it is not material. Power to prescribe the procedure is in section 96A(5A) and (9). Procedure is governed by section 96A and the Town and Country Planning (General Development Management Procedure) (Wales) Order 2012, article 28A:[55] as it is not itself an application for planning permission, the general provisions of the Order regarding such applications do not apply.

11.49 The Act contains no definition of material but states that in deciding whether a change is material, a local planning authority must have regard to the effect of the change, together with any previous changes made under this section, on the planning permission as originally granted.[56]

11.50 However, further assistance is in the Planning Guidance on the Order (published in July 2014), which says that it depends on a number of factors such as the context of the overall scheme, the amendments being sought to the original planning permission, the specific circumstances of the site and surrounding areas,

[51] See para. 11.40, above.

[52] DMP(W)O, art. 5(1)(c).

[53] See WGC 016/2014, para. 4.14.

[54] See the Town and Country Planning (Non-Material Changes and Corrections of Errors) (Wales) Order 2014 (SI 2014 No. 1770).

[55] Inserted by SI 2014 No. 1772.

[56] TCPA 1990, s. 96A(2).

which will vary from one application to another. What may be non-material in one context may be material in another.[57] It continues to list the following tests as a starting point:

(a) (i) is the scale of the proposed change great enough to cause an impact different to that caused by the original approved development scheme; and,
(ii) would the proposed change result in a detrimental impact either visually or in terms of local amenity?
(b) would the interests of any third party or body be disadvantaged in planning terms; or,
(c) would the proposed change conflict with national or development plan policies?

The change may only be made on application by a person with an interest in the land to which the permission relates.[58] A person has such an interest only if in relation to that land (or any mineral in, on or under it) the person is the estate owner of the fee simple, is entitled to a tenancy granted or extended for a term of years certain of which not less than two years remain unexpired, is the mortgagee of any interest or estate in the land or is a party to an estate contract within the meaning of section 2(4) of the Land Charges Act 1972.[59] 11.51

The power to amend includes power to impose new conditions or alter or remove conditions.[60] The application may be made before or after the development has been carried out. 11.52

Application must be made on the prescribed form and publicised by a site notice and notice to an adjoining owner or occupier and the local planning authority may consult and take into account representations received.[61] A fee is payable under the Town and Country Planning (Fees for Non-Material Changes) (Wales) Regulations 2014[62] unless exempted. 11.53

These applications, like a reserved matters application or for approval pursuant to a condition, are relevant applications under TCPA 1990, section 100A and a development order may provide for the time of decision and for matters regarding statutory consultees if a local planning authority has consulted them.[63] 11.54

A refusal to amend does not give rise to an appeal under section 78. Subject to any challenge that may be made where there is an error of law it would be necessary to apply for new permission or make a section 73 application as appropriate. 11.55

57 See para. 2.4.
58 TCPA 1990, s. 96A(4).
59 TCPA 1990, s. 96A(10).
60 TCPA 1990, s. 96A(3).
61 DMP(W)O, art. 28A.
62 SI 2014 No. 1761.
63 See paras 11.22–11.23, above.

Chapter 12

Application for Planning Permission – Procedural Steps

INTRODUCTION

This chapter considers the procedure to be followed by an applicant when applying for planning permission and the formal steps to be taken by the planning authority in determining the application. The legal constraints and framework of the decision-making process itself, that is, what considerations should be taken into account in determining the application, are considered in Chapter 13. 12.1

This chapter is concerned with all applications for planning permission made to local planning authorities. The procedures generally apply to applications for full permission, outline applications, applications under TCPA 1990, section 73 and retrospective applications under section 73A. The particular position of the latter applications, and relevant provisions regarding other types of application relating to an existing permission, have been considered in the previous chapter. Pre-application procedures, however, apply more restrictively, affecting only certain applications for full or outline permission. Where application is made in the first instance to the Welsh Ministers, different procedures apply. At present this extends only to developments of national significance under TCPA 1990, section 62D. These have been considered in Chapter 10. 12.2

The key provisions are in the Town and Country Planning (Development Management Procedure) (Wales) Order, as amended.[1] The Order sets out pre-application steps for an applicant and the formal process for making an application. It then specifies the steps to be followed by the decision-maker in accepting the application, publicising it and consulting as appropriate, and the duty to take into account representations duly received. 12.3

This chapter also refers to the procedure within the local planning authority to decide applications and rules regarding delegation to officers and the time within which a decision must be made. 12.4

The Crown is generally bound by TCPA 1990[2] and permission for development will be made by application to the local planning authority as for other development. However, there are certain special provisions taking account of the status of certain Crown development and these are referred to at the end of this 12.5

[1] SI 2012 No. 801 and see esp. amendments by SI 2015 No. 1330 and SI 2016 No. 59 ('DMP(W)O' in footnotes below).

[2] TCPA 1990, s. 292A.

chapter. Procedure where the development is by the local planning authority is also referred to at the end of this chapter.

PRE-APPLICATION PROCEDURE

12.6 One of the key features of applications for a development consent order for nationally significant infrastructure projects is the requirement for extensive consultation before application. One of the aims of the Planning (Wales) Act 2015 is to extend the use of such procedures and the provision of pre-application services, and this is the subject of sections 61Z, 61Z1 and 61Z2 of TCPA 1990. The provisions distinguish between an obligation to consult before making an application and a discretion to approach the local planning authority, in which event, however, the request obliges the authority to provide pre-application services.

12.7 Where an applicant proposes to make an application for permission for development specified by order, pre-application consultation must be carried out.[3] The operation of this in connection with developments of national significance has been considered in Chapter 10.[4] Separate provision is made for certain other applications made to local planning authorities.[5] This applies to proposed applications for planning permission, which therefore includes full and outline applications, but applications for development without complying with conditions previously imposed and for development already carried out are expressly excluded.[6]

12.8 Pre-application consultation must be carried out in accordance with TCPA 1990, s. 61Z(1) where the proposal is for major development.[7] There are five categories of major development.[8] They are: mineral developments; waste developments; the provision of dwelling houses numbering ten or more or on a site of half a hectare or more; buildings with a floor space of 1,000 square metres or more; and development on a site of one hectare or more.

12.9 The applicant must publicise a proposed application for this development by a site notice for at least twenty-eight days and by notice to owners and occupiers of adjoining land.[9] Information on the proposal must be available for inspection in the vicinity: this includes plans and drawings and those documents and particulars or evidence which would be required for an application.[10] The applicant must also consult community and specialist consultees[11] and the specialist consultees are

[3] TCPA 1990, s. 61Z(1) and (2).

[4] DMP(W)O, art. 7 and TCPA 1990, s. 61Z.

[5] See DMP(W)O, Part 1A and arts 2B–F, as inserted by the 2016 Amendment Order (SI 2016 No. 59).

[6] I.e. applications under TCPA 1990, ss. 73 and 73A excluded by s. 61Z(7)(b) and art. 2B(2).

[7] DMP(W)O, Part 1A, art. 2B.

[8] Defined in DMP(W)O, art. 2.

[9] DMP(W)O, art. 2C.

[10] DMP(W)O, art. 2C.

[11] TCPA 1990, s. 61Z(2) and (4) and DMP(W)O, art. 2D.

under a duty to provide a substantive response within twenty-eight days.[12] Specialist consultees are defined by reference to the category of development in the substituted Schedule 4 to the 2012 Order and mean those persons or bodies listed in the Schedule for the development in question.[13]

An application following this must include a pre-consultation report which gives details of the process, the responses and the account taken of those responses.[14] The report will be a necessary part of a valid application.[15] 12.10

To facilitate pre-application procedures and to enable a consistent approach across Wales, the Welsh Ministers may by regulations make provision for and in connection with the provision of pre-application services by a local planning authority or the Welsh Ministers.[16] Accordingly, the procedure may be applied to applications made in the first instance to the Welsh Ministers as well as to planning applications made in the ordinary course to the local planning authority. The regulations specify the circumstances in which pre-application services are to be provided, the nature of the services and publication of any advice provided. Under power granted by TCPA 1990, section 61Z2, regulations also require the keeping of records of pre-application services and the publication of a statement setting out the range of available services. 12.11

The purpose is for the local planning authority to assist a person in making an application and it provides a means for an applicant, if he wishes, to ascertain the initial view of the local planning authority in a structured manner rather than rely on the previous informal arrangements. 12.12

The relevant Regulations[17] apply to all applications for planning permission made to a local planning authority except those for development already carried out.[18] An applicant may request the services in writing, giving the required details and paying the appropriate fee and this is then a valid request for pre-application services which the local planning authority must acknowledge as soon as is reasonably practicable.[19] The local planning authority must then provide the pre-application services within twenty-one days.[20] 12.13

In the case of householder applications, the services are the provision of information about the relevant planning history of the land, any material development plan provisions and supplementary planning guidance and anything else considered material by the authority. The authority must also provide an initial assessment of 12.14

[12] DMP(W)O, art. 2E. A substantive response for these purposes is defined in the article.

[13] DMP(W)O, art. 2(1), as amended.

[14] DMP(W)O, art. 2F, which also sets out what the report must contain.

[15] See DMP(W)O, arts 8(1)(ba) and 22(3)(ba).

[16] TCPA 1990, s. 61Z1.

[17] The Town and Country Planning (Pre-Application Services) (Wales) Regulations 2016 (SI 2016 No. 61).

[18] Regulation 4.

[19] Regulation 5.

[20] Regulations 5(4) and 6(3).

the proposed development.[21] In the case of all other development the authority must in addition provide information on any section 106 obligation likely to be required, on any likely Community Infrastructure Levy and details of anything that would be required for a planning application to be valid.[22]

PLANNING APPLICATION PROCEDURE

12.15 The procedure for the planning application itself generally is in accordance with the Town and Country Planning (Development Management Procedure) (Wales) Order 2012.[23] This applies to applications for planning permission and therefore to full and outline applications and applications under TCPA 1990, sections 73 and 73A, although containing some variations of detail regarding each: these are noted here where appropriate. There are also provisions regarding appeals and applications made under a planning condition, which have been dealt with above.[24] The Order details how an application for approval of reserved matters is made and this has been considered above.[25]

12.16 Article 5 of the Order requires an application for planning permission to be made on the form published by Welsh Ministers[26] and be accompanied by prescribed plans and drawings, except in the case of applications further to TCPA 1990, sections 73 and 73A. It must give the particulars specified in the form, except that where it is an application for outline permission details of reserved matters need not be given.

12.17 A design and access statement must be submitted where required by article 7. The range of circumstances where a statement is required is now restricted and applies only to two categories of development. It does not apply to section 73 applications, to mining operations, a material change in use or to waste operations.[27] Subject to this it applies to major development, which has the same meaning as when considering the need for pre-application consultation.[28] It also applies to development in a conservation area or World Heritage Site if it is for more than one dwelling house or is for the provision of a building or buildings where the floor space created by the development is 100 square metres or more. Details of what the statement should contain is set out in the Order.

12.18 The local planning authority may require an application for planning permission to contain such information and be supported by such evidence as they think

[21] Regulation 7.

[22] Regulation 8.

[23] SI 2012 No. 801 as amended (see in particular SI 2016 No. 59), and see TCPA 1990, s. 62.

[24] See Chapter 11.

[25] See paras. 11.17–11.19, above, and art. 4.

[26] Form 1APP, see WGC 02/2012.

[27] DMP(W)O, art. 7(2).

[28] DMP(W)O, art. 7(1), and see art. 2 and above.

necessary[29] provided that it is not inconsistent with a development order.[30] The requirement for information must also be reasonable having regard, in particular, to the scale and nature of the development and applies only if it would be reasonable to think that the matter will be a material consideration in determining the application.[31] This power may be relied on at any stage before determination, and so applies during the decision-making process where an application has been accepted as valid, but in the case of major developments compliance will be necessary for acceptance of an application as valid.[32]

An applicant must give notice of the application to any owner or tenant of the land: the notice requirements are modified in the case of underground mineral workings.[33] The application must certify compliance with these provisions.[34] 12.19

Article 8 of the development order sets out what must be included in an application for planning permission. Use of the standard application form and provision of documents as listed in WGC 002/2012, Annex A1 would in practice meet the formal requirements and can be used as a checklist. This should then enable validation of the application by the authority, which is an essential part of the process. Introduction of the Community Infrastructure Levy means that additional information is needed to determine whether the charge is due and in what amount. The required ownership certificate is part of the standard application form. 12.20

Crown applications must be accompanied by a statement to that effect and the appropriate authorisation.[35] 12.21

FEES

On application, fees are payable dependent on the type of development in accordance with the Town and Country Planning (Fees for Applications, Deemed Applications and Site Visits) (Wales) Regulations 2015.[36] 12.22

Payment of any fee required is a requirement of a valid application and an application is not treated as received until the fee is paid (along with satisfying the other requirements of a valid application – see below).[37] Where the correct fee has not been paid the local planning authority must, as soon as reasonably practicable, 12.23

[29] TCPA 1990, s. 62(3).

[30] TCPA 1990, s. 62(4).

[31] TCPA 1990, s. 62(4A), applicable in Wales by amendment made by Planning (Wales) Act 2015, s. 28.

[32] See below.

[33] DMP(W)O, art. 10.

[34] DMP(W)O, art. 11.

[35] DMP(W)O, art. 6.

[36] SI 2015 No. 1552, as amended by SI 2016 No. 62.

[37] DMP(W)O, art. 22(3), as amended.

serve a notice that the application is invalid and give details of the fee and how to pay it.[38]

ACCEPTANCE OF THE APPLICATION – VALIDATION

12.24 A local planning authority 'shall not entertain' an application for planning permission unless it complies with the provisions of a development order.[39] Article 22(3) of the 2012 Order defines what is a valid application and the authority must acknowledge it as soon as reasonably practicable.[40] TCPA 1990, section 327A also states that an application shall not be entertained if it fails to comply with a requirement of the Act or regulations made under it as to the form or content of an application or accompanying document.

12.25 An application will be valid if it complies with articles 5, 6, 7 or 9 of the 2012 Order (as applicable, all as noted above), includes a certificate of compliance with the notice requirements to owners and those with an interest in the land, and the relevant fee is paid. Where it is for major development and pre-application consultation is required, a certificate of compliance is necessary.[41] In addition, where the application is for major development and the local planning authority have published a list of their requirements on their website the application must include the particulars or evidence so required.[42] Applications for antennae for an electronic communications network require a declaration in accordance with article 9.

12.26 The process of accepting an application as valid is meant to identify clear omissions and is concerned with the adequacy of information rather than its quality. Once accepted, the application and supporting information is entered in the register of applications maintained by the authority.[43] However, this does not prevent the authority requiring further information and if an omission is subsequently found the authority may then treat the application as invalid and notify the applicant to that effect.[44]

12.27 If the local planning authority think that the application or accompanying information does not comply with the validation requirement under section 62, they must notify the applicant, identifying the requirement and setting out their reasons, and inform the applicant of the right to, and time limit for, appeal.[45] Validation requirement is defined as one where the effect of non-compliance is

[38] DMP(W)O, art. 8(3).
[39] TCPA 1990, s. 65(5).
[40] DMP(W)O, art. 8.
[41] DMP(W)O, art. 8(1)(ba).
[42] DMP(W)O, art. 8.
[43] TCPA 1990, s. 69.
[44] DMP(W)O, art. 8(3).
[45] TCPA 1990, s. 62ZA and art. 8(3A).

that the application cannot be entertained or the time for an appeal has not begun to run.[46]

Where the application is for a consent, agreement or approval required by a condition or limitation on a planning permission, notice must be given where the application does not comply with the planning permission by virtue of a failure to provide information or documents, giving details of the failure.[47] It must also inform the applicant of the right to, and time limit for, appeal.[48] 12.28

An applicant has a right of appeal to the Welsh Ministers where the local planning authority give an applicant notice under TCPA 1990, section 62ZA.[49] In the case of a notice of invalidity relating to a planning application, appeal lies on one or more of the grounds set out in TCPA 1990, section 62ZB(2). The grounds are that the application complies with the validation requirement, that the application is not one to which the requirement applies, that it is not a validation requirement, or that the requirement is for further information which does not meet the reasonableness test under section 62(4A). In the case of applications for a consent, agreement or approval the grounds are in section 62ZB(3) according to the terms of the notice and essentially are that the application provided all necessary documents or information necessary to comply or that the time for determining the application or to appeal has begun to run in any event. 12.29

Appeal against non-validation is by notice in accordance with article 24C. In all cases the time limit for an appeal is two weeks from the date of service of the notice of invalidity.[50] Details of the form and supporting documents required are prescribed.[51] In addition, on a section 78 appeal the Welsh Ministers may decide whether a requirement imposed under section 62 complies with subsection (4A) of that section unless this has previously been decided on an appeal under section 62ZB. To that extent, therefore, the previous law on the extent to which a decision may be challenged on appeal on grounds relating to validation remains relevant. 12.30

Validation appeals are considered by a person appointed[52] on the basis of written representations. The appellant's notice and accompanying documents constitute his representations and the local planning authority's notice of invalidity constitutes their representations.[53] 12.31

46 TCPA 1990, s. 327A.

47 TCPA 1990, s. 62ZA(4) and (5).

48 DMP(W)O, art. 23(5).

49 TCPA 1990, s. 62ZB.

50 DMP(W)O, art. 24C(2).

51 DMP(W)O, art. 24C.

52 TCPA 1990, s. 62ZC: the Welsh Ministers may direct that the appeal is instead to be determined by them, TCPA 1990, s. 62ZD.

53 See Town and Country Planning (Validation Appeals Procedure) (Wales) Regulations 2016, SI 2016 No. 60.

STEPS AFTER VALIDATION

12.32 Following validation the local planning authority must give notice and consult in accordance with articles 12–14 as below.

12.33 The authority must determine the application within eight weeks or sixteen weeks where an environmental impact statement is required[54] and the time period runs from the date of receipt of a valid application and fee. Where an application is amended the period is the later of four weeks from the date of amendment or twelve weeks from the date of receipt of the original application.[55]

12.34 However, the authority may decline to determine the application where within the preceding two years the Welsh Ministers have refused a similar application on call-in under section 77 or where it was an application originally made to the Welsh Ministers under sections 60D, 60F, 60M or 60O or on appeal.[56] Note that these provisions exclude the amendments introduced by PCPA 2004, section 43, which do not apply in Wales.[57] Accordingly, it is the original section which applies but amended to take account of the additional powers of the Welsh Ministers to determine applications following the new provisions inserted by the Planning (Wales) Act 2015. Similarly, the provisions regarding overlapping applications made to local planning authorities under TCPA 1990, section 70B are not yet in force in Wales.[58]

PUBLICITY AND CONSULTATION

12.35 Publicity by the local authority is governed by article 12 of the Town and Country Planning (Development Management Procedure) (Wales) Order 2012. Consultation by the authority is in accordance with articles 14, 15 and 15ZA. Schedule 4 lists the appropriate consultees. These requirements are in addition to the notice requirements to be carried out by applicants and to any pre-consultation procedure which is applicable – see above. The rules vary according to the nature of the development.

12.36 The local planning authority must publicise an EIA application, those not in accordance with the development plan and those affecting public rights of way by a site notice for not less than twenty-one days and by notice in a locally circulating newspaper. Applications for major development must be publicised by a site

[54] DMP(W)O, art. 22.

[55] DMP(W)O, art. 22(2aa), or twenty weeks in the case of an EIA application – see SI 2016 No. 971.

[56] TCPA 1990, s. 70A(1)–(3). The applications made directly to the Welsh Ministers under sections 62D, 62F, 62M and 62O are themselves in force only insofar as relating to developments of national significance. The references to optional applications to the Welsh Ministers are not operative.

[57] See the amended TCPA 1990, section 70A, which extends the power to decline to refusals of similar applications by the local planning authority which have not been appealed.

[58] Except for TCPA 1990, s. 70B(4A) and (4B) although these apply only to planning authorities in England.

notice or by notice on any adjoining owner or occupier and in a locally circulating newspaper.

A section 73 application, except where it is for EIA development or affects rights of way, in which case the position above will apply, must be publicised by a site notice and in such other manner as the local planning authority consider appropriate. Any other application must be publicised by a site notice or notice to any adjoining owner or occupier.[59] Where the authority maintains a website for applications, information for each of these types of development must be publicised there.[60] 12.37

On call-in under section 77, the authority must inform the Welsh Ministers that the requirements have been satisfied and if they have not the obligations on the planning authority continue.[61] Account must be taken of representations duly made within twenty-one days of such notices.[62] Forms of notice are in Schedule 3 to the Order. Notice of referral to the Welsh Ministers must be given by the authority to the applicant.[63] 12.38

Consultation is governed by article 14[64] of and Schedule 4 to the Order. Again, section 73 applications have particular rules which will apply in place of the article 14 rules and are referred to below after the general provisions. Before granting planning permission for development which, in its opinion, falls within a category set out in the Table in Schedule 4, a local planning authority must consult the authority, body or person mentioned in relation to that category. This Schedule describes numerous types of development and identifies the relevant consultee. For example, where development is likely to affect the volume of traffic on a trunk road, the Welsh Ministers are consultees. Consultation does not apply where the authority, body or person mentioned is the local authority or, except where development has a risk of major accident,[65] has advised the authority that it does not wish to be consulted. In addition, the Welsh Ministers may give specific directions requiring consultation. 12.39

Unless already served with a copy of the application by the applicant, the authority must give notice to the consultee and must not determine the application until at least twenty-one days after the date on which relevant notice is given.[66] 12.40

In the case of section 73 applications, other than for EIA development,[67] the local planning authority may consult anyone within the Table in Schedule 4. The 12.41

[59] DMP(W)O, art. 12(2)–(5), as amended by SI 2016 No. 59.

[60] DMP(W)O, art. 12(7).

[61] DMP(W)O, art. 12(8) and (9).

[62] DMP(W)O, art. 21.

[63] DMP(W)O, art. 13.

[64] As amended by SI 2015 No. 1330, art. 6.

[65] See DMP(W)O, Sch. 4, para. (x).

[66] DMP(W)O, art. 14(4)(b), as amended.

[67] Unlike publicity, consultation requirements make no exclusion for applications affecting public rights of way.

authority must not determine the application for at least twenty-one days from the date of notice to the consultee or earlier service on him by the applicant.[68]

12.42 Where consultation is within either of the provisions above there is a duty on the consultee to respond[69] and a substantive response must be given within twenty-one days of the local planning authority's notice to him or, if earlier, service on him of the application by the applicant.[70] Any representations received from such a consultee must be take into account by the local planning authority in determining the application.[71]

12.43 Where an application relates to land in the area of a community council the council may request the local planning authority to notify it of any application or alteration to an application.[72] This applies equally to applications for the approval of reserved matters. On receipt of notification of an application covered by the request, the community council must say if it wishes to make representations and the representations in response must be made within fourteen days. Any representations made must be taken into account.[73]

12.44 Consultation with other bodies may be advised by policy or guidance although the body is not a statutory consultee for the particular development. Non-statutory consultees could include, for example, water and sewerage authorities, local health boards and archaeological trusts. The Welsh Government Information Report of September 2011, although noting that it may not be authoritative given that it pre-dates the Town and Country Planning (General Development Management) Order 2012, remains of value for information on non-statutory consultation.

12.45 In dealing with an application the local planning authority shall have regard to the provisions of the development plan so far as material and to any other material considerations[74] and this may include considerations relating to the use of the Welsh language so far as material.[75] The authority may grant planning permission for development which is not in accordance with the development plan further to directions given by Welsh Ministers under the Order:[76] this does not, of course, derogate from the general power to grant permission where appropriate under the Act. There is a duty to take into account all representations made under the notice and consultation arrangement of the Order.[77]

[68] DMP(W)O, art. 15ZA(3).

[69] PCPA 2004, s. 54(2)(b).

[70] DMP(W)O, art. 15A, which defines what constitutes a substantive response.

[71] DMP(W)O, arts 14(5) and 15ZA(4).

[72] TCPA 1990, Sch. 1A.

[73] DMP(W)O, art. 16.

[74] TCPA 1990, s. 70(2)(a) and (c).

[75] TCPA 1990, s. 70(2)(aa).

[76] DMP(W)O, art. 20.

[77] DMP(W)O, art. 21.

The authority may grant the application unconditionally or subject to conditions or may refuse it.[78] This is subject to the provision that all permissions must have time limits. An outline permission is subject to a condition that the approval of reserved matters must be made within three years and development begun within the later of five years from the grant of outline permission or two years of the final approval or such other periods as may be specified.[79] Full planning permission is subject to a condition that development shall be begun within five years or such other period as is specified.[80] 12.46

In the case of major development,[81] when the development granted by the permission is begun, notice must be given to the local planning authority and displayed at all times while the development is being carried out, in accordance with TCPA 1990, section 71ZB.[82] 12.47

PLANNING COMMITTEES AND DELEGATION

The mode of determining the application within the local planning authority is subject to the general powers of delegation under the Local Government Act 1972 and the particular rules in TCPA 1990, sections 319ZA–391ZD, inserted by section 39 of the Planning (Wales) Act 2015. 12.48

These were referred to in Chapter 4. The provisions confer power to make regulations regarding the exercise of functions by local planning authorities, in particular regarding the size and composition of committees and the extent to which decisions are by committees or officers. To date no regulations have been made. 12.49

It is of course necessary to follow prescribed standards of conduct and it should be noted that the governance provisions of the Localism Act 2011, section 26 and Schedule 4 and the provisions on standards do not apply to Welsh local authorities. The Conduct of Members (Model Code of Conduct) (Wales) Order 2008[83] contains a mandatory code in accordance with the Local Government Act 2000, section 50(2). 12.50

The publicity required for information relating to a decision generally is subject to the provisions of the Local Government Act 1972, section 100F, as amended by the Local Government (Access to Information) (Variation) (Wales) Order 2007.[84] This provides for relevant documents to be available for inspection by members of the council rather than the public. Public access may be via the public discussion at 12.51

[78] TCPA 1990, s. 70(1).

[79] TCPA 1990, ss. 92 and 91(4)(g).

[80] TCPA 1990, s. 91.

[81] See DMP(W)O, art. 2 and above.

[82] DMP(W)O, art. 24B.

[83] SI 2008 No. 788.

[84] SI 2007 No. 969.

the meeting or by reliance on section 100B, by which the report is to be available, or section 100D, referring to background papers.

THE DECISION NOTICE

12.52 A development order may include provisions as to the form of the decision notice.[85] It provides for the notice to specify any plans or other documents in accordance with which the development is to be carried out[86] and the permission will be deemed to be subject to a condition that it is so to be carried out.[87]

12.53 Where an application for planning permission or for approval of reserved matters is either granted subject to conditions or is refused, the notice must state clearly and precisely the full reasons for the refusal or for any condition imposed, specifying all policies and proposals in the development plan which are relevant to the decision.[88] The requirement does not extend to an approval as such and the difference between the two requirements may be significant if there is a legal challenge to a decision based on the adequacy of reasons.

12.54 Where the Welsh Ministers have given a direction restricting the grant of permission for the development or where the Welsh Ministers or a United Kingdom government department have expressed the view that the permission should not be granted (either wholly or in part) or should be granted subject to conditions, details of the direction or of the view expressed must also be given.[89]

12.55 The decision must be accompanied by a notification in the terms (or substantially in the terms) set out in Schedule 5: this refers to rights of appeal.[90]

12.56 Finally, where the applicant for planning permission has submitted an environmental statement and permission is granted, the notice must include a statement that environmental information has been taken into consideration by the authority.[91]

CROWN DEVELOPMENT

12.57 Particular provisions apply to planning permission for development by the Crown where the application is urgent. In addition, procedure may be modified where giving evidence in public at an inquiry has national security or defence implications and these are most likely to arise in Crown applications. These were introduced

85 TCPA 1990, s. 71ZA.

86 TCPA 1990, s. 71ZA(2).

87 TCPA 1990, s. 71ZA(3).

88 DMP(W)O, art. 24(1)(a).

89 DMP(W)O, art. 24(1)(b).

90 DMP(W)O, art. 24(1)(c).

91 DMP(W)O, art. 24(2).

on termination of the former Crown immunity by amendments introduced by PCPA 2004 and advice is in the Memorandum attached to the Welsh Assembly Government letter of 7 June 2006, 'Crown Application of the Planning Acts'.

TCPA 1990, section 292A simply says that TCPA 1990 applies to the Crown. 12.58
Pre-existing subordinate planning legislation was extended to the Crown by the Town and Country Planning (Application of Subordinate Legislation to the Crown) Order 2006.[92]

In addition, there are extended permitted development rights for the Crown 12.59
and specific enforcement requirements.

Crown land is any land in which there is a Crown interest or an interest of 12.60
the Duchy of Lancaster or Cornwall.[93] Applications will be by the relevant Crown or Government body (e.g. Crown Estate or government department) and such a body will be an appropriate authority within the definition in TCPA 1990, section 293(2) when making an application for planning permission. It should perhaps be noted that the functions regarding Crown land were transferred by the Transfer of Functions Order 1999 and are devolved matters, subject to those functions which are exercisable concurrently with the Secretary of State and save only that any dispute as to who is the appropriate authority remains to be determined by the Treasury under section 293(3) as this was excepted from transfer.

Where an appropriate authority certifies that the development is of national 12.61
importance and that it is necessary to carry it out as a matter of urgency, it may make the application for permission to the Welsh Ministers instead of an application under Part III of TCPA 1990.[94] A notice of such an application must be published in a newspaper[95] and must be in accordance with the relevant regulations and give the grounds for making the application.[96] The regulations in question are the Town and Country Planning (Development Management Procedure) (Wales) Order 2012, article 6 of which requires the application to be accompanied by a statement that it relates to Crown land and any written authorisation to the applicant from the appropriate authority.

The Welsh Ministers are to publicise the application and carry out consulta- 12.62
tion.[97] This is subject to restriction where national security is at issue. Consequential changes to the Inquiry Procedure Rules for urgent applications are in Part 2 of the Schedule to the Town and Country Planning (Inquiries Procedure) (Wales) Rules 2003.[98]

The Welsh Ministers may give a direction under TCPA 1990, section 321 12.63
which restricts publication and the extent of public disclosure where evidence

[92] SI 2006 No. 1282.

[93] TCPA 1990, s. 293.

[94] TCPA 1990, s293A, as amended by Planning (Wales) Act 2015, Sch. 4, para. 17(2).

[95] TCPA 1990, s. 293A(3).

[96] TCPA 1990, s. 293A(4).

[97] TCPA 1990, s. 293A and art. 15 of the 2012 Order.

[98] SI 2003 No. 1266.

relates to matters of national security or measures taken to protect the security of any premises or property. Further detail is in the Planning (National Security Directions and Appointed Representatives) (Wales) Regulations 2006[99] and relevant powers are exercised by the Counsel General where the matter in respect of which the local inquiry is held relates to Wales.[100] These apply to applications generally and to urgent Crown applications and the power to issue a direction can also be exercised by the Secretary of State.[101]

12.64 Consequential changes to the Inquiry Procedure Rules for restricting public evidence of information and for urgent applications are in Part 1 of the Schedule to the Town and Country Planning (Inquiries Procedure) (Wales) Rules 2003. Persons objecting to the making of a direction may be represented by a special advocate appointed by the Counsel General to make representations on that issue. If a direction is made a special advocate, being a different person from any appointed at the direction stage, is appointed to represent those excluded from access to the protected information.

12.65 Additional permitted development rights are granted to the Crown in respect of operational land by Parts 34–36 of the Town and Country Planning (General Permitted Development Order) 1995[102] and for all Crown land by Parts 37 and 38. Specific amendments were also made to the Town and Country Planning (Use Classes) Order 1987,[103] adding class CA2 so as to include certain defined secure institutions and adding law courts in class D1.

12.66 The specific enforcement provisions relating to the Crown are dealt with in Chapter 18.

LOCAL PLANNING AUTHORITY DEVELOPMENT

12.67 Development by or on the land of a local planning authority requires planning permission and the authority may grant itself permission. The provisions are, however, modified in certain respects by the Town and Country Planning General Regulations 1992,[104] regulations 2–11. In particular, permission granted to a local planning authority, except where the application is specifically made jointly with another developer, is for the benefit of the authority only and does not run with the land on transfer[105] and sections 70A (power to decline application), 78 and 79 (appeals) do not apply to applications by an interested local planning authority.[106]

99 SI 2006 No. 1387.

100 TCPA 1990, s. 321B.

101 See National Assembly for Wales (Transfer of Functions) Order 1999 (SI 1999 No. 672), Sch. 1.

102 SI 1995 No. 418.

103 SI 1987 No. 764.

104 SI 1992 No. 1492: see reg. 3.

105 Regulation 9.

106 Regulation 5.

TCPA 1990, section 316 accordingly provides that the control of development by the Act applies to land of an interested planning authority and to the development of any land by an interested planning authority either alone or jointly with others subject to any regulations made under the Act.[107] The power to make regulations is in addition to power under TCPA 1990, sections 319ZA–319ZC referred to above.[108] 12.68

An interested planning authority is defined as one which has any of the functions of a local planning authority in relation to the land in question and the Welsh Ministers.[109] 12.69

An application by an interested planning authority or for development of its land is to be determined by the local planning authority themselves.[110] This does not apply where the application is called-in by the Welsh Ministers[111] nor where it relates to its land but the authority is not itself intending to develop the land alone or jointly and, if it were not its land, it would be decided by another body.[112] It will therefore determine applications made by itself or in which it is interested but regulation 10 states that it is not to be decided by a committee, sub-committee or officer involved in the management of the land or buildings in question. 12.70

In addition to the modifications above, regulation 5 excludes the application of TCPA 1990, sections 94 and 95 (completion notices) and the certain other provisions are modified to the extent specified in Schedule 1 to the Regulations. For completeness it should be noted that, where government authorisation is required for development by a local authority or National Park Authority, that authorisation may direct that planning permission is deemed to be granted.[113] Authorisation in this context includes confirmation of compulsory purchase orders and so is of particular significance. 12.71

[107] TCPA 1990 s316

[108] TCPA 1990, s. 316(3), as amended by Planning (Wales) Act 2015.

[109] TCPA 1990, s. 316(6). Although the definition extends to the Welsh Ministers, the section is specifically excluded in its application to them in connection with certain powers to make regulations; and the particular matters in the text following do not apply to the Welsh Minsters as an interested planning authority.

[110] General Regulations 1992, reg. 3.

[111] Regulation 3.

[112] Regulation 4.

[113] TCPA 1990, s. 90(1).

Chapter 13

Planning Permission – Decision-making Framework

INTRODUCTION

In deciding whether to grant or refuse an application for planning permission the decision-maker must act in accordance with the development plan and any other material consideration.[1] What is material depends on the particular facts although in certain instances statute expressly provides that regard must be paid to some specific consideration. These statutes may apply generally or apply only to particular kinds of development. The requirements form the context or framework within which an individual decision is to be made. 13.1

This chapter looks at the general statutory framework before looking at the key provisions regarding the development plan and material considerations and then looks at certain general issues of what is or is not material. 13.2

STATUTORY CONTEXT AND PARTICULAR DUTIES

It has been seen above that the local planning authority have power to require information and this applies before and after accepting an application as valid and requests should obviously be made to enable the authority to discharge their statutory duties. The matters now considered concern specific duties imposed on the authority in the way they must approach their decision-making. These are of course additional to those legal duties placed on local authorities generally in carrying out their functions, for example, by the Equality Act 2010,[2] and planning decisions may often affect human rights and engage one or more of the Articles of the European Convention on Human Rights. 13.3

First, TCPA 1990, section 70(3) states that the general power to grant or refuse planning permission is subject to sections 66, 67, 72 and 73 of the Planning (Listed Buildings and Conservation Areas) Act 1990 and to section 15 of the Health Services Act 1976. The latter states that a permission relating to controlled premises as defined in that Act is of no effect unless accompanied by an authorisation for the works. The former Act is of more wide-ranging effect and is considered more fully in Chapter 24. The two central provisions of present concern are section 66 for listed buildings and section 72 for conservation areas. 13.4

1 TCPA 1990, s. 70 and PCPA 2004, s. 38(6).

2 An authority is under a duty to draw applicants' attention to their statutory obligations in this respect.

13.5 In considering whether to grant planning permission for development which affects a listed building or its setting, the local planning authority or the Welsh Ministers shall have special regard to the desirability of preserving the building or its setting or any features of special architectural or historic interest which it possesses.[3] In the exercise of any functions under the planning Acts with respect to any land or other buildings in a conservation area special attention shall be paid to the desirability of preserving or enhancing the character or appearance of that area.[4] Control over demolition in conservation areas is provided by sections 74–76: this was considered as appropriate in connection with demolition as development in Chapter 6.

13.6 *East Northamptonshire District Council and others v Secretary of State for Communities and Local Government and another*[5] held that the effect of section 66(1) was that decision-makers should give 'considerable importance and weight' to the desirability of preserving the setting of listed buildings when carrying out the balancing exercise required by law. It is therefore an example of those instances where the weight to be attached to an issue is prescribed and a failure to attach the prescribed weight would be an error enabling a court to set aside the decision; it is not simply a matter of judgment for the planning authority.

13.7 However, this should not be read as departing from the established principles concerning the adequacy of reasons and what needs to be established on any legal challenge. This was considered by the Court of Appeal in the *East Northamptonshire* case[6] and the judgment of Sullivan LJ was later referred to in *Mordue v Secretary of State for Communities and Local Government*,[7] where Sales LJ said:

> I do not consider that, read in the context of the judgment as a whole, Sullivan LJ and the court intended to state an approach to the reasons required to be given by a decision-maker dealing with a case involving application of section 66(1) of the Listed Buildings Act which was at variance from, and more demanding than, that stated in *Save Britain's Heritage* and *South Bucks DC v Porter (No. 2)*. Sullivan LJ's comments in para. [29] were made in the context of a decision letter which positively gave the impression that the inspector had *not* given the requisite considerable weight to the desirability of preserving the setting of the relevant listed buildings, where as a result it would have required a positive statement by the inspector referring to the proper test under section 66(1) to dispel that impression. In my judgment, the relevant standard to be applied in assessing the adequacy of the reasons given in the present case is indeed the usual approach explained in *Save Britain's Heritage* and *South Bucks DC v Porter (No. 2)*.

[3] Listed Buildings Act 1990, s. 66(1).

[4] Listed Buildings Act 1990, s. 72.

[5] [2014] EWCA Civ 137, [2015] 1 WLR 45. The reasoning referred to cases on s. 72 and there is no difference between the two sections in this respect.

[6] Above.

[7] [2015] EWCA Civ 1243, [2016] 1 WLR 2682 at para. 26.

Next there are a number of requirements which can be placed under the heading of nature conservation or protection. Some apply where there is a particular statutory designation but others are framed more generally. Section 71A of TCPA 1990 gives general power for the Welsh Ministers by regulation to make provision about the likely environmental effects of the proposed development before planning permission is granted. 13.8

Planning permission shall not be granted in the case of EIA development unless the planning authority or Welsh Ministers have first taken the defined environmental information into account and they shall state in the decision that they have done so.[8] Development is EIA development if the applicant submits an environmental statement for the development or the planning authority adopts a screening opinion to that effect.[9] Notice of a decision granting approval in such cases must comply with article 24(2) of the Town and Country Planning (General Management Procedure) (Wales) Order 2012. 13.9

Further, in exercising planning functions a local planning authority will be a competent authority in accordance with the Habitats Regulations.[10] As such it must have regard to the requirements of the Habitats Directive so far as they may be affected by those functions. This applies where development may affect a European Protected Site or a Protected Species.[11] In this respect the planning functions are distinct from the licensing functions of the Welsh Ministers, exercised through Natural Resources Wales, and the proper extent of the planning authority role was considered by the Supreme Court in *Morge v Hampshire CC*,[12] where Lord Brown said: 13.10

> the only obligation under regulation 3(4) [on the local planning authority] is . . . to 'have regard to the requirements of the Habitats Directive so far as [those requirements] may be affected by' their decision whether or not to grant a planning permission. I cannot see why a planning permission . . . should not ordinarily be granted save only in cases where the planning committee conclude that the proposed development would both (a) be likely to offend article 12(1) and (b) be unlikely to be licensed pursuant to the derogation powers.

Accordingly, the primary responsibility is on the licensing authority (NRW) and, if that body is satisfied, the local planning authority are entitled to presume compliance. 13.11

[8] The Town and Country Planning (Environmental Impact Assessment) (Wales) Regulations 2016 (SI 2016 No. 58), reg. 3. EIA development is defined in reg. 2.

[9] Regulation 4.

[10] Conservation of Species and Habitats Regulations 2010 (SI 2010 No. 490), reg. 3(4) and see Habitats Directive 92/43/EEC.

[11] E.g. Special Protection Areas, Special Areas of Conservation: potential or candidate sites are similarly protected and, as a matter of policy, Ramsar sites should be similarly treated: see PPW.

[12] [2011] UKSC 2, [2011] 1 WLR 268 at para. 29.

13.12 Where development is in or affects a National Park there is a duty to have regard to the purposes specified in section 5 of the National Parks and Access to the Countryside Act 1949, namely conserving and enhancing the natural beauty, wildlife and cultural heritage of the area and promoting opportunities for the understanding and enjoyment of the special qualities of those areas by the public.[13]

13.13 In exercising or performing any functions in relation to, or so as to affect, land in an area of outstanding natural beauty ('AONB'), a relevant authority shall have regard to the purpose of conserving and enhancing the natural beauty of the area of outstanding natural beauty.[14]

13.14 Where the exercise of its functions is likely to affect the flora, fauna or geological or physiographical features by reason of which a site of special scientific interest is of special interest, there is a duty to take reasonable steps, consistent with the proper exercise of the authority's functions, to further the conservation and enhancement of those features.[15]

13.15 More generally, a public authority must seek to maintain and enhance biodiversity in the exercise of its functions in relation to Wales and in so doing promote the resilience of ecosystems so far as consistent with the proper exercise of those functions.[16] A public body includes the Welsh Ministers,[17] a local planning authority and statutory undertakers. This duty where applicable replaces that in section 40(1) of the Natural Environment and Rural Communities Act 2006.

13.16 Section 11 of the Countryside Act 1968 requires all public bodies (including LPAs), in the exercise of their functions relating to land, to have regard to the desirability of conserving the natural beauty and amenity of the countryside, and natural beauty includes the conservation of its flora, fauna and geological and physiographical features.

13.17 Section 28G of the Wildlife and Countryside Act 1981 places a duty on public authorities (including local planning authorities), in exercising their functions so far as this is likely to affect the flora, fauna or geological or physiographical features by reason of which a site of special scientific interest is of special interest, to take reasonable steps, consistent with the proper exercise of their functions, to further the conservation and enhancement of those features.

13.18 In respect of each of these, relevant policy is in PPW Chapter 5 and TAN 5. PPW[18] says that National Parks and AONBs are of equal status in terms of landscape and scenic beauty and both must be afforded the highest status of protection from inappropriate developments. In development plan policies and development

[13] National Parks and Access to the Countryside Act 1949, s. 11A.

[14] Countryside and Rights of Way Act 2000, s. 85. A strategic planning panel has been added as a public body for this purpose: see s. 85(2)(d).

[15] Wildlife and Countryside Act 1981, s. 28G.

[16] Environment (Wales) Act 2016, s. 6 and see amendments to Natural Environment and Rural Communities Act 2006 by s. 27(2) and Sch. 2.

[17] The Welsh Ministers have additional responsibilities under the Act.

[18] At para. 5.3.6.

management decisions National Parks and AONBs must be treated as of equivalent status. In National Parks and AONBs, development plan policies and development management decisions should give great weight to conserving and enhancing the natural beauty, wildlife and cultural heritage of these areas.

Finally, in this respect, local planning authorities, in exercising planning functions, including determining planning applications, must have regard to specified provisions of the Waste Framework Directive.[19] 13.19

The third group of measures comprises two matters applying to the planning functions of a local authority and Welsh Ministers as a result of the Planning (Wales) Act 2015. 13.20

Section 2 of the Planning (Wales) Act 2015 applies to the Welsh Ministers, local planning authorities and any other public body in exercising any function in relation to the National Development Framework, a strategic development plan or a local development plan and any function under Part 3 of TCPA 1990 in relation to an application for planning permission. They must exercise that function as part of carrying out sustainable development in accordance with the Well-being of Future Generations (Wales) Act 2015 for the purpose of ensuring that the development and use of land contribute to improving the economic, social, environmental and cultural well-being of Wales. In so doing, the decision-maker must take into account guidance issued by the Welsh Ministers including relevant guidance issued under section 14 of the latter Act. It is expressly provided that this does not alter whether regard is to be had to any particular consideration under section 70 or the weight to be given to any such consideration.[20] 13.21

Clarification of the relationship between the Planning (Wales) Act 2015 and the Well-being of Future Generations (Wales) Act 2015 is contained in a set of three prospectus documents issued in January 2015. The intent is that the six well-being goals established by the latter Act inform and provide structure and that the sustainability appraisals required for all development plans will test plan policies against the sustainability objectives so that all planning decisions are taken in the context of sustainable development. 13.22

Section 31 of the Planning (Wales) Act 2015 then deals with individual applications for development, inserting a new paragraph (aa) into section 70(2) of TCPA 1990, requiring the local planning authority to have regard to any considerations relating to the use of the Welsh language so far as material to the application. Section 31(4) recites that the amendments do not alter whether regard is to be had to any particular consideration under section 70(2) or the weight to be given to any consideration. 13.23

[19] See the Waste (England and Wales) Regulations 2011 (SI 2011 No. 988), Part 6, as amended by the Waste (England and Wales) (Amendment) Regulations 2012 (SI 2012 No. 1889), the Waste (England and Wales) (Amendment) Regulations 2014 (SI 2014 No. 656) and the Waste (Miscellaneous Provisions) (Wales) Regulations 2011 (SI 2011 No. 971).

[20] Section 2(5).

TOWN AND COUNTRY PLANNING ACT 1990, SECTION 70 AND PLANNING AND COMPULSORY PURCHASE ACT 2004, SECTION 38(6)

13.24 Section 70(2) says that in dealing with an application for planning permission the local planning authority shall have regard to the provisions of the development plan, so far as material to the application, and to any other material considerations. In addition, PCPA 2004, section 38(6) provides that if regard is to be had to the development plan for the purpose of any determination to be made under the planning Acts, the determination must be made in accordance with the plan unless material considerations indicate otherwise.[21]

13.25 As has been seen above, the definition of development plan in section 38(4) will comprise the National Development Framework, any strategic development plan and the local development plan and so it may be necessary to have regard to three such plans. Where there is more than one development plan, the Planning and Compulsory Purchase Act 2008, section 38(5) provides that any conflict between plans is to be resolved in favour of the most recent plan.

13.26 The proper approach to the combined effect of sections 70 and 38(6) was considered by the House of Lords in *City of Edinburgh Council v Secretary of State for Scotland*[22] and the following passage from the speech of Lord Hope was cited in *R (Cala Homes (South) Ltd v Secretary of State for Communities and Local Government*[23] (the statutory references have been updated in the passage for clarity):

> It requires to be emphasised, however, that the matter is nevertheless still one of judgment, and that this judgment is to be exercised by the decision-taker. The development plan does not, even with the benefit of section [38(6)] have absolute authority. The planning authority is not obliged, to adopt Lord Guest's words in *Simpson v Edinburgh Corporation, 1960 S.C. 313* at p 318, 'slavishly to adhere to' it. It is at liberty to depart from the development plan if material considerations indicate otherwise. No doubt the enhanced status of the development plan will ensure that in most cases decisions about the control of development will be taken in accordance with what it has laid down. But some of its provisions may become outdated as national policies change, or circumstances may have occurred which show that they are no longer relevant. In such a case the decision where the balance lies between its provisions on the one hand and other material considerations on the other which favour the development, or which

[21] Note that article 20 of the Town and Country Planning (General Development Management) (Wales) Order 2012 states that a local planning authority may in such cases and subject to such conditions as may be prescribed by directions given by the Welsh Ministers under this Order grant permission for development which does not accord with the provisions of the development plan in force in the area in which the land to which the application relates is situated.

[22] [1997] 1 WLR 1447.

[23] [2011] EWCA Civ 639.

> may provide more up-to-date guidance as to the tests which must be satisfied will continue, as before, to be a matter for the planning authority.

The proper application of section 38(6) and section 70 was considered again by the Court of Appeal in *R (West Berkshire DC) v Secretary of State for Communities and Local Government*[24] on a challenge by the local planning authority to the lawfulness of planning policy on affordable housing made in a Written Ministerial Statement. Having referred to the *City of Edinburgh Council* case the court said: 13.27

> First, while the development plan is under section 38(6) the starting-point for the decision-maker (and in that sense there is a 'presumption' that it is to be followed), it is not the law that greater weight is to be attached to it than to other considerations: . . . Secondly, policy may overtake a development plan ('outdated and superseded by more recent guidance'). Both considerations tend to show that no systematic primacy is to be accorded to the development plan.

In the event, the court held that the terms of the policy statement did not countermand or frustrate the effective operation of section 38(6) or section 70(2) and was lawful. 13.28

The established uncontroversial general principles had earlier been summarised by Hickinbottom J in *Bayliss v Secretary of State for Communities and Local Government*[25] (they were accepted as accurate on appeal by the Court of Appeal).[26] They can usefully be repeated in full. Having referred to the two statutory provisions above, he said: 13.29

> That requires the proposed development to be in accordance with the development plan looked at as a whole, rather than with every policy in the plan, which may well pull in different directions and some of which may be more relevant to a particular application than others (*R v Rochdale Metropolitan Borough Council ex parte Milne (2001) 81 P. & C.R. 27* at [44]–[50]). Therefore, section 38(6) raises a presumption that planning decisions will be taken in accordance with the development plan, looked at as a whole; but that presumption is rebuttable by other material considerations.
>
> 'Material considerations' in this context include statements of central government policy set out in Planning Guidance Notes and Statements and, since March 2012, the National Planning Policy Framework ('the NPPF') which replaced many earlier policy documents. Any local guidance is also a material

24 [2016] EWCA Civ 441 at para. 20.

25 [2013] EWHC 1612 (Admin) at para. 3.

26 See [2014] EWCA Civ 347 at para. 9. The decision was on a s. 288 application and allowance must be made for the fact that the challenge may equally be to a local planning authority decision, not that of an inspector, and that the national guidance must be read as that of the Welsh Ministers not the NPPF.

> consideration. Whilst he must take into account all material considerations, the weight to be given to such considerations is exclusively a matter of planning judgment for the decision-maker, who is entitled to give a material consideration whatever weight, if any, he considers appropriate, subject only to his decision not being irrational in the sense of Wednesbury unreasonable (*Tesco Stores Ltd v Secretary of State for the Environment* at page 780F–G). The courts have consequently left such decisions to be taken by the appointed decision-maker on the basis of guidance promulgated by the Secretary of State (see, e.g., *R (Alconbury Developments Ltd) v Secretary of State for the Environment, Transport and the Regions [2001] UKHL 23* at [60] per Lord Nolan, [129] per Lord Hoffmann and [159] per Lord Clyde).
>
> However, the relevant policy may include guidance as to the weight to be given to a particular factor. Where it does so, weight is still a matter for the decision-maker; but he must take into account any policy guidance as to weight, which is itself a material consideration.
>
> A decision-maker must interpret national policy properly. The true interpretation of such policy is a matter of law for the court (*Tesco Stores Ltd v Dundee City Council [2012] UKSC 13*). Where a decision-maker has misunderstood or misapplied a plan or policy, that may found a challenge to his decision, if it is material, i.e. if his decision would or might have been different if he had properly understood and applied the guidance.

13.30 In *R (Hayes) v Wychavon DC*,[27] Lang J also confirmed:

> it is for the courts to decide whether a matter is a relevant consideration; but it is for the decision-maker to attribute to the relevant considerations such weight as he thinks fit. The courts will not interfere unless the decision-maker acts unreasonably in the *Wednesbury* sense (*Tesco Stores Ltd v Secretary of State for the Environment and others [1995] 1 W.L.R. 759*).

13.31 Where there is no adopted development plan, or its policies are considered outdated or superseded or there are no relevant policies, PPW states[28] that the decision should be taken in accordance with the key principles and key policy objectives of sustainable development in the planning system.

13.32 Where a plan is in the course of preparation it may be a material consideration, the weight to be attached to it depending on the stage reached in the adoption process but also the underlying evidence and policy background. It should be noted that on an appeal, if the development plan is adopted after evidence has been concluded, for example after the inquiry has been held, but before the decision has been given, the requirement will be to decide in accordance with the newly adopted development plan since decisions should be up to date when made.

27 [2014] EWHC 1987 (Admin) at para. 12.

28 At para. 4.2.4.

Where the development plan is still an emerging document it may be argued that a decision on an application should not be made until details of the adopted plan are known. This is the question of prematurity and is referred to in PPW at paragraphs 2.14.2–2.14.4 as follows: 13.33

> Refusing planning permission on grounds of prematurity will not usually be justified except in cases where a development proposal goes to the heart of a plan and is individually or cumulatively so significant, that to grant permission would predetermine decisions about the scale, location or phasing of new development which ought properly to be taken in the LDP context. Where there is a phasing policy in the plan that is critical to the plan structure there may be circumstances in which it is necessary to refuse planning permission on grounds of prematurity if the policy is to have effect. The stage which a plan has reached will also be an important factor and a refusal on prematurity grounds will seldom be justified where a plan is at the pre-deposit plan preparation stage, with no early prospect of reaching deposit, because of the lengthy delay which this would impose in determining the future use of the land in question.
>
> Whether planning permission should be refused on grounds of prematurity requires careful judgement and the local planning authority will need to indicate clearly how the grant of permission for the development concerned would prejudice the outcome of the LDP process.
>
> It is for the decision-maker, in the first instance, to determine through monitoring and review of the development plan whether policies in an adopted LDP are outdated for the purposes of determining a planning application. Where this is the case, local planning authorities should give the plan decreasing weight in favour of other material considerations such as national planning policy, including the presumption in favour of sustainable development (see section 4.2).

MEANING OF 'MATERIAL CONSIDERATIONS'

To be material the matter must be one where there is a real possibility that it might affect the ultimate conclusion.[29] In *R (Kides) v South Cambridgeshire District Council*,[30] Jonathan Parker LJ said: 13.34

> In my judgment a consideration is 'material', in this context, if it is relevant to the question whether the application should be granted or refused; that is to say if it is a factor which, when placed in the decision-maker's scales, would tip the balance to some extent, one way or the other. In other words, it must be a

[29] See *Bolton MBC v Secretary of State for the Environment* (1990) 61 P & CR 343 per Glidewell LJ, *Tesco Stores Ltd v Dundee City Council* [2012] UKSC 13 and *R (Watson) v Richmond upon Thames LBC* [2013] EWCA Civ 513 at para. 40.

[30] [2002] EWCA Civ 1370 at para. 121.

> factor which has some weight in the decision-making process, although plainly it may not be determinative. The test must, of course, be an objective one in the sense that the choice of material considerations must be a rational one, and the considerations chosen must be rationally related to land use issues.

13.35 In *R (Holder) v Gedling BC*[31] Kaye LJ observed that 'the disputed matters on this appeal are not rendered material considerations because the statute has expressly declared them to be so. Their materiality, if established, is based on their potential to have a legitimate bearing on the ultimate decision.' It must also be borne in mind that to say that an issue is potentially relevant, so that there is no error of law in referring to it is one thing, but it is quite another thing to say that an issue is necessarily relevant so that failure to refer to it is an error of law.[32]

13.36 Finally in this regard, reference should be made to the often-cited seven principles identified by Glidewell LJ in *Bolton MBC v Secretary of State for the Environment*[33] in the following terms:

> 1. The expressions used in the authorities that the decision maker has failed to take into account a matter which is relevant, which is the formulation for instance in Forbes J.'s judgment in *Seddon Properties*, or that he has failed to take into consideration matters which he ought to take into account, which was the way that Lord Greene put it in *Wednesbury* and Lord Denning in *Ashbridge Investments*, have the same meaning.
>
> 2. The decision maker ought to take into account a matter which might cause him to reach a different conclusion to that which he would reach if he did not take it into account. Such a matter is relevant to his decision-making process. By the verb 'might,' I mean where there is a real possibility that he would reach a different conclusion if he did take that consideration into account.
>
> 3. If a matter is trivial or of small importance in relation to the particular decision, then it follows that if it were taken into account there would be a real possibility that it would make no difference to the decision and thus it is not a matter which the decision maker ought to take into account.
>
> 4. . . . there is clearly a distinction between matters which a decision maker is obliged by statute to take into account and those where the obligation to take into account is to be implied from the nature of the decision and of the matter in question . . .
>
> 5. If the validity of the decision is challenged on the ground that the decision maker failed to take into account a matter in the second category, it is for the

31 [2014] EWCA Civ 599 at para. 7.

32 See e.g. in the context of alternative sites, Carnwath LJ in *Derbyshire Dales District Council v Secretary of State for Communities and Local Government* [2010] 1 P & CR 19.

33 (1991) 61 P & CR 343 at pp. 352–3.

judge to decide whether it was a matter which the decision maker should have taken into account.

6. If the judge concludes that the matter was 'fundamental to the decision,' or that it is clear that there is a real possibility that the consideration of the matter would have made a difference to the decision, he is thus enabled to hold that the decision was not validly made. But if the judge is uncertain whether the matter would have had this effect or was of such importance in the decision-making process, then he does not have before him the material necessary for him to conclude that the decision was invalid.

7. (Though it does not arise in the circumstances of this case.) Even if the judge has concluded that he could hold that the decision is invalid, in exceptional circumstances he is entitled nevertheless, in the exercise of his discretion, not to grant any relief.

What is material depends upon the particular facts but certain general guidance may be given. 13.37

LAND USE AND PERSONAL CHARACTERISTICS

First, to be material a matter must relate to use of the land. Planning permission runs with the land unless otherwise provided.[34] Personal characteristics of applicants are therefore not generally relevant. 13.38

Westminster City Council v Great Portland Estates Plc[35] concerned specific industrial protection policies in the City of Westminster district plan and held that the test of what was a material consideration was whether it served a planning purpose which related to the character of the use of the land and that on their true construction the industrial policies of the plan were concerned not with the protection of existing occupiers but with a genuine planning purpose, the continuation of industrial use important to the character and functioning of the city. However, Lord Scarman[36] pointed out: 13.39

> Personal circumstances of an occupier, personal hardship, the difficulties of businesses which are of value to the character of a community are not to be ignored in the administration of planning control. It would be inhuman pedantry to exclude from the control of our environment the human factor. The human factor is always present, of course, indirectly as the background to the consideration of the character of land use. It can, however, and sometimes should, be given direct effect as an exceptional or special circumstance. But such circumstances,

[34] TCPA 1990, s. 75.

[35] [1985] AC 661.

[36] At p. 670.

> when they arise, fall to be considered not as a general rule but as exceptions to a general rule to be met in special cases. If a planning authority is to give effect to them, a specific case has to be made and the planning authority must give reasons for accepting it. It follows that, though the existence of such cases may be mentioned in a plan, this will only be necessary where it is prudent to emphasise that, notwithstanding the general policy, exceptions cannot be wholly excluded from consideration in the administration of planning control.

13.40 This is applicable both to personal circumstances of the applicant (for example, gypsy status)[37] and to protection of the personal interests of persons affected by the development, as in *Westminster City Council v Portland Estates* itself. Generally, it is only where an individual or personal interest is considered as an element of the public interest that it is properly taken into account and here the rationale will be that wider general principle.

LOCAL CONCERN

13.41 One particular issue is the relevance of an expression of local concern over the impact of a development on the area. In *West Midlands Probation Committee v Secretary of State for the Environment, Transport and the Regions*,[38] Pill LJ stated the following propositions as having emerged from the authorities:

> (1) The impact of a proposed development upon the use of and activities upon neighbouring land may be a material consideration. (2) In considering the impact, regard may be had to the use to which the neighbouring land is put. (3) Justified public concern in the locality about emanations from land as a result of its proposed development may be a material consideration.

13.42 The point in question was the expressed concern of local residents relating to possible behaviour on and emanating from a bail hostel and it was held that:

> fear and concern felt by occupants of neighbouring land is as real in this case as in one involving polluting discharges and as relevant to their reasonable use of the land. The pattern of behaviour was such as could properly be said to arise from the use of the land as a bail and probation hostel and did not arise merely because of the identity of the particular occupier or of particular residents.[39]

[37] See e.g. *South Buckinghamshire DC v Porter (No. 1)* [2003] UKHL 26 at para. 31.

[38] (1997) 76 P & CR 589 at p. 597.

[39] (1997) 76 P & CR 589 at p. 597.

Referring to this in *Smith v First Secretary of State, Smith v Mid-Bedfordshire DC*,[40] Buxton LJ made clear that the 'fear and concern must be real, by which I would assume to be required that the fear and concern must have some reasonable basis, though falling short of requiring the feared outcome to be proved as inevitable or highly likely'. 13.43

FINANCIAL CONSIDERATIONS

Financial considerations may be material. This can arise in two different ways. First, the question may be whether considerations relating to financing the development itself are material, for example, what may be needed to enable the development to progress; secondly, the question may be one of planning gain, that is whether planning authorities are entitled to treat benefits secured by way of a requirement in or for the planning permission as a material consideration in deciding whether to grant planning permission. The second issue is best considered in the context of conditions, section 106 obligations and the Community Infrastructure Levy, and is dealt with in Chapters 15 and 16 below. Local financial considerations are not subject to any specific proviso as TCPA 1990, section 70(2)(b) is expressly excluded in Wales by section 70(2A). 13.44

The first issue was raised in *R v Westminster City Council, ex parte Monahan*.[41] The question was whether the local planning authority had been entitled, in deciding to grant planning permission for redevelopment of buildings including the Royal Opera House and the erection of offices, to balance the fact that the improvements to the opera house would not be financially viable if the permission for the offices were not granted against the fact that the office development was contrary to the development plan. Upholding the decision, it was held that since in reality financial constraints on the economic viability of desirable planning developments were unavoidable it would be unreal and contrary to common sense to exclude them from the range of considerations which might properly be regarded as material in determining planning applications. Provided that the ultimate determination of a planning application was based on planning grounds and not on some ulterior motive and was not irrational, financial considerations which fairly and reasonably related to the development were therefore capable of being material considerations which could be taken into account in reaching that determination. 13.45

CONSISTENCY

One of the purposes of development plan policies is to promote consistency and this should be reflected in the decision-making process. Decisions on other applications 13.46

[40] [2005] EWCA Civ 859 at para. 9.

[41] [1990] 1 QB 87.

are not binding but they can clearly be relevant and due account taken of them. The relevance of previous decisions may arise in the case of successive applications for the same site or for similar development on different sites.

13.47 In *North Wiltshire District Council v Secretary of State for the Environment and Clover*,[42] Mann LJ said:

> It was not disputed in argument that a previous appeal decision is capable of being a material consideration. The proposition is in my judgment indisputable. One important reason why previous decisions are capable of being material is that like cases should be decided in a like manner so that there is consistency in the appellate process. Consistency is self-evidently important to both developers and development control authorities. But it is also important for the purpose of securing public confidence in the operation of the development control system. I do not suggest and it would be wrong to do so, that like cases *must* be decided alike. An inspector must always exercise his own judgment. He is therefore free upon consideration to disagree with the judgment of another but before doing so he ought to have regard to the importance of consistency and to give his reasons for departure from the previous decision.

13.48 If an earlier decision is material then a failure to explain why it has not been followed is likely to result in the later decision being set aside on legal challenge. In *Dunster Properties Ltd v First Secretary of State*,[43] the Court of Appeal quashed a decision, Lloyd LJ saying that the inspector:

> did not adequately perform his obligation to give reasons for this decision in respect of his refusal to follow the basis of the earlier appeal decision which was a material consideration. In this respect it seems to me that by declining to comment, other than to refer to his own reasons already expressed, . . . [he] appears not to have faced up to his duty to have regard to the previous decision so far as it related to the point of principle as a material consideration.

13.49 There is no legal test that there must be a very good planning reason for departing from an earlier decision and ultimately the weight to be attached to a previous decision which is in point is a matter of planning judgment for the decision-maker.[44] In a recent case,[45] Lindblom J put it this way:

[42] (1992) 65 P & CR 137 at p. 145.

[43] [2007] EWCA Civ 236 at para. 23.

[44] See *St Albans City and District Council v Secretary of State for Communities and Local Government* [2015] EWHC 655 (Admin) considering *R (King's Cross Railway Land Group) v Camden LBC* [2007] EWHC 1515 (Admin).

[45] *Butterworth v Secretary of State for Communities and Local Government* [2015] EWHC 108 (Admin) at para. 33.

> the inspector had to face the 'practical test' posed by Mann LJ . . . in *North Wiltshire*,[46] namely whether, if she was to reject . . . [the Appellant's] proposal, she was necessarily agreeing or disagreeing with some critical aspect of the two previous appeal decisions. If she did not think that the principle of consistency applied in this case, she had to say so and make clear why this was her view. If, on the other hand, she accepted that the principle of consistency did apply but found herself unable to agree with the approach taken by the other inspectors, or if she agreed with their approach but was able to distinguish . . . [this] appeal from the other cases on its facts, again she had to say so, and explain why.

PRECEDENT EFFECT

It follows from the role of consistency above that concern may be raised that granting permission on an application would create a precedent for future development. It is clear that this concern can be a material consideration – see *Collis Radio Ltd v Secretary of State for the Environment*[47] and the more recent case of *R (Holder) v Gedling BC*.[48] 13.50

CONDITIONS AND SECTION 106 OBLIGATIONS

Planning permission should not be refused if the concern can be resolved by the imposition of a condition so the availability of a suitable condition is a material consideration. The tests to determine if a condition is appropriate are considered in Chapter 14. 13.51

In addition, the House of Lords held in *Tesco Stores v Secretary of State for the Environment*[49] that a planning obligation offered under section 106 of the Act of 1990 by a developer was a material consideration to which regard should be had under TCPA 1990, section 70(2) if it was relevant to the development. This must now be considered against the exclusion where the development is one in respect of which the authority intends funding to be by a Community Infrastructure Levy – see Chapter 16, below. 13.52

In each case there must be a connection with the development but the nature of the link required will depend on the contribution and matters relating to conditions may not be the same as for section 106 obligations. Further consideration of this aspect is in later chapters. 13.53

[46] See above.

[47] (1975) 29 P & CR 390.

[48] [2014] EWCA Civ 599.

[49] [1995] 1 WLR 759.

NATIONAL POLICY

13.54 National policy will in appropriate cases be a material consideration and its significance can increase where there is no directly applicable up-to-date development plan policy. Prior to adoption of the National Development Framework, PPW remains more widely pertinent and at the end of each Chapter it identifies national development plan policies relevant to each topic area and points out that local development plan policies should not need to repeat them.

'FALL-BACK'

13.55 In *R (Zurich Assurance Ltd (t/a Threadneedle Property Investments)) v North Lincolnshire Council*[50] Hickinbottom J accepted that the 'fall-back position' can be a material consideration so that a planning committee should compare the development for which planning permission is sought with what the applicants could do with the land and premises on the basis of the planning position as it stands without that planning permission. It was considered more comprehensively in *Gambone v Secretary of State for Communities and Local Government*,[51] where it was described as no more than an approach to material considerations where there may be an opportunity to use land in a particular way. Similarly, in *Carroll v Secretary of State for Communities and Local Government*[52] it was treated as part of the factual context where alternative proposals are raised. Both pointed to the distinction between the materiality of a consideration and the weight to be attached to it, and, in the former, Dove J[53] said:

> fall-back . . . involves a two-stage approach. The first stage of that approach is to decide whether or not the way in which the land may be developed is a matter which amounts to a material consideration. It will amount to a material consideration on the authorities, in my view, where there is a greater than theoretical possibility that that development might take place . . .
>
> Once the question of whether or not it is material to the decision has been concluded, applying that threshold of theoretical possibility, the question which then arises for the decision-maker is as to what weight should be attached to it. The weight which might be attached to it will vary materially from case to case and will be particularly fact sensitive.

50 [2012] EWHC 3708 (Admin) at para. 65.

51 [2014] EWHC 952 (Admin) at paras 25–6.

52 [2016] EWHC 2462 (Admin).

53 [2014] EWHC 952 (Admin) at para. 25.

Chapter 14

Conditions

INTRODUCTION

14.1 The local planning authority have general power under TCPA 1990, section 70 to grant an application unconditionally or subject to conditions or may refuse it. There is also express power to impose conditions conferred by section 72 of the Act. This is subject to the proviso that all permissions are subject to time limits. The Welsh Ministers have the same powers where the development is of national significance, is called-in and on appeal.[1]

14.2 Notwithstanding the generality of the powers, the courts have established key principles for what conditions may validly be imposed. Equally, the courts have laid down the proper approach to the construction of conditions. The constraints on and practical issues as to the use and drafting of conditions are the subject of detailed guidance given by WGC 016/2014 and this includes information on time limiting conditions and model conditions. It does not deal with mineral workings or the majority of waste management developments and for these reference should be made to MTANs and TAN21 Waste.

14.3 This chapter deals with the statutory context first and then looks at the tests for validity developed by the courts. The tests in government guidance are then identified before finally considering the proper approach to the construction of conditions.

POWER TO IMPOSE CONDITIONS – STATUTORY PROVISIONS

14.4 The local planning authority may grant an application unconditionally or subject to conditions or may refuse it.[2] Without prejudice to this, TCPA 1990, section 72(1) provides that conditions may be imposed on the grant of planning permission for regulating the development or use of any land under the control of the applicant (whether or not it is land in respect of which the application was made) or requiring the carrying out of works on any such land, so far as appears to the local planning authority to be expedient for the purposes of or in connection with the development authorised by the permission.

[1] See Developments of National Significance (Application of Enactments) (Wales) Order 2016 (SI 2016 No. 54), TCPA 1990, s. 77(4) and s. 79(4) respectively. References below to the local planning authority should accordingly be treated as referring also to the Welsh Ministers where appropriate.

[2] TCPA 1990, s. 70(1).

14.5 The sections apply to applications made to the local planning authority and planning permission means permission under Part III of TCPA 1990[3] and thus includes applications under sections 73 and 73A. The two sections regarding conditions are expressly applied to decisions of the Welsh Ministers on call-in[4] and to decisions on appeal.[5] Planning permission granted on an appeal against an enforcement notice is included as the permission is granted under Part III.[6] Operation of these sections where the application is made in the first instance to the Welsh Ministers under TCPA 1990, section 62D or 62M will depend on the terms of a development order made under TCPA 1990, section 75A.[7] In addition, it has been held that conditions may be imposed on applications for approval of reserved matters and on approval of other matters required by a condition.[8]

14.6 Conditions may require the removal of any buildings or works authorised by the permission, or the discontinuance of any use of land so authorised, at the end of a specified period, and the carrying out of any works required for the reinstatement of land at the end of that period. These are formally known as permissions granted for a limited period,[9] although in practice referred to as temporary permissions.

14.7 On an application to develop land without complying with conditions previously attached, permission may be granted subject to different conditions.[10]

14.8 These powers must be read subject to the requirements for time limits contained in sections 91 and 92 of TCPA 1990. Full planning permission is subject to a condition that development shall be begun within five years or such other period as is specified.[11] Outline permission shall be granted subject to a condition that application for approval of any reserved matter must be made not later than the expiration of three years from the date of grant of the permission[12] and that the development must be begun no later than the expiration of five years from the date of the grant of outline planning permission or, if later, the expiration of two years from the final approval of the reserved matters or, in the case of approval on different dates, the final approval of the last such matter to be approved.[13]

14.9 Conditions relating to mineral development are governed by Schedule 5 to TCPA 1990, which includes provision that section 72(2) is subject to the specific terms of paragraph 1(6)(a) of the Schedule regarding duration.

[3] TCPA 1990, s. 336(1).

[4] See TCPA 1990, s. 77(4).

[5] See TCPA 1990, s. 79(4).

[6] Section 179(3).

[7] See Planning (Wales) Act 2015, Sch. 4, para. 7.

[8] See Chapter 11.

[9] TCPA 1990, s. 72(2).

[10] TCPA 1990, s. 73(2).

[11] TCPA 1990, s. 91. Section 91 (3ZA) and (3ZB) contain further provisions on calculating the duration of a permission.

[12] TCPA 1990, s. 92(2)(a).

[13] TCPA 1990, s. 92(2)(c).

Planning permission is deemed to be subject to a condition that the development is to be carried out in accordance with the plans or documents which are specified for that purpose in the decision notice.[14] 14.10

In addition, where planning permission is granted for the erection of a building, the grant may specify the purposes for which the building may be used and if no purpose is so specified the permission is construed as including the use of the building for the purpose for which it is designed.[15] The particular use may be specified by a condition but otherwise the description of the development or the design use will determine the scope of the permission. Later development by a material change in use would require planning permission but is not a breach of condition and enforcement action cannot be taken on that basis.[16] 14.11

In *Wall v Winchester City Council*[17] it was said if a change from a permitted use to some other use is alleged in an enforcement notice: 14.12

> then in the absence of any condition limiting the use of the site to the permitted use, the question in every case will be: has the alleged change of use taken place and, if so, is it a material change of use for planning purposes? If the answer to either of these questions is 'no' there will have been no development, so planning permission will not be required. If the answer to both these questions is 'yes' there will have been development and planning permission will be required.

The Court of Appeal also confirmed[18] that the essential distinction was that a permission defines what can be done and a condition what cannot be done, what is forbidden. 14.13

It will be recalled that the written notice of the decision must state 'clearly and precisely the full reasons' for a refusal or for the imposition of any conditions.[19] 14.14

SCOPE OF THE POWER AND ABILITY TO SECURE COMPLIANCE

The powers in section 72 are additional express powers and do not prevent imposition of a condition which is lawful under section 70. 14.15

[14] TCPA 1990, s. 71ZA(3).

[15] TCPA 1990, s. 75(2) and (3).

[16] On the non-enforceability in the absence of an express condition, in a case relating to temporary or permanent use, see *R (I'm Your Man Ltd) v Secretary of State for the Environment, Transport and Regions* [1999] 77 P & CR 251 and *Wall v Winchester City Council* [2015] EWCA Civ 563.

[17] [2015] EWCA Civ 563 at para. 22.

[18] See para. 22.

[19] Town and Country Planning (Development Management Procedure) (Wales) Order 2012 (SI 2012 No. 801), art. 24.

14.16 In *Davenport v Hammersmith and Fulham LBC*[20] the court was concerned with the combined effect of the two sections and it was held that section 72 confers an express power to impose certain kinds of condition in relation to land under the control of the applicant. It does not, however, purport to cut down the generality of the power in section 70(1) as to the imposition of conditions and the reason why a condition requiring the carrying out of works on land not within the control of the applicant is invalid is the operation of a broader principle, namely that one cannot lawfully impose a condition requiring a person to secure a result that it does not lie wholly within his power to secure. Richards J said: 'There is nothing to show that a condition relating to land outside the application site and outside the control of the applicant is invalid unless that condition requires the carrying out of works on such land or is otherwise one with which the applicant could not be assured of securing compliance'.[21]

14.17 Grampian conditions have long been recognised as a proper means of controlling development where otherwise compliance with a condition might be outside an applicant's control. *Grampian RC v City of Aberdeen*[22] decided that there was a crucial distinction between a positive condition attached to planning permission that the applicant bring about some circumstance and a negative condition that the development should not commence until an event had occurred in that the latter was enforceable. The permission might therefore be conditional upon an event which the applicant does not control, nevertheless it is within his control not to take certain developments steps if and until some eventuality has occurred.

14.18 Such conditions may therefore relate to land outside the application or ownership of the applicant. Whether or not such a condition is unreasonable depends on the circumstances of the case. In *British Railways Board v Secretary of State for the Environment*,[23] Lord Keith said:

> The function of the planning authority was to decide whether or not the proposed development is desirable in the public interest. The answer to that question is not to be affected by the consideration that the owner of the land is determined not to allow the development so that permission for it, if granted, would not have reasonable prospects of being implemented. That did not mean that the planning authority, if it decided that the proposed development was in the public interest, was absolutely disentitled from taking into account the improbability of permission for it, if granted, being implemented. For example, if there were a competition between two alternative sites for a desirable development, difficulties of bringing about implementation on one site which were not present in relation to the other might very properly lead to the refusal of

20 (1999) 78 P & CR 421.

21 At p. 428. See, however, the further reasoning where the issue is the validity of an enforcement notice served on a person on the basis that he has control of the land.

22 1984 SC (HL) 58.

23 [1994] JPL 32 at p. 38.

planning permission for the site affected by the difficulties and the grant of it for the other. But there was no absolute rule that the existence of difficulties, even if apparently insuperable, had to necessarily lead to refusal of planning permission for a desirable development. A would be developer might be faced with difficulties of many different kinds, in the way of site assembly or securing the discharge of restrictive covenants. If he considered that it was in his interests to secure planning permission notwithstanding the existence of such difficulties, it was not for the planning authority to refuse it simply on their view of how serious the difficulties were.

VALIDITY GENERALLY

In addition to these statutory constraints, the courts have developed general principles controlling the use of conditions. 14.19

In *Pyx Granite Co. Ltd* v. *Ministry of Housing and Local Government*,[24] Lord Denning said: 14.20

> Although the planning authorities are given very wide powers to impose 'such conditions as they think fit,' nevertheless the law says that those conditions, to be valid, must fairly and reasonably relate to the permitted development. The planning authority are not at liberty to use their powers for an ulterior object, however desirable that object may seem to them to be in the public interest.

This statement was approved by the House of Lords in *Fawcett Properties Ltd v Buckingham County Council*.[25] 14.21

The principles were summarised in *Newbury DC v Secretary of State for the Environment*[26] where the House of Lords said (*per curiam*) that for conditions attached to the grant of a planning permission to be *intra vires* and valid the conditions imposed must be for a planning purpose and not for any ulterior one and they must fairly and reasonably relate to the development permitted. Also they must not be so unreasonable that no reasonable planning authority could have imposed them. 14.22

These three criteria have been cited in numerous authorities where the validity of conditions has arisen and establish the legal framework for the power to attach conditions. 14.23

[24] [1958] 1 QB 554 at p. 572.

[25] [1961] AC 636.

[26] [1981] AC 578.

PLANNING PURPOSE

14.24 The first criterion may appear straightforward and the need for planning decisions to be made on grounds relating to land use has been considered when looking at material considerations above. However, it may cause difficulties in marginal cases and it depends on the context. In *R v Bristol CC, ex parte Anderson*,[27] the court upheld a condition for a management scheme including a restriction on occupants keeping motor vehicles on a development of student residences. Laws LJ said that the welfare and support of students, viewed at large, may be said to be a social or moral concept, hardly having the appearance of a planning consideration or a consideration relevant to the development of land. However, the words have to be viewed in their context and he upheld the condition as the maintenance of support for students and the promotion of their welfare is objectively linked to the effects of this development upon neighbours and other interests.

'RELATED TO THE DEVELOPMENT'

14.25 It must be stressed that it is the specific development in question which must be considered under the second test: the fact that a condition may relate to the character of use of the land does not of itself mean that it is related to the particular development on that land.

14.26 In *Newbury* (above) the issue concerned an application for a material change of use of existing buildings where a condition was imposed for the removal of the buildings after a period of time. This was accepted as a proper planning purpose but the Secretary of State had found that as it related to long-term policy for industrial use in rural areas rather than the change of use as such it was not related to the particular development and the court found that in so doing he had not misdirected himself.

REASONABLENESS

14.27 The test here is the familiar one of unreasonableness in the *Wednesbury* sense, being so unreasonable that no reasonable person would have imposed the condition. In considering how this element of the principles has been interpreted, however, care must be taken to reflect changes in legislation and policy over time, in particular when considering planning gain.[28] Planning gain was considered in *R (Derwent Holdings Ltd) v Trafford BC*[29] and is specifically considered later in this text.

[27] (1999) 79 P & CR 358.

[28] See comments in *Tesco Stores Ltd v Secretary of State for the Environment* [1995] 1 WLR 759.

[29] [2011] EWCA Civ 832 – see Chapter 15.

Conditions cannot be imposed where the effect is to grant permission for something substantially different from that applied for. This is concerned with conditions cutting down or reducing the development and follows the decision in *Bernard Wheatcroft v Secretary of State for the Environment*.[30] These principles do not apply in the context of permissions and conditions arising on an enforcement appeal.[31] 14.28

IMPOSING CONDITIONS AND DEFERRAL FOR LATER APPROVAL

Although, as has been seen, matters may by condition be left for subsequent approval, it is important to deal with the key elements of the permission at the application stage and not simply defer them for decision under a condition, in particular as it may be necessary to ensure proper consultation. *Smith v Secretary of State for the Environment*[32] establishes that on an appeal the inspector cannot abdicate responsibility for key matters forming part of the consent by imposing a condition reserving approval of these to the local authority. Sedley LJ said that it is only if what is left over is so defined that it cannot modify or disrupt the terms on which planning permission is being granted that the handover of responsibility to the local planning authority is permissible. 14.29

Referring to this decision and the authorities there relied on, Elias J made clear in *R (Hereford Waste Watchers Ltd) v Herefordshire CC*[33] that: 14.30

> if the planning authority consider that a process or activity will have significant environmental effects then the [Environmental Statement] needs to include the detailed information identified in Sch.4 to the regulations.[34] It cannot leave the matter to be covered by conditions at a later stage. Even if that might otherwise be a satisfactory way of dealing with the problem, it frustrates the democratic purpose of the consultation process . . . However . . . it is a matter for the authority itself whether or not the development will have significant effects, and its decision on the point can only be challenged on traditional public law grounds.

[30] (1980) 43 P & CR 233.

[31] See *Ioannou v Secretary of State for the Environment* [2014] EWCA Civ 1432.

[32] [2003] EWCA Civ 262.

[33] [2005] EWHC 191 (Admin) at para. 25.

[34] At the relevant date the Town and Country Planning (Environmental Impact Assessment) (England and Wales) Regulations 1999 (SI 1999 No. 293).

14.31 Whether the matter may be left for subsequent approval depends upon the precise issue in question and its legal framework. In *R (Hayes) v Wychavon DC*,[35] Lang J said:

> Frequently, a condition requires an applicant to submit further details which have to be approved by the planning authority before the condition can be fulfilled. In this case, details relating to drainage and the disposal of manure have to be submitted and approved by the Defendant (this has not yet been done). There is no provision, either in TCPA 1990 or the Circular [11/95[36]], for a further stage of consultation with neighbours and objectors before the planning authority grants its approval for a scheme submitted pursuant to a condition. Nor is it the practice of planning authorities to consult generally at this stage. This is because the subject-matter of the conditions will usually have been consulted upon at the stage of the initial application. Here, the Claimant and other neighbours have already expressed their concerns on drainage and disposal of manure. It is the responsibility of the planning authority to determine the detail of the drainage and manure disposal schemes proposed by the applicant, having due regard to any concerns earlier expressed. I find no support in the statute, the Circular or the common law requirements of fairness for the Claimant's submission that it was unlawful for the Defendant to impose conditions for post-permission approval of details relating to drainage or manure disposal on the ground that the Claimant was thereby deprived of an opportunity to comment on the details proposed.

14.32 This must now be read in the light of TCPA 1990, section 100A, which provides for decisions on applications under a permission to take account of responses if the local planning authority do consult a person consulted on the original application, although not obliging an authority to consult.[37]

GUIDANCE

14.33 Guidance is given against the above legal background and serves to illustrate some of the practical issues that may arise. WGC 016/2014 is recent and cites relevant authority. It gives quite extensive guidance and the text below is only a brief summary of the key elements. The general aim is that conditions can enable many development proposals to proceed where it would otherwise be necessary to refuse planning permission.[38]

14.34 WGC 016/2014 states that conditions should not be imposed if there is no reasonable prospect of the required action being performed within the time limit

[35] [2014] EWHC 1987 (Admin) at para. 15.

[36] Equivalent to former WOC 35/95 on Use of Conditions; see now WGC 016/2014.

[37] See esp. paras. 11.22–11.23, above.

[38] See e.g. PPW 3.5.1.

imposed by the permission. On the identical wording in the predecessor circular it had been made clear not that there should be reasonable prospects of benefit accruing, but reasonable prospects of the action in question being performed within the specified time limit.[39]

The circular then refers to the formal tests of validity established by the courts, and states that the Welsh Government considers that conditions must satisfy six tests. The six are that the condition is necessary, relevant to planning, relevant to the development to be permitted, enforceable, precise and reasonable in all other respects. Some of these are not strictly issues of validity but go to the merits or desirability of a condition on granting permission and the circular is particularly useful in focusing on the wording of conditions and the practical effect of compliance. 14.35

The circular continues, saying that in considering if a condition is necessary the authority should ask if permission would have to be refused if the condition were not imposed. If it would not, then careful justification is required. A condition should be no wider than is required to achieve the specific objective and should not duplicate controls in other legislation without a good planning reason. It is said that conditions requiring the completion of the whole of the development should not normally be imposed. 14.36

Duplication of measures required by other enforcement regimes may also suggest that a condition is not relevant to planning and in this context it is said that a condition can however be justified, where another system of control exists, if the alternative control cannot be relied upon to secure planning objectives, or to prevent development being carried out in a way which would likely give rise to onerous requirements under other powers at a later stage. 14.37

Relevance also has a wider context and if the objective is to secure a purpose of the authority other than planning it should not be imposed. So a condition that first occupants be drawn from the authority's housing list furthers the objectives of the authority as housing authority and not planning purposes.[40] Clearly, given the social and economic objectives in development plans the distinction may not always be clear-cut and care needs to be taken in framing any condition. 14.38

A condition must also be justified as relating fairly and reasonably to the particular development. Accordingly, a condition may be imposed where the development creates an identified issue or has an additional impact on a particular feature. 14.39

The fourth requirement is that a condition should not be imposed if it cannot be enforced. This requires the authority to consider the way in which it would exercise its powers to issue an enforcement notice under TCPA 1990, section 172 or a breach of condition notice under section 187A. It has already been noted that a condition must be one which the applicant has the ability to comply with but it is equally necessary for the authority to be able to take effective action on any breach. 14.40

[39] See *R (Blyth Valley BC) v First Secretary of State* [2006] EWHC 3619 (Admin).

[40] This is based on *R v Hillingdon LBC, ex parte Royco Homes Ltd* [1974] 1 QB 720, although the actual decision was expressed in terms of reasonableness.

It will be necessary to consider the precise nature and timing of a requirement but difficulty of monitoring or detection is not decisive provided that what is or is not a breach can be properly distinguished.

14.41 The circular refers to the need for care where pre-commencement conditions and other conditions are both imposed. This stems from the *Whitley* principle,[41] namely that if the operations contravene the conditions on the planning permission they cannot properly be described as commencing the development authorised by the permission. If they do not comply with the permission they constitute a breach of planning control and for planning purposes will be unauthorised and thus unlawful.

14.42 In *Handoll v Warner Goodman & Streat*,[42] the Court of Appeal held that if a development does not comply in a material respect, or to a material extent, with the permission granted, an occupancy condition attached to that permission cannot apply to the unauthorised development. Accordingly, where the development itself is unlawful otherwise valid conditions on the permission are unenforceable. It follows that particular care must be taken to consider the interrelationship between conditions.

14.43 The requirement of precision simply means that the applicant should know exactly what he must do to comply and when any requirement comes into effect. Vague conditions are to be avoided and clear objectives or criteria are necessary. Nevertheless, as a matter of law a condition is only void if it can be given no sensible or reasonable meaning[43] and a 'mere ambiguity' will not necessarily render the permission itself void for uncertainty.[44]

14.44 Finally, a condition must be reasonable. In this regard, attention should be paid to the extent to which a condition interferes with an applicant's human rights.

CONSTRUCTION OF CONDITIONS

14.45 The meaning of a condition is for the courts as issues of construction are matters of law. The court is not concerned with the wisdom or merits of the condition.[45]

14.46 In *Hulme v Secretary of State for Communities and Local Government*,[46] Elias LJ summarised certain key principles to be applied when construing a condition. In *Telford and Wrekin Council v Secretary of State for Communities and Local Government*,[47]

[41] See *FG Whitley & Sons Co. Ltd v Secretary of State for Wales* (1992) 64 P & CR 296; and see Chapter 7, above.

[42] (1994) 70 P & CR 627.

[43] See *Fawcett Properties v Buckingham CC* [1961] AC 636.

[44] *R (Midcounties Co-operative Ltd) v Wyre Forest DC* [2010] EWCA Civ 841.

[45] See *Fawcett* above, per Lord Jenkins and *R (St Edmundsbury Borough Council) v Secretary of State for Communities and Local Government* [2008] EWHC 1913 (Admin).

[46] [2011] EWCA Civ 638.

[47] [2013] EWHC 79 (Admin).

Beatson LJ was concerned with the precision needed for a valid condition[48] in the context of the Town and Country Planning (Use Classes) Order 1987 and set out nine propositions. Both decisions, insofar as they deal with the proper approach to interpretation, and the earlier decision in *Sevenoaks DC v First Secretary of State*,[49] must now be read subject to the Supreme Court decision in *Trump International Golf Club Scotland Ltd v Scottish Ministers*,[50] in particular the analysis of Lord Carnwath,[51] pointing out the dangers of creating the impression that planning conditions were subject to special rules.

The *Trump* case was concerned with the construction of the Electricity Act 1989 and the validity of a condition attached to a consent under that Act. It was stated that the cases under the planning legislation were not directly applicable[52] but in submissions reliance was placed on the three planning cases above and the proper approach to the interpretation of conditions in a planning permission and the extent to which, thereafter, there is scope for implication were reviewed. On the general principle of uncertainty the court observed that the condition contained a mechanism enabling compliance and would not be uncertain on established principles from *Fawcett*, and then turned to principles of interpretation of documents, including planning permissions. 14.47

The view that planning permissions were subject to a materially different process of interpretation from other legal documents was rejected: 'they do not require a completely different approach to their interpretation'.[53] However, the particular context is relevant and includes such facts as the impact on third parties and the potential for criminal proceedings. 14.48

As with other documents, the conditions must be read in the context of the document as a whole and the court should seek to give them a sensible meaning if at all possible,[54] while the general approach to uncertainty of *Fawcett* was approved. However, the previous statements regarding implication were not accepted. The issue of implication could only arise later if the conclusion on interpretation was that the document was intended to have a particular effect but the words were absent to achieve that.[55] Subject to that, both leading judgments, however, doubted that implication was excluded altogether.[56] The result is as Lord Hope said:[57] 14.49

[48] He referred to the relevant English Guidance but the need to be precise is equally identified in Welsh Government Guidance.

[49] [2004] EWHC 771 (Admin).

[50] [2015] UKSC 74.

[51] At paras 45–66.

[52] See paras 32 and 45.

[53] See para. 66.

[54] See para. 55.

[55] See para. 35.

[56] See paras 35 and 60.

[57] See para. 34.

> When the court is concerned with the interpretation of words in a condition in a public document . . . it asks itself what a reasonable reader would understand the words to mean when reading the condition in the context of the other conditions and of the consent as a whole. This is an objective exercise in which the court will have regard to the natural and ordinary meaning of the relevant words, the overall purpose of the consent, any other conditions which cast light on the purpose of the relevant words, and common sense. Whether the court may also look at other documents that are connected with the application for the consent or are referred to in the consent will depend on the circumstances of the case, in particular the wording of the document that it is interpreting. Other documents may be relevant if they are incorporated into the consent by reference . . . or there is an ambiguity in the consent, which can be resolved, for example, by considering the application for consent.

14.50 The status and effect of conditions attached to a planning permission granted for a limited period once that limited period has expired and the development has become immune from enforcement action by lapse of time was raised in *Avon Estates Ltd v Welsh Ministers*[58] where the issue, in the words of Elias J, was: 'Can other restrictive conditions on the planning permission, such as an occupancy condition, still be enforced?' At paragraph 28 he answered it, saying:

> it is very difficult to conceive of a condition on a temporary permission under section 72 which could sensibly relate to a development, once that development has ceased to be authorised by the permission. The time limit and restoration condition itself does not provide an example which goes beyond its own scope, since that condition is expressly and precisely provided for by section 72(1)(b). One cannot derive a general approval from that for conditions which bind the land once the development itself has ceased to be authorised and has become immune from enforcement action. Such enduring conditions would, to be lawful, still have to relate fairly and reasonably to the permitted development, which was and is to be seen as a temporary development. So although I would not wish to be categoric as to the impossibility of such enduring conditions, I do regard it as very unlikely that the statutory scheme allows for what can be described as a permanent condition on a temporary permission, other than the time limit condition itself.

EFFECT OF INVALIDITY

14.51 Where a condition is invalid it may be possible to sever it from the permission so that the permission as a whole is not invalid. This was examined by Lord Morris in

[58] [2011] EWCA Civ 553.

Kent CC v Kingsway Investment (Kent) Ltd,[59] where he said that an invalid condition could be severed if that did no violence to the remaining language and did not affect the substance of the grant of permission.

Equally, part only of a particular condition may be severed by deleting the offending words if the remainder of the condition is valid. The position here refers to the situation where permission is granted dependent upon whether the local planning authority later approve or agree and has become known as 'tailpieces' after the first instance decision of Ouseley J in *R (Midcounties Co-operative Limited) v Wyre Forest DC*.[60] This was relied on in *Hubert v Carmarthenshire CC*[61] where an 'unless later approved' provision referring to the dimensions of the blade of a wind turbine was severed as it could have led to the permission which had been subject to public debate and democratic decision-making being sidestepped. 14.52

In *Barnett v Secretary of State for Communities and Local Government*,[62] the Court of Appeal considered the effect of section 75(3) and held that permission to construct a new dwelling on non-residential land will carry with it permission to use the new building for residential purposes so that there is in a sense a built-in application for a change of use of land in such cases, and the extent of the land covered by the implicit permission for a change of use will normally be ascertained by reference to the site as defined on the site plan. However, it was held that this is not the situation where there is an existing dwelling and the proposal is merely to alter or to extend it. The curtilage already exists. There is not necessarily any new use of land involved nor any extension to the existing curtilage. Whether there is an extension to the existing curtilage in any given case will depend upon the documents in question. Whether any resulting planning permission grants consent for a larger area than before to be used for purposes ancillary to the dwelling house depends on looking at the application form and the drawings. 14.53

[59] [1971] AC 72 at p. 114.

[60] [2009] EWHC 964 (Admin).

[61] [2015] EWHC 2327 (Admin).

[62] [2009] EWCA Civ 476.

Chapter 15

Section 106 Obligations

INTRODUCTION

Planning obligations are governed by section 106 of TCPA 1990. Guidance is still contained in WOC 13/97, supplemented by PPW.[1] The circular should be read to take account of the Community Infrastructure Levy Regulations 2010,[2] which give statutory force to the tests in the earlier circular and provide against overlap between obligations and the levy. Detailed guidance taking account of the levy has been published by the Planning Officers Society for Wales under the title 'Section 106: Guidance on the use of planning obligations for Welsh Local Authorities'. 15.1

The power to make regulations regarding the Community Infrastructure Levy is not at the time of writing a devolved matter[3] and the Community Infrastructure Levy Regulations 2010, as amended, apply equally to Wales and England: the relationship between the levy and section 106 obligations is considered here, with the specific rules regarding the levy being considered in the next chapter. 15.2

In certain cases a concern can be met by either a condition or a section 106 obligation but tests for validity are not the same and section 106 obligations have a discrete area of operation. Either can provide for meeting a commitment in kind, that is by the provision of a facility, but policy is that planning difficulties should be overcome by condition rather than by a planning obligation.[4] 15.3

Where contribution is by payment of a sum of money an obligation will be appropriate but this should not overlap with payments under the Community Infrastructure Levy and the regulations and policy statements provide generally for contributions to be met by the levy where the matter is within the local planning authority published list of infrastructure. It has been held that although the local planning authority must administer and monitor implementation of an obligation, they are not empowered to charge the cost of this to the developer.[5] 15.4

[1] At para. 3.5.5.

[2] SI 2010 No. 948 ('CIL Regs').

[3] It will become so when the Wales Act 2017 is in force as the reserved matters in Sch. 7A, M3 do not refer to the levy: see Chapter 16, below.

[4] See e.g. WGC 016/2014 at para. 4.21.

[5] *Oxfordshire CC v Secretary of State for Communities and Local Government* [2015] EWHC 186 (Admin) at para. 45: this may be contrasted with CIL where express provision is made by CIL Regulations, reg. 61.

NATURE AND FORM OF SECTION 106 OBLIGATIONS

15.5 Any person interested in land may, by agreement or otherwise, enter into an obligation restricting the development or use of the land in any specified way, requiring specified operations or activities to be carried out in, on, under or over the land, requiring the land to be used in any specified way or requiring a sum or sums to be paid to the authority on a specified date or dates or periodically.[6]

15.6 Accordingly, section 106 obligations may be bilateral (or multilateral), where they are agreed by both the interested party (or parties) and the local authority, or unilateral which bind the interested party or parties but are not enforceable against the local authority.[7] In either case they are enforceable by the local planning authority and run with the land, binding successors in title.[8] They may be both positive, requiring something to be done, or negative, that is restrictive, as in the case of covenants affecting land. Whether by agreement or undertaking, they are termed planning obligations.

15.7 Where the obligation is entered in connection with an application or proposed application for development consent under the Planning Act 2008, the obligation is known as a development consent obligation:[9] development for these purposes refers to development for the purposes of the 2008 Act and the deed creating the obligation must state that it is a development consent obligation.[10]

15.8 The obligation may be unconditional or subject to conditions and any restriction may be indefinite or for a specified period.[11] Payment of a sum may be of a specified amount or an amount determined in accordance with the obligation and may require the payment of periodical sums, either indefinitely or for a specified period.[12] There is power to make regulations providing for the payment of any sums under the section.[13]

15.9 The obligation may provide that a person shall not be bound by it in respect of any period during which he no longer has an interest in the land[14] but subject to this it is enforceable by the authority identified in accordance with subsection (9)(d) against the person entering into the obligation and against any person deriving title from that person.[15] Enforcement includes action by injunction[16] and where

[6] TCPA 1990, s. 106(1).

[7] A person interested in the land may include, for example, the developer and the owner and also leaseholders and mortgagees.

[8] TCPA 1990, s. 106(3)(b).

[9] TCPA 1990, s. 106(14).

[10] TCPA 1990, s. 106(1A) and (9)(aa).

[11] TCPA 1990, s. 106(2)(a) and (b).

[12] TCPA 1990, s. 106(2)(c).

[13] TCPA 1990, s. 106(12).

[14] TCPA 1990, s. 106(4).

[15] TCPA 1990, s. 106(3) and (4).

[16] TCPA 1990, s. 106(5).

it is to carry out any operations in, on, under or over the land to which the obligation relates, that authority may, subject to giving not less than twenty-one days' notice, enter the land and carry out the operations and recover from the person or persons against whom the obligation is enforceable any expenses reasonably incurred by them in doing so.[17] Obstructing a person entering and carrying out the operations is an offence.[18]

As regards injunctive relief for a breach, in *Newham LBC v Ali*[19] it was held that a planning obligation under TCPA 1990, section 106 was contractual in nature and that an injunction is appropriate as damages will generally not be an adequate remedy. In seeking an injunction the local planning authority were exercising a public function in the public interest and an injunction would normally be granted for a substantial breach unless the authority had been guilty of delay or unconscionable conduct such as might justify refusal of relief on ordinary equitable principles. The Court made clear that the factors relevant to seeking an injunction were not the same as the factors to be taken into account in enforcing against a breach of planning control, including those when seeking an injunction under TCPA 1990, section 187B and they should not be conflated. The purpose of an injunction under section 106(5) is to enforce an undertaking voluntarily given to the local planning authority. 15.10

A planning obligation must be entered into by a deed which states that the obligation is a planning obligation for the purposes of section 106, identifies the land in which the person entering into the obligation is interested, identifies the person entering into the obligation and states what his interest in the land is and identifies the local planning authority by whom the obligation is enforceable.[20] The obligation is a local land charge under the Local Land Charges Act 1975.[21] 15.11

The obligation is thus clearly distinguishable from a purely personal obligation which does not run with the land.[22] 15.12

STATUTORY TEST FOR REQUIRING AN OBLIGATION

A planning obligation can only be a material reason for the grant of planning permission if it meets the test in regulation 122 of the Community Infrastructure Levy Regulations 2010,[23] as amended by the Community Infrastructure Levy 15.13

[17] TCPA 1990, s. 106(6) and (7).

[18] TCPA 1990, s. 106(8).

[19] [2014] EWCA Civ 676, [2014] 1 WLR 2743.

[20] TCPA 1990, s. 106(9).

[21] TCPA 1990, s. 106(11).

[22] See e.g. *Westminster CC v Secretary of State for Communities and Local Government* [2013] EWHC 690 (Admin).

[23] SI 2010 No. 948.

(Amendment) Regulations 2011.[24] This provides that a planning obligation may only constitute a reason for granting planning permission for the development if the obligation is necessary to make the development acceptable in planning terms, directly related to the development and fairly and reasonably related in scale and kind to the development.

15.14 This applies to all grants under sections 70, 73, 76A or 77 of TCPA 1990.[25] It embodies the substance of the tests listed in WOC 13/97 that the obligation had to be necessary, relevant to planning, directly related to the proposed development, fairly and reasonably related in scale and kind to the proposed development and reasonable in all other respects.

15.15 Dealing with the first of these tests, in *Tesco Stores v Secretary of State for the Environment*,[26] Lord Hoffmann said:

> The test of acceptability or necessity . . . suffers in my view from the fatal defect that it necessarily involves an investigation by the court of the merits of the planning decision. How is the court to decide whether the effect of a planning obligation is to make a development acceptable without deciding that without that obligation it would have been unacceptable? Whether it would have been unacceptable must be a matter of planning judgment. It is, I suppose, theoretically possible that a Secretary of State or local planning authority may say in terms that he or it thought that a proposed development was perfectly acceptable on its merits but nevertheless thought that it was a good idea to insist that the developer should be required to undertake a planning obligation as the price of obtaining his permission. If that should ever happen, I should think the courts would have no difficulty in saying that it disclosed a state of mind which was Wednesbury unreasonable. But in the absence of such a confession, the application of the acceptability or necessity test must involve the courts in an investigation of the planning merits. The criteria in Circular 16/91[27] are entirely appropriate to be applied by the Secretary of State as part of his assessment of the planning merits of the application. But they are quite unsuited to application by the courts.

15.16 In *R (Welcome Break Group Limited) v Stroud District Council*,[28] Bean J said:

> There is nothing novel in regulation 122 except the fact that it is contained in a statutory instrument. Its wording derives from Departmental Circular 05/05, which in turn was the successor to previous circulars such as 16/91. Circular 16/91 required that the obligation to be imposed as a condition should be

[24] SI 2011 No. 987.

[25] Regulation 122(3).

[26] [1995] 1 WLR 759 at pp. 780–1.

[27] In Wales, WOC 13/97.

[28] [2012] EWHC 140 (Admin) at para. 48 and at para. 50.

> 'necessary to the grant of permission' or that it 'should be relevant to planning and should resolve the planning objections to the development proposal concerned'.

He then cited the passage above from *Tesco* and held:

> In my judgment this passage remains good law under the 2010 Regulations. So too does the ratio of the *Tesco* case. An offered planning obligation which has nothing to do with the proposed development apart from the fact that it is offered by the developer is plainly not a material consideration and can only be regarded as an attempt to buy planning permission. However, if it has some connection with the proposed development which is more than de minimis then regard must be had to it. The extent, if any, to which it affects the decision is a matter entirely within the discretion of the decision-maker.

Further, in *R (Hampton Bishop PC) v Herefordshire Council*,[29] Richards LJ said (at 15.17 paragraph 46): 'regulation 122 can be seen as part of a codification of principles developed in the case law'. The case concerned the offer by a rugby club to transfer its existing ground to the council for a nominal sum in connection with its application for planning permission elsewhere in the town for a new ground and residential development. The challenge was that the offer was not related to the development contrary to regulation 122(2)(b) as it was several kilometres away from the application site, the club would have no continued involvement with it and there was no restriction on use of the old ground. Rejecting this, Richards LJ said:

> The heart of the matter . . . is that the existing ground was going to be released as a direct result of the development for which planning permission was being sought. The future use of the ground was therefore one of the land use consequences of the very decision that the Council was taking. The continuation of the ground's existing use for sport and recreation might have been a practical likelihood in any event but the transfer to the Council, even without restriction, would help in practice to safeguard that outcome. All this is far removed from 'buying' planning permission. It fits comfortably within the requirement that the planning obligation be directly related to the development.

The principles concerning the relationship between off-site proposals and the 15.18 development had earlier been considered by the Supreme Court when applying them by analogy to compulsory purchase for development purposes,[30] and these were followed in *R (Derwent Holdings Ltd) v Trafford BC*,[31] where it was said that where the proposals for the two sites were part of the same application it can be

[29] [2014] EWCA Civ 878 at para. 50.

[30] See *R (Sainsbury's Supermarkets Ltd) v Wolverhampton CC* [2010] UKSC 20.

[31] [2011] EWCA Civ 832.

permissible to take into account the benefits of the one as offsetting the possible disadvantages of the other. Where a proposed development is likely to have significant harmful effects, an obligation which mitigates those effects may well meet the second test, relationship to the development, subject to the questions of scale in the third test. This follows from *R (Tesco Stores Ltd) v Forest of Dean DC*[32] where Sullivan LJ said:

> The package of measures in the section 106 agreement is fairly and reasonably related in kind to the development because it seeks to mitigate what is acknowledged to be a significant adverse impact of one of the major elements of that development. This is not a case of a local planning authority seeking funding through the imposition of a section 106 agreement for some extraneous planning benefit that is unrelated to any adverse impact of the development for which permission is sought. In terms of scale, measures that merely mitigate, but do not obviate, a significant adverse impact that would be caused by a proposed development are likely to be fairly and reasonably related in scale to that development. Each case will be fact sensitive. There might well be cases where the cost of such mitigation measures would be so excessive that the obligation would be out of scale with the proposed development even though they would not obviate its adverse effects, but there is nothing to suggest that the overall cost of these particular mitigation measures (£380,000) is out of scale with this substantial employment/retail proposal. It is the large scale of the retail element of this out of centre proposal which results in the significant adverse impact on the town centre.

15.19 Regulation 123 of the Community Infrastructure Regulations 2010 makes provision to avoid overlap so that where the funding is covered by the Community Infrastructure Levy it is not to be met by a planning obligation. Regulation 123(2)[33] provides that a planning obligation may not constitute a reason for granting planning permission for the development to the extent that the obligation provides for the funding or provision of relevant infrastructure. This is defined as any infrastructure or, where a list of infrastructure or projects wholly or partly funded by the levy has been published by the charging authority, any project or infrastructure within that list.[34]

GUIDANCE

15.20 Guidance sets out the appropriate relationship between section 106 obligations and the Community Infrastructure Levy. The levy is considered in the next chapter.

[32] [2015] EWCA Civ 800 at para. 11.

[33] As amended by SI 2011 No. 987, SI 2013 No. 982 and SI 2014 No. 385.

[34] CIL Regs, reg. 123(4).

Where the published list for the levy includes generic types of infrastructure, a section 106 obligation should not be sought on specific projects in that category, and, where the list is project specific, no planning obligation should be sought.

Pooled contributions towards items that may be funded via the levy are not to be collected via planning obligations and are precluded by regulation 123(4). This provides that a section 106 obligation may not constitute a good reason for granting planning permission if five or more obligations for that project or type of infrastructure have already been entered into since 6 April 2010 and it is a type of infrastructure that is capable of being funded by the levy. 15.21

As stated, generally a particular concern may be met by a condition or an obligation. In addition, in the case of highway works an agreement to execute the works under the Highways Act 1980, section 278 may be appropriate, although Planning Practice Guidance[35] states 'Planning obligations and conditions should not be used to require a developer to enter into section 278 agreements to provide items that appear on the charging authority's Regulation 123 infrastructure list.' 15.22

The remaining role of section 106 obligations is dealt with in PPW[36] and NPPF Planning Practice Guidance, *Community Infrastructure Levy* in identical terms. They state that the CIL is: 15.23

> intended to provide infrastructure to support the development of an area rather than to make individual planning applications acceptable in planning terms. As a result, there may still be some site specific impact mitigation requirements without which a development should not be granted planning permission. Some of these needs may be provided for through the CIL but others may not, particularly if they are very local in their impact. There is therefore still a legitimate role for development-specific planning obligations to enable a local planning authority to be confident that the specific consequences of development can be mitigated.

Generally, PPW[37] states that: 15.24

> Planning obligations should only be sought where they are necessary to make a proposal acceptable in land use planning terms. Planning permission may not be bought or sold and negotiations should be conducted in a way that is seen to be fair, open and reasonable. Unacceptable development should never be allowed because of unrelated benefits. Acceptable development should never be refused simply because an applicant is unwilling to offer such benefits.

35 NPPF Planning Practice Guidance, *Community Infrastructure Levy*, para. 107.

36 At para. 3.5.6.

37 At para. 3.5.7.

15.25 PPW continues[38] that, where there is a choice, the imposition of a condition is preferable to an obligation because 'Conditions are more transparent, offer greater flexibility in the light of changing circumstances and offer a developer the right of appeal to the Welsh Ministers against those conditions considered to be onerous'.

FAIRNESS AND PUBLICITY

15.26 The publicity required for information relating to a decision generally is subject to the provisions of the Local Government Act 1972, sections 100B (report), 100D (background papers) and 100F, as amended by the Local Government (Access to Information) (Variation) (Wales) Order 2007[39] (inspection by members of the council).

15.27 Regulation 29 of the Town and Country Planning (Development Management Procedure) (Wales) Regulations 2012[40] provides for copies of section 106 obligations to be entered on the register of applications and local development orders. On any application for planning permission or for approval of reserved matters the register must contain a copy of any section 106 obligation or Highways Act 1980, section 278 agreement either proposed or entered into. It must also contain a copy of any such agreement entered into in respect of the application land which the applicant considers relevant. A copy of any modification to these agreements is also to be entered in the register. Similar provisions apply for entry in the relevant part of the register (Part 2) following grant.

15.28 Thus the requirements should enable access to the information by the public or interested parties but they do not provide for consultation or notice as such notwithstanding the significance they may have. The Court of Appeal considered this in *R (Lichfield Securities Ltd) v Lichfield District Council*,[41] saying:

> It is fundamental to section 106 that it must be used only for legitimate planning purposes. A variety of people may have an interest in these—not only a potential financial beneficiary such as . . . [the Claimant] but, for example, local people who want to be sure that their community is going to benefit appropriately from a development. It is only in the run-up to the entry into the section 106 obligation that these interests can have any worthwhile say, for they have no right of appeal if the authority's eventual resolution adopts an unsatisfactory agreement.

15.29 The case concerned a section 106 agreement relating to road infrastructure costs challenged by another developer who had not been party to the negotiations but

[38] Paragraph 3.7.10.

[39] SI 2007 No. 969.

[40] SI 2012 No. 801.

[41] [2001] EWCA Civ 304 at para. 12.

who was potentially adversely affected by the formula used for the calculation. The Court of Appeal held that the exclusion from consultation was potentially unfair.

Publicity was considered extensively in *R (Perry) v Hackney LBC*.[42] This was a judicial review claim against the grant of permission brought by a local resident on a number of grounds and included consideration of sections 100D–100F of the Local Government Act 1972. One of the specific grounds was the claim that the local planning authority had acted unlawfully in failing to provide a copy of the proposed section 106 agreement to enable public comment. The claimant had enquired several times but the agreement was only placed on the register after the grant of permission. The matter was considered against overall fairness and the fact that the heads of terms of the agreement were clearly set out in the report to committee. Having recited the report's contents, Patterson J held:[43] 15.30

> Whilst those matters needed to be translated into phrasing appropriate for inclusion in a legal agreement, the full extent of what was intended within the section 106 agreement was quite clear. There was nothing which prevented the claimant making observations on any of the proposed heads of terms including that on the proposed twelve month review period.
>
> In those circumstances it is impossible for the claimant to say that he has suffered any substantial prejudice as a result of the procedural omission on the part of the defendant. This ground fails.

DURATION, MODIFICATION AND DISCHARGE

The Act provides a procedure for modifying or discharging an obligation and it is important to stress first that once entered into the obligation will on ordinary principles be binding subject to its terms and any conditions expressed. As noted above, an obligation runs with the land. In *Tesco Stores Ltd v Secretary of State for the Environment* Lord Hoffmann said:[44] 15.31

> it is normal for a planning obligation to be undertaken or offered in connection with an application for planning permission and to be expressed as conditional upon the grant of that permission. But once the condition has been satisfied, the planning obligation becomes binding and cannot be challenged by the developer or his successor in title on the ground that it lacked a sufficient nexus with the proposed development.

[42] [2014] EWHC 3499 (Admin).

[43] At paras 202 and 203.

[44] [1995] 1 WLR 759 at p. 779: see above.

15.32 This was relied upon in the context of an application to discharge an obligation in *R (Millgate Developments Ltd) v Wokingham BC*.[45]

15.33 A planning obligation may be modified or discharged by an agreement executed as a deed between the local planning authority and the person against whom it is enforceable.[46] In the case of a development consent obligation, where the application in connection with which the obligation was entered into was decided by the Secretary of State, agreement to modify or discharge it must similarly be with the Secretary of State.[47]

15.34 Specific power is also given for application to modify or discharge the obligation and the equivalent power regarding restrictive covenants affecting land contained in section 84 of the Law of Property Act 1925 is expressly excluded.[48]

15.35 Application is made by the person against whom it is enforceable after the expiry of the period of five years from the date on which the obligation was entered into.[49] Application for modification is for those modifications specified in the application which may not be a modification imposing an obligation on any other person against whom the obligation is enforceable.[50] The application must comply with the Town and Country Planning (Modification and Discharge of Planning Obligations) Regulations 1992,[51] which prescribe the form and content of applications, publicity requirements and procedures.

15.36 The applicant must give notice to every other person against whom it is enforceable, inviting representations within twenty-one days.[52] The local planning authority must post a site notice or serve owners and occupiers of adjoining land inviting representations within twenty-one days or publish a notice in a local newspaper inviting representations within fourteen days.[53] The application is not to be determined before expiry of those periods for representation but subject to this must be made within eight weeks. The period may be extended by agreement where an appeal has been made.[54]

15.37 On an application the authority may determine that the obligation shall continue without modification but shall discharge it where the obligation no longer serves a useful purpose. Where it does serve a useful purpose but that purpose would be served equally well by the modifications specified in the application the

45 [2011] EWCA Civ 1062.

46 TCPA 1990, s. 106A(1), (2) and (11).

47 TCPA 1990, s. 106A(1) and (11).

48 TCPA 1990, s. 106A(10).

49 TCPA 1990, s. 106A(3) and (4): the Act provides for an alternative period if prescribed but no such period has been prescribed.

50 TCPA 1990, s. 106A(3) and (5).

51 SI 1992 No. 2832 and see s. 106A(9).

52 1992 Regulations, reg. 4.

53 Regulation 5.

54 Regulation 6.

obligation shall have effect subject to those modifications.[55] It will be noted that there is no wider power to vary or impose different modifications.

Where the obligation is to continue without modification the decision must state clearly and precisely the full reasons for the decision and include details of the right of appeal.[56] Where the obligation is modified this takes effect from the date on which notice of the determination was given to the applicant.[57] 15.38

Appeal lies to the Welsh Ministers against a decision that an obligation continues without modification or against a failure to determine the application.[58] Written notice must be given within six months of the decision or of the expiry of the period for decision.[59] The notice must be on the prescribed form, contain the information there specified and be accompanied by a copy of the documents prescribed and a copy sent to the local planning authority as well as the Welsh Ministers.[60] 15.39

Appeals are heard by an appointed person in accordance with Schedule 6 to TCPA 1990[61] and the applicant and local authority shall be given the opportunity to appear and be heard if they so wish:[62] TCPA 1990, section 319B(7) does not include section 106B appeals within the appeals affected by the restriction of the right to be heard so that the right continues to apply. 15.40

Where the failure to give notice or refusal to modify the obligation is that of the Secretary of State in connection with a development consent order a challenge can only be brought by a claim for judicial review with a six-week time limit.[63] 15.41

55 TCPA 1990, s. 106A(6).

56 1992 Regulations, reg. 6(3).

57 TCPA 1990, s. 106(8).

58 TCPA 1990, s. 106B(1).

59 1992 Regulations, reg. 7.

60 1992 Regulations, reg. 7.

61 TCPA 1990, s. 106A(7) and reg. 8.

62 TCPA 1990, s. 106B(5).

63 TCPA 1990, s. 106C.

Chapter 16

Community Infrastructure Levy

INTRODUCTION

The power to make regulations regarding the Community Infrastructure Levy (CIL) is not a devolved matter and the Community Infrastructure Levy Regulations 2010,[1] as amended, apply equally to Wales and England. It will become a devolved matter when the substituted Schedule 7A M3 of GOWA 2006 is in force. This removes the levy from being a reserved matter, although no immediate changes to the regulations or practical application of the levy are anticipated. The relevant guidance is that issued by the Secretary of State for Communities and Local Government. The Welsh Ministers have, however, published guidance relating to infrastructure development in Wales to sit alongside the UK guidance in the form of the Community Infrastructure Levy (CIL) Preparation of a Charging Schedule. The relevant UK guidance is NPPF Planning Policy Guidance *Community Infrastructure Levy*. Planning Policy Wales refers to CIL at paragraphs 3.5.6–3.5.7. 16.1

CIL is a charge on new development to facilitate funding for infrastructure. Local planning authorities can impose the charge in accordance with their published charging schedule and spend it on the designated infrastructure. To date, three local planning authorities in Wales have introduced charging schedules. As the Welsh Government Guidance points out, local planning authorities are not bound to produce charging schedules and could continue to rely on section 106 obligations to the extent that they are permissible within the restrictions imposed by the CIL Regulations (see Chapter 15, above). 16.2

The interaction with section 106 obligations, to avoid a developer effectively bearing a double burden, has been referred to in the previous chapter, with the priority being for reliance on CIL where the requirement falls within the published charging schedule and where it is to meet general infrastructure needs, section 106 therefore being appropriate for certain site-specific measures and for affordable housing.[2] 16.3

[1] SI 2010 No. 948, as amended ('the CIL Regulations').

[2] TAN 2, Annex A says that affordable housing can be met by planning conditions or obligations as the local planning authority consider appropriate but the preference should be for conditions.

STATUTORY FRAMEWORK

16.4 The levy was introduced by Part 11 (sections 205–225) of the Planning Act 2008, which gave power to make regulations for the imposition of the charge: Part 11 was amended by the Localism Act 2011, section 114. The Regulations are the Community Infrastructure Levy Regulations 2010, as amended.[3] The Secretary of State has power to give guidance about any matter connected with CIL, and the local authority as charging authority and any appointed examiner (see below) must have regard to the guidance.[4]

16.5 Section 205(2) states: 'In making the regulations the Secretary of State shall aim to ensure that the overall purpose of CIL is to ensure that costs incurred in supporting the development of an area can be funded (wholly or partly) by owners or developers of land' in a way that does not make development of the area economically unviable. The stated intent was 'to create a simpler, fairer, more transparent and predictable system of standard charges, capable of unlocking additional funding for infrastructure that is required to deliver sustainable local communities. Intervention will also ensure better pooling of funding for larger items of infrastructure'.[5]

16.6 The levy is chargeable on development and a local planning authority is the charging authority for the levy.[6] Chargeable development is the development for which planning permission is granted[7] and planning permission is defined in regulation 5 and includes development consent under section 114 of the 2008 Act and general consents including consent by a development order. Development excludes work in connection with a building into which people do not normally go or go only intermittently to inspect or maintain fixed plant or machinery.[8] The commencement of development for CIL purposes is in accordance with regulation 7.

16.7 Liability to pay is provided by the Planning Act 2008, sections 208 and 209 and the CIL Regulations, subject to prescribed exemptions. Where liability to pay would arise in respect of a proposed development a person may assume liability to pay and power is given to make regulations for liability where nobody has assumed responsibility and in other specified cases. Only an owner or developer can be made liable: an owner is a person with a material interest in the land, defined as a legal freehold estate or a legal leasehold estate with more than seven years remaining from the date when the development is first permitted by the planning permission.[9]

[3] SI 2010 No. 948, as amended by SI 2011 No. 987, SI 2013 No. 982, SI 2014 No. 385 and SI 2015 No. 836.

[4] 2008 Act, s. 221.

[5] See Explanatory Memorandum to the 2010 Regulations.

[6] Planning Act 2008, s. 206.

[7] Regulation 9.

[8] Regulation 6.

[9] Regulation 4.

Development for the purposes of a charge is anything done for the creation of a new building or in respect of an existing building but this is subject to the exemptions in Part 6 of the CIL Regulations. These exempt minor development, that is generally a building of less than 100 square metres, but not including new residential units,[10] and defined self-build houses. The result is that the levy may be chargeable on a single dwelling whatever the size. Charities may be exempt or eligible for relief and social housing is also eligible for relief. There is a general power to grant relief in exceptional circumstances.[11] 16.8

CHARGING SCHEDULE

The amount is in accordance with the rates or criteria in the charging schedule published by each authority further to section 211.[12] The charging authority, in setting rates or other criteria, must have regard, to the extent and in the manner specified by CIL regulations, to actual and expected costs of infrastructure, matters specified by CIL regulations relating to the economic viability of development (which may include, in particular, actual or potential economic effects of planning permission or of the imposition of CIL) and other actual and expected sources of funding for infrastructure.[13] It will be charged in pounds per square metre on the net additional floor area. The rate to be set is for the authority subject to issues of viability but the Welsh Government Guidance states that a nil rate if set must be based on evidence of viability, not on policy grounds. 16.9

Part 3 of the CIL Regulations (regulations 11–30) provides for the content of the schedule and the procedure for publication and approval. Provision is made for production of the schedule by the authority, for consultation, receipt of representations, examination by an independent examiner and approval and publication of the schedule. Guidance on appropriate available evidence and the process to develop the schedule are in the Welsh Government Guidance, which deals with the relationship with the development plan process and with the content of the schedule and the examination process. 16.10

In particular, regulation 14 states that in setting rates (including differential rates) in a charging schedule, a charging authority must strike an appropriate balance between the desirability of funding from CIL (in whole or in part), the actual and expected estimated total cost of infrastructure required to support the development of its area, taking into account other actual and expected sources of funding, and the potential effects (taken as a whole) of the imposition of CIL on the economic viability of development across its area. A charging authority may also have regard to actual and expected administrative expenses in connection with 16.11

[10] Regulation 42.

[11] Regulation 55.

[12] 2008 Act, s. 209(1).

[13] 2008 Act, s. 211(2).

CIL to the extent that those expenses can be funded from CIL in accordance with regulation 61.

16.12 A schedule cannot be approved until it has been examined by an appointed examiner who must consider whether the authority has complied with Part 11 and the regulations, has used appropriate evidence and dealt with any other matter prescribed by the regulations.[14] Regulations as to what is appropriate evidence are made further to section 211(7A). Regulation 17 provides that any person may make representations on the draft charging schedule and the examiner must consider any such representation.[15] If the person making the representation so requests, he must be heard by the examiner,[16] who decides how the hearing is to be conducted.[17] The examiner has power to make recommendations to reject, modify or approve the schedule.[18]

16.13 In *R (Fox Strategic Land and Property Ltd v Chorley BC*,[19] the court stressed that a judicial review challenge to the examination was on traditional public law grounds and did not involve reconsideration of the merits of the evidence.

16.14 The schedule cannot be approved if rejected by the examiner. Where modifications are recommended, the authority has power to approve subject to the provisions of section 213(1)–(1D) depending on the reason for the modification. Approval and publication is in accordance with regulation 25 and regulation 28 provides that it takes effect on the date in the schedule, subject to prior publication.

16.15 Regulations must confer a right of appeal on a question of fact in relation to the application of methods for calculating CIL to a valuation officer or district valuer appointed by the Commissioners for Her Majesty's Revenue and Customs.[20]

16.16 The levy is to be applied in supporting development by funding the provision, improvement, replacement, operation or maintenance of infrastructure in accordance with section 216 and Part 7 of the Regulations. Infrastructure is defined as including roads and other transport facilities, flood defences, schools and other educational facilities, medical facilities, sporting and recreational facilities, and open spaces. Affordable housing contributions are not within the definition[21] and will therefore have to be met where appropriate via section 106 obligations or conditions.

16.17 The authority is empowered to add administrative expenses.[22]

16.18 Enforcement of the duty to pay is by regulations further to section 218. As soon as planning permission first permits development a liability notice is to be issued

[14] 2008 Act, s. 212.

[15] Regulation 20.

[16] Regulation 21(1).

[17] Regulation 21(12).

[18] 2008 Act, s. 212A.

[19] [2014] EWHC 1179 (Admin).

[20] 2008 Act, s. 215.

[21] See amendment of 2008 Act, s. 216 by CIL Regulations 2010, reg. 63(4).

[22] Regulation 61.

and served[23] and the authority must issue a demand notice.[24] By regulation 67 a commencement notice must be submitted to the collecting authority and served on owners of relevant land no later than the day before which the chargeable development is to be commenced. Payment is in accordance with regulations 70–76 and the further provisions for enforcing payment in Part 9, Chapters 2, 3 and 4 of the Regulations.

[23] Regulation 65.

[24] Regulation 69.

Chapter 17

Appeals

INTRODUCTION

An applicant may appeal to the Welsh Ministers where the local planning authority refuse planning permission or grant it subject to conditions. Refusal includes a failure to determine the application. The right extends to decisions made by local planning authorities on applications required under the terms of an existing planning permission: this includes applications for approval under the terms of an outline permission and cases where local planning authority approval is required for an element of the development which is not a reserved matter. 17.1

An applicant also has a right of appeal to the Welsh Ministers where the local planning authority give notice under TCPA 1990, section 62ZA, that is, where the authority give notice that the application does not comply with the validation requirements.[1] Consent applications under the Town and Country Planning (Control of Advertisements) Regulations 1992[2] carry a right of appeal to the Welsh Ministers in accordance with TCPA 1990, sections 78 and 79, subject to the modifications in Schedule 4, Part III of the Regulations.[3] 17.2

Other applications under the planning Acts which are not planning applications (for example, application for a certificate of lawful use and development), may carry rights of appeal. The right of appeal is dealt with in the text when considering the particular application in question. Appeals in connection with enforcement notices are considered separately in Chapter 19, below. 17.3

Appeal lies where the decision is that of the local planning authority and not where it is a decision at first instance of the Welsh Ministers. Accordingly, decisions where an application is called-in under section 77 or where an application for permission is made to the Welsh Ministers either because it is for development of national significance or is one made at the option of the applicant further to TCPA 1990, section 62M do not carry a right of appeal on the merits although there may be a right to challenge a decision by appropriate proceedings in the High Court under TCPA 1990, section 288.[4] Where an applicant has appealed to the Welsh Ministers under section 78 and the appeal has been dismissed that decision may be challengeable by an application under section 288.[5] 17.4

1 TCPA 1990, s. 62ZB: see Chapter 12.

2 SI 1992 No. 666.

3 Regulation 15: Pt IV of Sch. 4 sets out the modified ss. 78 and 79.

4 See Chapter 22, below.

5 TCPA 1990, ss. 284(1)(f) and (3)(b) and 288(1) and (4).

17.5 Where the application is for a major infrastructure project any challenge to the order granting development consent must be by judicial review in accordance with the Planning Act 2008, section 118.

17.6 The applicant may in addition have grounds to challenge a decision of the local planning authority by judicial review on one of the established grounds of review, for example, if bias is alleged, and the existence of a right of appeal on the merits for the applicant may not necessarily prevent such challenge where otherwise appropriate. Where the application to the local authority results in the grant of permission or consent or approval, a person with sufficient interest may challenge the decision in the High Court by judicial review but has no right of appeal on the merits.

17.7 Legal challenges under express statutory provision or by judicial review are dealt with below, in Chapter 22 and Chapter 23 respectively.

17.8 The Welsh Ministers have general power to prescribe the procedure for appeals which are to be decided by an inquiry, hearing or written representations.[6] The provisions governing appeals on the merits and the process and procedure on these appeals are dealt with below.

RIGHT OF APPEAL

17.9 A right of appeal to the Welsh Ministers is conferred by TCPA 1990, section 78 in the following circumstances.

17.10 First, the applicant may appeal where a local planning authority refuses an application for planning permission.[7] Where the application is granted subject to conditions, the applicant similarly has a right to appeal.[8] Thirdly, where the local planning authority refuse an application for any consent, agreement or approval required by a condition imposed on the grant of planning permission, or grant the application subject to conditions, the applicant may appeal to the Welsh Ministers.[9] This applies to applications for approval of reserved matters further to an outline permission and to other consents required by a condition attached to the grant of planning permission. Finally, an applicant for any approval required by a development order or local development order which is refused, or granted subject to conditions, may appeal to the Welsh Ministers.[10]

17.11 Refusal in each case includes non-determination, that is, failing to give notice of the decision on the application within the time allowed.[11] Refusal extends to

[6] TCPA 1990, s. 323A.

[7] TCPA 1990, s. 78(1)(a).

[8] TCPA 1990, s. 78(1)(a).

[9] TCPA 1990, s. 78(1)(b).

[10] TCPA 1990, s. 78(1)(c).

[11] TCPA 1990, s. 78(2).

failure to give notice that the authority declines to determine the application[12] or to give notice that an application has been called-in under section 77[13] within the prescribed time.

17.12 However, TCPA 1990, section 78(4AA)[14] seeks to restrict appeals where the merits have been determined in other proceedings. It provides that an appeal may not be brought or continued against the refusal of an application for planning permission if the land to which the application relates is in Wales, granting the application would involve granting planning permission in respect of matters specified in an enforcement notice as constituting a breach of planning control, and, on the determination of an appeal against that notice under TCPA 1990, section 174, planning permission for those matters was not granted under section 177. There is a similar restriction on an appeal against a conditional grant where the condition was not discharged on an appeal against an enforcement notice.[15]

17.13 In each of the above cases the requirements and procedure are laid down by the further provisions of TCPA 1990, section 78, and sections 78A and 79 and the relevant rules. The general procedure is in accordance with the Town and Country Planning (Development Management Procedure) (Wales) Order 2012, as amended,[16] with the details depending on the particular form of the appeal as below. The 2015 amendments made important changes distinguishing between different types of development.

TIME LIMITS

17.14 An appeal must be served within the period prescribed. The period depends upon the nature of the application, with an expedited procedure applying to appeals in respect of householder and minor commercial applications. Householder and minor commercial appeals exclude conditional grants on the relevant applications and so the expedited procedure is confined to actual refusal notices.[17]

17.15 A householder application is one for alterations, including those as to use, within or extending the curtilage of an existing dwelling. More precisely, it is an application for planning permission for the enlargement, improvement or other alteration of a dwelling house, or development within the curtilage of such a dwelling house, or the change of use to enlarge the curtilage of a dwelling house, for any purpose incidental to the enjoyment of the dwelling house. It does not include any

[12] TCPA 1990, s. 70(2)(aa).

[13] TCPA 1990, s. 78(2)(b).

[14] Inserted by Planning (Wales) Act 2015, s. 45 and brought fully into force from 16 March 2016 by SI 2016 No. 52, art. 8.

[15] TCPA 1990, s. 78(4AB).

[16] SI 2012 No. 801 ('DMP(W)O'), as amended by SI 2015 No. 1330 and SI 2016 No. 59.

[17] DMP(W)O, art. 26(7).

other application for change of use, an application for erection of a dwelling house, or an application to change the number of dwellings in a building.[18]

17.16 A minor commercial application refers to small alterations, including those as to use, to the ground floor of certain existing commercial buildings. The full definition is that it means an application for planning permission for the enlargement, improvement or other alteration of an existing building of no more than 250 square metres gross external floor space at ground floor level, or part of that building, currently in use for any of the purposes set out in the Order to another specified purpose or the carrying out of building or other operations to a shop front. The purposes in question are in Schedule 1A to the Order and refer to an application for the change of use from any of the purposes set out at paragraph 1 in Schedule 1A to the Order to any of the purposes set out in either paragraph 2 or paragraph 3 of that Schedule, and the change of use from any of the purposes set out at paragraph 2 in Schedule 1A to the Order to any of the purposes set out in paragraph 3 of that Schedule.[19]

17.17 In the case of these householder or minor commercial appeals, the period within which notice of appeal must be given is twelve weeks from the date of the notice of the decision. In any other case it is six months.[20] The period may be extended by the Welsh Ministers.[21] The time limit runs from the date of decision or determination or where additional information was required but not supplied from the date of service of the notice under article 3(2).[22]

17.18 As far as failure to determine is concerned, the 2015 amendments removed the time limit for such appeals to prevent applicants unknowingly losing the right of appeal. An appeal may therefore be made at any time where there has been a failure to make a decision.

17.19 Where an appeal is made against the refusal of planning permission on the basis of non-determination under TCPA 1990, section 78(2), the additional provisions of section 78A apply. These give the local planning authority an additional period of four weeks[23] within which to give notice of the decision and, thereafter, if the notice is a refusal, the appeal proceeds on that basis; if it is a conditional grant the appeal may proceed on that basis subject to the further options for the applicant to amend the appeal notice.

18 DMP(W)O, art. 2.1.

19 DMP(W)O, art. 2.1.

20 DMP(W)O, art. 26(2).

21 DMP(W)O, art. 26(2).

22 DMP(W)O, art. 26(2), as amended by SI 2015 No. 1330.

23 DMP(W)O, art. 26A.

APPEAL NOTICE

The form and content of the appeal notice again depend upon whether it is a householder or minor commercial appeal or any other category of appeal. In any case it must be on the form obtained from the Welsh Ministers.[24] If the required documents are not enclosed, the Welsh Ministers may refuse the application.[25] Appellants are encouraged to make an appeal online through the Planning Portal Welsh site.[26] 17.20

In the case of a householder appeal or a minor commercial appeal, the documents are: a copy of the application which was sent to the local planning authority, together with any plans, documents or drawings relating to the application which were not sent to the authority (excluding any relating to amendments proposed after the determination), and the notice of the decision or determination.[27] 17.21

In the case of any other appeal, the documents are: the application made to the local planning authority, all plans, drawings and documents sent to the authority in connection with the application, all correspondence with the authority relating to the application, any certificate provided to the authority under article 11, and any other plans, documents or drawings relating to the application which were not sent to the authority. In addition, the required documents include the notice of the decision or determination, if any, and, if the appeal relates to an application for approval of certain matters in accordance with a condition on a planning permission, the application for that permission, the plans submitted with that application, and the planning permission granted.[28] 17.22

The notice and documents must be served on the Welsh Ministers within the prescribed time and must also be served on the local planning authority as soon as reasonably practicable.[29] Notice must also be given to other persons as if the appeal were a planning application:[30] these refer to notice to the owner of the land, agricultural tenants, and with special provisions for mineral applications. 17.23

An appellant should set out the grounds of appeal fully so that the issues and arguments are apparent. The reasons for refusal will provide a focus and the grounds should respond to each of them. Annexe G of the Procedural Guide lists a number of points, of which key ones are the need to address planning merits and address all relevant development plan policies and explain how they are met. The planning history is unnecessary, as is a detailed description of the site, but, if case law is relied on, the full reference should be cited. 17.24

[24] DMP(W)O, art. 26(1)(a).

[25] DMP(W)O, art. 26(4).

[26] See Planning Inspectorate guidance.

[27] DMP(W)O, art. 26(3)(a).

[28] DMP(W)O, art. 26(3)(b).

[29] DMP(W)O, art. 26(1)(b).

[30] DMP(W)O, art. 25, applying arts 10 and 11.

PROCEDURE ON APPEAL

17.25 An appeal is a re-hearing on the merits. The Welsh Ministers may allow or dismiss the appeal or reverse or vary any part of the decision whether the appeal relates to that part of the decision or not and may deal with the application as if it had been made to them in the first instance.[31] It follows that an appeal against the grant of permission subject to conditions gives power to reconsider the whole decision. An appeal may be dismissed where the appellant is responsible for delay and fails to take the steps specified in a notice for expedition.[32]

17.26 Restriction on the power to vary an application for permission during the appeal process will be introduced on full implementation of section 47 of the Planning (Wales) Act 2015, which inserts a new section 78(4B) into TCPA 1990.[33] It provides that once notice of an appeal to the Welsh Ministers under this section has been served, the application to which it relates may not be varied, except in such circumstances as may be prescribed by a development order. The concern is the extent to which amendment may in effect deny meaningful consultation and representation by an affected party where the amendment changes the substance of the development sought as established by case law.[34] Regulations detailing when amendment may be allowed may make provision for further consultation.

APPOINTED PERSONS AND WELSH MINISTERS

17.27 The Welsh Ministers may by regulation prescribe classes of appeal which are to be determined by a person appointed by them[35] and in practice most appeals are decided by a planning inspector. The relevant regulation is the Town and Country Planning (Determination of Appeals by Appointed Persons) (Prescribed Classes) (Wales) Regulations 2015.[36] Regulation 3 provides for section 78 appeals to be determined by appointed persons subject to the exceptions in regulation 4, which include, for example, applications for planning permission under section 266 by statutory undertakers relating to operational land.

17.28 Where the appeal is to be decided by an appointed person he has the same powers and duties as the Welsh Ministers under TCPA 1990, section 79(1) and (4) and (6A):[37] these refer respectively to the general powers, notice as for applications and powers to deal with delay (see above). The Welsh Ministers do, however,

[31] TCPA 1990, s. 79(1).

[32] TCPA 1990, s. 79(6A).

[33] In force from 6 September 2015 insofar as necessary to make regulations or orders.

[34] The *Wheatcroft* principles: see *Bernard Wheatcroft Ltd v Secretary of State for the Environment* (1980) 43 P & CR 233 and *Ioannou v Secretary of State for Communities and Local Government* [2014] EWCA Civ 1432.

[35] TCPA 1990, s. 79(7) and Sch. 6.

[36] SI 2015 No. 1822.

[37] See TCPA 1990, Sch. 6, para. 2.

have power to direct that an appeal which would otherwise be determined by an appointed person shall instead be determined by them[38] and shall give reasons for that decision and in appropriate cases allow representations on that issue.[39]

Guidance is in circular NAW 07/2003 Planning (and analogous) Appeals and Call-in Procedures. Annex 5 refers to the procedure where jurisdiction has been recovered. It refers to the then position where functions remained with the National Assembly for Wales (not the Welsh Ministers) and the procedure before a Planning Decision Committee of the Assembly[40] but has not been formally withdrawn or replaced. However, there is updated guidance in the non-statutory Planning Inspectorate Procedural Guidance, *Planning appeals and called-in Planning applications – Wales* (dated June 2016). 17.29

The procedures on recovered jurisdiction on appeals and on call-in under section 77 have historically been treated as akin. The current edition of PPW no longer contains a section dealing with this[41] but the same criteria are in on-line updated guidance. This states that the powers may be used in relation to residential development of more than 150 houses or on more than 6 hectares of land, retail developments of over 10,000 square metres, major proposals for the winning and working of minerals, proposals for major developments which could have wide effects beyond their immediate locality, proposals giving rise to substantial controversy beyond the immediate locality, proposals which raise novel planning issues, proposals which raise significant legal difficulties, proposals to which a central government department has objected, or cases that can only be decided in conjunction with a case over which an Inspector has no jurisdiction. 17.30

DETERMINATION OF APPLICABLE PROCEDURE

Returning to appeals generally, the procedure to be followed in determining an appeal, that is whether it is by written representations, hearing or at a local inquiry, is to be determined by the Welsh Ministers.[42] This decision as to procedure must be made within seven days.[43] 17.31

The three distinct procedures are each governed by their own set of procedural rules, with a special expedited written representation procedure for householder 17.32

[38] TCPA 1990, Sch. 6, para. 3.

[39] TCPA 1990, Sch. 6, para. 3.

[40] See Chapter 1, above.

[41] Edition 9; it was dealt with in Edition 8 at para. 3.11.2.

[42] TCPA 1990, s. 319B. This follows amendments introduced by the Town and Country Planning (Determination of Procedure) (Wales) Order 2014 (SI 2014 No. 2773), inserting s. 319B and a new subsection (3A) into TCPA 1990, s. 79 so as to exclude the operation of s. 78(2), which gave the parties a right to be heard on an appeal to the Welsh Ministers.

[43] Town and Country Planning (Determination of Procedure) (Prescribed Period) (Wales) Regulations 2014, SI 2014 No. 2775.

and minor commercial appeals. The criteria by which the decision as to procedure is to be made must be published[44] and these are in Annex H to the guidance *Planning appeals and called-in Planning applications – Wales* (June 2016). They include factors such as the need and best means to test evidence, whether the status or personal circumstances of the applicant are at issue and the extent of local interest.

17.33 In all cases, the rules lay down a timetable and the intent is that it will be strictly adhered to. The general guidance is that although each case will be considered on its particular facts, late representations will only be considered in extraordinary circumstances. Examples of extraordinary circumstances include where representations are delayed because of a postal strike, or by the ill-health of an appellant, or to give a third party more time where the local planning authority are late in notifying them of the appeal, or where there has been a last-minute change in circumstances which the inspector ought to know about.[45]

WRITTEN REPRESENTATIONS

17.34 Procedure is governed by the Town and Country Planning (Referrals and Appeals) (Written Representations Procedure) (Wales) Regulations 2015.[46] Guidance is still contained in the main text and Annex 1 of circular NAW 07/03. Reference should also be made to the Planning Inspectorate guidance *Planning appeals and called-in Planning applications – Wales* (June 2016), of course noting the statement that it has no statutory status. The circular does not reflect the legislative status of the householder and minor commercial appeals but the guidance does.[47]

17.35 Part 1 of the Regulations applies to householder, advertisement consent and minor commercial appeals where it has been decided that the appeal is to be by written representations.[48] The procedure is for a more expedited decision, with a five-day period to respond and four weeks thereafter, although time limits may be extended.[49] The appeal notice should set out all matters fully as there is no right to comment on the local authority questionnaire.

17.36 As soon as practicable after the determination of procedure, the applicant must be notified in writing, including the starting date, and the local authority must then send a completed questionnaire and documents to the Welsh Ministers and appellant and give written notice to interested persons within five working days of the starting date.[50] The documents will include the representations on

[44] TCPA 1990, s. 319B(6).

[45] NAW 07/03, para. 13.

[46] SI 2015 No. 1331 (referred to in this section of the text as 'Written Representations Regs').

[47] The *Development Procedure Manual* deals with certain appeals, in particular validation appeals.

[48] Written Representations Regs, reg. 3(2).

[49] Written Representations Regs, reg. 19.

[50] Written Representations Regs, regs 4 and 5.

the application although they may be withdrawn.[51] The relevant appeal notice and documents comprise the appellant's representations and the questionnaire and documents sent with it comprise the local planning authority's representations in relation to the appeal.[52] Further information may be requested, subject to which the Welsh Ministers will determine the appeal, taking into account representations sent within the relevant time limits.[53]

The decision and the reasons for it must be notified in writing to the appellant, the local planning authority, any interested person and any other person so requesting where that is reasonable.[54] 17.37

All other appeals by written representation are subject to Part 2 of the Regulations[55] as detailed below. 17.38

As soon as practicable after the determination of procedure the applicant must be notified in writing of the starting date and formal appeal details.[56] The key stages are two, six and nine weeks from the starting date, although there is power for the time limits to be extended.[57] There is opportunity for the parties to send representations within the six-week period. 17.39

Within two weeks of the starting date the local authority must send a completed questionnaire and documents to the Welsh Ministers and appellant.[58] Within the same time the authority must give notice to interested parties containing the information prescribed, which includes notice that further representations may be sent, to be received within six weeks of the starting date.[59] Interested parties are statutory consultees and persons who made representations about the application. 17.40

The appeal notice and documents are the appellant's representations but an appellant who wishes to make further representations may do so and two copies[60] must be received within six weeks of the starting date.[61] The local authority may elect to treat the appeal questionnaire and supporting documents as its representations, in which case it must at the same time give notice of this.[62] If it does not so elect, two copies[63] of any further representations must be received within six weeks of the starting date.[64] The guidance states that normally the six-week representations 17.41

51 Written Representations Regs, reg. 10.

52 Written Representations Regs, reg. 7.

53 Written Representations Regs, regs 8 and 10.

54 Written Representations Regs, reg. 11.

55 Written Representations Regs, reg. 3(3).

56 Written Representations Regs, reg. 12.

57 Written Representations Regs, reg. 19.

58 Written Representations Regs, reg. 13.

59 Written Representations Regs, reg. 14.

60 Written Representations Regs, reg. 15(8); one if sent electronically.

61 Written Representations Regs, reg. 15(4).

62 Written Representations Regs, reg. 15(2).

63 Written Representations Regs, reg. 15(8); one if sent electronically.

64 Written Representations Regs, reg. 15(3).

should not contain new evidence or additional technical data. Further representations from either party are copied to the other by the Welsh Ministers and a party may send written comments on the other's representations to be received within nine weeks of the starting date.[65] Again, the guidance states that these should not contain new material or technical data. The Welsh Ministers may disregard further information from the appellant and local authority if it is not received within the nine weeks unless it has been requested by them.[66]

17.42 An interested person who has been notified under the Regulations may submit representations to be received within six weeks of the starting date and the parties may then comment within the period of not less than two weeks as specified by the Welsh Ministers.[67]

17.43 The decision is on the basis of the written representations received in accordance with regulation 17, and Annex 1(i) of NAW 07/03 gives guidance on the format and content of statements under these provisions.

17.44 In practice the inspector will carry out a site visit although there is no legal requirement to do so. It will generally be unaccompanied unless access is not otherwise practicable.

17.45 The decision and the reasons for it must be notified in writing to the appellant, the local planning authority, any interested person and any other person so requesting where that is reasonable.[68]

HEARINGS

17.46 Procedure is governed by the Town and Country Planning (Hearings Procedure) (Wales) Rules 2003.[69] Guidance is contained in the main text and Annex 2 of circular NAW 07/03. By rule 10, on a transferred appeal the inspector is to take relevant steps under rules 6(2) and (5), 7 and 18 in place of the Welsh Ministers. The position regarding the decision and criteria relevant to hearings are referred to above: see in particular Annexe H to the Planning Inspectorate guidance. Details of the hearings procedure are in Annexe D to this guidance.

17.47 If at any time before hearing the appellant or the local planning authority considers that the procedure is inappropriate and gives notice of this and the reasons for it, then, after consultation with the other party, the Welsh Ministers may arrange an inquiry instead.[70] If the hearing has started, the inspector has the like

[65] Written Representations Regs, reg. 15(5) and (6).

[66] Written Representations Regs, reg. 15(7).

[67] Written Representations Regs, reg. 16.

[68] Written Representations Regs, reg. 18.

[69] SI 2003 No. 1271, as amended by Town and Country Planning (Amendment of Appeals Procedures) (Wales) Rules 2007 (SI 2007 No 2285), and referred to in this section of the text as the 'Hearings Rules'.

[70] Hearings Rules, r. 8.

power after consultation with the parties where a party has informed him that a hearing is inappropriate or on his own initiative.

As in the case of other forms of appeal, there is a strict timetable based on the starting date, although the precise procedure will depend upon whether it is a transferred appeal (determined by the inspector) or not. On receipt of the correct appeal documents the inspectorate will notify the appellant and the local planning authority of the starting date, the appeal reference and the address for communications, and give further details to the planning authority.[71] 17.48

On receipt of notice from the inspectorate, the local planning authority must notify the inspectorate and the appellant of any statutory party[72] who has made representations and the inspectorate must notify the parties of any representations made to it by a statutory party.[73] Within two weeks of the starting date the local planning authority must serve a completed questionnaire and all relevant supporting documents on the inspectorate and the appellant[74] and give notice of the appeal to any statutory party or other person who made representations to it on the application.[75] 17.49

Within six weeks the appellant and the local planning authority must ensure that two copies of their hearing statements are received by the inspectorate and any statutory party.[76] Within the same time any statutory body or person who made representations who wants them to be taken into account on the appeal must provide three copies to the inspectorate.[77] Within nine weeks of the starting date, the appellant and local planning authority must provide two copies of their comments on the documents received to date.[78] Comments received after this date may be disregarded.[79] 17.50

There is no formal requirement for a statement of common ground as there is with inquiries but guidance states that it would be helpful for appellants and the local planning authority to cooperate and submit a short summary of agreed evidence including site description, planning history and a list of agreed policies.[80] 17.51

The hearing should take place within twelve weeks unless impracticable and not less than four weeks' written notice must be given to all persons entitled to take part.[81] 17.52

[71] NAW 07/03, paras 5 and 6.

[72] Defined by Hearings Rules, r. 2: it refers to those bodies whose representations must be taken into account in determining the application.

[73] Hearings Rules, r. 4(1).

[74] Hearings Rules, r. 4(2)(a).

[75] Hearings Rules, r. 4(2)(b).

[76] Hearings Rules, r. 6(1).

[77] Hearings Rules, r. 6(3).

[78] Hearings Rules, r. 6(4).

[79] Hearings Rules, r. 6(8).

[80] NAW 07/2003, Annex 2(i), para. 2.

[81] Hearings Rules, r. 7.

17.53 In general, participation, subject to the above, and procedure at the hearing is determined by the inspector and will normally be by discussion led by the inspector with no cross-examination, although participants are entitled to call evidence.[82] At the start of the hearing the inspector must identify what in his opinion are the main issues and the matters on which he requires further explanation.[83] A site visit must take place if either the appellant or the local planning authority requests; otherwise a visit may take place in accordance with rule 12.

17.54 At the conclusion of a non-transferred hearing the inspector writes a report for the Welsh Ministers to make their decision.[84] If they disagree with the report on a material fact or intend to admit new evidence or new matter of fact, the Welsh Ministers must give an opportunity to the participants to make written representations or request the re-opening of the hearing,[85] and similar provisions apply where the inspector himself wishes to consider new matters in a transferred appeal.[86] The requirement to notify the decision and the reason for it in the two classes of appeal are in rules 15 and 16.

17.55 Costs may be awarded in respect of unreasonable behaviour as detailed in WOC 23/93.

INQUIRIES

17.56 There is general power for the Welsh Ministers to hold a local inquiry for the purposes of exercising any of their functions under TCPA 1990 and the provisions of the Local Government Act 1970, section 250(2)–(5) will apply to the inquiry.[87] The inquiry must be held in public unless a direction is given in the interests of national security.[88]

17.57 Procedure at inquiries is governed by the Town and Country Planning (Inquiries Procedure) (Wales) Rules 2003,[89] where the Welsh Ministers are the deciding body. These rules also apply to inquiries on called-in applications. The Town and Country Planning (Determination by Inspectors) (Inquiries Procedure)

82 For procedure generally, see Hearings Rules, r. 11.

83 Hearings Rules, r. 11(4).

84 Hearings Rules, r. 13.

85 Hearings Rules, r. 13.

86 Hearings Rules, r. 14.

87 TCPA 1990, s. 320.

88 See TCPA 1990, s. 321. This power has been considered above in Chapter 12 in connection with Crown applications.

89 SI 2003 No. 1266, as amended by Town and Country Planning (Amendment of Appeals Procedures) (Wales) Rules 2007 (SI 2007 No. 2285), and referred to in this section of the text as the 'Inquiries Rules'.

(Wales) Rules 2003[90] govern procedure in the case of determinations by appointed persons. Guidance on each is in NAWC 07/2003 main text and Annex 3, and in the Planning Inspectorate guidance annexe E.[91] References below are to the Welsh Ministers or the inspector as used in the rules and this identifies which party is formally responsible but in practice all correspondence will be with the Planning Inspectorate.

17.58 As in the case of other appeals, the rules provide for a strict timetable from the starting date, the principal differences between the two sets of rules being in connection with the need for a pre-inquiry meeting and the timescale for statements of case following such meeting, and the precise circumstances relating to matters after close of the Inquiry. Time limits may be extended.[92]

17.59 On receipt of notice from the inspectorate, the local planning authority must notify the Welsh Ministers and the appellant of any statutory party[93] who has made representations, and the inspectorate must notify the parties of any representations made to it by a statutory party.[94] The local planning authority must ensure that within two weeks of the starting date the Welsh Ministers and the appellant have received a completed questionnaire and a copy of each of the documents referred to in it, and any statutory party and other person who made representations to the local planning authority about the application have been notified that an appeal has been made and of the address to which, and of the period within which, they may make representations.[95]

17.60 The Welsh Ministers or the inspector must cause a pre-inquiry meeting to be held where the inquiry is expected to last for eight or more days, unless considered unnecessary, and also where necessary in any shorter case[96] in accordance with the further provisions of rule 5. In the case of the rules where the Welsh Ministers determine the appeal (but only in those cases), the timescale thereafter is revised to date from the pre-inquiry meeting. The inspector has power where the Welsh ministers do not hold a pre-inquiry meeting to require one to be held.[97]

17.61 Then, within six weeks of the starting date, or, for recovered appeals where a pre-inquiry meeting was held, within four weeks of the meeting, the local planning authority and the appellant must ensure that two copies of its respective statement of

[90] SI 2003 No. 1267, as amended by Town and Country Planning (Amendment of Appeals Procedures) (Wales) Rules 2007 (SI 2007 No. 2285), and referred to in this section of the text as the 'Inspector Inquiries Rules'.

[91] References in this section of the text to a rule is to the applicable Rules depending on who is to determine the appeal.

[92] Inquiries Rules and Inspector Inquiries Rules, r. 21.

[93] Defined by r. 2 of each of the Inquiries Rules and Inspector Inquiries Rules – it refers to those bodies whose representations must be taken into account in determining the application. To avoid confusion the SI number is added, where appropriate.

[94] Inquiries Rules and Inspector Inquiries Rules, r. 4.

[95] Inquiries Rules and Inspector Inquiries Rules, r. 4.

[96] Inquiries Rules, r. 5 and Inspector Inquiries Rules, r. 7(2).

[97] Inquiries Rules, r. 7.

case is received by the Welsh Ministers and any statutory party.[98] The two principal parties may require a copy of any document referred to.[99] A person who has given notice of a wish to take part in the inquiry may be required to submit a statement of case[100] and the Rules provide for the distribution of statements and for further information where required.

17.62 Additional matters leading up to the inquiry are in the further provisions of the Rules. In particular, copies of written evidence and a summary of evidence must be submitted no later than four weeks before the date of the inquiry or, where a timetable has been arranged under rule 8, by the date specified.[101] In addition, the local planning authority and the appellant must together prepare a statement of common ground and ensure that it is received not less than four weeks before the date of the Inquiry.[102]

17.63 Procedure at the Inquiry is to be determined by the Inspector: he must at the start identify the main issues and, unless otherwise determined, the local planning authority will begin and the appellant has the final right of reply.[103] Evidence is by reading the summary of the written evidence and the full statement is treated as tendered in evidence and the whole of the evidence is subject to cross-examination. Written material received before the Inquiry opens may be taken into account provided that this is disclosed.[104] The inspector may allow any person to alter or add to a statement of case submitted so far as may be necessary for the purposes of the inquiry; but the inspector must, if necessary by adjourning the inquiry, give every other person entitled to, and who does, take part in the inquiry an adequate opportunity of considering any fresh matter or document.[105]

17.64 Closing submissions in an Inquiry 'expected to last' for eight days or more must be in writing,[106] although in practice closing submissions are almost invariably in writing. The inspector may make a pre-inquiry site inspection. He may make an accompanied site inspection during or after inquiry and must do so if requested by the local planning authority or the appellant.[107]

17.65 Each set of rules makes provision for further matters to be considered subsequently. If, after the close of an inquiry, an inspector proposes to take into consideration any new evidence or any new matter of fact (not being a matter of Welsh Government policy) which was not raised at the inquiry and which the inspector considers to be material to the decision, the inspector must not come to a decision

[98] Inquiries Rules and Inspector Inquiries Rules, r. 6.

[99] Inquiries Rules and Inspector Inquiries Rules, r. 6(5).

[100] Inquiries Rules and Inspector Inquiries Rules, r. 6(6).

[101] Inquiries Rules, r. 13 and Inspector Inquiries Rules, r. 14.

[102] Inquiries Rules, r. 14 and Inspector Inquiries Rules, r. 15.

[103] Inquiries Rules and Inspector Inquiries Rules, r. 15.

[104] Inquiries Rules, r. 15(12) and Inspector Inquiries Rules, r. 16(12).

[105] Inquiries Rules, r. 15(10) and Inspector Inquiries Rules, r. 16(10).

[106] Inquiries Rules, r. 15(14) and Inspector Inquiries Rules, r. 16(14).

[107] Inquiries Rules, r. 16 and Inspector Inquiries Rules, r. 17.

without first giving notice. He must notify the applicant, the local planning authority and the persons entitled to, and who did, take part in the inquiry of the matter in question and afford them an opportunity of making written representations or of asking for the re-opening of the inquiry. The response must be received within three weeks.[108]

If, after the close of an inquiry, the Welsh Ministers differ from the inspector on any matter of fact mentioned in, or appearing to them to be material to, a conclusion reached by the inspector, or take into consideration any new evidence or new matter of fact (not being a matter of Welsh Government policy), and are for that reason disposed to disagree with a recommendation made by the inspector, they must not come to a decision which is at variance with that recommendation without first giving notice. The notice is to the applicant, the local planning authority and the persons entitled to, and who did, take part in the inquiry, stating the disagreement and the reasons for it and affording those persons an opportunity of making written representations or, if any new evidence or new matter of fact has been taken into consideration, asking for the re-opening of the inquiry. The response must be received within three weeks.[109] 17.66

In either case the Inquiry must be re-opened if the appellant or local planning authority so requests in accordance with the rules, and may be re-opened in any other case.[110] 17.67

The appeal decision, and the reasons for it, must be notified in writing to the applicant and the local planning authority, all persons entitled to, and who did, take part in the inquiry and any other person who, having taken part in the inquiry, has asked to be notified of the decision.[111] 17.68

COSTS

Costs may be awarded. The power to make orders relating to costs is now section 322C of TCPA 1990, having been amended by the Planning (Wales) Act 2015. Subsection (6) gives the Welsh Ministers power to make orders as to costs of any party to an appeal. This power therefore applies to all appeals whatever procedure is followed. 17.69

No order has as yet been made under the amended provisions and in the meantime the guidelines in WOC 23/93 remain effective, although referable to the provisions as to costs prior to amendment. These set out the principle that a party will normally meet his own expenses of the appeal but that a party who has behaved unreasonably and has caused another party to incur unnecessary expense may be ordered to pay all or part of those costs. Examples of unreasonable conduct 17.70

[108] Inspector Inquiries Rules, r. 17.

[109] Inquiries Rules, r. 17.

[110] Inquiries Rules, r. 17(7) and Inspector Inquiries Rules, r. 18(4).

[111] Inquiries Rules, r. 18 and Inspector Inquiries Rules, r. 19.

are given relating both to procedural failings and conduct in connection with the substantive matters in the appeal.

17.71 In addition, the costs incurred by the Welsh Ministers in relation to an application, appeal or reference (or so much of them as the Welsh Ministers may direct) are to be paid by the applicant, appellant or person making the reference, or such local planning authority or other party to the application, appeal or reference, as the Welsh Ministers may direct.[112] This applies whether it is considered at an inquiry or hearing or on the basis of written representations.

17.72 A dispute over the amount of costs to be recovered may be referred for detailed assessment in accordance with the Civil Procedure Rules, Part 47. This, and steps to enforce a costs order, will require, as a necessary preliminary step, the making of a formal order for costs by the High Court.

17.73 Costs decisions on appeals were not formerly within the definition in TCPA 1990, section 284(3) and could not be challenged by an application under section 288 but only by judicial review, even where the substantive decision was challenged under section 288. Amendment has, however, been made, adding costs orders made in connection with the orders listed in section 284(2) or the actions in section 284(3) to enable a costs challenge to be brought under section 288.[113]

112 TCPA 1990, s. 322C.

113 TCPA 1990, s. 284(1)(g) and 284(3A), inserted by the Criminal Justice and Courts Act 2015, s. 91 and Sch. 16.

Chapter 18

Enforcement

INTRODUCTION

Part VII of TCPA 1990 (sections 171A–196D[1]), as amended in particular by PCPA 2004 and Planning (Wales) Act 2015, gives local planning authorities power to take action where there is a breach of planning control. The Welsh Ministers have reserve powers under TCPA 1990, sections 182 and 185. TCPA 1990, section 171A sets out what is a breach of planning control and what constitutes enforcement action. Action for breach must be taken within the time limits prescribed by section 171B. Ancillary powers are conferred to assist decision-making where there may be a breach of the Act, for example, power to require information and powers of entry,[2] and, in particular, the authority may issue a planning contravention notice.[3] 18.1

The local planning authority may issue an enforcement notice[4] or a breach of condition notice[5] and each of these constitutes taking enforcement action as legally defined.[6] Since 16 March 2016 there has been power to issue an enforcement warning notice[7] and this also will be classed as taking enforcement action.[8] In addition, the authority may issue a stop notice,[9] a temporary stop notice[10] or apply for an injunction.[11] The authority must keep a register of enforcement notices, stop notices, breach of condition notices and enforcement warning notices.[12] 18.2

Authority to take any action or issue a notice will depend on the individual scheme of delegation within the local planning authority but care must be taken to ensure that it does cover the precise action: in *Kirklees MBC v Brook*,[13] authority 18.3

[1] Not all of these provisions apply in Wales – see below.

[2] See s. 171C, ss. 196A–196C, s. 324(1)(c) and s. 330.

[3] Section 171C.

[4] See TCPA 1990, ss. 172–182.

[5] TCPA 1990, s. 187A.

[6] TCPA 1990, s. 171A(2).

[7] TCPA 1990, s. 173ZA.

[8] TCPA 1990, s. 171A(2)(aa).

[9] TCPA 1990, s. 183.

[10] TCPA 1990, ss. 171E–171H.

[11] TCPA 1990, s. 187B.

[12] TCPA 1990, s. 188 and SI 2012 No. 801 ('DMP(W)O'), art. 30.

[13] [2004] EWHC 2841 (Ch).

to delegate 'enforcement action' did not include proceedings for an injunction in the light of the definition of those words in TCPA 1990, s. 171A.

18.4 A person having an interest in the land or a relevant occupier may appeal against an enforcement notice, whether or not it has been served on him,[14] but there is no express right of appeal against any other form of notice; although, where appropriate, any notice may be challenged by an application for judicial review.[15] Appeals against an enforcement notice are dealt with in Chapter 19.

18.5 Failure to comply with an enforcement notice, a stop notice, a temporary stop notice, a breach of condition notice or a planning contravention notice is a criminal offence.[16] Criminal proceedings in these cases are considered in Chapter 20. In addition, where the local planning authority have issued a discontinuance order under TCPA 1990, section 102, measures to enforce the order are in TCPA 1990, sections 189 and 190.

18.6 Policy applying to enforcement proceedings is contained in PPW.[17] Guidance on the legislative provisions and procedures is to be found in the *Development Management Guide*.[18]

18.7 The enforcement provisions are modified in their application to the Crown or Crown land and this is considered at the end of this chapter.

BREACH OF PLANNING CONTROL AND TIME LIMITS

18.8 A breach of planning control consists of carrying out development without the required planning permission or failing to comply with a condition or limitation subject to which permission was granted.[19] In *R (I'm Your Man Ltd) v Secretary of State for the Environment*[20] it was held that there is no express or implied power for a local planning authority or the Secretary of State to impose limitations on a planning permission granted pursuant to an application. Such limitations are not capable of enforcement under the Act. The reference to limitations in the section therefore refers only to those imposed under a development order.

18.9 Enforcement action may only be taken against a breach of planning control within the set time limits. Where the breach is the carrying out of building, engineering, mining or other operations action must be taken within four years of the

[14] TCPA 1990, s. 174.

[15] See Chapter 23.

[16] See TCPA 1990, ss. 179, 187, 171G, 187A and 171D respectively.

[17] At para. 3.6; TAN 9, which dealt with enforcement, was cancelled and replaced by the *Development Management Guide*.

[18] WOC 24/97 is a pre-devolution document and the Guide is intended as updated guidance on procedure generally.

[19] TCPA 1990, s. 171A(1).

[20] (1999) 77 P & CR 251.

date on which the operations were substantially completed.[21] Change of use of any building to a single dwelling house requires action within four years of the breach.[22] In any other case, no enforcement action may be taken after the end of the period of ten years beginning with the date of breach.[23] Where the enforcement notice is directed at an unauthorised material change of use, it may lawfully require the removal of associated works as well as cessation of the unlawful use if the works are integral to or part and parcel of the unauthorised use, even if the works if viewed on their own would have been immune under the four-year rule.[24]

However, where an enforcement notice is in effect a breach of condition, 18.10
notice may be issued.[25] In addition, further enforcement action may be taken within four years of earlier enforcement or purported enforcement action for the same breach.[26] The latter rule should not be construed in an overly technical but in a pragmatic way and is concerned with the various acts of development which constitute the breaches of control, not the description of the substantive activities. In *Jarmain v Secretary of State for the Environment, Transport and Regions (No. 1)*,[27] the court accepted that 'the sub-section cannot be used to cover two different physical developments or two different changes of use, but it can be used to cover the same actual breach of development control which is described in different ways'.

The result is that after expiry of the relevant period the development is lawful. 18.11
This is expressly declared by TCPA 1990, section 191(2) and (3) as the consequence if no enforcement action may be taken.

The key question is the starting date for calculating the time period for action. 18.12
In the case of operations, time runs from the date when they were substantially completed. In the case of a change of use, it runs from the date of breach, which may be a matter of some difficulty where use is intermittent or where the change has been gradual. For all cases where the limit is ten years, the period runs from the date of breach.

Whether or not works have been substantially completed is not to be 18.13
approached over-technically. In *Sage v Secretary of State for the Environment, Transport and Regions*,[28] the House of Lords reversed the decision of the Court of Appeal. The Court of Appeal had held that works yet to be carried out on a building have to amount to development within the meaning of the 1990 Act if they are to be taken into account when deciding the issue of substantial completion, and accordingly all that was necessary was to complete those works which by statute required planning

[21] TCPA 1990, s. 171B(1).

[22] TCPA 1990, s. 171B(2).

[23] TCPA 1990, s. 171B(3).

[24] See *Murfitt v Secretary of State for the Environment* (1980) 40 P & CR 254 and *Kestrel Hydro v Secretary of State for Communities and Local Government* [2016] EWCA Civ 784 at para. 28.

[25] TCPA 1990, s. 171B(4)(a).

[26] TCPA 1990, s. 171B(4)(b).

[27] [2000] JPL 1063.

[28] [2003] UKHL 22, [2003] 1 WLR 983.

permission. In reversing this, the House of Lords held that an holistic approach must be taken and that regard must be had to the totality of the works which a person originally contemplated and intended to carry out.

18.14 Change of use to a single dwelling is singled out for particular attention because of the importance that is placed on certainty and the fact that it involves use of a building as a person's home. TCPA 1990, section 171B(2) simply says that where there has been a breach of planning control consisting in the change of use of any building to use as a single dwelling house, no enforcement action may be taken after the end of the period of four years beginning with the date of the breach; but the provisions have caused some difficulty in application. Such a change of use may be contrary to a condition attached to a permission and generally breach of condition has a ten-year, not four-year, time limit and an issue may also arise as to which period applies in other circumstances.

18.15 In *Arun DC v First Secretary of State*,[29] planning permission for an extension to a dwelling house contained a condition that it was only to be used for purposes ancillary to the main dwelling. An enforcement notice was served in respect of use as a separate dwelling, a use which had begun more than four but less than ten years earlier. It was held that the notice was out of time, the court finding that the words 'a breach of planning control' in TCPA 1990, section 171B(2) applied to both development without the required planning permission and failure to comply with any condition subject to which planning permission was granted, so that in either case, as the concern was a change in use to use as a single dwelling, the relevant period was four years.

18.16 In *Welwyn Hatfield Council v Secretary of State for Communities and Local Government*[30] the issue was whether there had been a change in use within section 171B(2) or whether the breach was within the 10-year limit of section 171B(3). Planning permission had been granted for a hay barn and the building as completed had the external appearance of such a barn but internally was fitted out as a single dwelling house. The owner moved in and lived there for four years, after which he applied for a certificate of lawful use, relying on the four-year time limit for change of use to a single dwelling. The certificate was refused and on appeal the Supreme Court held that the local planning authority was entitled to take enforcement action. It held that in considering whether for the purposes of change of use under TCPA 1990, section 171B(2) there had been a period of no use, it was appropriate to look at the matter in the round and ask what use the building had or of what use it was and that it was artificial to say that a building had had or been of no use at all or that its use was as anything other than a dwelling house when its owner had just built it to live in and had planned to and was about to move in within a few days. It followed that the short period between the end of July 2002 when the building had been completed and 9 August 2002 when it had been occupied

[29] [2006] EWCA Civ 1172, [2007] 1WLR 523.

[30] [2011] UKSC 15, [2011] 2 AC 304.

as a single dwelling house could not be relied to enable a claim of change of use under section 171B(2).

The court also considered the position of deliberate concealment and applied the general principle that a person was not entitled to benefit from his own wrongdoing so that positive and deliberately misleading false statements by an owner which successfully prevented discovery meant that the four-year period could not be relied on and the local planning authority was able to take enforcement action. Amendments[31] to deal with concealment have been introduced for land in England but not in Wales so that the matter still falls to be considered in accordance with the Supreme Court judgment without reference to planning enforcement orders, although it has recently been held that at any event these provisions did not remove the effect of the *Welwyn* decision.[32] 18.17

Action in respect of a material change of use can cause difficulties as there may not be a sharp dividing line between the old and the new but a gradual movement from one use to another. The approach is to require a rolling or continuous use. In *Thurrock BC v Secretary of State for the Environment, Transport and Regions*[33] it was said that: 18.18

> The problem in these cases arises from the fact that the wording of the enforcement legislation focuses on the carrying out of building operations and the making of a material change in the use of land whereas clearly what is of potential concern to the public is not primarily the process of building or the process of changing the use as such but the continued existence of the building or of the new use. That is made clear by section 173 which sets out what an enforcement notice can require as 'remedying the breach'. That section indicates that if the building is removed or the new activity ceases then the breach will be regarded as having been remedied . . . If there is a planning objection to the erection of a building the LPA must take enforcement action within 4 years of completion or lose the chance of taking such action. If there is a planning objection to a use which has been instituted without the grant of planning permission then again the LPA must take enforcement action within the appropriate time limit, 10 years in the present case. If the new use continues throughout that period then the LPA have lost their chance. Their position is much the same as that of a landowner who lets the world regularly walk along a path over his land. There comes a time when he has lost his right to object.

However, in *Trim v North Dorset DC*[34] Carnwath LJ said: 18.19

[31] TCPA 1990, ss. 171BA–171BC.

[32] See *Bonsall v Secretary of State for Communities and Local Government; Jackson v Secretary of State for Communities and Local Government* [2015] EWCA Civ 1246, [2016] 2 WLR 1407.

[33] [2002] EWCA Civ 226 at paras 24 and 25.

[34] [2010] EWCA Civ 1446, [2011] 1 WLR 1901, at para. 14.

> I should mention one point which is not in issue between the parties, in case it arises in another case. This concerns the application of the ten-year rule to breach of an occupancy condition such as in this case. Arguably, a distinction could be drawn between such a contravention and unauthorised development by a material change of use. The latter is a single event occurring at the time of the change. The ten-year period clearly runs from that date as 'the date of breach'. The former does not involve a single event of that kind. Arguably, there is fresh breach on each day on which the offending occupation continues. On that view, the ten-year period would start again each day, and in effect there would be no time limit for enforcement.
>
> It seems however to be the accepted view, and is not in issue before us, that in such a case also the ten-year period runs from the date when the offending use began, provided that there has been a continuing contravention since then: see *Nicholson v Secretary of State for the Environment [1998] J.P.L. 553*, 560, per Robin Purchas QC sitting as a deputy High Court judge, followed by Sullivan J in *R (North Devon District Council) v First Secretary of State [2004] 3 PLR 62*. This view is supported by Government guidance, which draws no distinction between unlawful development by a material change of use and breach of an occupancy condition: see Circular 10/97, Annex 2, para 2.4. As we have heard no argument, I express no view as to the correctness of the accepted approach, but simply reserve my position in case it should arise in a future case at this level.

PLANNING CONTRAVENTION NOTICES AND OTHER INVESTIGATORY POWERS

18.20 Where it appears to a local planning authority that there may have been a breach of planning control it may serve a planning contravention notice.[35] The notice may be served on the owner, occupier or a person who has any interest in the land or is carrying out operations or using the land for any purpose.

18.21 The power with its sanctions can be described as intrusive and, although minimally so, the authority must form its own view and it must appear that there is a breach; refusal to cooperate of itself is insufficient. In *R v Teignbridge DC, ex parte Teignmouth Quay Co.*,[36] a notice was quashed in judicial review proceedings, Judge J saying:

> the decision by the Council was based on a desire to obtain information which the company was not prepared to give and, on the available material, was reasonably entitled to refuse. In effect the Council was requiring the company to prove that it may not have been in breach of planning control and to justify the exercise of its rights under the GDO. The question whether to quash this decision is

[35] Section 171C(1).

[36] [1995] JPL 828 at p. 835.

> not answered simply by asking whether the Council behaved 'unreasonably' in the general sense: in the present case it is whether it behaved 'unreasonably' in the way it purported to exercise the powers granted and limited by statute. In my judgment no reasonable planning authority could have concluded that it appeared that there may have been a breach of planning control by the company on this land.

The notice may require information as to any operations, uses or activities being carried out on the land and any matter relating to conditions or limitations attached to planning permission relating to the land.[37] This may include, but is not limited to, information about specified operations or activities, the date when any use, operations or activities commenced, the name and address of the person using the land or carrying out such matters, information as to any planning permission or why it is not required and the nature of the recipient's interest in the land.[38] 18.22

The notice must contain details to enable a person to make any offer relating to planning permission or activities or works[39] or representations about the notice[40] and must give information of the likely consequences of failing to respond and that enforcement action may be taken.[41] A stop notice may entitle a person to compensation for loss under TCPA 1990, section 186 but no compensation is recoverable for loss if it is in respect of any loss or damage which could have been avoided by providing the information or otherwise cooperating when responding to a planning contravention notice.[42] The planning contravention notice must inform the recipient of this.[43] 18.23

A person who fails to comply with a planning contravention notice or gives false or misleading information in reply is guilty of an offence. This is considered in Chapter 20, below. 18.24

These provisions are in addition to the general power to require information as to interests in land to enable an order to be made or a notice issued conferred by TCPA 1990, section 330. This power applies to local planning authorities (including National Park Authorities[44]) and the Welsh Ministers enabling them to send a notice requiring information to the occupier and any person receiving rent, whether directly or indirectly, in respect of any premises. The matters on which information is required are the nature of the addressee's interest, the name and address of any other person known to have an interest, the use of the premises and when it began, the name and address of the user and the time when any activities 18.25

37 TCPA 1990, s. 171C(2).
38 TCPA 1990, s. 171C(3).
39 TCPA 1990, s. 171C(4)(a).
40 TCPA 1990, s. 171C(4)(b).
41 TCPA 1990, s. 171C(5)(a).
42 TCPA 1990, s. 186(5)(b).
43 TCPA 1990, s. 171C(5)(b).
44 TCPA 1990, s. 330(6).

began.[45] Failure without reasonable excuse to give the information is an offence,[46] as is knowingly making any misstatement.[47]

18.26 Powers of entry onto land in connection with enforcement are contained in TCPA 1990, sections196A–196C. There are separate powers for other specified purposes in section 324 of the Act. TCPA 1990, section 196A gives a power of entry without warrant for four purposes. These are to ascertain whether there is or has been a breach of planning control, to determine if any of the powers under Part VII (enforcement) of the Act should be exercised, to determine how any such power should be exercised and to ascertain if there has been compliance where any such power has been exercised.[48] The power of entry is conferred on any person duly authorised in writing by a local planning authority and only if there are reasonable grounds for entering the land for the purpose in question and only at a reasonable hour.[49] In addition, any person duly authorised in writing by the Welsh Ministers may at any reasonable hour enter any land to determine whether an enforcement notice should be issued in relation to the land or any other land, if there are reasonable grounds for entering for that purpose.[50] No authorisation can be granted without consulting the local planning authority.[51]

18.27 Admission to a dwelling house shall not be demanded as of right under either power unless twenty-four hours' notice of the intended entry has been given to the occupier.[52] A warrant may be issued to enter land where there are reasonable grounds for entering the land for any of the purposes mentioned above if the case is one of urgency or where admission has been refused or a refusal is reasonably apprehended.[53]

18.28 Section 196C contains additional provisions concerning exercise of the powers of entry (both with and without a warrant) and makes wilful obstruction a criminal offence. Certain restrictions on disclosure of manufacturing processes or trade secrets are in subsections (5)–(7).

ENFORCEMENT NOTICES

18.29 A local planning authority may issue an enforcement notice where it appears to it that there has been a breach of planning control and that it is expedient to issue the notice having regard to the development plan and to any other material

[45] TCPA 1990, s. 330(2).
[46] TCPA 1990, s. 330(4).
[47] TCPA 1990, s. 330(5).
[48] TCPA 1990, s. 196A(1).
[49] TCPA 1990, s. 196A(1).
[50] TCPA 1990, s. 196A(2).
[51] TCPA 1990, s. 196A(3).
[52] TCPA 1990, s. 196A(4).
[53] TCPA 1990, s. 196B(1).

considerations.[54] The meaning of breach of planning control has been considered above. The additional element is the expediency of issuing this form of notice and the extent to which that is challengeable.

An enforcement notice may be challenged by an appeal on one of the statutory grounds in TCPA 1990, section 174 but its validity may not be questioned on these grounds in any other proceedings.[55] Furthermore, the wording 'where it appears to them' that there has been a breach gives a substantial latitude to the local planning authority. Nevertheless, the decision to issue an enforcement notice is challengeable by judicial review and these circumstances were considered by Lindblom J in *Gazelle Properties Ltd, Sustainable Environmental Services Limited v Bath and North East Somerset Council.*[56] Having confirmed that the decision to issue a notice was amenable to judicial review on conventional grounds, he went on to consider the meaning of 'expediency', citing with approval Ousley J in the different context of a section 102 discontinuance order.[57] He distinguished the factual question of whether or not there had been a breach from the pragmatic question of what ought to be done about it and said:[58] 18.30

> the concept of 'expediency' in contexts which include the exercise of enforcement powers by a local planning authority goes wider than the concept of material planning considerations such as are engaged in the determination of an application for planning permission, extending, in the enforcement context, to the balance of advantage and disadvantage to the public interest and, in particular, the question of whether the potential gain in going ahead with enforcement action against an identified breach of planning control is worth the cost and time likely to be spent in doing so; and, secondly, that an authority's exercise of its discretion when making an 'expediency' decision is susceptible to review by the court on conventional public law grounds.

Equally, a decision not to issue an enforcement notice based upon errors of law may be subject to review leading to a mandatory order requiring issue of a notice.[59] 18.31

PPW makes clear that all enforcement action must be commensurate and that the purpose is to remedy the effects of breach and not to punish the person responsible.[60] It states that in all cases there should be dialogue with the owner or occupier and in some cases mediation may be possible so as to avoid taking 18.32

[54] TCPA 1990, s. 172.

[55] TCPA 1990, s. 285 – see later for consideration of this.

[56] [2010] EWHC 3127 (Admin).

[57] See *R (Usk Valley Conservation Group) v Brecon Beacons National Park Authority* [2010] EWHC 71 (Admin) at para. 56.

[58] [2010] EWHC 3127 (Admin) at para. 56.

[59] See *Ardagh Glass Ltd v Chester City Council* [2009] EWHC 745 (Admin), first instance decision, not appealed on this issue.

[60] At para. 3.6.3.

enforcement action. Overall, PPW states the test in these terms: 'The decisive issue for the authority is whether the breach of planning control would unacceptably affect public amenity or the existing use of land and buildings meriting protection in the public interest.'[61]

ENFORCEMENT NOTICES AND EIA DEVELOPMENT

18.33 Additional steps are required before issue of an enforcement notice if the unauthorised development is or may be EIA development within the Town and Country Planning (Environmental Impact Assessment) (Wales) Regulations 2016.[62] Where it appears to the local planning authority by whom or on whose behalf an enforcement notice is to be issued that the matters constituting the breach of planning control comprise or include Schedule 1 development or Schedule 2 development within the meaning of the Regulations they shall, before the enforcement notice is issued, adopt a screening opinion.[63] In addition, in such a case they shall serve with a copy of the enforcement notice a 'regulation 42 notice'. This notice must include the screening opinion and the written statement required by regulation 4(7) and shall require a person who gives notice of an appeal under section 174(2) to submit to the Welsh Ministers four copies of an environmental statement relating to that EIA development.[64]

18.34 The authority must send a copy of the regulation 42 notice to the Welsh Ministers together with a list of the other persons to whom a copy of the notice has been or is to be sent and also to the consultation bodies.[65]

18.35 Any person on whom a regulation 42 notice is served may apply to the Welsh Ministers for a screening direction. Where the Welsh Ministers direct that the matters which are alleged to constitute the breach of planning control do not comprise or include EIA development, they shall send a copy of the direction to every person to whom a copy of the regulation 42 notice was sent.[66] If they consider that the information provided in accordance with subparagraph (2)(c) is insufficient to enable them to make a direction, they shall notify the applicant and the authority of the matters in respect of which they require additional information and the information so requested shall be provided by the applicant within such reasonable period as may be specified in the notice.[67]

[61] PPW 3.6.1.

[62] SI 2016 No. 58 ('EIA Regs'): see Pt 10, reg. 40.

[63] EIA Regs, reg. 42.

[64] EIA Regs, reg. 42(2).

[65] EIA Regs, reg. 42(3).

[66] EIA Regs, reg. 43(6).

[67] EIA Regs, reg. 43.

18.36 In *R (Evans) v Basingstoke and Deane BC*[68] it was held that the ten-year time limit in section 171B(3) of the 1990 Act was not incompatible with Directive 85/337/EEC (projects with significant effects on the environment).[69] Accordingly, the general rules at to time limits for enforcement action apply to EIA development as for other unauthorised development.

ENFORCEMENT NOTICE – PROCEDURAL STEPS AND FORMALITIES

18.37 Authority to issue a notice depends upon the scheme of authority and delegation within the particular council.[70]

18.38 Once authorised a copy of the notice must be served on the owner and occupier of the land and on any other person having an interest in the land, which interest is in the authority's opinion materially affected by the notice.[71] The general definition of owner is in TCPA 1990, section 336: this excludes a mortgagee not in possession. However, the residual category of a person with an interest who is materially affected may necessitate service on a mortgagee as well as others who are not in actual occupation. There is no statutory definition of a person with an interest but the same phrase is used in TCPA 1990, section 174 conferring a right of appeal and in that context *R (Flynn) v Secretary of State for Communities and Local Government and another*[72] confirmed that 'a person having an interest in the land' meant a person having a legal or equitable interest in land and did not include a person who had no such interest but had some other link with the land. This is, of course, subject to the separate requirement to serve any occupier, which is a matter of fact.

18.39 Service must be not later than twenty-eight days after issue and not less than twenty-eight days before the notice takes effect.[73] Service is in accordance with the provisions of section 329 of TCPA 1990. An appeal may be made on the grounds of a failure to serve the notice as required by section 172,[74] although the failure may be disregarded if neither the appellant nor the person who was not served has been substantially prejudiced.[75]

18.40 As stated above, the local planning authority are required to keep a record of enforcement notices in a register[76] and detail of the information to be contained

[68] [2013] EWCA Civ 1635, [2014] 1 WLR 2034.

[69] Directive now superseded by 2011/92/EU.

[70] See para. 18.3, above.

[71] TCPA 1990, s. 172(2).

[72] [2014] EWHC 390 (Admin), [2014] 1 WLR 3270.

[73] TCPA 1990, s. 172(3).

[74] TCPA 1990, s. 174(2)(e).

[75] TCPA 1990, s. 176(5).

[76] See TCPA 1990, s. 188.

in the register is prescribed by article 30 of the Town and Country Planning (Development Management Procedure) (Wales) Order 2012.[77] Entry in the register is required within fourteen days of issue.[78]

CONTENT OF ENFORCEMENT NOTICE

18.41 An enforcement notice must state the matters which appear to be the breach of planning control and the paragraph of TCPA 1990, section 171 (1) under which the breach falls.[79] It must also specify the steps to be taken or the activities required to cease in order, wholly or partly, to remedy the breach by making the development comply with planning permission which has been granted, or discontinuing any use of the land, or restoring the land to its condition before breach or remedying any breach of amenity caused by the breach.[80] Particular examples of what may be required are given by section 173(5), including, for example, the alteration or removal of a building, and, where demolition is specified, construction of a replacement building may be required.[81]

18.42 The notice must state the date when it is to take effect[82] and the period at the end of which the steps are required to have been taken or the activities are required to have ceased: different periods may be specified for different steps or activities.[83]

18.43 Section 173(10) provides for the notice to contain such further information as is prescribed. A notice must specify the reasons why the local planning authority consider it expedient to issue the notice, all relevant development plan policies and proposals and the precise boundaries of the land, by plan or otherwise.[84] It must be accompanied by an explanatory note containing specified information which includes details of the right to appeal.[85]

18.44 Section 173(2) simply provides that the requirements of section 173(1)(a) to state the matters which appear to be a breach of planning control are complied with if the notice enables any person served to know what those matters are. Historically, the test framed by the courts was whether the notice told the person served 'fairly

[77] SI 2012 No. 801 ('DMP(W)O').

[78] DMP(W)O, art. 5.

[79] TCPA 1990, s. 173(1).

[80] Section 173(3) and (4). Restoration of the land to a condition before an unauthorised use took place may include the removal of associated works which are integral to the unauthorised use: see *Kestrel Hydro v Secretary of State for Communities and Local Government* [2016] EWCA Civ 784.

[81] TCPA 1990, s. 173(6) and (7).

[82] TCPA 1990, s. 173(8).

[83] TCPA 1990, s. 173(9).

[84] Town and Country Planning (Enforcement Notices and Appeals) (Wales) Regulations 2003 (SI 2003 No. 394), art. 3.

[85] SI 2003 No. 394, art. 4.

what he has done wrong and what he must do to remedy it'.[86] Notwithstanding this and judicial disapproval of the basis of challenges, attempts to draw fine distinctions continued both before and after the introduction of amended wording in 1991 and to an extent the practice remains today. The general approach of the courts has been to avoid artificial lawyerly distinctions and reference may be made to the brief overview by Munby LJ in *Westminster City Council v Davenport*:[87] he referred to case law historically abounding with hair-splitting technicalities and he declined to return to 'the bad old days'.

Although over-technical challenges are not favoured, clarity is needed in the wording of the notice. However, the degree of precision required may depend on the context in which a deficiency is alleged. The terms of a notice may fall for examination on an enforcement appeal, in challenges by judicial review or in criminal proceedings and the effect of any particular alleged failure in the notice may vary in each. The issue is whether a notice which contains an error is wholly ineffective. So, whether there is sufficient certainty or clarity may have to be judged in the context of the statutory grounds of appeal, against the inspector's powers of amendment on an appeal and when considering restrictions on raising matters on a prosecution for failing to comply with a notice stemming from section 285. 18.45

For present purposes it is sufficient to refer to the conventional approach exemplified by *Payne v National Assembly for Wales*,[88] where Wyn Williams J held that the distinction between enforcement notices which on their face were a nullity and those which were invalid until quashed was still one recognised by the higher courts. The decision in *Miller-Mead*[89] remained binding. Accordingly, a notice which was invalid on its face, being insufficiently certain, left the inspector no power to vary it because it was a nullity. The inspector should have notified the parties of his view and taken no further step in relation to the notice. However, the correctness of the distinction between nullity and validity was questioned (obiter) in *Broadland DC v Trott*[90] and this has been considered generally by the Court of Appeal in *Westminster City Council v Davenport*.[91] Reliance on the distinction may not therefore always be appropriate. 18.46

ENFORCEMENT NOTICES – FURTHER DRAFTING ISSUES

Care is necessary in framing the requirements of a notice to ensure that it does not have unintended effects. The wording may appear to involve either over or under enforcement. The former arises where the notice purports to take away an 18.47

[86] See Upjohn LJ in *Miller-Mead v Minister for Housing and Local Government* [1963] 2 QB 196 at p. 226.

[87] [2011] EWCA Civ 458, see esp. paras 55 and 57.

[88] [2006] EWHC 597 (Admin).

[89] See fn 86, above.

[90] [2011] EWCA Civ 301.

[91] See above.

established use. This would be challengeable on an appeal under section 174 and the notice may then be amended so as to safeguard the established use.[92] This is confined to cases of existing use and does not apply to the retention of buildings which had been altered or erected in breach of planning control.[93]

18.48 It should be stressed that it is necessary to take action to challenge the notice by an appeal, otherwise it will be effective according to its terms. In *Staffordshire CC v Challinor*[94] the Court of Appeal held that it was an over-simplification and a misinterpretation of the authorities to contend that an enforcement notice could not take away lawful use rights. It had long been established that lawful rights would be lost if an enforcement notice was served and existing rights not subsequently raised as grounds of appeal. That was the result of TCPA 1990, section 285(1).

18.49 Under-enforcement is expressly dealt with in TCPA 1990, section 173(11), which provides that where an enforcement notice in respect of any breach of planning control could have required any buildings or works to be removed or any activity to cease, but does not do so, and all the requirements of the notice have been complied with, then, so far as the notice did not so require, planning permission shall be treated as having been granted by virtue of section 73A in respect of development consisting of the construction of the buildings or works or, as the case may be, the carrying out of the activities. *Fidler v First Secretary of State*[95] held that the subsection only applies to activities or works included in the description of the breach in the enforcement notice. There, the enforcement notice had mentioned only one specific use but that did not mean that planning permission was deemed to have been granted to the various non-agricultural activities occurring at the time.

18.50 In addition, *Ioannou v Secretary of State for Communities and Local Government*[96] made clear that the only buildings, works or activities which could benefit from section 173(11) were those in existence when the enforcement notice was issued, and it could not extend to prospective development.

ENFORCEMENT NOTICES – DURATION

18.51 An enforcement notice remains in force notwithstanding that its requirements have been met.[97] Further, a requirement in an enforcement notice for a use of land to be discontinued is for it to be discontinued permanently and resumption after discontinuance is therefore a breach of the notice.[98] This leads to certain consequential

[92] See *Mansi v Elstree RDC* (1964) 16 P & CR 153 – and see appeals for further consideration.

[93] See *Mohammed v Secretary of State for Communities and Local Government* [2014] EWHC 4045 (Admin) – permission granted to appeal to Supreme Court.

[94] [2007] EWCA Civ 864.

[95] [2004] EWCA Civ 1295.

[96] [2014] EWCA Civ 1432.

[97] TCPA 1990, s. 181(1).

[98] TCPA 1990, s. 181(2).

provisions relating to carrying out the requirements of the notice and later works or use of the land, in particular regarding later attempts to 'undo' the steps taken to comply with the notice.

First, TCPA 1990, section 173(12) provides that where an enforcement notice requires the construction of a replacement building, and all the requirements of the notice with respect to that construction have been complied with, planning permission shall be treated as having been granted by virtue of section 73A in respect of development consisting of that construction. Where the requirements are to remove or alter any buildings or works and that is done, later development to reinstate or restore the buildings or works are treated as if the notice applied equally to the reinstated or restored building as to the original building.[99] Carrying out the development may then be a criminal offence.[100] Finally, if a local planning authority itself intends to take steps to alter or remove the reinstated or restored building, it shall give notice to that effect.[101] 18.52

Where, after the service of an enforcement notice, planning permission is granted for any development carried out before the grant of that permission, the notice shall cease to have effect so far as inconsistent with that permission.[102] This does not affect liability for an earlier breach.[103] *Havering LBC v Secretary of State for the Environment*[104] held that a planning permission would be effective to override an enforcement notice, even though it did not go precisely to the matters covered by the enforcement notice and even though it contained conditions, as long as it covered the same area of land and the use permitted by the permission embraced the use enforced against. However, it is not the case that the enforcement notice ceases to have effect altogether, only that it ceases to have effect to the extent that its requirements are inconsistent with the subsequent grant of planning permission.[105] 18.53

There is a right of appeal against an enforcement notice and this and the procedure and powers on appeal are considered separately.[106] Failure to comply with an enforcement notice is a criminal offence. This is considered in Chapter 20. 18.54

A local planning authority has power to withdraw a notice or waive or relax any requirement, including power to extend any period for compliance.[107] In addition, a local planning authority may by letter give a binding assurance to any person that he is not at risk of being prosecuted in connection with the enforcement notice or for specified matters relating to the notice.[108] The assurance may 18.55

[99] TCPA 1990, s. 181(3).

[100] See below.

[101] TCPA 1990, s. 181(4).

[102] TCPA 1990, s. 180(1).

[103] TCPA 1990, s. 180(3).

[104] (1983) 45 P & CR 258.

[105] *R (Rapose) v Wandsworth LBC* [2010] EWHC 3126 (Admin).

[106] See Chapter 19.

[107] TCPA 1990, s. 173A.

[108] TCPA 1990, s. 172A(1) and (5).

be withdrawn in whole or in part on giving a reasonable opportunity for steps to be taken to avoid prosecution.[109]

FAILURE TO COMPLY WITH ENFORCEMENT NOTICE – FURTHER MEASURES

18.56 In addition to, or instead of, bringing criminal proceedings for non-compliance, a local planning authority may seek to secure compliance by bringing injunction proceedings or take direct action under section 178. An injunction may be sought for anticipated and actual breaches of planning control and is more extensive therefore than action where an enforcement notice has been issued and not complied with, and is considered separately below.

18.57 Direct action, as it has been termed, refers to the power of the local planning authority themselves to execute the works required and recover the costs. Where any steps required by an enforcement notice to be taken are not taken within the period for compliance with the notice, the local planning authority may enter the land and take the steps and recover from the person who is then the owner of the land any expenses reasonably incurred by them in doing so.[110] The power to execute works is extended to development by way of reinstating or restoring a building or works where the original had been removed or altered to comply with a notice.[111] Regulations provide that ancillary powers in the Public Health Act 1936 apply to the exercise of this power as for other works executed by the local authority under statutory powers.[112]

18.58 The decision to rely on section 178 is amenable to judicial review and in appropriate cases may engage the human rights of the occupiers, for example where the steps involve eviction from their home.[113] Nevertheless, it will not be open to raise matters which amount to challenging the enforcement notice itself on one of the appeal grounds contrary to TCPA 1990, section 285 and the history of consideration of the site in the planning process may be relevant.[114] However, it is necessary that the action is properly action in accordance with the enforcement notice. Edwards-Stuart J held, in *Egan v Basildon BC*,[115] that the council cannot, when exercising its powers under section 178, demolish buildings or structures that had been erected unlawfully before the issue of the enforcement notice, which could have been but were not the subject of an enforcement notice or mentioned

[109] TCPA 1990, s. 172A(2) and (3).

[110] TCPA 1990, s. 178(1).

[111] TCPA 1990, s. 181(4).

[112] See s. 178(3) and Town and Country Planning General Regulations 1992 (SI 1992 No. 1492), reg. 14.

[113] See e.g. *R (O'Brien) v Basildon BC* [2006] EWHC 1346 (Admin).

[114] See e.g. *R (Sheridan) v Basildon BC* [2011] EWHC 2938 (Admin) at para. 45.

[115] [2011] EWHC 2416 (QB).

in an enforcement notice, under the rule in relation to enabling works which exists at common law or by virtue of section 111(1) of the Local Government Act 1972. Since the residents asserted that the buildings in question were constructed prior to the issue of the notices, it was for them to prove this in the case of each building.

Wilfully obstructing a person exercising the powers is a criminal offence.[116] 18.59

POWERS OF WELSH MINISTERS

If it appears to the Welsh Ministers to be expedient they may issue an enforcement notice but shall not do so without consulting the local planning authority. Such a notice has the same effect as a notice issued by the local planning authority and sections 178 and 181 apply as if referring to the Welsh Ministers.[117] 18.60

STOP NOTICES

Service of a stop notice is an additional power where immediate action is required in support of an enforcement notice. Where the local planning authority considers it expedient that any relevant activity should cease before the expiry of the period for compliance with an enforcement notice, it may, when it serves the copy of the enforcement notice or afterwards, serve a stop notice prohibiting the carrying out of that activity on the land to which the enforcement notice relates, or any part of that land specified in the stop notice.[118] 'Relevant activity' means any activity specified in the enforcement notice as an activity which the local planning authority require to cease and any activity carried out as part of that activity or associated with that activity.[119] 18.61

A stop notice shall not prohibit the use of any building as a dwelling house[120] nor prohibit the carrying out of any activity which has been carried on (whether continuously or not) for a period of more than four years,[121] with the exception of any activity consisting of, or incidental to, building, engineering, mining or other operations or the deposit of refuse or waste materials.[122] 18.62

The stop notice must refer to the enforcement notice to which it relates and have a copy of that notice annexed to it.[123] However, the stop notice is not invalid by reason that a copy of the enforcement notice to which it relates was not served 18.63

[116] TCPA 1990, s. 178(6).
[117] TCPA 1990, s. 182.
[118] TCPA 1990, s. 183(1).
[119] TCPA 1990, s. 183(2).
[120] TCPA 1990, s. 183(4).
[121] TCPA 1990, s. 183(5).
[122] TCPA 1990, s. 183(5A).
[123] TCPA 1990, s. 184(1).

as required if it is shown that the local planning authority took all such steps as were reasonably practicable to effect proper service.[124] The notice may not be served where the enforcement notice has already taken effect.[125] It must specify the date on which it will take effect and that date must not be earlier than three days from service, unless there are special reasons for an earlier date and these are specified in the notice, nor more than twenty-eight days from service.[126]

18.64 It may be served on any person who appears to a local planning authority to have an interest in the land or to be engaged in any activity prohibited by the notice.[127] Interest will here be construed as for service of an enforcement notice. The local planning authority may display details on the land by a site notice[128] and must enter a copy in its register.[129]

18.65 Being dependent on an enforcement notice, a stop notice ceases to have effect when the enforcement notice to which it relates is withdrawn or is quashed or the period for compliance with the enforcement notice expires. It ceases to have effect also if or to the extent that the activities prohibited by it cease, on a variation of the enforcement notice, to be relevant activities.[130] In addition, the stop notice may itself be withdrawn under TCPA 1990, section 183(7) and it then expires when notice of withdrawal is first served.[131] Where the stop notice was displayed by a site notice and is then withdrawn the authority must display a notice of the withdrawal.[132]

18.66 The local planning authority may also be liable to pay compensation in some of the above circumstances. It may be payable on the quashing of the enforcement notice or an activity ceasing to be a relevant activity under the stop notice, otherwise in either case as a result of the grant of planning permission or the discharge of a condition or limitation under section 174(2)(a). It may also be payable on the withdrawal of the enforcement notice, except as a consequence of the grant of planning permission for the development by the authority, or the withdrawal of the stop notice.[133]

18.67 Compensation is payable by the local planning authority to any person who, when the stop notice is first served, has an interest in or occupies the land to which the notice relates. It is payable in respect of any loss or damage directly attributable to the prohibition contained in the notice or, in the case of a variation of the enforcement notice so that activities cease to be relevant activities, the prohibition

[124] TCPA 1990, s. 184(8).
[125] TCPA 1990, s. 184(3).
[126] TCPA 1990, s. 184(2) and (3).
[127] TCPA 1990, s. 183(6).
[128] TCPA 1990, s. 184(6).
[129] TCPA 1990, s. 188(1).
[130] TCPA 1990, s. 184(5).
[131] TCPA 1990, s. 184(4).
[132] TCPA 1990, s. 184(7).
[133] TCPA 1990, s. 186(1).

of such of the activities prohibited by the stop notice as cease to be relevant activities.[134] It includes any sum payable in respect of a breach of contract caused by the taking of action necessary to comply with the prohibition.[135] Compensation is not payable, however, in respect of any activity which is or contributes to a breach of planning control if it could have been avoided by the provision of information or cooperation with requirements under sections 171C and 330 of the 1990 Act or section 16 of the Local Government (Miscellaneous Provisions) Act 1976.[136] Questions of disputed compensation are for the Upper Tribunal.[137]

If any person contravenes a stop notice after a site notice has been displayed or the stop notice has been served on him, he is guilty of an offence.[138] 18.68

If it appears to the Welsh Ministers to be expedient they may serve a stop notice but shall not do so without consulting the local planning authority. Such a notice has the same effect as a notice issued by the local planning authority.[139] 18.69

TEMPORARY STOP NOTICES

Temporary stop notices may be issued in accordance with sections 171E–171H of TCPA 1990. They are to meet cases of urgency where other action has not yet been taken. A notice may be issued where the local planning authority think that there has been a breach of planning control in relation to any land, and that it is expedient that the activity (or any part of the activity) which amounts to the breach is stopped immediately.[140] The notice must be in writing and must specify the activity which the authority thinks amounts to the breach, prohibit the carrying on of the activity (or of so much of the activity as is specified in the notice) and set out the authority's reasons for issuing the notice.[141] 18.70

The notice must be displayed on the land and has effect from that date[142] and ceases to have effect after twenty-eight days or shorter specified period or earlier withdrawal.[143] It may be served on the person who the authority thinks is carrying on the activity, is an occupier or has an interest in the land.[144] 18.71

134 TCPA 1990, s. 186(2).
135 TCPA 1990, s. 186(4).
136 TCPA 1990, s. 186(4).
137 TCPA 1990, s. 186(6).
138 TCPA 1990, s. 187(1).
139 TCPA 1990, s. 185.
140 TCPA 1990, s. 171E(2).
141 TCPA 1990, s. 171E(3).
142 TCPA 1990, s. 171E(5) and (6).
143 TCPA 1990, s. 171E(7).
144 TCPA 1990, s. 171E(4).

18.72 A temporary stop notice does not prohibit the use of a building as a dwelling house or prescribed activities,[145] nor the carrying out of any activity which has been carried out (whether or not continuously) for a period of four years[146] but can prohibit activity incidental to operations and the deposit of refuse or waste materials.[147]

18.73 A second or subsequent temporary stop notice must not be issued in respect of the same activity unless the local planning authority have first taken some other enforcement action, including obtaining an injunction, in relation to the breach of planning control which is constituted by the activity.[148]

18.74 A person commits an offence if a notice has been served on him or displayed on site and he contravenes it or causes or permits its contravention[149] but it is a defence to prove that the notice was not served on him and that he did not know and could not reasonably be expected to know of its existence.[150]

18.75 Compensation may be payable in accordance with TCPA 1990, section 171H in certain cases where the activity was lawful or the notice is withdrawn.

BREACH OF CONDITION NOTICES

18.76 Rather than issue an enforcement notice, a local planning authority may issue a breach of condition notice in any case where planning permission for development has been granted subject to conditions and any condition is not complied with.[151] Conditions includes limitations.[152] The provision is designed to provide a simpler process in appropriate cases. It is enforcement action within section 171A(2) and is therefore subject to the time limits prescribed by section 171B,[153] although where an enforcement notice is in effect in respect of the breach the limits do not prevent issue of a breach of condition notice.[154] In addition, a breach by development which is without permission and contrary to a condition may be subject to the four-year time period in accordance with *Arun DC v First Secretary of State*.[155]

18.77 Welsh Government guidance refers to enforcement action of all kinds and the policy cited above when considering enforcement notices applies equally here.

145 TCPA 1990, s. 171F(1).
146 TCPA 1990, s. 171F(2).
147 TCPA 1990, s. 171F(3).
148 TCPA 1990, s. 171F(5) and (6).
149 TCPA 1990, s. 171G(1) and (2).
150 TCPA 1990, s. 171G(5).
151 TCPA 1990, s. 187A(1) and (2).
152 TCPA 1990, s. 187A(13)(a); and see para. 8.8 above for construction of 'limitations'.
153 See above.
154 TCPA 1990, s. 171B(4).
155 [2007] 1WLR 523: see para. 18.15, above.

The notice may be served on any person who is carrying out or has carried out the development or any person having control of the land[156] and carrying out any development includes causing or permitting another to do so.[157] 18.78

The notice must require the person to secure compliance with such of the conditions as are specified in the notice,[158] although in the case of a notice served on a person in control of the land they must be conditions regulating the use of the land. It must also specify the steps which the authority considers ought to be taken, or the activities which the authority considers ought to cease, to secure compliance with the conditions specified.[159] The period for compliance is such period of not less than twenty-eight days beginning with the date of service as is specified but this may be extended by a further notice.[160] 18.79

Where, after the service of a breach of condition notice, planning permission is granted for any development carried out before the grant of that permission, the notice shall cease to have effect so far as inconsistent with that permission[161] and, if any condition to which the notice relates is discharged, the requirement to secure compliance with that condition ceases to have effect.[162] This does not affect liability for any earlier breach.[163] 18.80

There is no right of appeal against the issue of the notice. The issue of a breach of condition notice or the decision to prosecute for breach may be challenged by judicial review on established grounds. In addition, public law matters may be raised as a defence in criminal prosecutions as the restriction on raising matters in proceedings generally applicable to enforcement notices by TCPA 1990, section 285 does not apply equally to breach of condition notices. A person served may therefore seek to raise matters as to the validity and merits of the notice itself as a defence in the criminal proceedings. This is considered in Chapter 20, below. 18.81

INJUNCTIONS

Where a local planning authority considers it necessary or expedient for any actual or apprehended breach of planning control to be restrained by injunction, it may apply to the High Court or county court for an injunction.[164] This is so whether 18.82

[156] TCPA 1990, s. 187A(2): 'or' is to be read conjunctively.

[157] TCPA 1990, s. 187A(13)(b).

[158] TCPA 1990, s. 187A(2) and s. 187A(4).

[159] TCPA 1990, s. 187A(5).

[160] TCPA 1990, s. 187A(7).

[161] TCPA 1990, s. 180(1).

[162] TCPA 1990, s. 180(2).

[163] TCPA 1990, s. 180(3).

[164] TCPA 1990, s. 187B(1) and (4). An injunction is defined as a court order prohibiting a person from doing something or requiring a person to do something (see CPR Glossary) and the power is part of the general jurisdiction of the court to intervene to prevent unlawful conduct.

or not it has exercised or is proposing to exercise any of its other powers. On an application, the court may grant such an injunction as the court thinks appropriate for the purpose of restraining the breach.[165]

18.83 The application is governed by the general procedural rules for interim and final injunctions, and reference should be made to the Senior Courts Act 1981, section 37 and CPR Pt 8 and Pt 25 and PD25A. Where the injunction is to prevent environmental harm the additional provisions of CPD 8A, paragraph 20 will apply.

18.84 The principles to be applied in deciding whether or not to grant an injunction in planning matters were established by the House of Lords in *South Bucks DC v Porter*.[166] Here the local planning authority applied for an injunction to prevent the defendants, who were gypsies, from living in mobile homes and caravans on land acquired by them for that purpose but for which planning consent had been refused. In opposition, the defence raised planning grounds and the human rights of the occupiers, in particular their Article 8 right to respect for family life and their home. It was held that injunctive relief must be just and proportionate. The general principles from the judgment were conveniently summarised by Auld LJ in *Tonbridge and Malling BC v Davis*[167] as follows:

> 1) section 187B confers on the courts an original and discretionary, not a supervisory, jurisdiction, so that a defendant seeking to resist injunctive relief is not restricted to judicial review grounds; 2) it is questionable whether Article 8 adds anything to the existing equitable duty of a court in the exercise of its discretion under section 187B; 3) the jurisdiction is to be exercised with due regard to the purpose for which [it] was conferred, namely to restrain breaches of planning control, and flagrant and prolonged defiance by a defendant of the relevant planning controls and procedures may weigh heavily in favour of injunctive relief; 4) however, it is inherent in the injunctive remedy that its grant depends on a court's judgment of all the circumstances of the case; 5) although a court would not examine matters of planning policy and judgment, since those lay within the exclusive purview of the responsible local planning authority, it will consider whether, and the extent to which, the local planning authority has taken account of the personal circumstances of the defendant and any hardship that injunctive relief might cause, and it is not obliged to grant relief simply because a planning authority considered it necessary or expedient to restrain a planning breach; 6) having had regard to all the circumstances of the case, the court will only grant an injunction where it is just and proportionate to do so, taking account, inter alia, of the rights of the person or persons against whom injunctive relief is sought, and of whether it is relief with which that person or persons can and reasonably ought to comply.

[165] TCPA 1990, s. 187B(2).

[166] [2003] 2 AC 558.

[167] [2004] EWCA Civ 194 at para. 34.

The principles have been consistently applied by the courts and are well established. The balancing act required of course depends on the particular facts. In *Mid-Bedfordshire DC v Brown*,[168] Mummery LJ said: 18.85

> The authorities contain an informative debate on the variety of competing interests and discretionary considerations which the court should take into account: the decision of the council to seek an order; the practical problems of enforcement facing the court if the injunction is breached; the council's position on the planning merits; the possibility that the council might come to a different planning judgment; the planning history of the site; the degree of flagrancy of the breach of planning controls; the availability of suitable alternative sites for the defendants; the degree of urgency in the application; the need to act compatibly with the human rights of the defendants guaranteed by article 8 of the Convention for the Protection of Human Rights and Fundamental Freedoms as scheduled to the Human Rights Act 1998 with regard to respect for their home and private life; the personal circumstances of the defendants and the personal hardship likely to be inflicted on them as a result of an injunction enforcing the planning controls by requiring them to move on, including humanitarian considerations of health, safety and education, in particular those adversely affecting any children involved; the length of the defendants' occupation of the land; any delay on the part of the council in taking action; and any other relevant conduct and circumstances of the parties.

A court should not grant an injunction unless it would be prepared to take action for contempt if it were breached. However, the discretion as to sanctions on a committal hearing is not subject to the same principles as the initial decision to grant or refuse an injunction – see *South Cambridgeshire DC v Gammell*[169] and *Aylesbury Vale DC v Ilyas*.[170] 18.86

Section 187 is concerned with cases of breach of planning control and does not apply where the local planning authority otherwise have power to seek an injunction: for example, to enforce a section 106 obligation. In such a case, *Newham LBC v Ali*[171] held that the *South Bucks DC v Porter* principles do not apply. The Court of Appeal distinguished between the purpose of an injunction under section 187B which is to restrain a breach of planning control and the purpose of an injunction under section 106(5) which is to enforce an undertaking voluntarily given to a local planning authority. The Court held that the fact that a breach of the undertaking is also a breach of planning control does not justify a conflation of the factors that should or may be taken into account in deciding whether to grant 18.87

[168] [2005] 1 WLR 1460 at para. 8.

[169] [2005] EWCA Civ 1429.

[170] [2011] EWCA Civ 1377.

[171] [2014] 1 WLR 2743.

an injunction for breach in the two cases and they remain distinct. At paragraph 20, Lord Dyson MR said:

> where there has been a substantial breach of a planning obligation under section 106 of the 1990 Act, an injunction will normally be granted unless the local planning authority has acted in a way which justifies withholding relief on ordinary equitable principles. The fact that there is an outstanding planning appeal will usually be irrelevant. That is because the matters to which a local planning authority must have regard when making a planning decision concerning matters of planning control (for example, determining an application for planning permission, seeking an injunction under section 187B of the 1990 Act or taking direct action under section 178 of the 1990 Act) are not matters to which a local planning authority is required to have regard when deciding whether to seek an injunction under section 106(5) or to which the court should have regard when deciding whether to grant such an injunction. The distinction between matters that should be considered in the enforcement of planning control, as compared with other decisions (such as instituting criminal proceedings) was recognised by Ouseley J in *R (O'Brien) v Basildon District Council*.[172]

ENFORCEMENT WARNING NOTICES

18.88 TCPA 1990, section 173ZA was brought into force from 16 March 2016[173] and provides that an enforcement warning notice may be issued where it appears to the local planning authority that there has been a breach of planning control in respect of any land in Wales and there is a reasonable prospect that, if an application for planning permission in respect of the development concerned were made, planning permission would be granted. It constitutes formal enforcement action within TCPA 1990, section 171A(2).[174]

18.89 A copy of an enforcement warning notice is to be served on the owner and the occupier of the land to which the notice relates and on any other person having an interest in the land, being an interest that, in the opinion of the authority, would be materially affected by the taking of any further enforcement action. It must be entered in the register maintained under TCPA 1990, section 188. The notice must state the matters that appear to the authority to constitute the breach of planning control, and that, unless an application for planning permission is made within a period specified in the notice, further enforcement action may be taken.

18.90 The issue of an enforcement warning notice does not affect any other power exercisable in respect of any breach of planning control.

[172] [2006] EWHC 1346 (Admin) at paras 174–6.

[173] See Planning (Wales) Act 2015 (Commencement No. 3 and Transitional Provisions) Order 2016 (SI 2016 No. 52), art. 5, bringing ss. 43–46 of the 2015 Act fully into force.

[174] TCPA 1990, s. 173ZA(2)(aa).

DISCONTINUANCE AND OTHER ORDERS

The local planning authority can require use of land to be discontinued or impose conditions on continuance of its use. They can also require any buildings or works to be altered or removed. They do so by order where it appears to them to be expedient in the interests of the proper planning of their area which includes the interests of amenity.[175] Such an order may grant planning permission for any development of the land to which it relates subject to any specified conditions. 18.91

Where the requirements would displace persons residing in any premises the authority is obliged to secure the provision of suitable accommodation insofar as there is no suitable accommodation otherwise reasonably available.[176] These provisions do not apply in the case of mineral workings orders except to the extent specified in Schedule 9 to the Act. 18.92

Failure to comply is a criminal offence subject to a defence where a person proves that he took all reasonable measures and exercised all due diligence to avoid commission of the offence.[177] The local planning authority may themselves take any step required by the order where it has not been complied with in accordance with TCPA 1990, section 190. 18.93

Additionally, if it appears to the local planning authority that the amenity of a part of their area, or of an adjoining area, is adversely affected by the condition of land, they may serve on the owner and occupier a notice requiring specified steps for remedying the condition of the land to be taken within a period of not less than 28 days.[178] 18.94

THE CROWN AND CROWN LAND

TCPA 1990, section 296A contains provisions concerning enforcement in relation to the Crown. A local planning authority must not take any step for the purposes of enforcement in relation to Crown land unless it has the consent of the appropriate authority, which may be given subject to such conditions as it thinks appropriate. The appropriate authority is defined in section 293. Examples include the Crown Estate Commissioners in respect of the Crown Estate and government departments managing certain Crown land. 18.95

A step taken for the purposes of enforcement includes entering land, bringing proceedings and the making of an application. It does not include service of a notice or the making of an order (other than by a court). Accordingly, the local planning authority may make an enforcement order and issue any of a breach of condition notice, enforcement warning notice, stop notice and temporary stop 18.96

[175] TCPA 1990, s. 102.

[176] TCPA 1990, s. 102(6).

[177] TCPA 1990, s. 189.

[178] TCPA 1990, s. 215.

notice, and a planning contravention notice, although they will be unable to follow up any such action by entry or legal proceedings without consent. In addition, no act or omission done or suffered by or on behalf of the Crown constitutes an offence under TCPA 1990.

18.97 To allow for restricted access to information involving national security changes, equivalent to those for other inquiries, have been made with the addition of a Schedule to the Town and Country Planning (Enforcement) (Inquiries Procedure) (Wales) Rules 2003.[179]

[179] See amendments by the Town and Country Planning (Application of Subordinate Legislation to the Crown) Order 2006 (SI 2006 No. 1282), arts 35–43 and Sch. 6.

Chapter 19

Enforcement Notice Appeals

INTRODUCTION

A person having an interest in the land or a relevant occupier may appeal against an enforcement notice on one or more of the grounds specified in TCPA 1990, section 174. No other legal challenge may be made to a notice where one of these grounds applies. The appeal procedure is in accordance with TCPA 1990, sections 174–177 and the specific enforcement notice appeal regulations, although it is akin to appeals procedure generally with decisions following written representations, hearings or an inquiry. Guidance is in NAWC 08/2003, although, notwithstanding legislative changes, the guidance in WOC 24/97 except Annex 9, remains relevant. 19.1

RIGHT OF APPEAL AND STATUTORY GROUNDS

A person having an interest in the land or a relevant occupier, whether or not served with the notice, may appeal against an enforcement notice on one or more of seven specified grounds.[1] A relevant occupier is defined as a person occupying the land by licence at the date both when the notice is issued and when the appeal is brought.[2] In *R (Flynn) v Secretary of State for Communities and Local Government*[3] an inspector's decision that travellers had no right of appeal under section 174 was quashed in judicial review proceedings. The court held that a 'licence' within the meaning of section 174(6) meant a permission to enter and occupy the land in question, and could be a contractual licence or a bare licence and that the existence of an implied licence could be inferred from all the relevant circumstances, including the relationship between the parties involved and the circumstances in which the land was occupied. 19.2

The grounds on which an appeal may be brought under TCPA 1990, section 174(2) are (using the statutory alphabetical identification): 19.3

> (a) that, in respect of any breach of planning control which may be constituted by the matters stated in the notice, planning permission ought to be granted or, as the case may be, the condition or limitation concerned ought to be discharged;
> (b) that those matters have not occurred;

[1] TCPA 1990, s. 174(1).

[2] TCPA 1990, s. 174(6).

[3] [2014] EWHC 390 (Admin), [2014] 1 WLR 3270.

(c) that those matters (if they occurred) do not constitute a breach of planning control;
(d) that, at the date when the notice was issued, no enforcement action could be taken in respect of any breach of planning control which may be constituted by those matters;
(e) that copies of the enforcement notice were not served as required by section 172;
(f) that the steps required by the notice to be taken, or the activities required by the notice to cease, exceed what is necessary to remedy any breach of planning control which may be constituted by those matters or, as the case may be, to remedy any injury to amenity which has been caused by any such breach;
(g) that any period specified in the notice in accordance with section 173(9) falls short of what should reasonably be allowed.

19.4 However, provision is made to limit the right of appeal on ground (a), that is that planning permission ought to be granted, in relation to land in Wales by the Planning (Wales) Act 2015, section 46, which inserted a new subsection (2D) into section 174 of TCPA 1990. This provides that an appeal against an enforcement notice may not be brought on the ground specified in section 174(2)(a), if the enforcement notice was issued after a decision to refuse planning permission for a related development was upheld on an appeal under section 78. Development is 'related' if granting planning permission for it would involve granting planning permission in respect of the matter concerned. Upholding an appeal includes decisions to decline to determine or proceed with the appeal under section 79(6) or dismissal under that subsection. Similarly, section 174(2E) provides that an appeal may not be brought on the ground that a condition or limitation ought to be discharged[4] if the enforcement notice was issued after a decision to grant planning permission subject to the condition or limitation was upheld on an appeal under TCPA 1990, section 78.

19.5 Where an appeal is brought the appellant is deemed to have made an application for planning permission in respect of the matters stated in the notice as constituting a breach of planning control provided that the appeal notice specifies the ground under section 174(2)(a).[5] In addition, it is necessary to pay the prescribed fee.[6] Further consideration of the power to grant permission is set out below but at this stage it should be stressed that the planning permission which may be granted is limited to that alleged as a breach in the enforcement notice. A wider permission cannot be granted on an appeal. Equally, the deemed planning permission where building or works were not included for removal or activities were not ordered

[4] I.e. as specified in subsection (2)(a), as above.

[5] TCPA 1990, s. 177(5), inserted by Planning (Wales) Act 2015, s. 44.

[6] See the Town and Country Planning (Fees for Applications, Deemed Applications and Site Visits) (Wales) Regulations 2015 (SI 2015 No. 1522), as amended.

to cease when in either case they could have been[7] is confined to the breach of planning control alleged in the enforcement notice. Further, the power to vary the steps required in the enforcement notice on a ground (f) appeal cannot be used in conjunction with this deemed permission to obtain a more extensive permission.[8]

It is important to include all grounds of appeal which may be relied upon. 19.6
Where a matter is raised under one ground it may also be material to the issues under another ground but if there is no appeal under ground (a), for example, planning merits generally will not be admissible when considering whether the steps required are necessary under ground (f).[9]

METHOD OF APPEAL

An appeal is made by notice to the Welsh Ministers: the notice may be sent in 19.7
one of three ways and must be within the specified time.[10] The appeal may be by written notice to the Welsh Ministers before the date specified in the enforcement notice as the date on which it is to take effect, by sending notice to them in a properly addressed and pre-paid letter posted at such time that, in the ordinary course of post, it would be delivered before that date, or by sending notice using electronic communications at such time that, in the ordinary course of transmission, it would be delivered before that date. There is no prescribed notice of appeal but a form for electronic service is available on the Planning Portal (Welsh site).

Any document required or authorised to be sent by one person to another 19.8
under the Regulations may be sent by post or by means of electronic communication and any reference in the Regulations, however expressed, to writing is to be construed as including a reference to a form capable of being stored on, transmitted to and from, and read by means of, a computer.[11]

Where a person appeals, no person may claim in any other proceedings that 19.9
the appellant was not duly served with the enforcement notice.[12]

There is no power to extend the time limit for the appeal notice. It is import- 19.10
ant, therefore, to consider the scope of judicial review in cases where an appeal may be out of time as TCPA 1990, section 285 precludes any challenge to validity on the statutory appeal grounds except by an appeal under section 174. In *R (Stern) v*

[7] TCPA 1990, s. 173(11).

[8] *Tapecrown Ltd v First Secretary of State* [2006] EWCA Civ 1744 and *Ioannou v Secretary of State for Communities and Local Government* [2014] EWCA Civ 1432.

[9] See *Wyatt Brothers (Oxford) Ltd v Secretary of State for the Environment, Transport and Regions* [2001] EWCA Civ 1560 and explanation in *Ahmed*, below.

[10] TCPA 1990, s. 174(3).

[11] Town and Country Planning (Enforcement Notices and Appeals) (Wales) Regulations 2003 (SI 2003 No. 394), reg. 12.

[12] TCPA 1990, s. 175(5).

Horsham BC,[13] the appeal notice was lodged on the day the enforcement notices came into effect and was therefore out of time. Two enforcement notices had been issued but neither was served for several days after issue with the result that they failed to give the necessary minimum twenty-eight days before taking effect. The section 174 appeal was rejected as out of time. The appellant then sought to challenge the validity of the enforcement notices to be met by the response that section 285 precluded the challenge, which could only have been by an appeal under section 174 and that the section 174 appeal was out of time. The High Court quashed the enforcement notices, holding that section 174(2)(e), which allows an appeal on the ground that the notice was not served as required, referred only to the situation where the enforcement notice had not been served at all. Therefore, section 285 did not prevent a challenge to validity by judicial review where the failure was a failure to serve the enforcement notice in time. In the event, the late service of the enforcement notice, being partly the cause of the late appeal, had caused substantial prejudice and the enforcement notices were quashed.

PROCEDURE

19.11 The notice must specify the grounds of appeal and set out briefly the facts in support of each ground on which the appellant intends to rely. The grounds must be sent with the appeal notice or not later than fourteen days from the date on which the Welsh Ministers send a notice requiring this to be done.[14] Where more than one ground is specified in the appeal, the appeal may be determined without considering any ground as to which the appellant has failed to give the required information within that time limit.[15] Further, where there is a failure to provide the information required under section 174(4), the Welsh Ministers may dismiss the appeal.[16]

19.12 Section 175 gives power to make regulations prescribing the procedure on appeal. The Town and Country Planning (Enforcement Notices and Appeals) (Wales) Regulations 2003,[17] regulations 5–9 set out the procedural steps. The requirements as to the appeal notice have been noted above and on receipt of the notice the Welsh Ministers must notify the local planning authority and send it a copy.[18] The authority must then within fourteen days send the Welsh Ministers a certified copy of the enforcement notice and a list of the persons on whom it

[13] [2013] EWHC 1460 (Admin).

[14] TCPA 1990, s. 174(4) and Town and Country Planning (Enforcement Notices and Appeals) (Wales) Regulations 2003, reg. 5.

[15] TCPA 1990, s. 174(5).

[16] TCPA 1990, s. 176(3)(a).

[17] SI 2003 No. 394 ('Appeals Regs').

[18] Appeals Regs, reg. 6.

was served.[19] A deemed application is subject to payment of the specified fee save where there is a pending application or appeal for the development to which the enforcement notice relates.[20]

The procedure on appeal is determined by the Welsh Ministers.[21] As with other appeals, the procedure can be a local inquiry, a hearing or by written representations, or a combination of them, as considered appropriate. The Welsh Ministers must determine the procedure within the prescribed period and notify the appellant and local planning authority of which procedure has been selected. There is a general requirement to publish the criteria that are to be applied in determining the procedure to be followed. 19.13

The criteria, which are not fully determinative, are to be found in the Planning Inspectorate guidance on completing an enforcement appeal (Wales) at Annexe 1. They are identical to those for appeals generally[22] except that the intent to apply for costs is not a relevant factor in the case of written representations in enforcement cases. They include factors such as the need and best means to test evidence, whether the status or personal circumstances of the applicant are at issue and the extent of local interest. 19.14

The procedure to be followed in each type of appeal is detailed in the appropriate Regulations, that is the Town and Country Planning (Enforcement) (Written Representations Procedure) (Wales) Regulations 2003,[23] the Town and Country Planning (Enforcement) (Hearings Procedure) (Wales) Rules 2003,[24] the Town and Country Planning (Enforcement) (Inquiries Procedure) (Wales) Rules 2003[25] and the Town and Country Planning (Enforcement) (Determination by Inspectors) (Inquiries Procedure) (Wales) Rules 2003.[26] Essentially they mirror the steps applicable to section 78 appeals. 19.15

Appeals will generally be determined by planning inspectors although cases may be recovered depending upon the breach alleged and the circumstances. In this respect, the Town and Country Planning (Determination of Appeals by Appointed Persons) (Prescribed Classes) (Wales) Regulations 2015 apply to section 78 and section 174 appeals.[27] 19.16

In each case, when the Welsh Ministers are satisfied that they have received all the documents necessary to entertain the appeal they must send notice to this 19.17

[19] Appeals Regs, reg. 7.

[20] See the Town and Country Planning (Fees for Applications, Deemed Applications and Site Visits) (Wales) Regulations 2015 (SI 2015 No. 1522), reg. 10.

[21] TCPA 1990, s. 319B, inserted by Town and Country Planning (Determination of Procedure) (Wales) Order 2014 (SI 2014 No. 2773).

[22] Annexe H of the Appeals Procedural Guide.

[23] SI 2003 No. 395 ('Written Representations Regs').

[24] SI 2003 No. 1268 ('Hearings Rules').

[25] SI 2003 No. 1269 ('Inquiries Rules').

[26] SI 2003 No. 1270 ('Inspector Rules').

[27] See the Prescribed Classes Regs, reg. 3 and Chapter 17, above.

effect to the appellant and to the local planning authority[28] and the date of this notice is the starting date.[29] Within two weeks of the starting date the local planning authority must send a completed copy of the questionnaire and supporting documents to the Welsh Ministers and the Appellant.[30]

19.18 In written representation cases, within six weeks of the starting date the local planning authority must send a statement of the submissions it proposes to put forward to the Welsh Ministers and to all persons served with the enforcement notice: this is to include a summary of its grounds of opposition to each ground of appeal and a statement of whether it would be prepared to grant planning permission and, if so, the conditions it would wish to impose.[31]

19.19 The local planning authority may elect to treat the questionnaire, supporting documents and regulation 8 statement as its representations and give notice accordingly but at any event within six weeks of the starting date the statement containing the required details of the authority's case must be sent to the Welsh Ministers.[32] Any further representations which the appellant wishes to make must similarly be sent to be received within six weeks of the starting date.[33] Each of them may then make comments on the opposing party's representations to be received within nine weeks of the starting date.[34] An interested party who has received notice of the appeal may make representations to be received by the Welsh Ministers within six weeks of the starting date.[35]

19.20 The procedure is similar in the case of hearings although there the six-week statement is referred to as a hearing statement and the particular requirements, including those for interested parties, are all in regulation 5 of the relevant Regulations. These also provide for details of the hearing, attendance and participation and the procedure at the hearing.[36] The hearing may be conducted at the site and otherwise a site visit must be made if so requested by the appellant or the local planning authority.[37]

19.21 The Inquiries procedure follows the same pattern save that provision is made for pre-inquiry meetings, statements of evidence and for a statement of common ground. A pre-inquiry meeting may, or in some cases must, be held and the timetable for statements of case in that event is four weeks from conclusion of the pre-inquiry meeting.[38] Where a person has notified the Welsh Ministers of an

28 Appeals Regs, reg. 9.

29 Appeals Regs, reg. 8(3).

30 Written Representations Regs, reg. 5; r. 4 of each of the Rules.

31 Written Representations Regs, reg. 8(1) and (2).

32 Written Representations Regs, reg. 7.

33 Written Representations Regs, reg. 7.

34 Written Representations Regs, reg. 7.

35 Written Representations Regs, reg. 8.

36 See Hearings Rules, rr. 6–11.

37 Hearings Rules, r. 12.

38 Inquiries Rules, r. 8.

intention to take part, his statement must be received within four weeks of the date specified in writing to him by the Welsh Ministers[39] and such person may comment on another person's statement of case so as to be received not less than four weeks before the inquiry date.[40] Written statements of evidence must be sent so as to be received not less than four weeks before the inquiry or in accordance with the timetable laid down for the particular appeal.[41]

The local planning authority and the appellant must together prepare a statement of common ground so as to be received not less than four weeks before the inquiry.[42] Procedure at the inquiry is regulated by the inspector and unless otherwise determined the appellant begins and has the final right of reply.[43] 19.22

UNAUTHORISED EIA DEVELOPMENT

Where it appears that the appeal is in respect of unauthorised development which is Schedule 1 or Schedule 2 development within the Environmental Impact Assessment Regulations[44] and there is no screening opinion or direction the Welsh Ministers shall issue such direction[45] and can require additional information for that purpose.[46] Failure to provide the information means that the deemed planning application and any ground (a) appeal lapses.[47] If it appears, when considering the appeal, that the alleged breach includes unauthorised EIA development and no environmental statement is submitted with the appeal, the Welsh Ministers may require one to be submitted within a period as specified.[48] Failure to provide the statement means that the deemed planning application and any ground (a) appeal lapses.[49] 19.23

Where the appeal is accompanied by an environmental statement the procedure and power to require further information is laid down by regulation 47 and following regulations, with publicity requirements in regulation 49 and a right of public inspection in regulation 50. 19.24

[39] Inquiries Rules, r. 8, Inspector Rules, r. 6.

[40] Inquiries Rules, r. 8(15), Inspector Rules, r. 6.

[41] Inquiries Rules, r. 16, Inspector Rules, r. 15.

[42] Inquiries Rules, r. 17, Inspector Rules, r. 16.

[43] Inquiries Rules, r. 18, Inspector Rules, r. 17. It differs therefore from the procedure on s. 78 appeals where the local planning authority will generally begin.

[44] Town and Country Planning (Environmental Impact Assessment) (Wales) Regulations 2016 (SI 2016 No. 58).

[45] EIA Regs, reg. 45.

[46] EIA Regs, reg. 45(6).

[47] EIA Regs, reg. 45(7).

[48] EIA Regs, reg. 45(2).

[49] EIA Regs, reg. 45(2)(e).

EFFECT OF APPEAL AND POWERS ON APPEAL

19.25 Where an appeal is brought, the enforcement notice is of no effect pending final determination or withdrawal of the appeal.[50] This is subject to the express powers if an appeal is made under TCPA 1990, section 289: here the High Court or Court of Appeal may order that the notice shall have effect, or have effect to such extent as may be specified in the order, pending the final determination of those proceedings and any re-hearing and determination by the Welsh Ministers.[51]

19.26 On the determination of an appeal under section 174, the Welsh Ministers may grant planning permission in respect of the matters stated in the enforcement notice as constituting a breach of planning control, whether in relation to the whole or any part of those matters or in relation to the whole or any part of the land to which the notice relates.[52] In so doing they shall have regard to the provisions of the development plan, so far as material to the subject matter of the enforcement notice, and to any other material considerations.[53] Where the permission is for EIA development, it shall not be granted unless they have first taken into consideration environmental information and the decision shall state that this has been done.[54] They may also discharge any condition or limitation subject to which planning permission was granted[55] and may substitute another condition or limitation for it, whether more or less onerous.[56]

19.27 In addition they may determine whether, on the date on which the appeal was made, any existing use of the land was lawful, any operations which had been carried out in, on, over or under the land were lawful or any matter constituting a failure to comply with any condition or limitation subject to which planning permission was granted was lawful and, if so, issue a certificate of lawful use and development in accordance with TCPA 1990, section 191.[57] This will apply only to appeals on grounds (c) and (d) and the effect of section 177(1A) in applying certain parts of sections 191–194 is to require a specific application that the use or development is lawful. A fee is payable.[58] This power is for exceptional circumstances only as all facts may not be known and it may more appropriately be dealt with by quashing the notice and advising that a section 191 application can be made.[59]

[50] TCPA 1990, s. 175(4).

[51] TCPA 1990, s. 289(4A).

[52] TCPA 1990, s. 177(1)(a).

[53] TCPA 1990, s. 177(2).

[54] EIA Regs, reg. 25(1).

[55] TCPA 1990, s. 177(1)(b).

[56] TCPA 1990, s. 177(4).

[57] TCPA 1990, s. 177(1)(c). TCPA 1990, ss. 191(5)–(7), 193(4) (so far as it relates to the form of the certificate), (6) and (7) and 194 apply as they apply to s. 191 applications.

[58] Town and Country Planning (Fees for Applications, Deemed Applications and Site Visits) (Wales) Regulations 2015 (SI 2015 No. 1522), reg. 10.

[59] See guidance on enforcement appeals, p. 9.

On appeal, the Welsh Ministers may correct any defect, error or misdescription in the enforcement notice, or vary the terms of the enforcement notice, if satisfied that it will not cause injustice to the appellant or the local planning authority.[60] As noted above when considering enforcement notices generally, the law has developed so as to establish a category of enforcement notices which are a nullity, or so much 'waste paper'. This dates back to *Miller-Mead v Minister of Housing and Local Government*,[61] where it was held, in connection with the predecessor legislation, that if a misrecital in the notice went to the substance of the matter, the notice must be quashed, but if the misrecital did not go to the substance and could be amended without injustice, it should be amended. In *Koumis v Secretary of State for Communities and Local Government*,[62] Sullivan LJ referred to section 176(1) and said: 19.28

> This statutory power to correct error is somewhat broader than the power which was contained in the earlier legislation which was considered in *Miller-Mead*. Given the breadth of the current statutory power to correct error on appeal to the Secretary of State, it seems to me that the *Miller-Mead* approach to nullity should be confined to those cases where the failure to comply with the statutory requirements in section 173 is apparent on the face of the enforcement notice itself.

One particular use of this power is to vary the steps required to be taken so as to preserve established rights following the principles in *Mansi v Elstree RDC*.[63] The *Mansi doctrine* concerns the protection of an existing use or uses and how obvious it is that an enforcement notice will be construed so as to protect them. Consideration of it may be found in *R (Reid) v Secretary of State for Transport, Local Government and the Regions*,[64] citing *Kinnersley Engineering Limited v Secretary of State for the Environment, Transport and the Regions*.[65] More recently it was considered in *Turner v Secretary of State for Communities and Local Government, South Buckinghamshire District Council*,[66] where it was made clear that the doctrine does not extend to protect any intensification of use that may occur from inclusion in a notice but is confined to cases where the actual intensification is lawful as not being a material change of use. 19.29

More generally, the extent of the power of variation was considered by the Court of Appeal in *Tapecrown Ltd v First Secretary of State*,[67] where the potential breadth of the discretion conferred was identified. Carnwath LJ commented: 19.30

60 TCPA 1990, s. 176(1).

61 [1963] 2 QB 196.

62 [2014] EWCA Civ 1723 at para. 80.

63 (1964) 16 P & CR 153.

64 [2002] EWHC 2174 (Admin).

65 [2001] JPL 1082.

66 [2015] EWHC 1895 (Admin).

67 [2006] EWCA Civ 1744 at paras 31–3.

> Section 173(3) allows the steps required by the enforcement notice to be directed to achieving 'wholly or partly' any of the purposes referred to in subs.(4). Those purposes are, in summary, remedying the breach, or remedying 'any injury to amenity' caused by the breach. In so far as the notice requires less than a full remedy of the alleged breach, there is provision for a deemed permission for what is left after compliance (s.173(11)).
>
> There is a possible gap here. Repairing the damage to amenity may be only part of what is needed. Even a physically unobtrusive development may be objectionable in planning terms, but it may be made more acceptable by steps short of total demolition. That is the province of ground (a), which needs to be read with s.177. The latter makes clear that, on an enforcement appeal, planning permission may be granted in respect of the matters alleged in the notice 'in relation *to the whole or any part* of those matters' (s.177(1)(a)); that for this purpose ordinary planning considerations (including the development plan) must be taken into account (s.177(2)), and that the permission is to be treated as though granted on an application (s.177(3)(6)), and so (at least by implication) may be subject to any necessary conditions.
>
> In short, the inspector has wide powers to decide whether there is any solution, short of a complete remedy of the breach, which is acceptable in planning terms and amenity terms. If there is, he should be prepared to modify the requirements of the notice, and grant permission subject to conditions (or to accept a s.106 agreement, if offered). I would emphasise, however, that his primary task is to consider the proposals that have been put before him. Although he is free to suggest alternatives, it is not his duty to search around for solutions.

19.31 The extent to which something was an 'obvious alternative' which the inspector should take into account was considered further in *Ahmed v Secretary of State for Communities and Local Government*[68] where again the concern was the relationship of the duty to consider the ground (a) application for planning permission and the ground (f) issue that the steps should be varied to give effect to the appellant's case. The court here accepted that the fact that a matter was raised under one ground of appeal does not mean that it should not also be considered as material when considering another ground (i.e. a matter raised under ground (a) was material to ground (f)).

19.32 However, the power to vary the steps required to be taken under ground (f) cannot be used so as to enable the development after compliance to be granted deemed permission, so it cannot secure development beyond that which is existing and within the power to grant permission on a ground (a) appeal. If the development is beyond that which is alleged as the breach of planning control in the notice but may be acceptable in planning terms it may be appropriate to extend the time for compliance under ground (g) to allow the appellant to make an application

[68] [2014] EWCA Civ 566.

for permission.[69] In the absence of a ground (a) appeal the outcome which can be achieved under ground (f) is more restricted.[70]

The Welsh Ministers have in addition power to give any directions necessary to give effect to the determination of the appeal.[71] These should be properly exercised to give effect to the decision where allowing an appeal on a particular ground and a failure to do so may be an error of law.[72] 19.33

Procedural defects in the appeal process may be relied on to decide the appeal. Failure by the appellant to provide a written statement of grounds and the further information required under section 174(4) within the prescribed time may lead to dismissal[73] and the appeal may be allowed and the enforcement notice quashed where the local planning authority fail to comply with any requirements imposed on it under section 175(1) in the required time.[74] 19.34

TCPA 1990, section 176(1) confers a general power to quash the notice where the appeal is allowed. 19.35

Any decision of the Welsh Ministers in relation to the grant of permission or in discharging any condition or limitation or in issuing a certificate of lawful use on the appeal is final.[75] 19.36

COSTS

The costs provisions of TCPA 1990, section 322C, inserted by the Planning (Wales) Act 2015, section 49, apply to enforcement notice appeals as well as to section 78 appeals. They replace the former provisions in TCPA 1990, section 175(7), although no rules have as yet been made. The amending provisions will bring into one place the provisions to order costs in all types of planning procedures and thus introduce a unified structure. 19.37

The current position is that costs may be awarded in all enforcement appeals, whatever procedure has been followed, subject to the general principles contained in WOC 23/1993. 19.38

69 *Ioannou v Secretary of State for Communities and Local Government* [2014] EWCA Civ 1432.

70 *Miaris v Secretary of State for Communities and Local Government* [2016] EWCA Civ 75.

71 TCPA 1990, s. 176(2A).

72 See *Koumis v Secretary of State for Communities and Local Government* [2014] EWCA Civ 1723 at paras 58–61.

73 TCPA 1990, s. 176(3)(a).

74 TCPA 1990, s. 176(3).

75 TCPA 1990, s. 177(7).

Chapter 20

Criminal Proceedings for Breach of Enforcement and Other Notices

INTRODUCTION

Failure to comply with an enforcement notice, a stop notice, a temporary stop notice, a breach of condition notice or a planning contravention notice is a criminal offence.[1] Failure to comply with a discontinuance order is also a criminal offence.[2] Where an offence is proved to have been committed by a body corporate any person acting, or purporting to act as a director, manager, secretary or similar officer shall also be guilty of the offence if it was committed with his consent or connivance or is attributable to any neglect on his part.[3] 20.1

The particular problem encountered is the extent to which the validity of the underlying notice may be challenged as a defence in criminal proceedings. Here enforcement notices may be distinguished from the other notices because of the provisions of TCPA 1990, section 285 which preclude challenge except by an appeal further to TCPA 1990, section 174. 20.2

FAILURE TO COMPLY WITH ENFORCEMENT NOTICE – CRIMINAL PROCEEDINGS

Where, at any time after the end of the period for compliance with an enforcement notice, any step required by the notice to be taken has not been taken or any activity required by the notice to cease is being carried on, the person who is then the owner of the land is in breach of the notice and is guilty of an offence.[4] In addition, it is an offence for a person who has control of or an interest in the land to which an enforcement notice relates (other than the owner) to carry on any activity which is required by the notice to cease or cause or permit such an activity to be carried on.[5] 20.3

It is important to stress that as to ownership liability, it is the owner at the time of the contravention who is liable. The definition is that in TCPA 1990, section 336, referring to entitlement to the rack rent. Where there was a sale but 20.4

[1] See TCPA 1990, ss. 179, 187, 171G, 187A and 171D respectively.

[2] TCPA 1990, s. 189.

[3] TCPA 1990, s. 331.

[4] TCPA 1990, s. 179(1) and (2).

[5] TCPA 1990, s. 179(4) and (5).

registration of title had not been completed by the relevant date, issues may arise as to who was the owner. This was considered by the courts in connection with the previous land registration provisions where it was held that, as section 336 refers to entitlement to receipt of rent 'in his own right or as trustee', the person registered as owner would remain liable.[6]

20.5 The offences are continuing ones and there may be a second or subsequent conviction for a later breach.[7] The offences are either way offences punishable by a fine[8] and any financial gain shall be taken into account in deciding the level of the fine.[9]

20.6 Section 179 contains certain statutory defences. It is a defence for an owner to show that he did everything he could be expected to do to secure compliance with the notice.[10] This means, for example, that an owner not in possession may be able to rely on any inability to require an occupier (e.g. a tenant) to comply with the notice. The leading case is *R v Beard*,[11] where it was said:

> Where it is within the power of the owner of the land to comply with the notice without the assistance of others, no question of a defence under subsection (3) arises. Before a defence can arise under that subsection, the owner must show that compliance with the notice is not within his own unaided powers, otherwise no question of his having to secure compliance with the notice can arise.

20.7 This was followed in *R v Clarke*,[12] which held that the introduction of the Human Rights Act had made no difference and that the question of the defendant's human rights did not have to be looked at again as they had been considered during the planning procedure.[13]

20.8 In addition, in all cases where a person charged with an offence has not been served with a copy of the enforcement notice and the notice is not contained in the appropriate register kept under TCPA 1990, section 188, it is a defence for him to show that he was not aware of the existence of the notice.[14] This is relevant, for example, where the person charged as the 'then owner' of the land was not

[6] *East Lindsey District Council v Thompson* [2001] EWHC 81 (Admin). The Land Registration Act 2002 contains differently worded provisions but the registered owner would remain a person in receipt of the rack rent within section 336.

[7] TCPA 1990, s. 179(6).

[8] TCPA 1990, s. 179(8): on summary conviction the fine shall not exceed £20,000.

[9] TCPA 1990, s. 179(9).

[10] TCPA 1990, s. 179(3).

[11] [1996] EWCA Crim 396.

[12] [2002] EWCA Crim 753.

[13] Consideration of the authorities may be found in *Sevenoaks DC v Harber* [2008] EWHC 708 (Admin).

[14] TCPA 1990, s. 179(7) – see also TCPA 1990, s. 285(2), which enables an owner to raise non-service notwithstanding the general restriction on challenges imposed by s. 285(1).

the owner when the notice was issued: he should have relied on his searches, and therefore on the register, at the time of purchase to be informed of the planning status of the land and can therefore raise a failure to make the entry.

The Divisional Court considered a number of technical matters regarding defences to prosecution in *Sanger v Newham LBC*.[15] It was held that once service had been proved in accordance with the requirements, receipt did not have to be proved and it was for the defendant to show that he was unaware of the notice under section 179(7). Further, the offence crystallises at the date for compliance and is thereafter a continuing one subject to the defences although the relevant date for the defences was the date of the alleged offence, so that if after the date for compliance but by that date the defendant had done everything he reasonably could to comply the defence was available. 20.9

ENFORCEMENT NOTICES – VALIDITY AS A DEFENCE

The question then arises of the scope of any residual defences. TCPA 1990, section 285 provides that the validity of an enforcement notice shall not, except by way of an appeal under Part VII (i.e. section 174), be questioned in any proceedings whatsoever on any of the grounds on which such an appeal may be brought. The statutory grounds were considered in Chapter 19 and the effect is significantly to limit the scope of defences which might otherwise be applicable. 20.10

In *R v Wicks*,[16] the appellant had been convicted of failing to comply with an enforcement notice. At trial he had sought to challenge the notice as having been issued in bad faith and motivated by immaterial considerations. The House of Lords held that whether a person was entitled to challenge the validity of an act under statutory authority in criminal proceedings was a matter of statutory construction and that the 1990 Act did not make the matters raised ones for a criminal court: in section 179(1) 'enforcement notice' meant simply a notice issued by the local planning authority that was formally valid and had not been set aside on appeal or quashed on judicial review. Lord Hoffmann said,[17] 'the duty of the landowner is perfectly clear: if the enforcement notice has not been quashed, he must obey it'. 20.11

This has been applied and considered in numerous authorities. In *Bracken v East Hertfordshire District Council*,[18] it was said: 20.12

> In his speech in *R. v. Wicks* Lord Hoffmann construed the planning legislation as merely requiring an enforcement notice which appears formally valid and which has not been quashed on appeal or by judicial review. In such a case, nothing but the formal validity of the notice will be relevant to an issue before

[15] [2014] EWHC 1922 (Admin), [2015] 1 WLR 332.

[16] [1998] AC 92.

[17] At p. 121.

[18] [2000] All ER(D) 579.

> the justices, see page 117C. In short, a defendant charged with an offence against section 179(2) of the Act can still raise the issue that the piece of paper served on him was not an enforcement notice, it was simply so much waste paper. On the other hand if it is a notice issued by a planning authority which is formally valid and has not been quashed, then the fact that the notice contains defects which could have been corrected by the Secretary of State under section 176(1) or the decision to issue it was flawed in one of the ways for which the remedy is judicial review, will not be matters that a defendant can raise by way of defence.

20.13 *Wicks* was also considered in *Palacegate Properties Ltd v Camden LBC.*[19] Laws LJ held that the general principle is that no one is to be prevented from relying upon any legally relevant question[20] but that not everything is legally relevant. The Court confirmed that it is not open to a court in a criminal trial to go behind a notice which is valid on its face and show that the decision to issue the notice could be (or could have been) invalidated and confirmed that the standard judicial review grounds, including *Wednesbury* or procedural review, cannot be raised in a criminal prosecution. *Irvine v Carmarthenshire County Council*[21] confirms that the introduction of the Human Rights Act had made no difference. Further, in *R v Clayton*[22] the Court of Appeal confirmed that *Wicks* was equally applicable to a complaint of abuse of process in the criminal prosecution where the validity of the enforcement notice was at the heart of the abuse complaint.

20.14 However, in *Badcock v Hertfordshire CC*[23] the court made clear that it was not designed to impinge on the criminal process to such an extent as to preclude a defence or reverse the burden of proof in relation to the factual ingredients of an alleged failure to comply with the requirements of an enforcement notice once it has been issued. Here the issue was whether or not certain material was waste. The court ruled that, although it was not open to the appellant to say that at the date of the notice the land was not being used for the processing of waste, that did not mean that the issues of what materials were in fact being processed at the date of breach and whether they were 'waste', as legally defined, were not relevant, notwithstanding the fact that what was taking place at the time of issue of the notice and what was taking place and relied on as breach were the same. The essential task of the prosecution was to prove in respect of each count: (1) the service and effect of the notice; (2) the acts complained of; (3) that the acts constitute a breach of the notice.

20.15 The latter case also held that the restrictions applicable to enforcement notice prosecutions do not apply equally to proceedings for failure to comply with a stop notice.

[19] (2001) 82 P & CR 199.

[20] See judgment, para. 7.

[21] [2008] EWHC 2866 (Admin).

[22] [2014] EWCA Civ 1030, [2014] 1 WLR 3994.

[23] [2002] EWCA Crim 1941, esp. at para. 26.

REINSTATEMENT OR RESTORATION OF BUILDINGS OR WORKS

It is also an offence where without planning permission a person carries out any development on land by way of reinstating or restoring buildings or works which have been removed or altered in compliance with an enforcement notice.[24] It is a summary offence subject to a fine not exceeding level 5 on the standard scale. Failure to remove or alter the works or restoration or reinstatement (as opposed to the restoration or reinstatement development itself) is not covered by this provision although if there is development consisting of a change of use in breach of the notice (i.e. a resumption of the use enforced against) there may be an offence under section 179.[25] 20.16

STOP NOTICE

If any person contravenes a stop notice after a site notice has been displayed or the stop notice has been served on him he is guilty of an offence.[26] Contravention includes causing or permitting its contravention.[27] It is a defence for the accused to prove that the stop notice was not served on him and that he did not know, and could not reasonably have been expected to know, of its existence.[28] The offence is an either way offence punishable by a fine.[29] The offence may be committed over a period of time and there may be a second or subsequent conviction for a later breach.[30] 20.17

Where a person has been served with the stop notice in accordance with TCPA 1990, section 183(6) the matter is relatively straightforward and there will be a contravention by carrying out the relevant activity at any time within the period when the stop notice is in effect. Where liability is based on posting a site notice, it is still necessary to prove that the person contravened the notice in the sense above and that the notice was in effect: the burden is then on the defendant to establish the statutory defence. The uncertain element is the extent to which valid service of the notice on some appropriate person is necessary. TCPA 1990, section 184(6) gives power to display a site notice 'where a stop notice has been served' and the date on which the stop notice takes effect 'must not be earlier than three days after the date when the notice is served' unless there are special 20.18

[24] TCPA 1990, s. 181(5).

[25] See TCPA 1990, s. 181(5) and *Pathfield Estates Ltd v Haringey LBC* [2013] EWHC 2053(Admin): change of use is not within s. 181(5).

[26] TCPA 1990, s. 187(1).

[27] TCPA 1990, s. 187(1B).

[28] TCPA 1990, s. 187(3).

[29] TCPA 1990, s. 187(2).

[30] TCPA 1990, s. 187(1A).

reasons. The service provisions of section 329 and the Local Government Act 1972, section 233 apply. It will, it appears, be necessary to apply these and prove actual service in an appropriate manner or rely on the deemed service provisions of the Interpretation Act 1978, section 7.

STOP NOTICES – VALIDITY AS A DEFENCE

20.19 The extent to which challenges to the stop notice itself, in particular its validity, can be raised as a defence to a criminal prosecution raises similar questions to the issues for planning contravention notices as neither carries a right of appeal and TCPA 1990, section 285 does not restrict the scope of challenge. However, there is of course a right to appeal against the enforcement notice to which the stop notice relates.

20.20 In *Badcock v Hertfordshire CC*,[31] the fact that section 285 refers to enforcement notices and not to stop notices did lead to a distinction in the limitation on what could be raised in criminal proceedings relating to each type of notice.

TEMPORARY STOP NOTICE

20.21 A person commits an offence if a temporary stop notice has been served on him or displayed on site and he contravenes it or causes or permits its contravention[32] but it is a defence to prove that the notice was not served on him and that he did not know and could not reasonably be expected to know of its existence.[33]

BREACH OF CONDITION NOTICE

20.22 A person who has been served with a breach of condition notice is in breach if at any time after the end of the period allowed for compliance with the notice any of the conditions specified in the notice is not complied with and the steps specified in the notice have not been taken or, as the case may be, the activities specified in the notice have not ceased.[34] Breach is a criminal offence.[35] The offence may be committed over a period of time and there may be a second or subsequent conviction for a later breach.[36]

[31] [2002] EWCA Crim 1941.

[32] TCPA 1990, s. 171G(1) and (2).

[33] TCPA 1990, s. 171G(5).

[34] TCPA 1990, s. 187A(8).

[35] TCPA 1990, s. 187A(9).

[36] TCPA 1990, s. 187A(10).

It is a defence for a person to prove that he took all reasonable measures to secure compliance with the conditions specified in the notice, or, where the notice was served on him as a person having control of the land, that he no longer had control.[37] 20.23

BREACH OF CONDITION NOTICES – VALIDITY AS A DEFENCE

The issue of a breach of condition notice or the decision to prosecute for breach may be challenged by judicial review on established grounds but public law matters may also be raised as a defence to prosecution as the restriction on raising matters in proceedings generally applicable to enforcement notices by TCPA 1990, section 285 does not apply. A person served may therefore seek to raise matters as to the validity and merits of the notice itself as a defence in the criminal proceedings. 20.24

In *Dilieto v Ealing LBC*[38] it was pointed out that the issues on a prosecution for non-compliance with a breach of condition notice would usually involve fact-finding for which no planning expertise was required and that hardship could be involved in requiring all challenges to be by judicial review. The reasons for the restrictions on raising public law matters given in *R v Wicks* in connection with enforcement notices were not necessarily applicable with equal force. Accordingly, although some challenges may only be appropriate for judicial review, some, specifically an issue as to service within the time limits of TCPA 1990, section 171B, could be raised as a defence to a prosecution. A notice served out of time was not a breach of condition notice within the section. 20.25

This was considered by the Court of Appeal in *Trim v North Dorset District Council*,[39] which concerned a private law claim for a declaration that service of a breach of condition notice was out of time so that non-compliance would be lawful. The authority argued that the private law claim was an abuse of process and the means of challenge was by judicial review. The Court upheld this and stressed the public law nature of service of a breach of condition notice. It held that once a breach of condition notice is served, the person responsible has a choice if he wishes to regularise his planning position. He may seek judicial review promptly to challenge the validity of the notice or he may apply to the local planning authority under section 73 of the 1990 Act to discharge the condition. If he does neither, he must accept the consequent uncertainty affecting his property. The authority is under no duty to prosecute nor to assist the person responsible to escape the consequences of his unlawful actions. 20.26

The court upheld the general exclusivity principle that in general it is an abuse of process to challenge the validity of public law decisions other than by judicial review. However, in the specific context of defences to a breach of condition notice 20.27

[37] TCPA 1990, s. 187A(11).

[38] [2000] QB 381.

[39] [2010] EWCA Civ 1446, [2011] 1 WLR 1901.

prosecution, the Court disagreed with any view that *Dilieto* might be intended to suggest that judicial review was inappropriate and treated it as an example of an established exception to the exclusivity principle where the authority itself had initiated the action.[40]

PLANNING CONTRAVENTION NOTICE

20.28 A person who fails to comply with a planning contravention notice at any time after the period of twenty-one days from service is guilty of an offence[41] and this is a continuing offence so that there may be a second or subsequent conviction for ongoing failure.[42] It is a defence to prove that there was a reasonable excuse for the failure.[43] In addition, it is an offence knowingly or recklessly to make a false or misleading statement.[44]

[40] See judgment at paras 28 and 29. The scope for the defence is therefore in accordance with *Wandsworth LBC v Winder (No. 1)* [1985] AC 461 where the scope of judicial review as excluding a defence, there in civil proceedings, was considered, with an exception in those cases where it is the public authority itself which has initiated the legal proceedings.

[41] TCPA 1990, s. 171D(1).

[42] TCPA 1990, s. 171D(2).

[43] TCPA 1990, s. 171D(3).

[44] TCPA 1990, s. 171D(5)(a) and (b).

Chapter 21

Certificates of Lawfulness of Use or Development

INTRODUCTION

Allied to the enforcement provisions of the local planning authority considered above are two specific means of obtaining certainty as to the lawfulness of particular development. TCPA 1990, section 191 enables an applicant to apply for a certificate that existing development or development already carried out is lawful. Section 192 enables an applicant to apply for a certificate that proposed development is lawful. Examples would include an applicant served with an enforcement notice who disputes the unlawfulness alleged and persons simply seeking to clarify or confirm the status of development where no formal grant of permission exists. 21.1

The procedure in each case is prescribed by the Town and Country Planning (Development Management Procedure) (Wales) Order 2012.[1] If the application is refused the applicant may appeal and affected third parties may have a right to challenge a grant by judicial review. Notwithstanding legislative changes the current specific guidance remains Annex 8 of WOC 24/97 but supplemented by NAWC 08/2003. 21.2

SECTION 191 CERTIFICATE OF LAWFULNESS OF EXISTING USE OR DEVELOPMENT

This section refers to a certificate of lawfulness of existing use or development. It provides that any person (not necessarily the landowner) who 'wishes to ascertain whether (a) any existing use of buildings or other land is lawful; (b) any operations which have been carried out in, on, over or under land are lawful; or (c) any other matter constituting a failure to comply with any condition or limitation subject to which planning permission has been granted is lawful' may make an application for a certificate to the local planning authority specifying the land and describing the use, operations or other matter. 21.3

It differs from a planning application as no question of the planning merits applies; it is a simple question of what has in fact taken place. The description of use must be specific and precise and simply referring to a use class is not sufficient. 21.4

'Lawful' in respect of uses or operations means that no enforcement action may then be taken, whether because the uses or operations did not involve development or require planning permission or because the time for enforcement action 21.5

[1] SI 2012 No. 801, see art. 28.

has expired or for any other reason. In addition, the uses or operations must not constitute a contravention of any of the requirements of any enforcement notice then in force.[2] For the purposes of any failure to comply with any condition or limitation any failure is lawful at any time if the time for taking enforcement action in respect of the failure has then expired and it does not constitute a contravention of any of the requirements of any enforcement notice or breach of condition notice then in force.[3]

21.6 The subsections are comprehensive and lawful thus means lawful in planning terms: the fact that the use or operations might be unlawful under other legislation so that a person is seeking to rely on his own illegality does not prevent the issue of a certificate and the certificate creates no immunity from proceedings under any other statutory system of regulatory control.[4]

21.7 Further, any breach of planning control relied on must still be subsisting at the time of the application otherwise the necessary period for immunity would not be established.[5] The breach must be continuous and have subsisted for the full immunity period.[6] If it is contrary to the terms of a current enforcement notice, that notice will necessarily prevail. Lawful use may be ended by abandonment, the creation of a new planning unit or a material change of use.

21.8 It is for the applicant to provide information which satisfies the local planning authority of the lawfulness of the matter described in the application at the time of the application although the authority may modify or substitute a description of the development. If the local planning authority is satisfied of the lawfulness it must issue a certificate otherwise it must refuse it.[7] It was made clear in *Panton v Secretary of State for the Environment, Transport & the Regions and Vale of White Horse District Council*[8] that this means that there is a duty on the authority to issue a certificate in respect of the premises applied for where a lawful use is demonstrated and, if the facts and circumstances so require, to modify the description of the use from that described in the application.

21.9 The extent of what was there referred to as a power to modify the description was considered in *R (Freedman) v Wiltshire Council*,[9] where Lewis J said that a local planning authority is entitled, in principle, to substitute a description of a different use from that described in the application form provided that the authority is satisfied, on a balance of probability, that the evidence demonstrates that the use as substituted has been carried on continuously for a period of ten years or more.

[2] TCPA 1990, s. 191(2).

[3] TCPA 1990, s. 191(3).

[4] *Epping Forest DC v Philcox* [2002] EnvLR 2.

[5] See *Nicholson v Secretary of State for the Environment and Maldon DC* (1998) 76 P & CR 191 and *Ellis v Secretary of State for Communities and Local Government* [2009] EWHC 634 (Admin).

[6] *North Devon CC v Secretary of State for the Environment* [1998] PLCR 356.

[7] TCPA 1990, s. 191(4).

[8] [1999] 1 PLR 92.

[9] [2014] EWHC 211 (Admin), at para. 25.

The authority in this case, therefore, had power to substitute a description of 'vehicular parking' for 'ancillary vehicular parking', provided that the evidence established ten years' or more continuous use for the parking.

A certificate must specify the land to which it relates, describe the use, oper- 21.10
ations or other matter in question, give the reasons for determining the use, operations or other matter to be lawful and specify the date of the application for the certificate.[10] Where the lawfulness is because the use is not development by reason of TCPA 1990, section 55(2)(f), that is, it falls within the same use class as another purpose for which the building in question was used and is in accordance with the further provisions of the Use Classes Order, the certificate must specify the class in question.[11]

The wording of the certificate requires a degree of precision and it is this which 21.11
prevails (see *Hannan* below) although the degree of detail will vary according to the circumstances.[12] In *R (Sellars) v Basingstoke and Deane BC*[13] it was held that identification of the correct planning unit is an essential part of the decision under section 191. The lawfulness of any use, operations or other matter for which a certificate is in force under this section shall be conclusively presumed.[14]

In *Hannan v Newham LBC*[15] the court made clear that it is the description in 21.12
the certificate which matters. It rejected a submission that a certificate is granted in respect of the use as it was actually being undertaken at the date of the application so that if the use continues to be the use that was then undertaken and which led to the grant of the certificate, such use is lawful. It was held that:

> The crucial features of s.191 concern the effect of the certificate. Subsection 4 makes it clear that the certificate is granted in relation to the use described in the application. It is the lawfulness of the use described in the application which matters. Subsection 5 requires the certificate to describe the use 'in question'. The use in question, by reference back to subs.4, is the use described in the application. It is the lawfulness of the use for which a certificate is in force which is conclusively presumed.[16]

A certificate shall also have effect, as if it were a grant of planning permission, for 21.13
the purposes of section 3(3) of the Caravan Sites and Control of Development Act 1960, section 7(1) of the Mobile Homes (Wales) Act 2013, section 5(2) of the

[10] TCPA 1990, s. 191(5).

[11] TCPA 1990, s. 191(5)(b).

[12] See e.g. *Hillingdon LBC v Secretary of State for Communities and Local Government* [2008] EWHC198 (Admin).

[13] [2013] EWHC 3673 (Admin).

[14] TCPA 1990, s. 191(6).

[15] [2014] EWHC 1424 (Admin).

[16] See para. 23.

Control of Pollution Act 1974 and section 36(2)(a) of the Environmental Protection Act 1990.

21.14 An application is made following the procedure laid down by article 28 of the Town and Country Planning (Development Management Procedure) (Wales) Order 2012. The same procedure applies to applications under TCPA 1990, section 192 and is referred to later in this chapter after considering the substantive provisions of that section.

SECTION 192 CERTIFICATE OF LAWFULNESS OF PROPOSED USE OR DEVELOPMENT

21.15 Section 192 contains provisions regarding a proposed use equivalent to those relating to an existing use. If any person (again, it is not confined to the landowner) wishes to ascertain whether any proposed use of buildings or other land, or any operations proposed to be carried out in, on, over or under land, would be lawful, he may make an application for this purpose to the local planning authority specifying the land and describing the use or operations in question. Lawful has the same meaning as for section 191 and is as prescribed by section 191(2) and (3).[17]

21.16 If the local planning authority are provided with information satisfying them that the use or operations described in the application would be lawful if instituted or begun at the time of the application, they shall issue a certificate to that effect and in any other case they shall refuse the application.[18]

21.17 In *Broads Authority v Secretary of State for the Environment, Transport and Regions*[19] it was held permissible to grant a certificate where the application sought confirmation that the completion of development permitted by an existing planning permission would be lawful subject to compliance with conditions on the permission.

21.18 A certificate must specify the land to which it relates, describe the use or operations in question, give the reasons for determining the use or operations to be lawful and specify the date of the application for the certificate.[20] Where the lawfulness is because the use is not development by reason of TCPA 1990, section 55(2)(f) of the Act, that is, it falls within the same use class as another purpose for which the building in question was used and is in accordance with the further provisions of the Use Classes Order, the certificate must specify the class in question.[21] A local planning authority does not have the power under section 192 itself to require a modification of the description of the proposed use or development although it could encourage the applicant to submit a more restricted form of application.[22]

[17] See paras. 21.5 and 21.6, above.

[18] TCPA 1990, s. 192(2).

[19] (2001) 81 P & CR 3.

[20] TCPA 1990, s. 192(3).

[21] TCPA 1990, s. 192(3)(b).

[22] *R (Tapp) v Thanet DC* [2001] EWCA Civ 559.

The lawfulness of any use or operations for which a certificate is in force under this section shall be conclusively presumed unless there is a material change, before the use is instituted or the operations are begun, in any of the matters relevant to determining such lawfulness.[23] 21.19

APPLICATION PROCEDURE

The procedure for applying for an order under both sections 191 and 192 is laid down by TCPA 1990, section 193 and the Town and Country Planning (Development Management Procedure) (Wales) Order 2012.[24] 21.20

An application for a certificate under either section must be made on a form published by the Welsh Ministers or a form substantially to the like effect.[25] By article 28(1) the application must include the particulars specified or referred to in the form and specify the land and describing the use, operations or other matter in question in accordance with sections 191 or 192 as the case may be. The form must be accompanied by a plan identifying the land to which the application relates drawn to an identified scale and showing the direction of north.[26] Where two or more uses, operations or matters are specified the plan must identify the part of the land to which each relates.[27] In addition, it shall be accompanied by such evidence verifying the information included in the application as the applicant can provide and a statement setting out the applicant's interest in the land, the name and address of any other person known to the applicant to have an interest in the land and whether any such other person has been notified of the application.[28] 21.21

The application form prescribed includes the obvious formal details of the applicant and site and also precise details of the grounds of the application and, where applicable, details of the use class relied on. In the case of a section 191 application the precise basis of the claim (e.g. that the use began more than ten years before) is needed together with relevant dates and, if residential use is claimed, the nature and number of residential units. The description of development proposed under a section 192 application must be particularised. Further documents are required where a section 192 application relates to Crown land.[29] The appropriate fee must be paid with the application[30] and the application may be by electronic communication in accordance with article 32.[31] 21.22

[23] TCPA 1990, s. 192(4).

[24] SI 2012 No. 801 ('DMP(W)O').

[25] DMP(W)O, art. 28(1).

[26] DMP(W)O, art. 28(2).

[27] DMP(W)O, art. 28(4).

[28] DMP(W)O, art. 28(2).

[29] DMP(W)O, art. 28(3).

[30] DMP(W)O, arts 28(6) and 8(1)(g).

[31] See DMP(W)O, art. 28(5).

21.23 An application complying with all the above formalities is a valid application[32] and as soon as reasonably practicable after receipt of a valid application the local planning authority must send an acknowledgement in the terms, or substantially the terms, of Schedule 1 to the Order.[33] If the application is subsequently found to be invalid the applicant must be notified[34] and the local planning authority may require further information to enable it to deal with the application.[35]

21.24 Written notice of the decision on the application must be given within the period of eight weeks of receipt of a valid application or, unless an appeal has been made, within an agreed extended period.[36] A certificate under section 191 or 192 of the 1990 Act must be in the form set out in Schedule 7 to the 2012 Order, or in a form substantially to the like effect.[37]

21.25 Where an application is refused, in whole or in part (including a case in which the local planning authority modify the description of the use, operations or other matter in the application or substitutes an alternative description for that description), the notice of decision must state clearly and precisely the authority's full reasons for its decision. It must also include a statement to the effect that if the applicant is aggrieved by the decision the applicant may appeal to the Welsh Ministers under section 195 of TCPA 1990.[38]

21.26 A certificate may be revoked in accordance with section 193(7) and the requirements of article 28(15)–(17).

21.27 Knowingly or recklessly making a false or misleading statement for the purpose of procuring a decision on an application under section 191 or 192 is an offence.[39] Using a false or misleading document, or withholding material information, with intent to deceive for the same purpose is also an offence.[40]

APPEAL

21.28 Where an application is made to a local planning authority for a certificate under section 191 or 192 and the application is refused or is refused in part, or notice of the decision is not given within the prescribed time period, the applicant may by notice appeal to the Welsh Ministers.[41]

32 DMP(W)O, art. 28(12).
33 DMP(W)O, art. 28(7).
34 DMP(W)O, art. 28(8).
35 DMP(W)O, art. 28(9).
36 DMP(W)O, art. 28(10).
37 DMP(W)O, art. 28(14).
38 DMP(W)O, art. 28(11).
39 TCPA 1990, s. 194(1)(a).
40 TCPA 1990, s. 194(1)(b) and (c).
41 TCPA 1990, s. 195(1B)–(1C).

A notice of appeal must be served within such time, being not less than twenty-eight days, and in such manner as may be prescribed by a development order and be accompanied by the information prescribed by such an order. No period has, however, been prescribed. Procedure on section 195 appeals, that is whether it is by written representations, hearing or inquiry, is determined by the Welsh Ministers as for other appeals.[42] The criteria in aid of this decision are also as for those other appeals.[43] The procedural rules applying to each of the appeal procedures is as for enforcement appeals[44] and reference should be made to the details in Chapter 19, above. The Planning Inspectorate has issued specific guides on completing the forms and the different procedures for lawful development certificates and enforcement appeals. TCPA 1990, Schedule 6 and the Town and Country Planning (Determination of Appeals by Appointed Persons) (Prescribed Classes) (Wales) Regulations 2015[45] apply to these appeals as to other appeals. 21.29

In addition, when fully in force there will be restrictions on the ability to vary the application following similar provisions for appeals under TCPA 1990, section 78.[46] Once notice of an appeal under section 195 has been served, the application to which it relates may not be varied, except in such circumstances as may be prescribed by a development order, and a development order which makes provision under subsection (1DA) must provide for an application which is varied to be subject to such further consultation as the Welsh Ministers consider appropriate.[47] 21.30

If satisfied that the authority's refusal is not well founded, or would not have been well founded if a decision had been made, the Welsh Ministers shall grant the appeal, or in the case of a refusal in part modify the certificate otherwise it shall be dismissed. The Welsh Ministers' decision on appeal is final.[48] 21.31

[42] TCPA 1990, s. 319B and the Town and Country Planning (Determination of Procedure) (Wales) Order 2014 (SI 2014 No. 2773).

[43] The criteria are in Annexe 1 to the Planning Inspectorate guide to completing the s. 191 or 192 appeal form.

[44] See application rules of each of the relevant 2003 Orders.

[45] SI 2015 No. 1822.

[46] Subsections (1DA) and (1DB), inserted into s. 195 by Planning (Wales) Act 2015, s. 47(2).

[47] TCPA 1990, s. 195(1DA) and (1DB).

[48] TCPA 1990, s. 196(3).

Chapter 22

Statutory Challenge and Appeals

INTRODUCTION

Part XII of TCPA 1990 is concerned with the validity of certain planning decisions and orders. It provides a statutory procedure to challenge these actions and prohibits challenge through any other legal proceedings. Similarly, section 113 of PCPA 2004 provides that documents, including development plans, may not be questioned in any legal proceedings except in accordance with its provisions. The commonest examples of these challenges relate to decisions made by the Welsh Ministers (including, of course, planning inspectors as the appointed person for the appeal) on appeals against the refusal or conditional grant of planning permission and against the issue of an enforcement notice. 22.1

Where a decision or action falls outside the scope of these provisions a challenge may be made where appropriate on general public law grounds by judicial review. This enables challenge to the legality of decisions of public bodies where they have exceeded or abused their powers on grounds concerned with the decision-making process, not the merits of the decision. Judicial review is considered in the next chapter. However, more detailed consideration of judicial review generally and the role and procedure of the Administrative Court, which deals with statutory and judicial review claims, is outside the scope of this work. Reference should be made to *Administrative Law and the Administrative Court in Wales* by David Gardner[1] for more comprehensive analysis. In addition, the exclusion of other legal challenge can impact on the availability of a defence to a criminal prosecution. The scope of this has been considered in connection with enforcement.[2] 22.2

TCPA 1990, sections 284, 285 and 286 identify the decisions and actions which cannot be challenged except in accordance with Part XII. Part XII provides for challenge by proceedings in the High Court in accordance with sections 287, 288 and 289. Section 113 of PCPA 2004 makes similar provision for the actions there listed. Although largely assimilated procedurally it is important to distinguish the different provisions.[3] However, procedural failures may be capable of cor- 22.3

[1] University of Wales Press, 2016, part of the Public Law of Wales series. Greater detail of the procedural requirements for judicial review is in Chapter 5 and for statutory review is in Chapter 6 of that work.

[2] See Chapter 20, above.

[3] The claim must be brought in the Planning Court in accordance with the relevant rules, that is the Civil Procedure Rules. These and the nature of the Planning Court are considered below.

rection under powers in the Civil Procedure Rules depending on the particular circumstances.[4]

22.4 Section 288 enables a challenge in the High Court to those matters listed in section 284(2) and (3). This includes a challenge to a decision of the Welsh Ministers on a section 78 appeal or on an application called-in under section 77 against the refusal or conditional grant of planning permission, although extending to a number of other particular decisions of the Ministers or the local planning authority. It will extend to decisions made by Welsh Ministers following applications at first instance to them under TCPA 1990, sections 62D–62F (developments of national significance) and 62M–62O (option of applicant) when fully in force.[5]

22.5 Section 285 restricts challenges to the validity of enforcement notices and similar orders except further to section 289 if one of the statutory grounds for appeal in TCPA 1990, section 174 applies. These grounds have been considered in Chapter 19, above. The Welsh Ministers' decision on a section 174 appeal may therefore be challenged under section 289 of TCPA 1990. The two remaining sets of provisions, TCPA 1990, section 287 and PCPA 2004, section 113, are concerned with other orders, decisions and directions, and provide separate rules regarding applications to the High Court to question validity. Notably these provisions apply to challenges to development orders.

22.6 Permission (leave) is required for all forms of challenge under TCPA 1990, sections 287, 288 and 289 and PCPA 2004, section 113.[6]

SECTION 284

22.7 TCPA 1990, section 284 states that the validity of certain decisions and orders may not be questioned in any legal proceedings whatsoever except in accordance with Part XII of the Act. The provisions refer to actions both by Welsh Ministers and by a local planning authority.

22.8 Three categories of decision or order are identified under section 284(1). They are: first, simplified planning zone schemes, highway orders under Part X and orders relieving statutory undertakers of obligations under section 277; secondly, orders listed in subsection (2); and, thirdly, action by the Welsh Ministers under subsection (3). The first group is best considered in conjunction with section 287 and PCPA 2004, section 113 and is dealt with later. Those acts listed in section 284(2)

[4] See generally *Secretary of State for Communities and Local Government v Vicente* [2013] EWCA Civ 817, [2014] 1 WLR 966.

[5] The relevant provisions are TCPA 1990, section 284(3)(aa)–(ac), which are in force only to the extent necessary to make regulations and the substantive provisions to which they refer are not all fully operational: see relevant text above.

[6] This follows amendment by the Criminal Justice and Courts Act 2015 with effect from 26 October 2015.

include orders revoking or modifying planning permission,[7] orders requiring discontinuance under section 102, tree preservation orders, orders for special control of advertisements under section 221 and certain orders relating to discontinuance of mineral workings under Schedule 9. These are challengeable only further to section 288.

Notable examples of actions of the Welsh Ministers listed in section 284(3)[8] are decisions on applications called-in under section 77, on appeals further to both section 78 (planning applications) and section 195 (certificate of lawful use or development) and decisions granting planning permission or discharging conditions on appeals against enforcement notices.[9] In addition to these, it includes decisions confirming completion notices under section 95, decisions on purchase notices and certain tree preservation and advertisement consents.[10] Challenge to all of these actions is similarly only by proceedings under TCPA 1990, section 288. Interim decisions in the course of a determination have been held not to be a decision on appeal, which refers only to final decisions and only these are within section 288.[11] Amendments by the Planning (Wales) Act 2015, Schedule 4, paragraph 15 when fully in force will add to the list actions of the Welsh Ministers' decisions under the additional powers under TCPA 1990, sections 62D, 62F, 62M and 62O introduced by the 2015 Act.[12] Accordingly, the actions will include decisions on applications of national significance, secondary consents in those cases and applications made at the applicant's option to the Welsh Ministers in the first instance and to connected consents. 22.9

In the case of decision or action which relates to a statutory undertaker, where it would fall within section 284(3) except for the fact that it is required to be taken by both the Welsh Ministers and the appropriate minister as relating to the operational land of a statutory undertaker,[13] sections 284–288 equally apply.[14] 22.10

Costs decisions on appeals were not formerly within the definition in section 284(3) and could not be challenged by an application under section 288 but only by judicial review even where the substantive decision was challenged under section 288. Amendment has, however, been made adding costs orders made in connection with the orders listed in TCPA 1990, section 284(2) or the actions in section 284(3) to enable a costs challenge to be brought under section 288.[15] 22.11

[7] I.e. under TCPA 1990, s. 97.

[8] Amendment by s. 15 of the Planning (Wales) Act 2015 generally is to add express reference to the Welsh Ministers in the text although the section is not yet in force.

[9] See TCPA 1990, s. 177(1).

[10] For details, see TCPA 1990, s. 284(3)(h).

[11] *Cooperative Retail Services Ltd v Secretary of State for the Environment* [1980] 1 WLR 271.

[12] See Chapter 2, above.

[13] Further to Part XI (ss. 262–283) – see Chapter 4, above.

[14] TCPA 1990, s. 291.

[15] TCPA 1990, s. 284(1)(g) and (3A), inserted by Criminal Justice and Courts Act 2015, s. 91 and Sch. 16.

22.12 It should be noted that a decision of the Welsh Ministers to refuse planning permission on the deemed application on an appeal against an enforcement notice is not, unlike the grant of permission in such a case, within subsection (3)(e) and is not therefore within section 288. Challenge to a refusal is therefore by proceedings under TCPA 1990, section 289. The refusal or failure of the Welsh Ministers to take any of the specified actions is expressly excepted from operation of the section, so any general jurisdiction to challenge by legal proceedings remains.[16]

22.13 As far as actions by local authorities are concerned, in general, for the avoidance of any doubt, note that local authority decisions on an application for planning permission are not caught by the prohibition so that a challenge to the grant of permission would have to be by way of judicial review.

22.14 In addition, TCPA 1990, section 286 protects certain actions taken without jurisdiction, that is by the 'wrong' authority. The validity of any permission, determination or certificate granted, made or issued or purporting to have been granted, made or issued by a local planning authority under various powers including an application for planning permission, an application for non-material changes to planning permission under section 96A, an application for a certificate of lawful use and development under section 191 or 192 and an application for consent to the display of advertisements under section 220 shall not be called in question in any legal proceedings, or in any proceedings under TCPA 1990 which are not legal proceedings, on the ground that the permission, determination or certificate should have been granted, made or given by some other local planning authority.

RIGHT OF CHALLENGE UNDER SECTION 288

22.15 A right to challenge any order within section 284(2) or action by the Welsh Ministers within section 284(3) is conferred by TCPA 1990, section 288(1) and (4), which is thus the only means of legal challenge. In addition, a relevant costs order may be challenged, whether or not part of another application.[17]

22.16 Proceedings may be brought by a person aggrieved[18] or by the authority directly concerned.[19] In *Ashton v Secretary of State for Communities and Local Government*,[20] Pill LJ said:

[16] TCPA 1990, s. 284(4).

[17] TCPA 1990, s. 288(1A).

[18] TCPA 1990, s. 288(1).

[19] TCPA 1990, s. 288(2).

[20] [2010] EWCA Civ 600 at para. 53. The relevant references cited are article 10a of the Environmental Impact Assessment Directive (85/337/EEC), *Attorney General of the Gambia v N'Jie* [1961] AC 617, *Eco-Energy (GB) Ltd v First Secretary of State* [2005] 2 P & CR 5, *Lardner v Renfrewshire Council* [1997] SCLR 454, *Cumming v Secretary of State for Scotland* [1992] SCLR 831, *Morbaine Ltd and Roberts v First Secretary of State and others* [2005] JPL 377 and *Commission of the European Communities v Ireland* (Case C-427/07).

> The following principles may be extracted from the authorities and applied when considering whether a person is aggrieved within the meaning of s.288 of the 1990 Act: 1. Wide access to the courts is required under s.288 (art.10a, *N'Jie*). 2. Normally, participation in the planning process which led to the decision sought to be challenged is required. What is sufficient participation will depend on the opportunities available and the steps taken (*Eco-Energy*, *Lardner*). 3. There may be situations in which failure to participate is not a bar (*Cumming*, cited in *Lardner*). 4. A further factor to be considered is the nature and weight of the person's substantive interest and the extent to which it is prejudiced (*N'Jie* and *Lardner*). The sufficiency of the interest must be considered (art.10a). 5. This factor is to be assessed objectively. There is a difference between feeling aggrieved and being aggrieved (*Lardner*). 6. What might otherwise be a sufficient interest may not be sufficient if acquired for the purpose of establishing a status under s.288 (*Morbaine*). 7. The participation factor and the interest factor may be interrelated in that it may not be possible to assess the extent of the person's interest if he has not participated in the planning procedures (*Lardner*). 8. While recognising the need for wide access to the courts, weight may be given, when assessing the prior participation required, and the interests relied on, to the public interest in the implementation of projects and the delay involved in judicial proceedings (A.G. Kokott in *Ireland*).

Subsequently, the general meaning of 'person aggrieved' was extensively reviewed in *Walton v Scottish Ministers*.[21] Here, Lord Reed stated[22] that ordinarily persons will be regarded as aggrieved if they made objections or representations as part of the procedure which preceded the decision challenged, and their complaint is that the decision was not properly made, but that a person who did not so object may still be regarded as a person aggrieved. He then reviewed case law regarding standing in judicial review, distinguishing a mere busybody from a person with a legitimate concern, and emphasised the importance of context before concluding:[23] 22.17

> I have listed the various factors which support Mr Walton's entitlement to bring the present application as a 'person aggrieved'. Mutatis mutandis, those factors would also have given him standing to bring an application for judicial review if, for example, he had sought to challenge the Ministers' decision to restrict the remit of the inquiry so that some of his objections were, as he contended, unlawfully excluded from its scope.

A local planning authority may be a person aggrieved within subsection (1) depending on the circumstances but there is an additional express right to challenge orders 22.18

[21] [2012] UKSC 44.

[22] At paras 86–7.

[23] At para. 96.

or actions within the section given to the authority directly concerned.[24] This is defined as the authority who made the order or decision in question or served the notice to which the proceedings relate or who referred the matter or who was otherwise named in the order or notice.[25]

GROUNDS

22.19 The permitted grounds of challenge refer to substantive invalidity and to procedural failure. Section 288 provides that a claim may be made where the relevant order or action is not within the powers of TCPA 1990 or that any of the relevant requirements have not been complied with. Relevant requirements are in turn defined by section 288(9) as any requirements of TCPA 1990 or the Tribunals and Inquiries Act 1992 or of any applicable order, regulations or rules made under either Act. The grounds are not concerned with the planning merits of the decision or with the facts except to the extent that there is no reasonable factual basis as recognised by established heads of challenge. It is not, of course, a re-hearing and evidence will normally be confined to establishing the formal basis of the decision.

22.20 The grounds are akin to the grounds of challenge in judicial review proceedings. In *E v Secretary of State for the Home Department*[26] Carnwath LJ referred to the history of judicial review and statutory challenge on a point of law in an appeal concerning an asylum decision and expressed the general principle, saying:

> Thus, in spite of the differences in history and wording, the various procedures have evolved to the point where it has become a generally safe working rule that the substantive grounds for intervention are identical . . . The main practical dividing line is between appeals (or review procedures) on both fact and law, and those confined to law. The latter are treated as encompassing the traditional judicial review grounds of excess of power, irrationality, and procedural irregularity.

22.21 In *Walton v Scottish Ministers*,[27] Lord Carnwath returned to the principles when considering the two statutory grounds in the Roads (Scotland) Act 1984, the wording of which was materially the same as in the planning Acts, and said:

> In the modern law, in my view, it would be wrong to construe such provisions too rigidly, or without regard to the parallel development of principles of judicial review. In *Woolf, Jowell and Le Sueur, De Smith's Judicial Review, 6th ed (2006)*, paras 17–025 et seq the two statutory grounds are helpfully related to Lord Diplock's now well established categorisation of the grounds for judicial review in *Council*

[24] TCPA 1990, s. 288(2).

[25] TCPA 1990, s. 288(10).

[26] [2004] EWCA Civ 49, [2004] QB 1044 at para. 42.

[27] [2012] UKSC 44 at para. 111.

> *of Civil Service Unions v Minister for the Civil Service [1985] AC 374*. It is suggested that ground (a) is equivalent to 'the grounds of judicial review known as illegality and unreasonableness'; while ground (b) is 'close to the ground of judicial review of procedural propriety', treated by Lord Diplock as including 'both the common law rules of natural justice and the breach of statutorily required procedures'. The authors add: 'Normally in applications to quash, for the claimant to succeed in quashing the decision he must have been "substantially prejudiced" by the failure to comply with the statute's procedural conditions. Under both substantive and procedural grounds of review the courts possess a residual discretion not to quash a decision where there has been no prejudice or detriment to the claimant and to refuse relief in exceptional circumstances.'
>
> I find this a useful general guide, which gives appropriate, but not unduly legalistic, effect to the distinction drawn by the legislature between substantive and procedural grounds. The applicant will be refused a remedy, where he complains only of a procedural failure (whether under statutory rules or common law principles), if that failure has caused him personally no substantial prejudice. Where, however, a substantive defect is established, going either to the scope of the statutory powers under which the project was promoted, or to its legality or rationality in the sense explained by Lord Diplock, the court's discretion to refuse a remedy will be much more limited. These general principles must of course be read in the context of the statutory framework applicable in a particular case.

Brief consideration of the general principles of judicial review is in Chapter 23. 22.22
However, in the immediate context of a section 288 appeal the principles of challenge have been stated in well known authorities and established over many years.

In *Ashbridge Investments Ltd v Ministry of Housing and Local Government*,[28] Lord 22.23
Denning was concerned with a challenge to a ministerial decision under the Housing Act 1957 and said:

> The court can only interfere on the ground that the Minister has gone outside the powers of the Act or that any requirement of the Act has not been complied with. Under this section it seems to me that the court can interfere with the Minister's decision if he has acted on no evidence; or if he has come to a conclusion to which on the evidence he could not reasonably come; or if he has given a wrong interpretation to the words of the statute; or if he has taken into consideration matters which he ought not to have taken into account, or vice versa; or has otherwise gone wrong in law. It is identical with the position when the court has power to interfere with the decision of a lower tribunal which has erred in point of law.

[28] [1965] 1 WLR 1320 at p. 1326.

22.24 This has been cited numerous times in planning cases, including *Seddon Properties Ltd v Secretary of State for the Environment*[29] where a number of principles were identified, including that the Secretary of State must not act perversely, must not take into account irrelevant material or fail to take into account that which is relevant, must abide by statutory procedures, which include the duty to give reasons that are clear and intelligible and deal with the substantial points raised, and he must not depart from the rules of natural justice.

22.25 More recently, the proper approach was usefully summarised by Lindblom J in *Bloor Homes East Midlands Limited v Secretary of State for Communities and Local Government, Hinckley and Bosworth Borough Council*[30] as follows:

> The relevant law is not controversial. It comprises seven familiar principles: (1) Decisions of the Secretary of State and his inspectors in appeals against the refusal of planning permission are to be construed in a reasonably flexible way. Decision letters are written principally for parties who know what the issues between them are and what evidence and argument has been deployed on those issues. An inspector does not need to 'rehearse every argument relating to each matter in every paragraph' (see the judgment of Forbes J. in *Seddon Properties v Secretary of State for the Environment (1981) 42 P. & C.R. 26*, at p.28).
>
> (2) The reasons for an appeal decision must be intelligible and adequate, enabling one to understand why the appeal was decided as it was and what conclusions were reached on the 'principal important controversial issues'. An inspector's reasoning must not give rise to a substantial doubt as to whether he went wrong in law, for example by misunderstanding a relevant policy or by failing to reach a rational decision on relevant grounds. But the reasons need refer only to the main issues in the dispute, not to every material consideration (see the speech of Lord Brown of Eaton-under-Heywood in *South Bucks District Council and another v Porter (No. 2) [2004] 1 W.L.R. 1953*, at p.1964B–G).
>
> (3) The weight to be attached to any material consideration and all matters of planning judgment are within the exclusive jurisdiction of the decision-maker. They are not for the court. A local planning authority determining an application for planning permission is free, 'provided that it does not lapse into *Wednesbury* irrationality' to give material considerations 'whatever weight [it] thinks fit or no weight at all' (see the speech of Lord Hoffmann in *Tesco Stores Limited v Secretary of State for the Environment [1995] 1 W.L.R. 759*, at p.780F–H). And, essentially for that reason, an application under section 288 of the 1990 Act does not afford an opportunity for a review of the planning merits of an inspector's decision (see the judgment of Sullivan J., as he then was, in *Newsmith v Secretary of State for Environment, Transport and the Regions [2001] EWHC Admin 74*, at paragraph 6).

[29] (1978) 42 P & CR 26.

[30] [2014] EWHC 754 (Admin) at para. 19.

(4) Planning policies are not statutory or contractual provisions and should not be construed as if they were. The proper interpretation of planning policy is ultimately a matter of law for the court. The application of relevant policy is for the decision-maker. But statements of policy are to be interpreted objectively by the court in accordance with the language used and in its proper context. A failure properly to understand and apply relevant policy will constitute a failure to have regard to a material consideration, or will amount to having regard to an immaterial consideration (see the judgment of Lord Reed in *Tesco Stores v Dundee City Council [2012] P.T.S.R. 983*, at paragraphs 17 to 22).

(5) When it is suggested that an inspector has failed to grasp a relevant policy one must look at what he thought the important planning issues were and decide whether it appears from the way he dealt with them that he must have misunderstood the policy in question (see the judgment of Hoffmann L.J., as he then was, *South Somerset District Council v The Secretary of State for the Environment (1993) 66 P. & C.R. 80*, at p.83E–H).

(6) Because it is reasonable to assume that national planning policy is familiar to the Secretary of State and his inspectors, the fact that a particular policy is not mentioned in the decision letter does not necessarily mean that it has been ignored (see, for example, the judgment of Lang J. in *Sea Land Power & Energy Limited v Secretary of State for Communities and Local Government [2012] EWHC 1419 (Q.B.),* at paragraph 58).

(7) Consistency in decision-making is important both to developers and local planning authorities, because it serves to maintain public confidence in the operation of the development control system. But it is not a principle of law that like cases must always be decided alike. An inspector must exercise his own judgment on this question, if it arises (see, for example, the judgment of Pill L.J. *R (Fox Strategic Land and Property Ltd v Chorley BC*[31] at paragraphs 12 to 14, citing the judgment of Mann L.J. in *North Wiltshire District Council v Secretary of State for the Environment*[32] at p.14).

The established principles concerning material considerations and the standard of reasoning were also summarised by Lang J in *Villages Action Group v Secretary of State for Communities and Local Government.*[33] 22.26

The Court of Appeal recently considered procedural irregularity and natural justice in the context of section 288 in *Hopkins Development Ltd v Secretary of State for Communities and Local Government.*[34] The Court emphasised that what was required was that parties had a reasonable opportunity to present evidence and deal 22.27

[31] [2014] EWHC 1179 (Admin).

[32] (1992) 65 P & CR 137.

[33] [2015] EWHC 2729 (Admin).

[34] [2014] EWCA Civ 470 at para. 61.

with material issues and that each knew the case it had to face. The Court distilled principles from the authorities as follows:

> From reviewing the authorities I derive the following principles: (1) Any party to a planning inquiry is entitled (i) to know the case which he has to meet and (ii) to have a reasonable opportunity to adduce evidence and make submissions in relation to that opposing case. (2) If there is procedural unfairness which materially prejudices a party to a planning inquiry that may be a good ground for quashing the inspector's decision. (3) The . . . Rules are designed to assist in achieving objective (1)(i), avoiding pitfall (1)(ii) and promoting efficiency. Nevertheless the Rules are not a complete code for achieving procedural fairness. (4) A [statement under the rules] . . . identifies what the inspector regards as the main issues at the time of his statement. Such a statement is likely to assist the parties, but it does not bind the inspector to disregard evidence on other issues. Nor does it oblige him to give the parties regular updates about his thinking as the Inquiry proceeds. (5) The inspector will consider any significant issues raised by third parties, even if those issues are not in dispute between the main parties. The main parties should therefore deal with any such issues, unless and until the inspector expressly states that they need not do so. (6) If a main party resiles from a matter agreed in the statement of common ground . . . the inspector must give the other party a reasonable opportunity to deal with the new issue which has emerged.

PROCEDURE

22.28 Proceedings under TCPA 1990, section 288 are claims for what is known as planning statutory review. This is defined to include also challenges under TCPA 1990, section 287 and PCPA 2004, section 113 as well as challenges under the Planning (Listed Buildings and Conservation Areas) Act 1990, section 63 and the Planning (Hazardous Substances) Act 1990, section 22. There is a separate Practice Direction, CPR PD8C, relating solely to planning statutory review.

22.29 Section 288 cases are Planning Claims assigned to the Planning Court. The Planning Court is a specialist list of the High Court, technically part of the Administrative Court which is itself part of the Queen's Bench Division, and was set up in 2014, the intent being both to ensure relevant expertise and to expedite decisions.[35] The Planning Court regularly sits in Wales and there is a Planning Court Office, where claims may be lodged, based in the Civil Justice Centre in Cardiff. These cases share certain procedural formalities with High Court challenge by judicial review and are begun by a claim under CPR Pt 8. Since 26 October 2015 permission is required to bring a section 288 challenge and the principal difference between the two regimes now concerns an extension of time for bringing

[35] Target timescales are set out in CPR PD54E, para. 3.4.

proceedings. However, planning statutory review and judicial review are distinct with only those provisions referring to venue and planning court claims (CPR Pt 54.21–24 and CPR PD54D and 54E) expressly applying to both sorts of claim.

CPR PD54E relates exclusively to the Planning Court, applying to judicial review and planning statutory review, and introduces a category of Significant Planning Court claims with expedited target hearing timescales. A party wishing to make representations that a case is within this category must include representations in the claim form or acknowledgement.[36] 22.30

Application under section 288 must be made within six weeks. This dates from the date when the action was taken or, in the case of orders, from the date on which the order is confirmed or takes effect.[37] The date of receipt by a party is not the relevant date but, for example, the date which a decision letter bears. The period cannot be extended. This has been expressly held in connection with the statutory limitation in PCPA 2004, section 113.[38] However, failure to comply with further time limits, for example for service of the claim form if a claim is issued in time, can be met by the courts extending time under CPR Pt 3.1(2)(a) – see e.g. *Corus UK Ltd v Erewash BC*[39] (section 287 appeal) and *Harrogate BC v Secretary of State for Communities and Local Government and Zammitt*[40] (section 288 appeal). 22.31

Amendment after the time period prescribed was considered in *Secretary of State for Communities and Local Government v Vicente*,[41] where it was held that amendment was not governed by CPR Pt 17.4 but by Pt 17.1(2)(b) so that amendment could be permitted to add a new ground after the end of the six-week period. Permission is required to add a ground additional to those for which permission was granted.[42] 22.32

An application is by a claim under CPR Pt 8[43] and must be by the statutory form.[44] This is subject to the additional matters in CPR PD8C, which applies specifically to statutory planning review and expressly excludes CPR PD8A and also CPR Pt 8.3(1) and (2), 10.3(2) and Part 15 (defence and reply). As stated above, CPR Pt 54.21–24 and CPD54D and 54E also apply specifically to the claim being an application under the Planning Acts. The claim form must contain the information specified in CPR Pt 8.2 and also the additional matters listed in CPR PD8C, paragraph 2.2 and be accompanied by the documents listed in paragraph 2.3. The specified matters are the names of any person who may need to be served in accordance with paragraph 4.1, a request for permission to bring the claim, detailed grounds of claim, a statement of facts, any directions sought and 22.33

36 CPR PD54E, para. 3.2.

37 Section 288(4B).

38 See *R (Barker) v Hambleton DC* [2012] EWCA Civ 610.

39 [2006] EWCA Civ 1175.

40 [2014] EWHC 1506 (Admin).

41 [2013] EWCA Civ 817, [2014] 1 WLR 966.

42 CPR PD8C, para. 13.

43 See CPR PD8A, Section B.

44 CPR PD8C, para. 2.1.

the relief claimed. Any evidence to be relied on must be filed and served within fourteen days of service of the claim form unless it accompanied the claim form.[45] All necessary documents should be attached including legal materials and a list of essential documents for advance reading. Additional provisions as to service and evidence are within CPR Pt 8 and PD8C, paragraph 4 and written evidence may not be relied upon unless it accords with paragraph 14. The Ministry of Justice Administrative Court Guidance document on section 288 applications sets out the key procedural requirements and lists the documents needed.

22.34 A person served with the claim form who wishes to take part in the proceedings must file an acknowledgement of service in accordance with CPR PD8C, paragraphs 5.3–5.6, which replace the general rules for claims in CPR 8.3(1) and (2).[46] If the person served fails to file an acknowledgement he may only take part in the permission hearing if the court so allows and may take part in the review hearing only if he complies with the rules regarding the provision of detailed grounds of opposition or support and for written evidence.[47] Permission is generally considered on the papers without a hearing but a person refused permission may request that a decision be reconsidered at a hearing in accordance with CPR PD8C, paragraphs 7 and 8.

POWERS OF HIGH COURT

22.35 The High Court may by interim order suspend the operation of the order or action, the validity of which is questioned by the application, until the final determination of the proceedings.

22.36 At the final hearing the High Court, if satisfied that the order or action in question is not within the powers of TCPA 1990, or that the interests of the applicant have been substantially prejudiced by a failure to comply with any of the relevant requirements in relation to it, may quash that order or action.[48] There is accordingly a distinction between substantive and procedural irregularity, with substantial prejudice needed to be shown in the latter.

22.37 Where all parties agree, the review may be decided without a hearing[49] and provisions regarding agreed final orders are at CPR PD8C, paragraph 18.

45 CPR PD8A, para. 22.8.

46 CPR PD8C, paras 5.1 and 5.2.

47 CPR PD8C, para. 6, which replaces the general rules for Pt 8 Claims in CPR 8.4.

48 TCPA 1990, s. 288(5)(b).

49 CPR PD8C, para. 17.

ENFORCEMENT NOTICES – SECTIONS 285 AND 289

An enforcement notice shall not be questioned in any legal proceedings whatsoever on any ground on which an appeal may be brought under Part VII of the Act, except by an appeal under TCPA 1990, section 289.[50] Section 289 states that the appellant or the local planning authority or any other person having an interest in the land to which the notice relates may appeal against the Welsh Ministers' decision on an appeal against an enforcement notice. The appeal may be either to the High Court on a point of law or require the Ministers to state and sign a case for the opinion of the High Court. 22.38

This therefore excludes judicial review where the issue concerns one of the section 174 grounds, whether or not such an appeal was actually made. Where an appeal was made, a challenge to the appeal decision falls within section 289, but where the grounds of challenge are not themselves grounds within section 174, the prohibition on other proceedings in section 285 will not apply. It will also exclude defences to criminal proceedings for breach of enforcement notices where the grounds are within section 174. However, in the latter case there is a specific exception where the enforcement notice was not served on a person with an interest at the time of issue and who did not know and could not reasonably have been expected to know of its issue where his interests have been substantially prejudiced by the failure.[51] 22.39

The extent to which matters may be raised as a defence in criminal proceedings was considered in Chapter 20, above, and reference should be made in particular to *R v Wicks*. Where the statutory grounds of appeal are not in issue legal proceedings are not barred. This was made clear in *Davy v Spelthorne*.[52] The extent to which judicial review is available for these residual matters was also considered in *R v Wicks* where *mala fides*, bias or other procedural impropriety were expressly identified as examples. In general terms, matters affecting the existence of grounds to issue an enforcement notice will be within section 174 and therefore not challengeable by judicial review, which will accordingly be confined to examination of whether the issue of a notice was 'expedient'.[53] 22.40

As noted above, the decision of the Welsh Ministers to grant planning permission on an enforcement appeal can only be challenged under section 288 as such a decision is within section 284(3), but a refusal is governed by section 285 and will be within section 289,[54] as will a decision quashing the enforcement notice itself. 22.41

Challenges to interim or interlocutory decisions are also within section 289, which refers to giving 'a decision in proceedings on an appeal': this may be 22.42

[50] TCPA 1990, s. 285(1).

[51] TCPA 1990, s. 285(2).

[52] [1984] AC 262 at p. 272.

[53] See para. 18.30, above.

[54] See e.g. *De Souza v Secretary of State for Communities and Local Government* [2015] EWHC 2245 (Admin).

contrasted with section 288 where the applicable wording in section 284(3) is 'a decision on an appeal', which has been held to be confined to the final determination.[55]

22.43 The challenge is a statutory appeal and subject to the CPR appeal provisions in Part 52, and CPR PD52D with the provisions of paragraphs 4 and 26 specifically referring to section 289. No appeal may be brought without permission of the High Court.[56] Application for permission must be brought within twenty-eight days of the date on which notice of the decision was given to the appellant.[57] The time may be extended in accordance with the general rules in civil proceedings. CPR PD54D governing venue applies and the enforcement of planning control is a Planning Court claim[58] and subject to the particular provisions of that court. Permission is always dealt with at a hearing and not on the papers, unlike section 288 appeals, and if granted the court may give directions on the future conduct of the appeal.[59] If permission to appeal is refused, there is no right of appeal against the refusal.[60]

22.44 Pending final determination of the proceedings, the court may, on such terms, if any, as it thinks fit, order that the enforcement notice shall have effect, or have effect to such extent as may be specified in the order. The terms may include requiring the local planning authority to give an undertaking as to damages or any other matter and the order may extend until the conclusion of any re-hearing and determination by the Welsh Ministers.[61]

22.45 Where, on hearing the appeal, the court is of the opinion that the decision appealed against was erroneous in point of law, it will not set aside or vary that decision but will remit the matter to the Welsh Ministers for re-hearing and determination in accordance with the opinion of the court.[62]

DEVELOPMENT PLANS AND OTHER SCHEMES AND ORDERS

22.46 PCPA 2004, section 113 provides for challenges to development plans and other actions. Similar but not identical measures apply to orders and schemes further to section 287(2) of TCPA 1990, as amended by PCPA 2004. In each case the actions covered are referred to as 'relevant documents'. Section 113 applies to the Wales Spatial Plan, development plan documents and the local development plan. The section applies equally to a revision of any such document. When the relevant provisions of the Planning (Wales) Act 2015 are fully in force the reference to

[55] See para. 22.9, above.

[56] TCPA 1990, s. 289(6).

[57] CPR PD52D, para. 26.

[58] CPR Pt 54.21.

[59] CPR PD52D, para. 26.

[60] *Walsall MBC v Secretary of State for Communities and Local Government* [2013] EWCA Civ 370.

[61] TCPA 1990, s. 289(4A).

[62] CPR PD52D, para. 26.15.

the Wales Spatial Plan will be omitted and it will expressly apply to the National Development Framework for Wales and in addition to strategic development plans.

The relevant document may not be questioned in any legal proceedings whatsoever except as provided by the section[63] but may be challenged by a person aggrieved by application to the High Court on the ground that the document is not within the appropriate power or a procedural requirement has not been complied with. The section makes further express provision as to the meaning of appropriate power and procedural requirements. The meaning of 'person aggrieved' has been considered above. In the specific context of section 113 applications, *Ashton v Secretary of State for Communities and Local Government*[64] was followed in *Zurich Assurance Ltd v Winchester City Council*,[65] where Sales J said: 22.47

> Factors relevant to the assessment whether a person who objects to a planning decision qualifies as a 'person aggrieved' by that decision include the nature of the decision and the directness of its impact on him, the grounds on which he claims to be aggrieved, whether he had a fair opportunity to participate in the relevant decision-making process to raise such grounds of objection and whether he did in fact make use of such opportunity to make those objections before the decision was taken.

Application must be made within six weeks of the relevant date.[66] Claims under both TCPA 1990, section 287 and PCPA 2004, section 113 are claims for planning statutory review subject to the procedural provisions of CPR PD8C considered above. The court also has power to make interim orders. An application may not be brought without leave of the court, which must be sought within six weeks.[67] 22.48

If the High Court is satisfied that a relevant document is to any extent outside the appropriate power or that the interests of the applicant have been substantially prejudiced by a failure to comply with a procedural requirement it may quash the relevant document or remit the relevant document to a person or body with a function relating to its preparation, publication, adoption or approval. If it remits the relevant document it may give directions as to the action to be taken in relation to the document including requiring the document to be treated (generally or for specified purposes) as not having been approved or adopted, or it may require specified steps in the process that has resulted in the approval or adoption to be treated as having been taken or as not having been taken, as the case may be. It may also require action to be taken by a person or body with a function relating to the preparation, publication, adoption or approval of the document (whether or not 22.49

63 PCPA 2004, s. 113(2).

64 [2010] EWCA Civ 600; see para. 22.16, above.

65 [2014] EWHC 758 (Admin) at para. 82.

66 Defined in PCPA 2004, s. 113.

67 PCPA 2004, s. 113(3A), (3B) and (5A), as inserted by Criminal Justice and Courts Act 2015, s. 91 and Sch. 16, para. 8.

the person or body to which the document is remitted) or requiring action to be taken by one person or body to depend on what action has been taken by another person or body. These powers are exercisable in relation to the relevant document wholly or in part or generally or as it affects the property of the applicant.

22.50 Section 287(2) of TCPA 1990 makes essentially similar provisions regarding relevant documents falling within subsection (1): this refers to simplified planning zone schemes and certain highway orders[68] and orders relieving statutory undertakers from impracticable obligations.[69] Application may be made by a person aggrieved and the grounds are that the relevant document is not within the appropriate power or a procedural requirement has not been complied with.

22.51 The six-week time limit applies equally as for section 113 documents and newly inserted provisions section 287(2A), (2B) and (3ZA) require leave to proceed and deal with interim orders. The power at final hearing does not, however, extend to remitting the document but is confined to quashing the relevant document wholly or in part or generally, or as it affects the property of the applicant.[70]

[68] I.e. those under TCPA 1990, ss. 247, 248, 249, 251, 257 or 258.

[69] Made under TCPA 1990, s. 277.

[70] TCPA 1990, s. 287(3A) and (3B).

Chapter 23

Judicial Review

INTRODUCTION

Planning decisions are subject to the general supervisory jurisdiction of the High Court by judicial review, that is by application in accordance with the Senior Courts Act 1981, section 31 and CPR Pt 54 for a mandatory, prohibiting or quashing order. In addition, this procedure may be used for a declaration or an injunction.[1] The claim may include a claim for damages, restitution or the recovery of a sum due but may not seek such a remedy alone.[2] 23.1

Judicial review may not be brought to the extent that TCPA 1990, Part XII or PCPA 2004, section 113 make specific provision for legal challenge. This exclusion and the specific rights of challenge have been considered above. Where a challenge falls outside the specific terms of the preclusive provisions judicial review may be sought. Judicial review is the appropriate means of challenge, for example, where the local planning authority grant planning permission and the fact that section 285 states that the validity of an enforcement notice shall not be challenged in any proceedings on any of the grounds on which an appeal may be brought under Part VII of the Act does not prevent review on other grounds.[3] 23.2

Judicial review may exceptionally be appropriate where an applicant is aggrieved by a local planning authority refusal of permission, although generally the right of appeal under TCPA 1990, section 78 will be relied on. Misconduct by the decision-maker is an example of the potential applicability of judicial review in this situation although it is always the case that save in the most exceptional circumstances judicial review will not be granted where other available remedies have not been used.[4] 23.3

Decisions on major infrastructure projects under the Planning Act 2008 are expressly made subject to challenge by judicial review in accordance with the procedure set out in section 118 of the Act, which provides that this is the only means to question the consent.[5] This applies equally to the grant and the refusal 23.4

[1] See CPR Pt 54.2 and 3.

[2] CPR Pt 54.3(2) and Senior Courts Act 1981, s. 31.

[3] See *R v Wicks (Peter Edward)* [1998] AC 92, *Davy v Spelthorne BC* [1984] AC 262 and see the discussion in *Gazelle Properties Ltd, Sustainable Environmental Services Ltd v Bath and North East Somerset Council* [2010] EWHC 3127 (Admin).

[4] See e.g. *R v Epping and Harlow General Commissioners, ex parte Goldstraw* [1983] 3 All ER 257 and D. Gardner, *Administrative Law and the Administrative Court in Wales*.

[5] Section 118 prescribes a six-week time limit for bringing these claims.

of consent and amendments and any other action or omission of the Secretary of State in connection with development consent applications.

23.5 The procedural provisions for a High Court statutory review or challenge, which were considered in the previous chapter, and for judicial review are similar but it is necessary to adopt the correct procedure and key differences affect the power to extend time periods and there are differences in the wording regarding who may bring proceedings and the scope of review which may be important in the individual case. In addition, the costs-capping provisions of CPR Pt 54.41 where the claim is an Aarhus Convention claim are confined to judicial review.[6] In *Venn v Secretary of State for Communities and Local Government*,[7] the Court of Appeal held that this exclusion of other proceedings was a deliberate expression of legislative intent which should not be side-stepped judicially, although it was said that the costs protection regime did not comply with the Convention.

23.6 All cases involving planning permission, other development consents, the enforcement of planning control and the enforcement of other statutory schemes, whether by judicial review or statutory challenge, are dealt with by the Planning Court.[8] A party wishing to make representations that a case is a Significant Planning Court claim within CPR PD54E must include representations in the claim form or acknowledgement.[9]

PROCEDURE – GENERAL REQUIREMENTS

23.7 A claim can only be brought within the specified time, with the permission (leave) of the court and by a person with a sufficient interest. The Pre-Action Protocol for Judicial Review[10] applies and should be complied with although because of the shorter time limit for planning claims it is recognised that it may not be appropriate. The parties should seek to comply but the court will not apply normal cost sanctions where it is satisfied that it has not been possible to comply because of the shorter time limits.[11] Where this is not applicable the court expects all parties

[6] The Aarhus Convention of June 1998 is the UNECE Convention on Access to Information, Public Participation in Decision-making and Access to Justice in Environmental Matters. Article 9(3) provides for states to ensure that members of the public have access to administrative or judicial procedures to challenge acts or omissions contravening national law relating to the environment and the costs-capping provisions of the CPR are to implement its terms. See, generally, D. Gardner, *Administrative Law and the Administrative Court in Wales*, 7-24.

[7] [2014] EWCA Civ 1539, [2015] 1 WLR 2328.

[8] See para. 22.29, above. CPR Pt 54.21: the full list includes other disputes of a similar nature, e.g. compulsory purchase and highway matters.

[9] CPR PD54E, para. 3.2.

[10] Pre-action protocols explain the conduct and set out the steps the court would normally expect the parties to take in particular civil proceedings: see Practice Direction Pre-Action Conduct and Protocols.

[11] Protocol, paragraph 6.

to comply with the protocol and will take this into account in case management and costs decisions. Even in emergency cases, it is stated that it is good practice to send to the defendant the draft Claim Form which the claimant intends to issue and a claimant is also normally required to notify a defendant when an interim mandatory order is being sought.[12]

In the case of a claim challenging the decision of the Welsh Ministers or local planning authority under the planning Acts, the claim form must be filed not later than six weeks after the grounds to make the claim first arose.[13] Challenges relating to development consent must also be brought within six weeks.[14] This is thus shorter than the maximum period for judicial review claims generally but it is not subject to the overall test of promptness in CPR Pt 54.5(1). The period cannot be extended by agreement between the parties[15] but application can be made for an extension of time under the general civil procedure provisions of CPR Pt 3.1(2)(a). In the case of a challenge to the grant of planning permission, the claim arises when the permission was actually granted and not on the date of an earlier resolution to grant it.[16] 23.8

A claim for judicial review can only proceed with the court's permission.[17] Granting permission depends upon there being an arguable case which should be considered further by the court and on there being no bar to proceeding. Permission can only be granted to someone with sufficient interest – see below. In addition, the Criminal Justice and Courts Act 2015, section 85(2) inserts a new subsection (3A) into the Senior Courts Act 1981, section 31 to restrict leave where relevant financial information has not been given. This provision is not yet in force. 23.9

Permission is generally considered at first instance without a hearing,[18] although the court may require a hearing. At the permission stage, the court must consider if the outcome for the applicant would have been substantially different if the conduct complained of had not occurred if asked to do so by the defendant and may consider this question of its own motion.[19] If it appears highly likely that the outcome would not have been substantially different, leave must be refused unless it is appropriate to disregard this for reasons of exceptional public interest.[20] The court will give notice of the decision to grant or refuse permission, which will include any directions given[21] and will include its reasons.[22] Permission may 23.10

[12] See Protocol, paragraph 7.

[13] CPR Pt 54.5(4) and (5).

[14] Planning Act 2008, section 118(1)(b).

[15] CPR Pt 54.5(2).

[16] *R (Burkett) v Hammersmith and Fulham LBC and another* [2002] UKHL 23, [2002] 1 WLR 1593.

[17] Senior Courts Act 1981, s. 31(3) and CPR Pt 54.4.

[18] CPR PD54A, para. 8.4.

[19] Senior Courts Act 1981, s. 31(3C). Procedural rules for a hearing on the issue are in CPR Pt 54.11A.

[20] Senior Courts Act 1981, s. 31(3D) and (3E).

[21] CPR Pt 54.11.

[22] CPR Pt 54.12(2).

be limited to certain of the grounds of application. Permission is required if an applicant later wishes to rely on grounds additional to those for which permission was granted.[23] Where a claim is brought within time, the power of the court to permit subsequent amendment was considered in *Secretary of State for Communities and Local Government v Vicente*.[24]

23.11 The Senior Courts Act 1981, section 31(3) states that the court shall not grant leave to make an application for judicial review unless it considers that the applicant has a sufficient interest in the matter to which the application relates. In cases brought under the Human Rights Act 1998, section 7 requires a claim to be by a victim of the unlawful act. The requirement of standing ('sufficient interest') is not identically worded to that for section 288 appeals where it is 'person aggrieved', although the two terms may on the facts be co-extensive. Both were considered in the Supreme Court in *Walton v Scottish Ministers*.[25]

23.12 The general approach is that the words should not be interpreted restrictively but be construed to give effect to the supervisory role of the court in maintaining the rule of law as well as redressing individual grievances. As was stated in *Walton*, 'the rule of law would not be maintained if, because everyone was equally affected by an unlawful act, no one was able to bring proceedings to challenge it.' The busybody is to be excluded but not a person reasonably concerned. The focus is on those 'directly affected' (those words being found in the definition of 'interested party' in CPR 54.1) and a personal interest need not be shown if the individual is acting in the public interest and can genuinely say that the issue directly affects the section of the public that he seeks to represent. The court in *Walton* made clear that a person would normally be regarded as a 'person aggrieved' by a decision if he had made objections or representations as part of the procedure which preceded the decision challenged. However, the fact that a prior objection had been lodged is not essential. In general, in all cases the context is critical.

23.13 Furthermore, standing is relevant at two stages, that is both at the preliminary stage of deciding whether to grant permission and also at the later stage when exercising the discretion to grant relief on the merits of the claim – see *Walton*,[26] *Inland Revenue Commissioners v National Federation of Self-Employed and Small Businesses Ltd*[27] and *R v Monopolies and Mergers Commission, ex parte Argyll Group Plc*.[28]

23 CPR Pt 54.15.

24 [2013] EWCA Civ 817, [2014] 1 WLR 966. See Chapter 22, above.

25 [2012] UKSC 44 at paras 82–96; see para. 22.21, above.

26 At para. 103.

27 [1982] AC 617.

28 [1986] 1 WLR 763.

PROCEDURE – FORMAL STEPS

Proceedings are commenced by the issue of a claim form which must be served within seven days of issue on the defendant and, unless the court otherwise directs, on any interested party.[29] Claim forms are issued at an Administrative Court Office of the High Court as specified in CPR PD54D. There is an office in Cardiff and issue in Cardiff will normally lead to a hearing in Wales. Transfer to another court area is in accordance with the further provisions of this Practice Direction. Service on the Welsh Ministers is via the Director of Legal Services to the Welsh Assembly Government, Cathays Park, Cardiff CF10 3NQ.[30] Proceedings regarding devolved decisions will ordinarily be heard in Wales as convenient to the parties – see *R (Deepdock Ltd) v Welsh Ministers*.[31] The decision will be taken in accordance with the general considerations in determining venue listed in CPR PD54D. 23.14

The information and documents to accompany the form are set out in CPR PD54A, paragraph 5.6. Note that if it is claimed that the matter is an Aarhus Convention claim then details of this should be given[32] as these claims are subject to special provisions limiting recoverable costs. Given the wide scope of the Convention where planning matters are concerned, as found in *Venn*,[33] this is likely to apply widely in judicial review claims in planning matters. In *Venn*[34] it was held that the national law relating to the environment in the Convention included national and local policy. Additional information is also required where the claim seeks to raise any issue under the Human Rights Act 1998.[35] 23.15

Further, if the claimant intends to raise a devolution issue, the claim form must specify that the applicant wishes to raise this issue and identify the relevant provisions of the Government of Wales Act 2006, and contain a summary of the facts, circumstances and points of law on the basis of which it is alleged that it arises. 'Devolution issue' has the same meaning as in paragraph 1 of Schedule 9 to the 23.16

[29] CPR 54.7.

[30] See Crown Proceedings Act 1947, s. 17, addresses for service from which are in Annex 2 to CPR PD66.

[31] [2007] EWHC 3347 (Admin).

[32] CPR 54.6; the definition is found in CPR 45.41 and the specific costs rules in CPR 45.42–44 and CPR PD45. See para. 23.5 fn 6, above for the Convention.

[33] See para. 23.5, above.

[34] At paras 16–17.

[35] CPR PD54A, para. 5.3.

Government of Wales Act 2006, which essentially means that action was outside the devolved powers given to the Assembly or Welsh Ministers.[36]

23.17 If any person served wishes to take part in the review he must file an acknowledgement of service within twenty-one days and serve it on the claimant and any other party named in the claim within seven days of filing.[37] A person failing to acknowledge may not take part in any permission hearing unless the court allows but may take part in the judicial review hearing itself by filing full details and complying with the further rules.[38]

23.18 The application for permission is generally considered without a hearing and, if permission is given, the court may give directions.[39] The defendant and any interested person must then file detailed grounds contesting the claim and any written evidence within thirty-five days if it is intended to contest the claim.[40] If permission is refused, granted conditionally or granted on certain grounds only, the claimant may ask for that decision to be reconsidered at a hearing by filing a request within seven days, unless the court certifies that the case is totally without merit.[41] In appropriate cases the court may order a 'rolled-up' hearing, that is, one where the issue of permission and the final hearing on the grounds of the claim are heard together.

23.19 Evidence throughout the review process, other than in exceptional cases, is in writing and must be in accordance with CPR 54.17; and further procedural guidance is in CPR PD54A.

23.20 At the conclusion of the proceedings the court may make a mandatory order, that is one requiring the defendant to act in a particular way, a quashing order setting aside the order or decision in question, or make an order prohibiting particular

[36] For requirement, see CPR PD54A, para. 5.4. The full definition is that a devolution issue means

(a) a question whether an Assembly Measure or Act of the Assembly, or any provision of an Assembly Measure or Act of the Assembly, is within the Assembly's legislative competence,

(b) a question whether any function (being a function which any person has purported, or is proposing, to exercise) is exercisable by the Welsh Ministers, the First Minister or the Counsel General,

(c) a question whether the purported or proposed exercise of a function by the Welsh Ministers, the First Minister or the Counsel General is, or would be, within the powers of the Welsh Ministers, the First Minister or the Counsel General (including a question whether a purported or proposed exercise of a function is, or would be, outside those powers by virtue of section 80(8) or 81(1)),

(d) a question whether there has been any failure to comply with a duty imposed on the Welsh Ministers, the First Minister or the Counsel General (including any obligation imposed by virtue of section 80(1) or (7)), or

(e) a question of whether a failure to act by the Welsh Ministers, the First Minister or the Counsel General is incompatible with any of the Convention rights,

[37] CPR 54.8.

[38] CPR 54.9.

[39] CPR 54.10.

[40] CPR 54.14.

[41] CPR 54.12. Totally without merit means 'bound to fail': see *R (Grace) v Secretary of State for the Home Department* [2014] EWCA Civ 1091, [2014] 1 WLR 3432 at para. 19.

action in the future. Each of these is a discretionary remedy so that the court may grant relief or decline to make an order as appropriate in the circumstances of the case. It may also make a declaration as to the lawfulness of the matter in issue or grant an injunction. In appropriate cases it can make a combination of these orders. A declaration may be made or an injunction granted where claimed if the court considers that it would be just and convenient, having regard to the nature of the matters in respect of which relief may be granted by mandatory, prohibiting or quashing orders, the nature of the persons and bodies against whom relief may be granted by such orders and all the circumstances of the case.[42]

Damages, restitution or the recovery of a sum due may be ordered but the application cannot seek such a remedy alone.[43] They may be ordered where the application includes a claim for an award arising from any matter to which it relates and the court is satisfied that such an award would have been made if the claim had been made in an action begun by the applicant at the time of making the application. However, the High Court must refuse to grant relief on an application for judicial review, and may not make a financial award on such an application, if it appears to be highly likely that the outcome for the applicant would not have been substantially different if the conduct complained of had not occurred.[44] This may be disregarded if it is appropriate to do so for reasons of exceptional public interest.[45] 23.21

If the court makes a quashing order it may remit the matter to the decision-maker, direct re-consideration in accordance with the judgment or, where permitted, substitute its own decision.[46] 23.22

GROUNDS OF JUDICIAL REVIEW

This is intended as only a brief introduction to this topic, referring to some issues of particular relevance to planning. As has been seen, the general principles which apply to the statutory challenges and decisions under TCPA 1990, Part XII may be equally relevant here and reference should be made to Chapter 22. In addition, the legal context of decision-making and what is or is not a material consideration was considered in Chapter 13 and should be referred to. 23.23

The classic formulation identifies three broad grounds of judicial review: illegality, irrationality and procedural impropriety.[47] Illegality refers to errors of law, irrationality to *Wednesbury* unreasonableness, and the latter to the particular procedural rules as well as general principles of fairness or natural justice. *Wednesbury* 23.24

[42] Senior Courts Act 1981, s. 31(2).

[43] CPR Pt 54.3(2).

[44] Senior Courts Act 1981, s. 31(2A).

[45] Senior Courts Act 1981, s. 31(2B).

[46] CPR 54.19.

[47] *Council of Civil Service Unions v Minister for the Civil Service* [1985] AC 374, per Lord Diplock at p. 410D.

unreasonableness means that material considerations must be taken into account and immaterial ones disregarded and that the decision overall is not so unreasonable that no reasonable body could have come to it.[48] This classification is not exhaustive.

23.25 The planning Acts form a comprehensive code and planning applications raise issues of public interest and of concern to third parties: accordingly, the occasions when a legitimate expectation can arise from the conduct or representations of the local planning authority will be rare.[49]

23.26 In addition, a claim that a public body has acted in a way incompatible with the Convention for the Protection of Human Rights and Fundamental Freedoms may be brought in judicial review proceedings. In these cases the test of proportionality may need to be applied and that generally requires a more intensive review than traditional common law unreasonableness.[50] However, *R (Association of British Civilian Internees: Far East Region) v Secretary of State for Defence*[51] held that proportionality had not replaced the test of reasonableness traditionally applicable on judicial review claims which raised no human rights or European Community law issues.[52]

23.27 The jurisdiction is a supervisory not an appellate one and it is not concerned with the merits of the decision but with the decision-making process. So in *Tesco Stores Ltd v Secretary of State for the Environment*,[53] Lord Hoffmann said that it is:

> a fundamental principle of British planning law . . . that the courts are concerned only with the legality of the decision-making process and not with the merits of the decision. If there is one principle of planning law more firmly settled than any other, it is that matters of planning judgment are within the exclusive province of the local planning authority or the Secretary of State.

23.28 Key relevant formulations of the general principles in the context of planning may be found in particular in cases which have been referred to earlier and are not considered further at this point. Key cases are: *Ashbridge Investments Ltd v Ministry of Housing and Local Government*,[54] *Seddon Properties v Secretary of State for the Environment*,[55] *Bolton MBC v Secretary of State for the Environment*,[56] *Tesco Stores Ltd v Secretary of State for the Environment and others*,[57] *South Bucks District Council*

48 See *Associated Provincial Picture Houses Ltd v Wednesbury Corporation* [1948] 1 KB 223.

49 See *Henry Boot Homes Ltd v Bassetlaw DC* [2002] EWCA Civ 983.

50 *R v Secretary of State for the Home Department, ex parte Daly* [2001] AC 532.

51 [2003] EWCA Civ 473, [2003] QB 1397.

52 In *R (Lumsdon and others) v Legal Services Board* the Supreme Court considered the test of proportionality and set out a summary to clarify the principle of proportionality as it applies in EU law.

53 [1995] 1 WLR 759 at p. 780.

54 [1965] 1 WLR 1320.

55 (1981) 42 P & CR 26.

56 (1991) 61 P & CR 343.

57 [1995] 1 WLR 759.

and another v Porter (No. 2)[58] and *Tesco Stores Ltd v Dundee City Council.*[59] Helpful summaries of established principles are in *Bayliss v Secretary of State for Communities and Local Government*[60] and *Bloor Homes East Midlands Ltd v Secretary of State for Communities and Local Government, Hinckley and Bosworth Borough Council,*[61] again, as cited earlier.

Important issues which may need to be resolved therefore include the distinction between matters of law and those of fact, the latter being for the decision-maker not the courts, although a decision may nevertheless be legally wrong where the finding was essential to jurisdiction. Where the construction of policy is concerned the decision must be based on a proper interpretation of policy and the meaning of policy is a question of law as a decision cannot be in accordance with a development plan if the plan is misunderstood – see *Tesco Stores Ltd v Dundee City Council.*[62] Other common grounds of challenge refer to procedural irregularity including compliance with consultation requirements. What is material in the light of the above depends upon a proper reading of the decision and the courts have repeatedly held that the decision should be read fairly rather than subject to over-rigorous examination. 23.29

Where the challenge is based on an alleged inadequacy in the reasons given by the decision-maker for the decision, the principles were stated by the House of Lords in *Save Britain's Heritage v Number 1 Poultry Ltd*[63] and *South Bucks District Council v Porter (No. 2).*[64] Relevant summary of the principles applied to section 288 challenges has been made earlier but the essential points bear repetition. In the latter case, Lord Brown said:[65] 23.30

> The reasons for a decision must be intelligible and they must be adequate. They must enable the reader to understand why the matter was decided as it was and what conclusions were reached on the 'principal important controversial issues', disclosing how any issue of law or fact was resolved. Reasons can be briefly stated, the degree of particularity required depending entirely on the nature of the issues falling for decision. The reasoning must not give rise to a substantial doubt as to whether the decision-maker erred in law, for example by misunderstanding some relevant policy or some other important matter or by failing to reach a rational decision on relevant grounds. But such adverse inference will not readily be drawn. The reasons need refer only to the main issues in the dispute, not to every material consideration. They should enable disappointed

[58] [2004] 1 WLR 1953.

[59] [2012] UKSC 13.

[60] [2013] EWHC 1612 (Admin) and see [2014] EWCA Civ 347.

[61] [2014] EWHC 754 (Admin).

[62] [2012] UKSC 13.

[63] [1991] 1 WLR 153.

[64] [2004] 1 WLR 1953.

[65] At para. 36.

> developers to assess their prospects of obtaining some alternative development permission, or, as the case may be, their unsuccessful opponents to understand how the policy or approach underlying the grant of permission may impact upon future such applications. Decision letters must be read in a straightforward manner, recognising that they are addressed to parties well aware of the issues involved and the arguments advanced. A reasons challenge will only succeed if the party aggrieved can satisfy the court that he has genuinely been substantially prejudiced by the failure to provide an adequately reasoned decision.

23.31 Judicial review is, as stated, the means of third party challenge to a local authority grant of planning permission and for residual grounds perhaps involving natural justice in decision-making, although the latter may fall within TCPA 1990, sections 287–289. Where the challenge is to the grant of planning permission by the local planning authority, the principles governing the approach to a committee report to seek to establish whether or not there may have been an error of law were stated by Hickinbottom J in *R (Zurich Assurance Ltd t/a Threadneedle Investments) v North Lincolnshire Council*[66] as follows:

> i. In the absence of contrary evidence it is a reasonable inference that members of the planning committee follow the reasoning of the report, particularly where a recommendation is adopted. ii. When challenged such reports are not to be subjected to the same exegesis that might be appropriate for the interpretation of a statute: what is required is a fair reading of the report as a whole consequently: 'An application for Judicial Review based on criticisms of the planning officer's report will not normally begin to merit consideration unless the overall effect of the report significantly misleads the committee about material matters which thereafter are left uncorrected at a meeting of the planning committee before the relevant decision is taken.' (*Oxton Farms, Samuel Smiths Old Brewery (Tadcaster) v Selby District Council (18th April 1997) 1997 WL 1106106* per Judge LJ as he then was.) iii. In construing reports it has to be borne in mind that they are addressed to a 'knowledgeable readership', including council members 'who, by virtue of that membership, may be expected to have a substantial local and background knowledge' (*R v Mendip District Council ex parte Fabre (2000) 80 P and CR 500* per Sullivan J as he then was). That background knowledge includes 'a working knowledge of the statutory tests' for determination of a planning application (*Oxton Farms* per Pill LJ).

23.32 Turning to potential residual or general grounds of challenge concerning impropriety, procedural irregularity includes breach of the principles of natural justice, for example bias. Alleged bias by an inspector was recently considered by the Court of Appeal in *Turner v Secretary of State for Communities and Local Government*,[67] in the

66 [2012] EWHC 3708 (Admin) at para. 15.

67 [2015] EWCA Civ 582.

context of TCPA 1990, section 288. The court reiterated that the appropriate test of apparent bias is the standard of the notional fair-minded and informed observer. Where decisions are those of Ministers, reference can be made to *Broadview Energy Development v Secretary of State for Communities and Local Government*[68] and *R (Condron) v National Assembly for Wales*[69] (both section 288 cases).

Where the allegation includes that of direct pecuniary interest, a person may be automatically disqualified. The principles were recently considered in *Kelton v Wiltshire CC*[70] where a challenge was made on grounds that a councillor voting in favour of the application for planning permission was a director of the housing association which had been identified as the applicant's preferred bidder for the affordable housing component of the development. It was held that there was no direct pecuniary interest as there were too many contingencies between the grant of permission and any benefit as director. Nor was the councillor disqualified as taking an active role as promoting a cause which would require more exceptional facts. 23.33

[68] [2016] EWCA Civ 562. That part of the decision referring to disclosable pecuniary interests under Localism Act 2011, s. 31 is not considered here as the section does not apply to local planning authorities in Wales.

[69] [2006] EWCA Civ 1573.

[70] [2015] EWHC 2853 (Admin).

Chapter 24

Historic Environment

INTRODUCTION

Listed buildings and conservation areas are amongst the subjects specified in the Government of Wales Act 2006, Schedule 7, paragraph 18, together with town and country planning, as within the legislative competence of the National Assembly for Wales.[1] In addition, paragraph 2 of Schedule 7 allows Acts to be passed concerning archaeological remains, ancient monuments and buildings, and places of historic or architectural interest. Functions under the Act relating to all these subjects have been transferred to the Welsh Ministers.[2] 24.1

The statutory framework is established by the Ancient Monuments and Archaeological Areas Act 1979 ('the 1979 Act') and the Planning (Listed Buildings and Conservation Areas) Act 1990 ('Listed Buildings Act 1990'). The former provides for Welsh Ministers to maintain a schedule of ancient monuments and contains regulation to prevent unauthorised works to scheduled monuments and enables designation of archaeological sites. Over 4,000 monuments are scheduled in Wales. 24.2

The Listed Buildings Act gives special protection to buildings or areas of special architectural or historic interest. It provides for a code for listing and control of works to particular buildings and for the designation of conservation areas. These measures provide a self-contained code but also guide decisions under TCPA 1990 and the enforcement and appeal provisions largely mirror those in TCPA 1990. Responsibility under the Act falls to the Welsh Ministers and to local planning authorities. There are nearly 30,000 listed buildings and 523 conservation areas in Wales.[3] 24.3

The Planning (Listed Buildings and Conservation Areas) (Wales) Regulations 2012[4] contain the detailed provisions for listing and enforcement. Policy on conserving the historic environment is set out in PPW Chapter 6, together with three pre-devolution circulars.[5] The circulars are acknowledged to need updating – see 24.4

[1] See s. 108.

[2] See National Assembly for Wales (Transfer of Functions) Order 1999 (SI 1999 No. 672), art. 2 and Schedule 1 and Government of Wales Act 2006, s. 58, subject to two minor exceptions for certain decisions relating to Crown land and information contrary to the national interest.

[3] See National Assembly for Wales Bill Summary (June 2015), Research Service.

[4] SI 2012 No. 793.

[5] WOC 60/96, WOC 61/96 and WOC 1/98.

Revised Explanatory Memorandum to Historic Environment (Wales) Act 2016 – and a new TAN will be issued to supersede them in due course.

24.5 The Historic Environment (Wales) Act 2016 amends both the 1979 Act and the Listed Buildings Act. Important changes include giving greater power to halt unauthorised works and protect scheduled monuments and historic buildings, improving administrative control as well as creating a statutory register of historic parks and gardens and establishing an independent advisory body. At the date of writing the 2016 Act is generally in force, although in certain cases this is limited to rule-making powers and formal matters only, in particular the provisions concerning the listing of buildings of special architectural or historic interest.[6]

ANCIENT MONUMENTS AND ARCHAEOLOGICAL AREAS ACT 1979

24.6 For present purposes the key structures of the 1979 Act provide for the Welsh Ministers to maintain a schedule of ancient monuments and power to control works and grant consent, with the execution of unauthorised works being a criminal offence. Such a consent is a secondary consent to be determined by the Welsh Ministers as part of an application for development of national significance.[7] The impact on an ancient monument, whether or not scheduled,[8] may be a material consideration in a planning application and may trigger specific consultation requirements.

24.7 An ancient monument is defined as one which is scheduled or which is in the opinion of the Welsh Ministers of public interest by reason of the historic, architectural, traditional, artistic or archaeological interest attaching to it.[9] A monument is any building, structure or work, whether above or below the surface of the land, and any cave or excavation, any site comprising such remains and any site comprising, or comprising the remains of, any vehicle, vessel, aircraft or other movable structure or part thereof which is not otherwise a work within the definition.[10] Any machinery attached to a monument shall be regarded as part of the monument if it could not be detached without being dismantled. There is an exception for ecclesiastical buildings used as such.[11]

24.8 The definition has been extended by the Historic Environment (Wales) Act 2016, section 22, with effect from 21 May 2016: this amended section 61 to include sites evidencing previous human activity generally. The 2016 Act will also introduce

[6] See s. 41 of the Act.

[7] See Chapter 10, above.

[8] PPW 6.5.1.

[9] Section 61(12).

[10] Section 61(7).

[11] Section 61(7).

a duty to consult appropriate persons as part of the scheduling process.[12] The duty extends to proposals to exclude a monument or make a material amendment to the schedule and section 1AA of the 1979 Act generally equates this action to the initial inclusion. A notice inviting representations on the proposed inclusion of a monument in the schedule must be served on the owner, occupier, the local authority or authorities for the location and any other person considered appropriate as having special knowledge or interest.[13] Coupled with this are provisions to give interim protection to a site during the consultation process under section 1AA.[14]

Works are authorised where carried out in accordance with the terms and any 24.9
conditions of a written consent of the Welsh Ministers.[15] Consent to works to a scheduled monument is dealt with by section 3 and may be subject to conditions imposed under section 2. Applications are in accordance with Schedule 1 to the 1979 Act, with a simplified procedure applying in accordance with regulations to be made under the Historic Environment (Wales) Act 2016.[16]

Carrying out unauthorised works to a scheduled monument is an offence.[17] 24.10
Works within the section are works of demolition, destruction or damage, removal or repair to the monument or any alteration or addition to it and flooding or tipping on land in or under which there is a scheduled monument.[18]

Where the works result in the demolition, destruction or damage to the sched- 24.11
uled monument it is a defence for a person to prove that he had taken all reasonable precautions and exercised all due diligence to avoid or prevent damage.[19] In the case of such works or works of tipping or flooding it is additionally a defence for the accused to prove that, before executing the works or before causing or permitting their execution, he had taken all reasonable steps to find out whether there was a scheduled monument in the area affected by the works and he did not know, and had no reason to believe, that the monument was within the area affected by the works or (as the case may be) that it was a scheduled monument.[20] When the interim protection provisions are in force an additional defence will be available in such cases where there was a reasonable failure to know of the interim protection.[21]

Failure to comply with conditions of the consent is also an offence under 24.12
section 2(6) of the 1979 Act, subject to a defence where a person can prove that he had taken all reasonable steps to find out if there was a scheduled monument in

[12] The details are by provisions inserted into the 1979 Act by s. 3 of the 2016 Act. Section 3 is in force for the purposes of making regulations but not otherwise: see s. 41.

[13] 1979 Act, s. 1AA.

[14] See 1979 Act, s. 1AB: in force only for the purposes of making regulations.

[15] 1979 Act, s. 2(3).

[16] See sections 5–10.

[17] 1979 Act, s. 2(1).

[18] 1979 Act, s. 2(2).

[19] 1979 Act, s. 2(7).

[20] 1979 Act, s. 2(8A).

[21] 1979 Act, s. 2(6A).

the area and that he took all reasonable precautions and exercised all due diligence to avoid contravening the condition.

24.13 It is a defence to any offence under section 2 where the works are urgently necessary in the interests of health and safety and notice was given to the Welsh Ministers as soon as reasonably practicable.[22]

24.14 Enforcement where works have been or are being carried out in breach of section 2(1) or (6) is the subject of new provisions operative from 21 May 2016. Sections 9ZC–9ZM, inserted into the 1979 Act, give power to issue an enforcement notice or a temporary stop notice or take injunctive proceedings and deal with supplementary matters, for example as to the content of notices, date of operation, appeals and prosecution for failure to comply. The stated intent is to give the Welsh Ministers enforcement powers in respect to scheduled monuments broadly equivalent to those for listed buildings.

24.15 Turning to the other subject matter of the 1979 Act, either the Welsh Ministers or a local authority may designate an area as one of archaeological importance where it appears to merit treatment as such for the purposes of the Act.[23] It is an offence to carry out operations on land in an area of archaeological importance without first giving notice to the Welsh Ministers.[24] Operations are those which disturb the ground and flooding and tipping operations.[25] This is subject to the exemptions contained in section 37 of the Act.

PLANNING (LISTED BUILDINGS AND CONSERVATION AREAS) ACT 1990

24.16 The Listed Buildings Act 1990 requires the Welsh Ministers to compile a list of buildings of special architectural or historic interest and provides for works to listed buildings to be undertaken only if authorised by the local planning authority or Welsh Ministers. It is an offence to execute unauthorised works and the local planning authority have power to issue an enforcement notice. This is subject to a right of appeal and for decision by the Welsh Ministers with procedural provisions broadly mirroring planning appeals. Local planning authorities are responsible for designating conservation areas and for publishing proposals for their preservation and enhancement[26] and demolition of a building in a conservation area is subject to specific protection.

24.17 In considering whether to grant planning permission for development which affects a listed building or its setting, the local planning authority or the Welsh Ministers shall have special regard to the desirability of preserving the building or its

[22] 1979 Act, s. 2(9).

[23] 1979 Act, s. 33.

[24] 1979 Act, s. 35.

[25] 1979 Act, s. 35(2).

[26] Listed Buildings Act 1990, ss. 69 and 71.

setting or any features of special architectural or historic interest which it possesses.[27] Further, in the exercise of any functions under the planning Acts with respect to any land or other buildings in a conservation area, special attention shall be paid to the desirability of preserving or enhancing the character or appearance of that area.[28]

Generally, as stated, the historic environment may be a material consideration in planning matters and reference should be made to PPW, which deals with the protection of designated and non-designated sites and buildings in the development plan process, in determining planning applications and also where appropriate in carrying out specific functions under the Listed Buildings Act. Control over demolition in conservation areas ('conservation area consent') is provided by sections 74–76. Where an application for planning permission, other than a retrospective application under section 73A, is made for development which would affect the setting of a listed building or the character or appearance of a conservation area, additional publicity requirements are imposed on the local planning authority.[29] 24.18

LISTING PROCESS

Listing is the responsibility of the Welsh Ministers[30] and the relevant functions are carried out by Cadw. In making the assessment they shall take into account not only the building itself but also any respect in which its exterior contributes to the architectural or historic interest of any group of buildings of which it forms part and the desirability of preserving, on the ground of its architectural or historic interest, any feature of the building consisting of a man-made object or structure fixed to the building or forming part of the land and comprised within the curtilage of the building.[31] Once entered on the approved list, the building is a listed building and this includes any object or structure fixed to the building or within the curtilage of the building which, although not fixed to the building, forms part of the land and has done so since before 1 July 1948.[32] 24.19

The list must be published and there is power for the local planning authority to make a temporary listing by a building preservation notice where the building is in danger of demolition or alteration so as to affect its character as of special architectural or historic interest. The current provisions are in section 3 of the Listed Buildings Act but a new provision, section 3A to similar effect but exclusive to Wales, will replace this from a date to be appointed further to section 25 of the Historic Environment (Wales) Act 2016. 24.20

[27] Listed Buildings Act 1990, s. 66(1); see paras. 13.5–13.7, above and cases there cited.

[28] Listed Buildings Act 1990, s. 72; see paras. 13.5–13.7, above and cases there cited.

[29] Listed Buildings Act 1990, ss. 67(1) and (2) and 73.

[30] Listed Buildings Act 1990, s. 1.

[31] Section 1(3).

[32] Section 1(5).

24.21 Amendments are made by the Historic Environment (Wales) Act 2016, which inserts new provisions regarding consultation and protection during the consultation stage equivalent to those referred to above for scheduled monuments. They are in force only to the extent that they confer power to make regulations.[33] The duty to consult extends to proposals to include or to exclude a building from listing. A notice inviting representations on the proposed inclusion of a building in the schedule must be served on the owner, occupier, the local authority or authorities for the location and any other person considered appropriate as having special knowledge or interest.[34] There is a separate provision, when in force, for application to the Welsh Ministers for a certificate that a building is not intended to be listed.[35] Interim protection during consultation will be given by the Listed Buildings Act 1990, section 2B as if the building were listed. Where a building has been listed, section 2D will give power to review the listing on application by the owner or occupier. The review must be carried out by a local inquiry, a hearing or by written representations.

EFFECT OF LISTING

24.22 No person shall execute or cause to be executed any works for the demolition of a listed building or for its alteration or extension, unless the works are authorised.[36] Contravention of this is a criminal offence.[37] Executing or causing to be executed any works in breach of a condition attached to a consent is equally an offence.[38] Both are subject to a defence where specified conditions relating to urgent works for safety or health or for preservation of the building are proved.[39] Works for the alteration or extension of a listed building are authorised if the written consent for their execution has been granted by the local planning authority or the Welsh Ministers and they are executed in accordance with the terms of the consent and of any conditions attached to it.[40] In the case of demolition, consent is subject to

[33] Historic Environment (Wales) Act 2016, s. 41.

[34] Listed Buildings Act 1990, s. 2A.

[35] See Listed Buildings Act 1990, s. 6A.

[36] Listed Buildings Act 1990, s. 7. (The following references are to the 1990 Act unless otherwise stated.)

[37] Section 9(1).

[38] Section 9(2).

[39] Section 9(3). The conditions are: (a) that works to the building were urgently necessary in the interests of safety or health or for the preservation of the building; (b) that it was not practicable to secure safety or health or, as the case may be, the preservation of the building by works of repair or works for affording temporary support or shelter; (c) that the works carried out were limited to the minimum measures immediately necessary; and (d) that notice in writing justifying in detail the carrying out of the works was given to the local planning authority as soon as reasonably practicable.

[40] Section 8(1).

additional requirements for notice and access to the Royal Commission on Ancient and Historical Monuments in Wales.[41]

Application for consent is made to the local planning authority in accordance with the Listed Buildings Act 1990, section 10 and the Planning (Listed Buildings and Conservation Areas) Regulations 2012, reg. 3. Conditions may be attached to the grant of consent.[42] The consent endures for five years or for any different specified period.[43] There is also power to apply to discharge or vary any condition attaching to a consent.[44] 24.23

APPEALS

There is a right of appeal to the Welsh Ministers against a refusal or conditional grant of consent or of an application to discharge or vary conditions.[45] Where a condition requires an application for later approval of the details of works (such a condition is authorised by section 17(2)), there is also a right of appeal against a refusal as there is against a failure or refusal to give notice of the decision.[46] An appeal must be brought within twenty-eight days of the decision and specify the grounds.[47] Appeals may be determined by an appointed person further to Schedule 3 to the Listed Buildings Act and the Town and Country Planning (Determination of Appeals by Appointed Persons) (Prescribed Classes) (Wales) Regulations 2015.[48] 24.24

Appeals will be by written representations, hearings or inquiry. The procedure in each case is as for planning appeals under TCPA 1990, section 78 as each of the relevant regulations or rules, that is the Town and Country Planning (Referrals and Appeals) (Written Representations Procedure) (Wales) Regulations 2015,[49] the Town and Country Planning (Hearings Procedure) (Wales) Rules 2003,[50] the Town and Country Planning (Inquiries Procedure) (Wales) Rules 2003[51] and the Town and Country Planning (Determination by Inspectors) (Inquiries Procedure) 24.25

[41] Section 8(2) and (5).

[42] Section 17, which details nonexhaustive purposes for which conditions may be imposed.

[43] Section 18.

[44] Section 19.

[45] Section 20 and see SI 2012 No. 793, reg. 12.

[46] Section 20.

[47] Section 21.

[48] SI 2015 No. 1822.

[49] SI 2015 No. 1331.

[50] SI 2003 No. 1271.

[51] SI 2003 No. 1266.

(Wales) Rules 2003[52] apply equally to listed building applications and appeals.[53] Reference should therefore be made to Chapter 17.

24.26 A challenge to the decision of the Welsh Ministers on appeal can only be made by an application to the High Court on the grounds that it is not within the powers of the Act or that any of the relevant provisions have not been complied with.[54] The application must be made within six weeks of the decision.

ENFORCEMENT

24.27 Although there is the additional sanction that unauthorised works are a criminal offence, specific enforcement powers exist to secure compliance as they do for breach of planning control. A listed building enforcement notice may be issued where it appears to the local planning authority that any works have been or are being executed to a listed building in their area involving a contravention of section 9(1) or (2) if they consider it expedient to do so having regard to the effect of the works on the character of the building as one of special architectural or historic interest.[55] The Historic Environment (Wales) Act 2016 will add new powers to issue a temporary stop notice.

24.28 A listed building enforcement notice shall specify the alleged contravention and require such steps as may be specified in the notice to be taken for restoring the building to its former state or for bringing the building to the state in which it would have been if the terms and conditions of any listed building consent which has been granted for the works had been complied with. If the authority considers that restoration as above would not be reasonably practicable or would be undesirable, steps may be specified for executing such further works specified in the notice as it considers necessary to alleviate the effect of the works which were carried out without listed building consent.[56] The notice must also specify the date on which it is to take effect and the period within which the prescribed steps must be taken.[57] In addition, the notice must state why it is considered expedient to issue it and specify all relevant development plan policies and proposals and identify the land precisely.[58] It must also be accompanied by an explanatory notice containing prescribed information.[59]

[52] SI 2003 No. 1267.

[53] See reg. 3 of each of the respective regulations.

[54] Sections 62 and 63.

[55] Section 38(1).

[56] Section 9(2).

[57] Section 9(3).

[58] Town and Country Planning (Enforcement Notices and Appeals) (Wales) Regulations 2003 (SI 2003 No. 394), reg. 3.

[59] SI 2003 No. 394, reg. 4.

The notice must be served on the owner, occupier and any other person whose interest in the building is materially affected within twenty-eight days and not less than twenty-eight days before the date on which it is to take effect.[60] 24.29

A person having an interest in the listed building in question or an occupier of it may appeal to the Welsh Ministers by written notice before, or as would in the ordinary course of post be delivered before, the date on which the enforcement notice takes effect.[61] The notice must specify the grounds, although where it does not do so they are to be specified within fourteen days of a notice requiring them.[62] 24.30

The grounds are specified in section 39(1) and the validity of a listed building enforcement notice shall not be questioned in any other proceedings whatsoever on any of the grounds on which an appeal may be brought.[63] The grounds, using the statutory designation, are: 24.31

(a) that the building is not of special architectural or historic interest;
(b) that the matters alleged to constitute a contravention of section 9(1) or (2) have not occurred;
(c) that those matters (if they occurred) do not constitute such a contravention;
(d) that works to the building were urgently necessary in the interests of safety or health or for the preservation of the building, that it was not practicable to secure safety or health or, as the case may be, the preservation of the building by works of repair or works for affording temporary support or shelter, and that the works carried out were limited to the minimum measures immediately necessary;
(e) that listed building consent ought to be granted for the works, or that any relevant condition of such consent which has been granted ought to be discharged, or different conditions substituted;
(f) that copies of the notice were not served as required by section 38(4);
(g) except in relation to such a requirement as is mentioned in section 38(2)(b) or (c), that the requirements of the notice exceed what is necessary for restoring the building to its condition before the works were carried out;
(h) that the period specified in the notice as the period within which any step required by the notice is to be taken falls short of what should reasonably be allowed;
(i) that the steps required by the notice for the purpose of restoring the character of the building to its former state would not serve that purpose;
(j) that steps required to be taken by virtue of section 38(2)(b) exceed what is necessary to alleviate the effect of the works executed to the building;

60 Section 9(4) and (5).

61 Section 39(2).

62 See s. 39(4) and reg. 5 of SI 2003 No. 394.

63 Section 64.

(k) that steps required to be taken by virtue of section 38(2)(c) exceed what is necessary to bring the building to the state in which it would have been if the terms and conditions of the listed building consent had been complied with.

24.32 Further procedure on appeals is in accordance with the Town and Country Planning (Enforcement Notices and Appeals) (Wales) Regulations 2003: these apply to listed building enforcement notices and enforcement notices issued under TCPA 1990, section 172 and reference should be made to Chapter 19. Appeals may be determined by an appointed person further to Schedule 3 to the Listed Buildings Act.

24.33 Determination of the appeal is by a local inquiry, hearing or by written representations and the appropriate procedure is determined by the Welsh Ministers in accordance with section 88E of the Listed Buildings Act 1990. Procedure for each of these is governed by the same set of regulations as for planning enforcement appeals, that is the Town and Country Planning (Enforcement) (Written Representations Procedure) (Wales) Regulations 2003,[64] the Town and Country Planning (Enforcement) (Hearings Procedure) (Wales) Rules 2003,[65] the Town and Country Planning (Enforcement) (Inquiries Procedure) (Wales) Rules 2003[66] and the Town and Country Planning (Enforcement) (Determination by Inspectors) (Inquiries Procedure) (Wales) Rules 2003.[67]

24.34 Any defect, error or misdescription in the listed building enforcement notice may be corrected on appeal or the terms of the notice may be varied where the Welsh Ministers are satisfied that the correction or variation will not cause injustice to the appellant or the local planning authority.[68] Where the appeal is allowed the notice may be quashed.[69] There is power for the Welsh Ministers to grant listed building consent for the works to which the listed building enforcement notice relates or for part only of those works and to discharge any condition or limitation subject to which listed building consent was granted and substitute any other condition, whether more or less onerous. Further, if they think fit, they may amend any list compiled or approved by removing from it the building to which the appeal relates.[70]

24.35 Power to issue temporary stop notices to require the immediate cessation of unauthorised works where expedient for a period of twenty-eight days will be introduced by sections 44B–44D, inserted by section 29 of the 2016 Act with effect from 21 May 2016. Breach is a criminal offence and compensation may be recovered for loss or damage directly attributable to the notice.

[64] SI 2003 No. 395.

[65] SI 2003 No. 1268.

[66] SI 2003 No. 1269.

[67] SI 2003 No. 1270.

[68] Section 41(1).

[69] Section 41(2).

[70] Section 41(3).

Where a local planning authority considers it necessary or expedient for any actual or apprehended contravention of section 9(1) or (2) to be restrained by injunction, it may apply to the court for an injunction, whether or not it has exercised or is proposing to exercise any of its other enforcement powers. 24.36

CONSERVATION AREAS

Further provisions of the Listed Buildings Act 1990 provide for conservation areas. 24.37
Local planning authorities are required to determine which parts of their area are of special architectural or historic interest, the character of which it is desirable to preserve or enhance and to designate them as conservation areas.[71] They are then under a duty to formulate and publish proposals for their preservation and enhancement.[72] When exercising any functions under the planning Acts in respect of any buildings or land in a conservation area, special attention shall be paid to the desirability of preserving or enhancing the character or appearance of that area.[73] Preserving the character or appearance may be achieved by a positive contribution to preservation or by development which leaves the character or appearance unharmed, so that where there is no adverse effect and no other planning objection the development is permitted.[74]

Demolition within a conservation area can only be carried out with consent[75] 24.38
and key provisions regarding listed buildings apply to buildings in conservation areas but subject to modification by regulation.[76] This conservation area consent is a separate consent, additional to planning permission. Buildings which are listed, ecclesiastical buildings, scheduled monuments and buildings subject to a specific direction are excepted.[77] The important provisions made applicable as for listed buildings are those relating to offences, authorisation of works and appeals (sections 7–26) and enforcement notices and appeals (sections 38–46).

The modifications are by regulation 16 of and Schedule 3 to the Planning 24.39
(Listed Buildings and Conservation Areas) (Wales) Regulations 2012.[78] The essential effect of these is that conservation area buildings are protected from demolition where this would affect the character or appearance of the conservation area.[79]

[71] Section 69.

[72] Section 71.

[73] Section 72(1).

[74] *South Lakeland DC v Secretary of State for the Environment* [1992] 2 AC 141.

[75] Section 74.

[76] Section 74(3).

[77] Section 75.

[78] SI 2012 No. 793.

[79] Consequent modification is made to the s. 38 ground (a) appeal to refer to the character or appearance of the conservation area.

Subject to this, the provisions above regarding listed buildings can be read as applying to buildings in a conservation area.

24.40 Finally, where a tree in a conservation area is not otherwise protected by the terms of a tree preservation order, it is an offence to carry out certain works without the consent of the local planning authority.[80]

[80] TCPA 1990, s. 211.

Index

D

E

T